¡Encuentra aquí tu próxima lectura!

Escanea el código con tu teléfono móvil o tableta.
Te invitamos a leer los primeros capítulos
de la mejor selección de obras.

Rites of Spring

The Great War
and the
Birth of the Modern Age

Modris Eksteins

BLACK SWAN

RITES OF SPRING

A BLACK SWAN BOOK 0 552 99406 5

Originally published in Great Britain
by Bantam Press, a division of Transworld
Publishers Ltd

PRINTING HISTORY

Bantam Press edition published 1989
Black Swan edition published 1990

This book is set in 11/12 pt Mallard
by Colset Private Limited, Singapore.

Black Swan Books are published by
Transworld Publishers Ltd, 61–63
Uxbridge Road, Ealing, London W5 5SA, in
Australia by Transworld Publishers
(Australia) Pty. Ltd, 15–23 Helles Avenue,
Moorebank, NSW 2170, and in
New Zealand by Transworld Publishers
(N.Z.) Ltd., Cnr. Moselle and Waipareira
Avenues, Henderson, Auckland.

Made and printed in Great Britain by
Cox & Wyman Ltd., Reading, Berks.

For Jayne

Contents

List of Illustrations   11

Map of the Western Front   13

Preface   15

Prologue: Venice   23

ACT ONE

I Paris

Vision   31

29 May 1913   32

Le Théâtre Des Champs-Élysées   40

Diaghilev and the Ballets Russes   46

Rebellion   62

Confrontation and Liberation   69

Audience   76

Scandal as Success   83

II Berlin

Ver Sacrum   90

Overture   101

Technique   108

Capital   113

Kultur   116

Culture and Revolt   122

War as Culture   134

III In Flanders' Fields

A Corner of a Foreign Field   141

Guns of August   145

Peace on Earth   159

The Reason Why   166

Victorian Synthesis   183

Is There Honey Still for Tea?   187

ACT TWO

IV Rites of War

Battle Ballet   195

Themes   199

Transvaluation   216

V Reason in Madness

Theirs was not to Reason Why   234

Duty   242

VI Sacred Dance

War God   263

Congregation   276

VII Journey to the Interior

War as Art   283

Art as Form   292

Art and Morality   303

Avant-Garde   307

ACT THREE

VIII Night Dancer

The New Christ   326

Star   333

Lest We Forget   339

Itinerary and Symbol   350

New Worlds and Old   359

Associations   364

IX Memory

War Boom   368

Life or Death   371

Fame   380

Cloud Juggler   397

X Spring Without End

Germany, Awake!   399

Victim Hero   405

Art as Life   413

Myth as Reality   418

'Es Ist Ein Frühling Ohne Ende!'   431

Acknowledgements   441

Notes   444

Selected Sources   482

Index   485

Illustrations

Stravinsky and Nijinsky (Bibliothèque nationale)
Diaghilev and Cocteau (Bettmann/BBC Hulton)
Le Théâtre des Champs-Élysées
Corps de ballet in *Le Sacre du printemps* (*Comoedia Illustré*, June 1913)
Berlin, imperial palace, 1 August 1914 (Bettmann/BBC Hulton)
Paris, Gare de l'Est, 2 August 1914 (Bettman/BBC Hulton)
Petrograd, Nevsky Prospekt, 3 August 1914 (Mansell Collection)
London, Trafalgar Square, 4 August 1914 (Bettmann/BBC Hulton)
German Christmas, 1914 (Ullstein)
Peace on earth: Christmas Day, 1914 (Imperial War Museum)
Battle ballet (ECPA)
Christmas, 1916 (Imperial War Museum)
Menin Road (Imperial War Museum)
Menin Road by Paul Nash (Imperial War Museum)
Armored lookout man (Times Newspapers, Ltd.)
Dada dancers (Fondation Arp)
Cubist war (Imperial War Museum)
Victory! (Bettmann/BBC Hulton)
Berlin dances (Bildarchiv Preussischer Kulturbesitz)
Tanz in Baden-Baden by Max Beckmann (Staatsgalerie moderner Kunst, Munich)

11

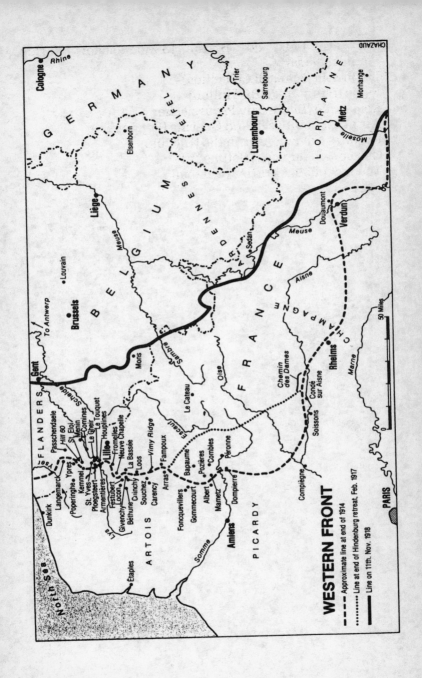

WESTERN FRONT

--- Approximate line at end of 1914
.... Line at end of Hindenburg retreat, Feb. 1917
——— Line on 11th. Nov. 1918

CHAZAUD

Preface

As one approaches the outskirts of Verdun on the Route Nationale 3 from Mertz, having enjoyed a serene Vosges countryside of rolling hills and meadows, and a steady honor guard of sturdy oak trees, one is struck suddenly, a few kilometers outside the town, by a dreary sight. A blot on the surroundings. A graveyard. Piled high and in full view of the road are smashed corpses, crumpled bodies, glistening skeletons. This is, however, a graveyard without crosses, without headstones, without flowers. There are few visitors. Most travelers probably do not even notice the place. But it is a prominent memorial to the twentieth century and our cultural references. Many would say that it is a symbol of modern values and aims, of our striving and our regrets, the contemporary interpretations of Goethe's invocation *stirb und werde*, die and become. It is an automobile graveyard.

If you continue into Verdun, pass through the town, and then proceed northeast by minor roads, you can find your way to a larger graveyard. This one has crosses. Thousands of them. Row upon symmetrical row. White. All the same. More people today pass the automobile graveyard than this one. More people can identify with the crushed cars than with the now impersonal horror that this cemetery recalls. This is the memorial cemetery for those who fell during the battle of Verdun in the First World War.

This is a book about death and destruction. It is a

discourse on graveyards. As such it is also, however, a book about 'becoming.' It is a book about the emergence, in the first half of this century, of our modern consciousness, specifically of our obsession with emancipation, and about the significance of the Great War, as it was called prior to the outbreak of the Second World War, in the development of that consciousness. And while it would appear, on the surface at least, that an automobile graveyard, with all its implications – 'I think cars today are the cultural equivalent of the great Gothic cathedrals,' wrote Roland Barthes – has far more significance for the contemporary mind than a First World War cemetery, this book will try to show that the two graveyards are related. For our preoccupation with speed, newness, transience, and inwardness – with life lived, as the jargon puts it, 'in the fast lane' – to have taken hold, an entire scale of values and beliefs had to yield pride of place, and the Great War was, as we shall see, the single most significant event in that development.

Our title, adapted from a ballet that is a landmark of modernism, is suggestive of our main motif: movement. One of the supreme symbols of our centrifugal and paradoxical century, when in striving for freedom we have acquired the power of ultimate destruction, is the dance of death, with its orgiastic-nihilistic irony. *The Rite of Spring*, which was first performed in Paris in May 1913, a year before the outbreak of war, is, with its rebellious energy and its celebration of life through sacrificial death, perhaps the emblematic *oeuvre* of a twentieth-century world that, in its pursuit of life, has killed off millions of its best human beings. Stravinsky intended initially to entitle his score *The Victim*.

To demonstrate the significance of the Great War, one must of course deal with the interests and emotions involved in it. This book approaches those interests and emotions in the broad terms of cultural history. This genre of history must concern itself with more than

16

music, ballet, and the other arts, with more even than automobiles and graveyards; it must in the end unearth manners and morals, customs and values, both articulated and assumed. As difficult as the task may be, cultural history must at least try to capture the spirit of an age.

That spirit is to be located in a society's sense of priorities. Ballet, film, and literature, cars and crosses, can provide important evidence of these priorities, but the latter will be found most amply in the social response to these symbols. In modern society, as this book will argue, the audience for the arts, as for hobbits and heroes, is for the historian an even more important source of evidence for cultural identity than the literary documents, artistic artifacts, or heroes themselves. The history of modern culture ought then to be as much a history of response as of challenge, an account of the reader as of the novel, of the viewer as of the film, of the spectator as of the actor.

If this point is apposite to the study of modern culture, then it is also pertinent to the study of modern warfare. Most history of warfare has been written with a narrow focus on strategy, weaponry, and organization, on generals, tanks, and politicians. Relatively little attention has been paid to the morale and motivation of common soldiers in an attempt to assess, in broad and comparative terms, the relationship of war and culture. The unknown soldier stands front and center in our story. He is Stravinsky's victim.

Like all wars, the 1914 war, when it broke out, was seen as an opportunity for both change and confirmation. Germany, which had been united as recently as 1871 and within one generation had become an awesome industrial and military power, was, on the eve of war, the foremost representative of innovation and renewal. She was, among nations, the very embodiment of vitalism and technical brilliance. The war for her was to be a war of liberation, a *Befreiungskrieg*, from the hypocrisy of bourgeois form and convenience, and Britain was to her the principal representative of the order against which she was rebelling. Britain was in fact the major conservative power of the *fin-de-siècle* world. First industrial nation, agent of the Pax Britannica, symbol of an ethic of enterprise and progress based on parliament and law, Britain felt not only her pre-eminence in the world but her entire way of life threatened by the thrusting energy and instability Germany was seen to typify. British involvement in the 1914 war was to turn it from a continental power struggle into a veritable war of cultures.

At the same time that tensions were developing between states in this turn-of-the-century world, fundamental conflicts were surfacing in virtually all areas of human endeavor and behavior: in the arts, in fashion, in sexual mores, between generations, in politics. The whole motif of liberation, which has become so central to our country – be it the emancipation of women, homosexuals, proletariat, youth, appetites, peoples – comes into view at the turn of the century. The term *avant-garde* has usually been applied simply to artists and writers who promoted experimental techniques in their work and urged rebellion against established academies. The notion of *modernism* has been used to subsume both this avant-garde and the intellectual impulses behind the quest for liberation and the act of rebellion. Very few critics have ventured to extend these notions of the avant-garde and modernism to the social and political as well as artistic agents of revolt, and to the act of rebellion in general, in order to identify a broad wave of sentiment and endeavor. This book attempts to do so. Culture is regarded as a social phenomenon and modernism as the principal urge of our time. The book argues in the process that Germany has been the modernist nation *par excellence* of our century.

Like the avant-garde in the arts, Germany was swept by a reformist zeal at the *fin de siècle* and by 1914 she had come to represent both to herself and to the international community the idea of spirit at war. After the trauma of military defeat in 1918, the radicalism in Germany, rather than being subdued, was accentuated. The Weimar period, 1918 to 1933, and the Third Reich, 1933 to 1945, were stages in a process. Avant-garde has for us a positive ring, storm troops a frightening connotation. This book suggests that there may be a sibling relationship between these two terms that extends beyond their military origins. Introspection, primitivism, abstraction, and myth making in the arts, and introspection, primitivism, abstraction, and myth making in politics, may be related manifestations. Nazi kitsch may bear a blood relationship to the highbrow religion of art proclaimed by many moderns.

Our century is one in which life and art have blended, in which existence has become aestheticized. History, as one theme of this study will try to show, has surrendered much of its former authority to fiction. In our post-modernist age a compromise may, however, be possible and necessary. In search of this compromise our historical account proceeds in the form of a drama, with acts and scenes, in the full and diverse sense of those words. In the beginning was the event. Only later came consequence.

Rites of Spring

Prologue: Venice

Venice, city of the doges, city of Renaissance splendor, city of lagoons, reflections, and shadows, is the city of imagination. It is a city of spirits beyond measurable time. It is a city of sensations and, above all, inwardness.

Venice, with its mirrors and mirages, is where Richard Wagner found inspiration for his opera *Tristan und Isolde*, that tortured celebration of life, love, and death, and where he died in February 1883, in the Palazzo Vendramin Calerghi, in a room overlooking the Grand Canal. Venice was the favorite city also of Sergei Pavlovitch Diaghilev. He died in the Grand Hôtel des Bains de Mer on the Lido in August 1929. Wagner tried to unite all the arts in his grand opera; Diaghilev tried to unite all the arts in his grand ballet. The one created; the other crafted. Both were symbols of their eras. They both found inspiration in Venice. They both came to Venice to die.

Diaghilev was born in Russia's Novgorod province in March 1872, in a military barracks. His father was an officer in the imperial guard, a devoted and loyal servant of the tsar. The son first visited Venice in 1890 at the age of eighteen with his cousin and lover Dmitri

Filosofov. He took Vaslav Nijinsky, the young Polish dancer, there after their first great Paris season in 1909. Diaghilev was thirty-seven, Nijinsky twenty-one. They stayed at the Grand Hôtel des Bains, the impresario and his new young lover. Vaslav went bathing, often, and sunned himself. Diaghilev watched. He never bathed in public.

Two years later, in 1911, Thomas Mann, who was three years Diaghilev's junior, who attributed to Wagner the greatest influence on his youthful sensibility, and who in 1902 devoted a story to the Tristan theme, stayed at the Grand Hôtel des Bains and shortly afterward completed *Death in Venice*, his novella about a famous artist from Munich, Gustav Aschenbach, who did not bathe publicly either but who loved 'this most improbable of cities,'[1] Venice, and yet another young Polish boy, Tadzio. Aschenbach would sit on the beach, admiring the Polish lad, the symbol to him of perfect beauty. As the admiration turned to passion, Venice was invaded by Asiatic cholera.

Like Diaghilev, Aschenbach was born in the provinces, in a small town in Silesia. Like Diaghilev, he was the son of a servant of the state, in this case an upper official in the judicature, and his family, too, was full of officers, judges, and functionaries. Aschenbach, like Diaghilev, stayed at the Hôtel des Bains on the Lido.

In the long mornings on the beach his heavy gaze would rest, a fixed and reckless stare, upon the lad; towards nightfall, lost to shame, he would follow him through the city's narrow streets where horrid death stalked too, and at such time it seemed to him as though the moral law were fallen in ruins and only the monstrous and perverse held out a hope.

On the morning of the day Tadzio was due to leave, Aschenbach observed him in a fight on the beach with another foreign boy, a sturdy fellow, Jaschiu. Tadzio was quickly vanquished. 'He made spasmodic efforts to shake the other off, lay still, and then began a feeble twitching.' Moments later, Aschenbach died.

Some minutes passed before anyone hastened to the aid of the elderly man sitting there collapsed in his chair. They bore him to his room. And before nightfall a shocked and respectful world received the news of his decease.

Diaghilev knew Mann's story well. He gave copies of it to his intimates. Anton Dolin received a copy on his birthday in July 1924.

In August 1929, Diaghilev, aged fifty-seven, left his latest protégé, the sixteen-year-old Igor Markevitch, in Munich, where the two had attended a performance of *Tristan*, and returned to Venice to the Grand Hôtel des Bains. The dancers Boris Kochno and Serge Lifar, two of Diaghilev's recent lovers, joined him a few days later. On 19 August, Diaghilev, a diabetic, died. Misia Sert was present, along with Kochno and Lifar. After the nurse had pronounced death, Kochno, with a terrible roar, suddenly flung himself on Lifar, and a vicious struggle ensued, with biting, tearing, and kicking. 'Two mad dogs were fighting over the body of their master,' commented Misia.[2] Two days later a gondola ferried Diaghilev's body to the funeral isle of San Michele, where he lies buried. The inscription on his tombstone reads:

Venise, Inspiratrice Éternelle de nos Apaisements
SERGE DE DIAGHILEV
1872–1929

Serge Diaghilev and Thomas Mann never met, it seems. Yet the life of one and the imagination of the other overlapped to an obviously extraordinary degree. Coincidence is our term for concurrence that is not consciously willed and that we cannot explain in any definitive sense. However, if we retreat from the restrictive world of linear causality and think in terms of context and confluence rather than cause, then it is undeniable that there were many influences – to begin with, those of Venice and Wagner – at work on the imaginations of Mann and Diaghilev, two giants of twentieth-century aesthetic sense, influences that led one to create a certain fiction and the other actually to live strikingly near that fiction.

Moreover, one must ask whether Mann's story was any less real than Diaghilev's life. Heinrich Mann, in a review of his brother's novella, saw that the central issue of *Death in Venice* was 'Which came first, reality or poetry?'[3] In his *Life Sketch* of 1930 Thomas Mann spoke of the 'innate symbolism and honesty of composition' of *Death in Venice*, a story that, he asserted, was 'taken simply from reality.' Nothing was invented, he claimed, none of the settings, none of the characters, none of the events. Tadzio, it has since been established, was in fact a certain Wladyslaw Moes, a young Polish boy on holiday in Venice. Jaschiu was one Janek Fudakowski. Aschenbach bore a distinct resemblance to Gustav Mahler, who died in 1911. Thomas Mann, whose art as a whole is striking in its fusion of autobiographical and imaginative experience, called his novella 'a crystallization.'[4]

And so where does the fiction cease and the reality begin? Perhaps even to ask that question is to posit a false antithesis. For Mann the external world was of interest only as a source of art; life was subordinate to art. And Diaghilev tried to live the life of a character of fiction, a latter-day Rastignac in the guise of a Des Esseintes or a Charlus. At the turn of the century Theodor Herzl wrote that 'dream is not so different from deed as many believe. All activity of men begins as dream and later becomes dream once more.' And at roughly the same time Oscar Wilde could take a charac-

26

teristically provocative position on the issue: 'One should so live that one becomes a form of fiction. To be a fact is to be a failure.'[5] Marcel Duchamp, despite proclaiming the opposite intention, would blur the distinction between art and life by inserting actual objects into his work. Man Ray, by juxtaposing a European face and an African mask in his photography, would blend time, culture, and history. Truman Capote and Norman Mailer would write 'nonfiction novels,' and Tom Wolfe in his 'new journalism' would introduce his readers to what one critic has called 'fables of fact.'[6] If there has been a single principal theme in our century's aesthetics, it is that the life of imagination and the life of action are one and the same.

Are they? Is such fusion not simply the twentieth-century artist's self-justifying postulation? A latter-day plagiarism of Shelley's poet-legislator? Yet maybe there is some truth to the claim. Perhaps for much of the eighteenth and throughout the nineteenth century the realm of ideas was more distinct from the world of action and social reality. The two spheres were separated by a moral sense, a social code. Ideas were much more likely to rise from a prescribed set of moral principles, derived essentially from Christianity and parenthetically from humanism. Action and behavior were to be interpreted in terms of the same principles. That buffer, between thought and action, a positive moral code, has disintegrated in the twentieth century, and in the process, in the colossal romanticism and irrationalism of our era, imagination and action have moved together, and have even been fused.

Sensation is everything. The ghost has become reality and reality a ghost. John Ruskin in fact described Venice as a 'ghost':

> upon the sands of the sea, so weak – so quiet – so bereft of all but her loveliness, that we might well doubt, as we watched her faint reflection in the

mirage of the lagoon, which was the City, and which the Shadow.[7]

We shall all become Venetians, predicted Friedrich Nietzsche: 'A hundred profound solitudes make up the city of Venice – that is its magic. A symbol for future mankind.'[8]

In 1986, as Venice continued to slide into the sea at a disturbing rate, a lavish three-million-dollar exhibition titled 'Futurism and Futurists' ran at the Grassi Palace on the Grand Canal.

Act One

1

Paris

New meditations have proved to me that things should move
ahead with the artists in the lead, followed by the scientists,
and that the industrialists should come after these two classes.

HENRI DE SAINT-SIMON

1820

I'm terribly sensitive to certain physical beauties – dancing
girls, etc., and out of them I shape a sort of artificial paradise on
earth. I've got to be close to dancing to live. As I think Nietzsche
wrote, 'I'll have faith in God only if he dances.'

LOUIS-FERDINAND CÉLINE

Who wrote this fiendish Rite of Spring?
What right had he to write this thing?
Against our helpless ears to fling
Its crash, clash, cling, clang, bing, bang, bing?

Letter to the Boston Herald
1924

VISION

A libretto, in Igor Stravinsky's hand, reads in translation:

The Rite of Spring is a musical choreographic work. It
represents pagan Russia and is unified by a single
idea: the mystery and great surge of the creative
power of Spring. The piece has no plot . . .
  First Part: The Kiss of the Earth. The spring celebration . . . The pipers pipe and young men tell

31

fortunes. The old woman enters. She knows the mystery of nature and how to predict the future. Young girls with painted faces come in from the river in single file. They dance the spring dance. Games start . . . The people divide into two groups, opposing each other. The holy procession of the wise old men. The oldest and wisest interrupts the spring games, which come to a stop. The people pause trembling . . . The old men bless the spring earth . . . The people dance passionately on the earth, sanctifying it and becoming one with it.

Second Part: The Great Sacrifice. All night the virgins hold mysterious games, walking in circles. One of the virgins is consecrated as the victim and is twice pointed to by fate, being caught twice in the perpetual dance. The virgins honor her, the chosen one, with a marital dance. They invoke the ancestors and entrust the chosen one to the old wise men. She sacrifices herself in the presence of the old men in the great holy dance, the great sacrifice.[1]

29 MAY 1913

Many have claimed to describe it, that opening night performance of *Le Sacre du printemps* on 29 May 1913, a Thursday, at the Théâtre des Champs-Élysées: Gabriel Astruc, Romola Nijinsky, Igor Stravinsky, Misia Sert, Marie Rambert, Bronislava Nijinska, Jean Cocteau, Carl Van Vechten, Valentine Gross. Their accounts conflict on significant details. But one thing they all agree on: the event provoked a seismic response.

Many in the audience were exceptionally elegant that evening as they arrived for the 8:45 curtain. All were excited. For weeks rumors had circulated about the artistic delights that the Russian ballet company had prepared for the new Paris season. Advance publicity talked of the 'real art,' the 'true art,' an art not confined by space and time, that Paris would experience. Seat prices had been doubled. There was certainly an air of expectation. Debussy's *Jeux*, choreographed and danced by Nijinsky, had premièred a fortnight earlier, the first ballet ever performed in modern dress – sports clothes of the day, in this case – and had been given a cool reception even by those sympathetic to modern art. Great virtuosity had been expected of the new Vestris, Nijinsky; only childish movements, so many thought, had been performed. A 'haphazard essay in affectation' Henri Quittard called the performance in *Le Figaro*, and suggested that the audience would have been happier just listening to the music.[1] Many now anticipated that *Le Sacre* would make up for that disappointment and revive the enchantment and sensation of previous 'Russian seasons,' when Parisian high society, together with the artistic and intellectual community, had been intoxicated by oriental bacchanals and other exotica.

This evening the *beau monde* was well represented. Against the black and white background of tails and the plush amaranth of the theater décor, tiaras sparkled and silk flowed. In addition to lavishly attired social snobs, there were aesthetic snobs too, who had come in ordinary suits, some with *bandeaux*, some with soft hats of one sort or another, which were considered a mark of revolt against the stiff toppers and bowlers of the upper classes. Gabriel Astruc claimed that there were about fifty passionate fans of the Russians present, including those he called 'some radical Stravinskyites in soft caps.'[2] Long hair, beards, and mustaches were also in abundance. Of the crowd of aesthetes, whether becapped or hirsute, who attended this and similar events Cocteau said that 'they would applaud novelty at random simply to show their contempt for the people in the boxes.'[3] In short, a readymade cheering section was present, prepared to do battle against sterility.

Dress, nonetheless, was no foolproof means of identifying artistic or any other inclination in 1913.

Unpredictability was the smartest fashion. At a subsequent performance of Le Sacre, Gertrude Stein was to observe the poet Guillaume Apollinaire – who proclaimed himself the 'judge of this long quarrel between tradition and innovation' – in the seats below.

> He was dressed in evening clothes and was industriously kissing various important looking ladies' hands. He was the first one of his crowd to come out into the great world wearing evening clothes and kissing hands. We were very amused and very pleased to see him do it.[4]

Shock and surprise, in other words, were the ultimate chic.

Regardless of attire, the audience on that opening night played, as Cocteau noted, 'the role that was written for it.' And what was that role? To be scandalized, of course, but, equally, to scandalize. The brouhaha surrounding Le Sacre was to be as much in the reactions of members of the audience to their fellows as in the work itself. The dancers on stage must have wondered at times who was performing and who was the audience.

Shortly after the wistful bassoon melody of the opening bars, the protests began, first with whistling. When the curtain went up and the dancers appeared, jumping up and down and toeing, against all convention, inward rather than outward, the howling and hissing started. 'Having already made fun of the public once,' wrote Henri Quittard in Le Figaro, referring to Jeux, 'a repeat of the same joke, in such a heavy-handed way, was not in very good taste.'[5] To turn ballet, the most effervescent and fluid of art forms, into grotesque caricature was to insult good taste and the integrity of the audience. That was the attitude of the opposition. It felt offended. It jeered. Applause was the response of the defenders. And so the battle was joined.

Personal insults were certainly exchanged; probably

some punches too; maybe cards, to arrange a semblance of satisfaction afterward. Whether a duel was fought the next morning as a result of the exchanges, as the melodramatic Romola Nijinsky asserts; whether a society lady actually spat in a man's face; whether the Comtesse de Pourtalès did in fact, as Cocteau tells it, get up, coronet askew, waving her fan, and exclaim, 'I am sixty years old and this is the first time anyone has dared to make fun of me'; all of these details are froth on the meaning of the agitation. Of outrage and excitement there was plenty. Indeed, there was such a din that the music may have been almost drowned out at times.

But drowned out completely? Some reports leave the impression that no one, apart from the musicians in the orchestra and Pierre Monteux, the conductor, heard the music after the opening bars – not even the dancers. Cocteau first and then Stravinsky have left us with a picture of Nijinsky standing in the wings, on a chair, shouting numbers to the dancers.[6] But he did so because of the difficulty of the choreography and the lack of conventional rhythms in the musical score – Nijinsky had done this consistently in rehearsal – rather than, as Cocteau and Stravinsky would have us believe, because of any problems the dancers had in hearing the orchestra. Valentine Gross, whose sketches of the Ballets Russes were being exhibited that night in the foyer, has given us a delightfully airy but slightly preposterous account:

I missed nothing of the show which was taking place as much offstage as on. Standing between the two middle boxes, I felt quite at ease at the heart of the maelstrom, applauding with my friends. I thought there was something wonderful about the titanic struggle which must have been going on in order to keep these *inaudible* musicians and these *deafened* dancers together, in obedience to the laws of their

35

invisible choreographer. *The ballet was astoundingly beautiful.*[7]

Does the picture she paints here – musicians who cannot be heard, dancers who cannot hear – not have an abstract and absurd quality to it? And yet while, as she implies, she could not hear the music and while she did not know what rhythms the dancers were dancing to, Valentine Gross says she found the ballet 'astoundingly beautiful'! Was she responding to what she heard and saw in the work of art presented, or was she responding in retrospect to the whole delicious *affaire*?

A touch of the modern dramatist is also present in Carl Van Vechten's accounts. He had been music and dance critic – the first such creature in the United States – for the *New York Times* before going to Europe in 1913 as drama critic of the *New York Press*. Some months earlier he had helped Mabel Dodge launch her famous salon in New York. 'Cat-calls and hisses succeeded the playing of the first few bars,' he wrote about the première of *Le Sacre*,

and then ensued a battery of screams, countered by a foil of applause. We warred over art (some of us thought it was and some thought it wasn't) . . . Some forty of the protestants were forced out of the theater but that did not quell the disturbance. The lights in the auditorium were fully turned on but the noise continued and I remember Mlle Piltz [the chosen maiden] executing her strange dance of religious hysteria on a stage dimmed by the blazing light in the auditorium, seemingly to the accompaniment of the disjointed ravings of a mob of angry men and women.[8]

The image of the dancers dancing to the noise of the audience is wonderful, and telling. The audience was as much a part of this famous performance as the corps de ballet. And to which side did the ejected protesters belong? Forty of them? Surely that number would have required a whole detachment of security men to clear. And no-one, not even the manager of the theater, Gabriel Astruc, makes any mention of such precautionary personnel in attendance or of such a large-scale evacuation. Moreover, Bronislava Nijinska claims, contrary to Van Vechten, that Maria Piltz's 'dance of the chosen maiden' met with relative quiet.[9]

Another version of the opening night excitement, which Van Vechten gave elsewhere, reveals that he is hardly a reliable source for detail. He apparently attended both the first and second performances of Le Sacre, and, to put it kindly, seems to have confused incidents from both.

> I was sitting in a box in which I had rented one seat. *Three ladies sat in front of me* and a young man occupied the place behind me. He stood up during the course of the ballet to enable himself to see more clearly. The intense excitement under which he was laboring, thanks to the potent force of the music, betrayed itself presently when he began to beat rhythmically on the top of my head with his fists. My emotion was so great that I did not feel the blows for some time. They were perfectly *synchronized with the beat of the music.* When I did, I turned around. His apology was sincere. We both had been carried beyond ourselves.[10]

In this account the music obviously could be heard! Van Vechten would like us to believe that his is a description of the raucous opening night, but we know from Gertrude Stein that she was one of the 'three ladies' sitting in front of Van Vechten, and she attended only the second performance on Monday! And according to Valentine Gross, who was present at all four performances of Le Sacre in Paris that May and June, the battle of the first night was not repeated. This merely suggests that Gertrude Stein's account is no more credible than the rest: 'We could hear nothing . . . one literally could not, throughout the whole performance, hear the sound of music.'[11] Literally? A score for over a hundred instruments could not be heard? Gertrude Stein went home with Alice B. Toklas and wrote not an article about the ballet but a poem, 'The One,' inspired by the stranger in her box, Carl Van Vechten. Perhaps she simply had not been listening.

Whom are we to believe? Gabriel Astruc claims in his memoirs that he shouted from his box shortly after the beginning, on opening night, *'Ecoutez d'abord! Vous sifflerez après!'** and that immediately, as if in response to the trident of Neptune, the storm abated: 'The end of the work was heard in distinct quiet.' Despite all the evident contradictions in the memoir accounts, these have been cited indiscriminately in all the secondary literature describing that opening night on 29 May 1913.

But what about the press reports? They are no more reliable than the memoirs in helping us determine exactly what happened. They were written by critics in attendance rather than by reporters in the strict sense, and consequently all displayed *parti-pris* attitudes similar to the divisions in the audience. The critical comments addressed themselves more thoroughly to Stravinsky's score than to Nijinsky's choreography – a reflection of the training of the critics – but this at any rate would suggest that much of the music had in fact been audible.

Where does all this confusion leave us? Is there not sufficient evidence to suggest that the trouble was caused more by warring factions in the audience, by their expectations, their prejudices, their preconceptions about art, than by the work itself? The work, as we shall see, certainly exploited tensions but hardly

*Listen first! You can whistle afterward!

caused them. The descriptions of the memoirists and even the accounts of the critics are immersed in the *scandale* rather than the music and ballet, in the event rather than the art. None of the witnesses ever mentions the rest of the program that first evening, the reception accorded *Les Sylphides*, *Le Spectre de la Rose*, and *Prince Igor*. Some people, like Gertrude Stein, so captivated, even if in retrospect, by this early twentieth-century 'happening,' have implied that they were present when they clearly were not. Can one blame them? To have been in the audience that evening was to have participated not simply at another exhibition but in the very creation of modern art, in that the response of the audience was and is as important to the meaning of this art as the intentions of those who introduced it. Art has transcended reason, didacticism, and a moral purpose: art has become provocation and event.

Thus, Jean Cocteau, who in his staccato prose – which corresponds so well with the percussive diction of *Le Sacre* – has given us many of our lasting images of that opening night, did not hesitate to admit that he was more concerned with 'subjective' than 'objective' truth; in other words, with what he felt, what he imagined, not with what actually occurred. His account of what happened after the performance of *Le Sacre* – his claim that he, along with Stravinsky, Nijinsky, and Diaghilev, drove out at two o'clock in the morning to the Bois de Boulogne and that Diaghilev, tears streaming down his face, started reciting Pushkin – has been denied by Stravinsky and is a passage that is a piece of theater, poetry, and prose combined. But most of our other witnesses are of a similar kind.

Valentine Gross's images are equally literary: the composers Maurice Delage, 'beetroot-red with indignation,' and Maurice Ravel, 'truculent as a fighting cock,' and the poet Léon-Paul Fargue 'spitting out crushing remarks at the hissing boxes.' The composer Florent Schmitt is said to have called the society ladies of the

Sixteenth Arrondissement 'whores' and the ambassador of the Austro-Hungarian Empire 'an old bum.' Some have claimed that Saint-Saëns went storming out early; Stravinsky has said that he was not even present. All this is the stuff of literature, or fact fermented by ego and memory and turned into fiction.

But what about the other camp, les pompiers, or philistines, as they were called by the aesthetes? Their testimony is naturally more limited. Most of the criticism poured out in the press almost immediately, yet it too was thoroughly engrossed in the event, in the social implications of the art, rather than the art itself.

Where does the fiction end and the fact begin? That boisterous evening rightly stands as a symbol of its era and as a landmark of this century. From the setting in the newly constructed, ultramodern Théâtre des Champs-Élysées, in Paris, through the ideas and intentions of the leading protagonists, to the tumultuous response of the audience, that opening night of Le Sacre represents a milestone in the development of 'modernism,' modernism as above all a culture of the sensational event, through which art and life both become a matter of energy and are fused as one. Given the crucial significance of the audience in this culture, we must look at the broader context of La Sacre.

LE THÉÂTRE DES CHAMPS-ÉLYSÉES

The avenue Montaigne runs between the Champs-Élysées and the place d'Alma in the Eighth Arrondissement. In an area of Paris that was redeveloped toward the end of the last century, the quarter had become fashionable with the haute bourgeoisie even before 1914. They lived there, as well as in Parc Monceau, Chaillot, Neuilly, and Passy. At number 13 on the arbored avenue stands the Théâtre des Champ-Élysées. Today the world's greatest artists perform there.

The theater is one of the finer examples of the work of Auguste Perret, whom some consider 'the father of modern French architecture.'[1] Constructed between 1911 and 1913, it belongs to the first generation of buildings to be erected with reinforced concrete. But in addition to the use of new materials, steel and concrete in place of brick or stone, a major concern of Perret was to incorporate and project in his work what he regarded as a new honesty and simplicity of style. Together with his contemporary Tony Garnier, he reacted against the prevailing heavy composite styles from the past or the current mannered mode of *art nouveau*, with its ornamentation and pretense. Clean lines and a new openness in the use of material were essential. 'Like all architecture based on false principles,' Garnier wrote, 'ancient architecture is an error. Truth alone is beautiful. In architecture, truth is the result of calculations made to satisfy known necessities with known materials.'[2]

For its ostentatious age this was a bold and aggressive formulation which echoed similar statements by architects and urban planners elsewhere, especially in Germany and Austria. 'Ornament is crime,' insisted Adolf Loos. A young associate who worked mornings in Perret's office in 1908 and studied in the afternoons was a twenty-one-year-old Swiss, Charles-Édouard Jeanneret. One day Perret asked the young man, who was later to take the name Le Corbusier, whether he had been to see the palace at Versailles yet. 'No, I shall never go!' was the reply. 'And why not?' 'Because Versailles and the classical epoch are nothing but decadence!'[3]

In 1902–1903, Perret had constructed an eight-story block of flats, at 25bis rue Franklin, that was revolutionary in its use of materials and its spatial effects. Two columns of prominent bay windows seemed to hang suspended without support and focused attention on the radical application of glass and concrete rectangular patterns. There was some *relief* on the façade, but contrary to *art nouveau* style, it did not impose itself on the

41

eye. Graduates of the tradition-minded École des Beaux-Arts regarded the new composition, in light of its startling simplicity, as more a matter of engineering than of art. The Théâtre des Champs-Élysées met with a similar response.

Most of the expensive construction of the era was straightforward imitation of a seventeenth- or eighteenth-century style, with little imagination. That style itself was based on classical patterns revived first in Italy and then exported north. The syncretic mode of the Grand and Petit Palais, both a stone's throw from the avenue Montaigne and built for the international exhibition of 1900 – when Paris celebrated herself – exemplified this imitative tendency. By comparison, the Théâtre des Champs-Élysées looked barren. Its lines were clean, even cold. The ferroconcrete construction, with smooth surfaces and sharp edges, exuded strength. Spaces for billboards were in perfect geometric relation to the other rectangular patterns in the façade, to the windows, the entrances, and the panels of sculptured *hauts-reliefs*, by Antoine Bourdelle, that constituted the only decoration on the exterior. In the vestibule an abundance of marble intensified the impression of cool reticence.

This was an architecture which was concerned, its designers claimed, with social needs and not individual whims, which preoccupied itself with authenticity and sincerity as opposed to pretense and hypocrisy. The overall austerity, compared with other public buildings, particularly the Opéra, built only forty years earlier, surprised and offended many people, however. Even the main auditorium, while rich in color, amaranth and gold, with painted frescoes by Maurice Denis, left a sense of uncluttered space. Denis, one of the theoreticians of postimpressionism, urged art to move away from mimesis, the interpretation of reality through imitation. 'We must close the shutters,' he said.[4]

Many were prone to denounce the new theatre as a

product of foreign influence. After all, Auguste Perret was born in Belgium, at Ixelles near Brussels, whither his father, a mason, had fled, under sentence of death, because he had fired on the Louvre during the Commune of 1871. The family was by definition obviously hostile to the French tradition. The Flemish architect Henry Van de Velde, who had been involved in the initial planning for the building, was also an early reformer who, steeped in the ideas of the British arts and crafts movement, had turned from fine to applied arts, developing notions of what he called 'free aesthetics.' Most of his patrons were German and he taught in Germany. Because of all these foreign associations J.L. Forain, the artist, derided the new theater as 'the Zeppelin on the avenue Montaigne.' Émile Bayard, the prolific art critic, was reminded of a 'funeral monument,' and Alphonse Gosset, the architect, scoffed at the construct, alluding, too, to a German influence:

> That the Germans, highly susceptible to sonorous singing, and hypnotic music, should accept this sort of reclusion, is perhaps understandable, but Parisians, avid of bright lights and elegance, no!

The inclination was to regard the building as an architectural affront to Parisian good taste, conviviality, and civility.[5]

The German reference is to be explained not merely in terms of hatred for an enemy in an era of resurgent nationalism. Germany did indeed lead the way in the development of a new architectural style based on an acceptance of industry and of the inevitability of urban growth. Though still confronted with extensive opposition, in Germany the new architectural aesthetic had nevertheless passed the bounds of an avant-garde style embraced by a few individuals. By the end of the first decade of this century many of the leading schools and academies of art were under the direction of such

43

progressive-minded people as Peter Behrens in Düsseldorf, Hans Poelzig in Breslau, and Henry Van de Velde in Weimar. The influential German Werkbund, with its aggressive concern for quality, utility, and beauty in all industrial work, was founded in 1907 and profoundly affected a whole generation of students, among them Walter Gropius and Ludwig Mies van der Rohe. In that same year, 1907, the mammoth German electrical company, Allgemeine Elektrizitäts-Gesellschaft, appointed Peter Behrens its architectural adviser, an indication of how far the new ideas had already spread. In Austria developments were similar. One can see then that Auguste Perret was, in the minds of many Frenchmen, an *agent provocateur* in the spiritual employ if not outright pay of the Germans.

Charges similar to those leveled at Perret were also laid against Gabriel Astruc, the Parisian impresario who openly confessed that he, contrary to most Frenchmen in the years before 1914, was a xenophile, a lover of foreigners.[6] An emotionally crapulous character, whose great passion was always the circus and who in his memoirs recounted with equal relish and animation his witnessing the execution by guillotine of four criminals on the one hand and his managerial accomplishments on the other, Astruc was descended from the Spanish Sephardim and was the son of a grand rabbi. He married into the music publishing firm of Enoch and, with financial help from the music lover and cultural benefactor Count Isaac de Camondo and his Turkish banking family, he established in April 1904 a promotion agency, the Société Musicale.

Astruc brought to Paris a steady stream of outstanding foreign artists, such as Wanda Landowska and Artur Rubinstein from Poland; Enrico Caruso, Lina Cavalieri, and Titta Ruffo to present in 1905 an 'Italian season'; and the entire Metropolitan Opera from New York, with Arturo Toscanini, in 1910. Astruc also demanded credit for bringing to Paris a touring group of

44

American blacks who introduced Parisians to Negro spirituals and the cakewalk.

From this base Astruc laid the foundations for an 'international committee of artistic patronage,' which provided distinguished moral support for visits and exchanges of international artists. The French section was headed by the beautiful and active Comtesse Greffuhle, whom Proust used as part model for both his Duchesse and his Princesse de Guermantes and whom another admirer considered a 'goddess' who would have inspired Veronese and Tiepolo.[7] The American representation included William K. Vanderbilt, John J. Astor, Clarence Mackay, James Stillman, and Pierpont Morgan. In London Lady de Grey enlisted the duchesses of Portland and Rutland and Sir Ernest Cassel, financier and friend of the king.

It was in 1906 that Astruc began developing his plans for a new theater, and in the seven years it took for the idea to become reality he encountered a barrage of opposition: the management of the Opéra and the Opéra Comique feared competition, for the star system that Astruc promoted would raise prices and thin out audiences; furthermore, his emphasis on novelty would encourage the frivolous and ephemeral. Municipal and state officials questioned the wisdom and purpose of the theater. Anti-Semites maligned him as a money-grubbing Jew interested in eroding established values. 'It would take me a whole volume,' Astruc wrote in typical turns of phrase in his memoirs, 'to tell the true story, miraculous and disheartening, of the construction of "my theater." I know, not each stone because it is built of cement, but each metal fiber.'[8] Yet the theater was built and it had luminous financial backing – Vanderbilt, Morgan, Stillman, Rothschild, Cassel – as well as support, both moral and financial, from Otto H. Kahn, president of the New York Opera.

The theater opened on 30 March 1913. Lights projected on to the façade emphasized the building's

45

whiteness, its simplicity, and high-lighted the reliefs of Bourdelle's frieze, *Apollo and the Muses*. Astruc observed the first-night audience arriving to hear the inaugural concert devoted to Berlioz's *Benvenuto Cellini* and Weber's *Der Freischütz*.

> On entering the hall, people seemed first to be blinded. Then they looked. Some became excited. Others sniggered. The majority, before voicing an opinion, waited to hear that of their neighbor. The words 'Munich,' 'neoclassical German' blended here and there.

Jacques-Émile Blanche heard similar responses – 'Theosophist temple,' 'Belgian' – but he was astute enough to note that both certain artistic motifs in the theater and its programs bowed noticeably to tradition. The whole enterprise was a symbolic attempt to synthesize modern and traditional impulses.[9] Paris, however, was not yet prepared for such a resolution.

DIAGHILEV AND THE BALLETS RUSSES

'I am firstly a great charlatan,' Serge Diaghilev wrote to his step-mother in 1895, in a statement that has become justly famous because of its exuberance and its accuracy as a self-assessment,

> though *con brio*; secondly, a great *charmeur*; thirdly, I have any amount of cheek; fourthly, I am a man with a great quantity of logic, but with very few principles; fifthly, I think I have no real gifts. All the same, I think I have just found my true vocation – being a Maecenas. I have all that is necessary save the money – *mais ça viendra*.[1]

Diaghilev's background was a welter of contraries, real and imagined. Perhaps the most profound of these contraries was that his birth occasioned his mother's death. Misia Sert, an equally extravagant character who was to become his close friend, had a similar fate. Both seemed to be plagued throughout their lives with a sense of guilt for simply existing. Diaghilev's father was a provincial aristocrat who nonetheless indulged in business; he owned some large distilleries. A military man, he nevertheless had a serious and deep love for music. In the Russian context neither combination was regarded as unusual, but as the son became increasingly westernized, he began to labor under what he sensed were contradictions in his past and in his upbringing. Even though he tried as he grew older to adopt a cosmopolitan air, Diaghilev never renounced his provincial roots. Thus a tension always remained in him between the formative experience of his early life and the aspirations of his adult years.

Diaghilev began his studies at the university in St Petersburg with the intention of becoming a lawyer; he continued them at the conservatory, studying composition. He wrote some songs and even a scene for an opera on the theme of Boris Godunov. He played the piano with panache and had a fine baritone voice, singing arias from *Parsifal* and *Lohengrin* in concert on at least one occasion. He dabbled in painting as well. He did not become a lawyer or a composer or an artist. Romola Nijinsky relates that the musicians said of Diaghilev that he was not a musician, and the painters said that he was a dilettante, but both had generous comments about his abilities in the other art, in the same way that statesmen had said of Disraeli that he was a fine writer, and writers had acknowledged that he was a grand statesman. Still, Diaghilev's legal training and his interest in all the arts were to be combined in an astonishingly productive manner.[2]

With his family background, his education, and his social connections – he had an uncle who was minister of the interior to the tsar in the 1890s and who introduced him to court society – Diaghilev had strong roots in a conservative imperial tradition. However, he was also clearly driven by countervailing instincts: the sense of having destroyed his mother and hence a sympathy for matriarchy; his homosexuality, which he accepted relatively early in life and which he seems to have enjoyed flaunting; and his aesthetic sensibility in general, which led him in his twenties to cultivate a dandyish appearance – a gray streak in his otherwise jet-black hair, a neat mustache, a monocle and chain. He also encouraged the legend that his family was an illegitimate line from Peter the Great. There is nonchalance and anxiety here, posturing and guilt. He tried to combine the divergent tendencies for a time, working, for instance, as adviser to the administrator of the imperial theaters, but Diaghilev was not willing to repress, and the Russian establishment was not flexible enough to absorb, his antiestablishment sentiments and other extravagant behavior, which were interpreted as intolerable disrespect toward the imperial authorities, and he was fired in 1901. His departure was probably inevitable, because he was already extensively involved in entrepreneurial activities. He began to talk, like Peter the Great, about opening a window on Europe.

Having traveled through much of Europe in the early 1890s and having inherited his mother's money in 1893, when he reached the age of twenty-one, Diaghilev began his activities on a modest scale, initially as an art impresario, organizing exhibitions first of British and German watercolors for St Petersburg, next of Scandinavian art, and then of Russian paintings, which he displayed in Russia and was later to bring to the rest of Europe. In 1898, with a group of friends, he founded a lavish and expensive publication called Mir iskusstva (The World of Art), a journal that was to survive for six years and that, despite its relatively brief life and small circulation, which never exceeded four thousand, provoked intense debate in Russian art circles by attacking both conservative academicism and radical social utilitarianism, and by promoting new trends in Western art, from impressionism to futurism. In 1899 he brought to St Petersburg a show of French impressionists and other moderns that elicited great interest.

Diaghilev's international recognition began in 1905 with another of the paradoxes that marked his early years. In that year of war and revolution for Russia, when the Japanese devastated both the tsar's armies and his fleet, when protesting workers in St Petersburg were massacred on 'Bloody Sunday' by Cossack cavalry, when peasants burned and pillaged manor houses in the countryside, and when workers called a general strike that Trotsky would later term the Bolshevik 'dress rehearsal for revolution,' in this remarkable year Diaghilev, the dandy and aesthete, opened at the Tauride Palace in St Petersburg – Catherine the Great had had it built for her lover Potemkin – an astonishing display of Russian historical portraits he had assiduously collected in the provinces and borrowed from other parts of Europe. The exhibition, which received a generous subsidy from the tsar, opened in February and contained four thousand canvases, including thirty-five portraits of Peter the Great, forty-four of Catherine the Great, and thirty-two of Alexander I. Before the show closed in May it had been visited by forty-five thousand people.[3] Even the inaugural exhibition of the Museum of Modern Art in New York in 1929, with all its publicity, would attract only five thousand more visitors. Russia had never seen such an imposing public statement on its official history. It must be emphasized that Diaghilev, the budding experimentalist who was to become manager extraordinary of the 'modern spirit,' launched himself from the foundations of the Russian past.

In the following year he organized a Russian exhibit for the Salon d'Automne in the Petit Palais in Paris. The presentation contained a cross section of material ranging from icons through eighteenth-century portraits to works by the *World of Art* circle, Mikhail Vrubel, Valentine Serov, Alexandre Benois, Léon Bakst, Mstislav Dobujinsky, Nicholas Roerich, and Mikhail Larionov. The committee of patrons for the exhibition was headed by the Grand Duke Vladimir and included the Comtesse Greffuhle, who had probably the most elegant salon in Paris and whom Diaghilev met, impressed, and enlisted in supporting his project for the next year, a festival of Russian music.

Thereafter one success followed another. In 1907, between 16 and 30 May, five concerts were given at the Opéra, presenting a wide range of Russian music, with Rimsky-Korsakov, Rachmaninov, and Glazunov conducting their own compositions. Among the singers were Chaliapin and Cherkasskaya. The sonorous and dramatic bass baritone in particular was an enormous success. The next year, 1908, Mussorgsky's *Boris Godunov*, in a revised version by Rimsky-Korsakov, was taken to Paris. The opera about the tsar who ruled from 1598 to 1605 and about the pretender Dmitri was not popular in St Petersburg. Court society especially found offensive the parts of the story that called into question legitimacy, justice, and authority. Paris, however, seemed to love the work, above all Chaliapin's Boris. Misia Sert was spellbound: 'I left the theater stirred to the point of realizing that something had been changed in my life. The music was with me always.'[4]

It was through the Comtesse Greffuhle that Diaghilev met Gabriel Astruc. Diaghilev had now presented to Paris Russian painting, Russian music, Russian opera, and, as he was to put it later, 'from opera to ballet was but a step.' The existence of outstanding Russian dancers who were completely unknown outside Russia was an important reason for the move into ballet. But there was a theoretical side that was perhaps even more important.

In a Wagnerian sally toward ultimate art Diaghilev claimed that ballet contained in itself all the other art forms. Wagner had conceived of opera as a higher form of drama and a further evolution of the Greek synthesis of music and word. In the opera, however, claimed Diaghilev, there were visual impediments, like stationary singers, and aural barriers, like the need to concentrate on words, all of which interfered with the necessary fluidity of art. 'In the ballet,' wrote Alexandre Benois, who exercised a great influence on Diaghilev, 'I would point to the elemental mixture of visual and aural impressions; in the ballet is attained the ideal of the *Gesamtkunstwerk* about which Wagner dreamed and about which every artistically gifted person dreams.'[5]

In June 1911, Stravinsky, very much under the spell of Diaghilev, would cite the new gospel to Vladimir Rimsky-Korsakov, son of the composer:

> I am interested in and love the ballet more than anything else . . . If some Michelangelo were alive today – so I thought looking at his frescoes in the Sistine Chapel – the only thing that his genius would admit and recognize is choreography . . . The only form of theatre-art that makes its cornerstone the *problems of beauty* and nothing more is the ballet.[6]

The search for the *Gesamtkunstwerk* – for the holy grail that is the 'total art form' – was actually a universal one by the end of the nineteenth century. The arts, in part because of the enormous influence of Wagner, had moved steadily toward each other. Debussy, to introduce an example here to which we shall return later, would take a symbolist poem by Mallarmé and use it as a basis for a tone painting not dissimilar in effect from impressionism in pictorial art.

Diaghilev and Astruc reached agreement, and on 19 May 1909, the Ballets russes – consisting of fifty-five dancers trained exclusively in the imperial ballet school and on temporary leave from the imperial theaters of St

Petersburg and Moscow – opened in Paris at the Théâtre du Châtelet. That opening night, when the program consisted of *Le Pavillon d'Armide*, the act of the opera *Prince Igor* that includes the Polovetsian dances, and *Le Festin*, is enshrined in the annals of ballet, and that whole Russian season of 1909 was a sensation. Ballet in Paris, as in most of Europe, had sunk by the end of the nineteenth century to a display merely of prettiness; pleasant, controlled steps and charming costumes; 'a little Italian virtuosity,' as Richard Buckle has put it, 'tricked out with a lot of French coquetterie.'[7] Stage decoration was not an art, only a craft left to artisans. The Russians changed all this. The sets of Bakst, Benois, and Roerich, with their bright and provocative colors and lavish features, such as authentic Georgian silk, were stunning, no longer merely a backdrop but an integral part of the spectacle. The choreography of Fokine called for a new energy and physical ability, captured breathtakingly in Nijinsky's leaps and Pavlova's and Karsavina's grace. Karsavina in her autobiography has an anecdote to relate about Nijinsky that reveals as much about the latter's mentality as it does about the effect of his agility.

Somebody was asking Nijinsky if it was difficult to stay in the air as he did while jumping; he did not understand at first, and then very obligingly: 'No! No! not difficult. You have to just go up and then pause a little up there.'[8]

The themes were exotic, usually Russian or oriental. The music was different. And the dance was not simply an attempt to relate movement to sound but to express sound in movement.

So, in 1909, fifteen years after a diplomatic alliance had been ratified between the Quai d'Orsay and St Petersburg in response to the German threat, Paris finally encountered the Russians. Proust commented:

This charming invasion, against whose seductions only the most vulgar critics protested, brought on Paris, as we know, a fever of curiosity less acute, more purely aesthetic, but perhaps just as intense as that aroused by the Dreyfus case.[9]

In 1910 the Russians returned to Paris and then played the Theater des Westens in Berlin. In 1911, to escape from the perpetual problems of borrowing dancers from their regular companies and to achieve some independence, Diaghilev formed his own company, the Ballets russes de Diaghilev, and over the next years, 1911 to 1913, the ballet toured Europe – Monte Carlo, Rome, Berlin, London, Vienna, Budapest – and left a trail of excitement, incredulity, and rapture. Many young aesthetes recorded their exuberance. Of the first performance of *Schéhérazade*, Proust told Reynaldo Hahn that he had never seen anything quite so beautiful.[10] Harold Acton described that production:

. . . the heavy calm before the storm in the harem: the thunder and lightning of negroes in rose and amber; the fierce orgy of clamorous caresses; the final panic and bloody retributions: death in long-drawn spasms to piercing violins. Rimsky-Korsakov painted the tragedy; Bakst hung it with emerald curtains and silver lamps and carpeted it with rugs from Bokhara and silken cushions; Nijinsky and Karsavina made it live. For many a young artist *Schéhérazade* was an inspiration equivalent to Gothic architecture for the Romantics or Quattrocento frescoes for the Pre-Raphaelites.[11]

Rupert Brooke, the handsome and gifted young poet who became a symbol of the spiritual confusion and yearning of his generation, was ecstatic after first seeing the Russians in 1912: 'They, if anything, can redeem our civilization. I'd give everything to be a ballet designer.'[12]

In 1911 London was introduced to the Russian company. On 26 June, Diaghilev's troupe performed at Covent Garden at the coronation gala for King George V amidst 100,000 roses used as decoration and before an audience that included ambassadors and ministers, African kings, Indian chiefs, maharajahs and mandarins, and the cream of British society. 'Thus, in one evening,' Diaghilev quipped, 'the Russian ballet conquered the whole world.' *The Illustrated London News* was so taken by the Russian achievement that it called for the creation of a permanent dance company at Covent Garden; and the *Times* was so enthusiastic that it began to print regular articles on dance. In its issue of 5 July, *Punch* had three cartoons related to dance, an indication of how striking the impact of the Russians had been. Kaiser Wilhelm of Germany and King Alfonso of Spain eventually became patrons of the Ballets russes.

With every season Diaghilev became more daring. The eroticism became more overt. It was there from the start, in *Cléopatre* in the 1909 season – the tale about a queen who seeks a lover willing to die at dawn after a night of love – with its wild bacchanal scene of quickening *tempi*, great leaps of the Ethiopians, tossing flesh, and waves of silk and gold. But it became bolder. That caused the excitement to turn in some quarters to disquietude.

The *scandale* of the 1912 season was the première in Paris on 29 May of Debussy's *L'Après-midi d'un faune*, inspired by Mallarmé's poem, choreographed and danced by Nijinsky, with *art nouveau* sets and costumes by Bakst. The story is about a Roman deity, a faun, with horns and a tail, who falls in love with a young wood nymph. Nijinsky, dressed in leotards at a time when skin-tight costumes were still thought to be improper, provoked in the audience a collective salivation and swallowing as he descended, hips undulating, over the nymph's scarf, and quivered in simulated orgasm. That was simply the culmination of a ballet that broke all the rules of traditional taste. The entire work was staged in profile in an attempt to reproduce the images of classical *bas-reliefs* and vase paintings. Movements, both walking and running, were almost entirely lateral, always heel to toe, followed by a pivot on both feet and a change of position of arms and head. Gaston Calmette, editor of *Le Figaro*, refused to publish the review prepared by the regular dance correspondent, Robert Brussel, and instead penned a front-page article himself in which he denounced *Faune* as 'neither a pretty pastoral nor a work of profound meaning. We are shown a lecherous faun, whose movements are filthy and bestial in their eroticism, and whose gestures are as crude as they are indecent.'[13]

Calmette was to move from one onslaught to the next in 1912–13. When Auguste Rodin sprang to the defense of Nijinsky, Calmette berated him as an immoral dilettante who squandered public funds. In December 1913 Calmette would begin his last campaign, an attack this time against Joseph Caillaux, former prime minister and now minister of finance in the new Doumergue government. On 16 March 1914, Henriette Caillaux, the minister's wife, took a taxi to the *Figaro* offices in rue Drouot, waited patiently for an hour to see the chief editor, then walked with him into his private office and emptied her automatic pistol at him. Hit by four of six shots, he died that evening.

Other members of the public were apparently also offended by *Faune*, and the final scene was modified slightly in subsequent performances. But the aesthetes were elated by the beauty of this 'offense against good taste.' Léon Bakst thought the choreography the work of a genius, and Diaghilev himself, at first hesitant about even accepting this extraordinary manifestation of Nijinsky's independence, nonetheless recognized its brilliance. The artist and designer Charles Ricketts even celebrated Calmette's murder.[14] The wits of course worked overtime. One quip to surface: '*Faune y soit qui mal y pense.*'

Nijinsky's deliberate provocation in *Faune* was symptomatic of an ever-increasing boldness in the choreography and musical language of the Russians. Fokine had led the departure from the conventions of classical ballet by cutting down on brilliant steps and virtuosity and by emphasizing interpretation of the music. He despised meaningless displays of strength. 'The dance,' he insisted, 'need not be a *divertissement*. It should not degenerate into mere gymnastics. It should, in fact, be the plastic word. The dance should express . . . the whole epoch to which the subject of the ballet belongs.'[15]

Nijinsky then added a new dimension to the revolt and reached a new stage in the quest for a 'plasticity' of movement and image. In addition to *Faune* and *Le Sacre* he choreographed *Jeux*, which opened the season in 1913. It was a mixture of classical steps and 'anti-classical' poses. At the beginning Nijinsky arrived onstage, with a traditional grand jeté, in pursuit of a somewhat oversized tennis ball, but some of the unusual positions that were to dominate *Le Sacre* now appeared, poses, for instance, with arms rounded and feet turned inward. The public was hardly enthusiastic about what was purported to be a new verisimilitude in dance. Where was that honesty? it asked. Perhaps in Nijinsky's mind, certainly not on the stage. Although the ballet was supposed to revolve around a tennis match, the choreography bore little resemblance to any game. Even Debussy, a musical reformer himself, was astounded by the audacity. He called Nijinsky

a perverse genius . . . a young savage . . . This fellow adds up triple crochets with his feet, checks them on his arms, then suddenly, half-paralyzed, he stands crossly watching the music slip by. It's awful.[16]

When *Jeux* came to London, *Punch* took one of its pokes at both the disenchanted audience and Nijinsky.

Nijinsky, there are certain souls
More blind to beauty than a hen is,
Who, jarred not by the caracoles
In all your other ballet roles,
Take umbrage at your 'Tennis.'[17]

The music chosen by Diaghilev for his ballet company became more abstract as well. The Russian composers whom he used early on were relatively orthodox, though the melodic line usually consisted of exotic themes to which western ears were not accustomed. Debussy's impressionistic compositions marked a departure in a more experimental direction, with their new harmonic patterns and interest in sounds for their own sake without reference to melody. Debussy's concern was with 'delicate feelings,' with 'elusive moments,' rather than with the overwhelming harmonic patterns of the German school of the era. Fleeting emotions, wisps of sensation, the bubbles in the champagne, these were attributes of the impressionists, who marked an important stage in the breakdown of romantic music and in the move toward an internalized music of expressionism.

By the end of the first decade of the new century, with the help of the impressionists, the manner of composition was changing radically. From Mozart until the late nineteenth century, music was put together with relatively large building blocks: scales, arpeggios, long cadences. However, by the end of the century these units were being discarded. Music had been reduced to individual notes or, at most, short motifs. As in architecture, the arts and crafts movement, and painting, there was a new emphasis on basic materials, primary colors, and elemental substance.

There was nothing accidental about the scandals caused by Diaghilev and his Ballets russes. This 'charlatan con brio' was a master mind at provocation. 'It is success and only success, my friend,' he wrote to Benois in 1897, 'that saves and redeems all . . . I do have

57

a rather vulgar insolence and I am accustomed to telling people to go to hell.'[18] He was a Nietzschean creation, a supreme egotist out to conquer, and he succeeded in becoming the despot of a cultural empire that affected, primarily through the medium of ballet, all the arts of his time, including fashion, literature, theater, painting, interior design, and even cinema. Jacques-Émile Blanche called him a 'professor of energy, the will that gives body to others' conceptions.'[19] Benois was to say 'Diaghilev had in him everything it takes to be a *duce*.'[20] His public importance was in his achievement as a manager, as a propagandist, as a *duce*, and less as a creative person. As a theorist he plundered other people's ideas; as an impresario, he plundered, in Napoleonic *dragonnades*, the world of art. His creation was his management, his shaping of shapes, and in this role he was a brilliant artistic *condottiere*. As such he became central to twentieth-century aesthetic sense, to the enshrinement of attitudes and styles rather than substance. He was a figurehead of the aesthetics of technique. People wrote long letters to him; he replied by telegram.

This does not mean, however, that Diaghilev did not have a positive view of art. He did, but his approach was intuitive, not analytical. Many have noted how he would seize upon an idea or project immediately, before he had had an opportunity to examine it. While the *World of Art* journal forced him constantly to formulate aesthetic ideas and to make decisions on the basis of these ideas, he never succeeded in assembling a clear and consistent philosophy of art. He did, nevertheless, build on certain premises.

He conceived of art as a means of deliverance and regeneration. The deliverance would be from the social constraints of morality and convention, and from the priorities of a western civilization – of which Russia was becoming increasingly a part – dominated by a competitive and self-denying ethic. The regeneration would involve the recovery of a spontaneous emotional life, not simply by the intellectual elite, although that was the first step, but ultimately by society as a whole. Art, in this outlook, is a life force; it has the invigorating power of religion; it acts through the individual but in the end is greater than that individual; it is in fact a surrogate religion.

Social conscience did not motivate this thinking. Like Nietzsche, Diaghilev believed that autonomy of the artist and morality were mutually exclusive. A man obsessed with morality, with socially acceptable behavior, could never be free, and like Gide, Rivière, and Proust, he believed that the artist, to achieve freedom of vision, must have no regard for morality. He must be amoral. Morality, as the avant-garde was wont to say, was an *invention des laids*, the revenge of the ugly. Liberation to beauty would come not through collective effort but through egotism, through a personal salvation and not through social works.

Although Diaghilev paid homage to history and the accomplishments of western culture, he did see himself essentially as a pathfinder and liberator. Vitality, spontaneity, and change were celebrated. Anything was preferable to stultifying conformism, even moral disorder and confusion. Oscar Wilde's sally that 'there is no sin except stupidity' expressed Diaghilev's sentiments too. Social and moral absolutes were thrown overboard, and art, or the aesthetic sense, became the issue of supreme importance because it would lead to freedom.

Diaghilev was of course merely a part, though an immensely significant one, of a much broader cultural and intellectual trend, a revolt against rationalism and a corresponding affirmation of life and experience that gained strength from the 1890s on. The romantic rebellion, which, with its distrust of mechanistic systems, extended back over a century, coincided at the *fin de siècle* with the rapidly advancing scientific demolition of the Newtonian universe. Through the discoveries of

Planck, Einstein, and Freud, rational man undermined his own world. Science seemed thus to confirm important tendencies in philosophy and art. Henri Bergson developed his idea of 'creative evolution,' which rejected the notion of 'objective' knowledge: the only reality is the *élan vital*, the life force. He became a veritable star in fashionable circles in Paris. And the Italian futurist Umberto Boccioni, reflecting the widespread preoccupation with machines and change, declared, 'There is no such thing as a nonmoving object in our modern perception of life.' Diaghilev was attuned to these developments, which hailed a will to constant metamorphosis and praised the beauty of transitoriness. He grasped the new wave with exhilaration. '*Qui n'avance pas recule*,' he decided.*

In this context, where rationalist notions of cause and effect were rejected and the importance of the intuitive moment stressed, shock and provocation became important instruments of art. For Diaghilev art was not meant to teach or imitate reality; above all, it was to provoke genuine experience. Through the element of shock he hoped to achieve in his audience what Gide tried to elicit from his protagonist Lafcadio in *Les Caves du Vatican*, which was published in 1914: an *acte gratuit*, behavior free of motivation, purpose, meaning; pure action; sublime experience free of the constraints of time or place. '*Étonne-moi, Jean!*'** Diaghilev said to Cocteau on one occasion, and the latter came to look on that moment and utterance as a road-to-Damascus experience. Surprise is freedom. The audience, in Diaghilev's view, could be as important to the experience of art as the performers. The art would not teach – that would make it subservient; it would excite, provoke, inspire. It would unlock experience.

In his belief that art had to draw more of its content

**He who does not advance retreats.
*Surprise me, Jean!

60

from popular folk traditions and that only in this way could the gap be bridged between popular and high culture, Diaghilev followed in the footsteps of Rousseau, Herder, and the romantics. It was in the Russian countryside, primitive and unaffected by mechanization, that Diaghilev and his circle found much of their inspiration, in the designs and colors of peasant costumes, the paintings on carts and sleighs, the carvings around windows and doors, and the myths and fables of an unassuming rural culture. It was, according to Diaghilev, from this Russian soul that salvation would come for western Europe. 'Russian art,' he wrote in March 1906 before his first exhibition there, 'will not only begin to play a role; it will also become, in actual fact and in the broadest meaning of the word, one of the principal leaders of our imminent movement of enlightenment.'[21]

Diaghilev acknowledged his intellectual debts: to a conservative Russian culture rooted in an aristocratic tradition; to a wave of modern thought that stretched back a century and that had a strong German component, in E.T.A. Hoffmann, Nietzsche, and Wagner, among others; and to a growing appreciation, particularly in Russia, Germany, and eastern Europe, of what the Germans called *Volk* culture. But while he possessed a strong sense of history, his sights were set on the future. He followed the manifestoes and exploits of the futurists with interest, and showed a special fondness for the art of the Russian futurists Larionov and Goncharova. He did not despise technology as some aesthetes did but looked on the machine as a central component of the future. On New Year's Day 1912, Nijinsky and Karsavina danced *Le Spectre de la Rose* at the Opéra in Paris at a gala honoring French aviation. As an impresario, Diaghilev was keenly aware of the importance of modern methods of publicity and advertisement, and he had no compunction in resorting to exaggeration, ambiguity, and impertinence in his pursuit of success.

The goal of his grand ballet was to produce a synthesis – of all the arts, of a legacy of history and a vision of the future, of orientalism and westernism, of the modern and the feudal, of aristocrats and peasants, of decadence and barbarism, of man and woman, and so on. He wished to fuse the double image of contemporary life – an age of transition – into a vision of wholeness, with emphasis, however, on the vision rather than the wholeness, on the quest, the striving, on the pursuit of wholeness, continuing and changing though this had to be. He meant, in Faustian temper, to overcome and integrate. The 'either-or' decision that ethics called for he rejected in favor of an aesthetic imperialism that, like Don Giovanni, craved everything. Here was a hunger for wholeness that nevertheless, because of its emphasis on experience, celebrated the hunger more than the wholeness.

REBELLION

Diaghilev's ballet enterprise was both a quest for totality and an instrument of liberation. Perhaps the most sensitive nerve it touched – and this was done deliberately – was that of sexual morality, which was so central a symbol of the established order, especially in the heart of political, economic, and imperial power, western Europe. Again, Diaghilev was simply an heir to a prominent, accumulating tradition. For many intellectuals of the nineteenth century, from Saint-Simon through Feuerbach to Freud, the real origin of 'alienation,' estrangement from self, society, and the material world, was sexual. 'Pleasure, joy, expands man,' wrote Feuerbach; 'trouble, suffering, contracts and concentrates him; in suffering man denies the reality of the world.'[1]

The middle classes, in particular, of the Victorian age interpreted pleasure in primarily spiritual and moral rather than physical or sensual terms. Gratification of the senses was suspect, indeed sinful. Will, based on moral fervor, was the essence of successful human endeavor; pure passion, its opposite. That the issue of sexual morality should become a vehicle of rebellion against bourgeois values for the modern movement was inevitable. In the art of Gustav Klimt, in the early operas of Richard Strauss, in the plays of Frank Wedekind, in the personal antics of Verlaine, Tchaikovsky, and Wilde, and even in the relaxed morality of the German youth movement, a motif of eroticism dominated the search for newness and change. 'Better a whore than a bore,' mused Wedekind, while in the United States Max Eastman shouted, 'Lust is sacred!'[2] The sexual rebel, particularly the homosexual, became a central figure in the imagery of revolt, especially after the ignominious treatment Oscar Wilde received at the hands of the establishment. Of her Bloomsbury circle of gentle rebels Virginia Woolf said, 'The word bugger was never far from our lips.'[3] André Gide, after a long struggle with himself, denounced publicly *le mensonge des moeurs*, the moral lie, and admitted his own predilections. Passion and love, he had concluded, were mutually exclusive. And passion was much purer than love.[4]

Diaghilev's sexual proclivities were well known, and he made no attempt to mask them; quite the reverse. Stravinsky said later that Diaghilev's entourage was 'a kind of homosexual Swiss Guard.'[5] Not surprisingly, a sexual tension pervaded the whole experience of the Ballets russes, among performers, managers, hangers-on, and audience. Some of the ballet themes were openly erotic, even sadomasochistic, as in *Cléopatre* and *Schéhérazade*: in both, young slaves pay for sexual pleasures with their lives. In others the sexuality was veiled. In *Petrushka* the puppet dies frustrated in his love for a cruel doll. Nijinsky was to claim later in his diary, written six years after the first performance, that *Jeux*, with its cast of one man and two girls, was

Diaghilev's way of presenting, without danger of outright censure, his own fantasy, apparently often stated to Nijinsky, of making love to two men.[6] Whether or not this was a fabrication of Nijinsky's dementia – the diary was written at the end of the Great War as Nijinsky was slipping into madness – it is not inconsistent with Diaghilev's behavior.

In all the ballets, the colors of the sets, the boldness of the costumes, and the sustained energy of the dancing accentuated the passion. Poets wrote odes to Anna Pavlova; they sang praises to the beautiful Karsavina and Rubinstein; but every aesthete in Europe seemed to be in love with the 'grace and brutality,' to use Cocteau's words,[7] of Nijinsky. Appropriately, he was barred from dancing at the Imperial Theater in Moscow after a performance before the dowager empress in 1911 in *Giselle*, in which he wore nothing over his tights and displayed, in Peter Lieven's words, his '*rotundités complètement impudiques.*'[8] From his extraordinary levitation in *Le Spectre de la Rose* to the scandalous finale of *L'Après-midi d'un faune* to the provocative choreography of *Jeux*, Nijinsky with his physical prowess and his mental audacity, with his combination of innocence and daring, caught the imagination of an entire generation. The erotic thrill Parisians derived was underlined by the full-page picture of him in *L'Illustration* with the caption 'Dancer Nijinsky more talked of than debates in the Chamber.'[9] 'An idiot of genius' the highly sexed Misia Sert called him in a telling phrase. Diaghilev, always aroused by public acclaim, took Nijinsky as his lover after the outstanding success of the 1909 season. The two men lived together for a time, and when Nijinsky suddenly married in 1913, the dancer seemed genuinely not to have understood the reason for Diaghilev's outrage. 'If it is true that Serge does not want to work with me – then I have lost everything,' Nijinsky wrote to Stravinsky in December 1913. 'I cannot imagine what has happened, what is the reason for his behavior. Please ask Serge what is the matter, and write to me about it.'[10] It was this stunning naïveté – the suggestion that he was not burdened by the moral baggage of centuries, what Gide called the moral lie – combined with the venturesomeness of his artistic imagination that excited Proust, Cocteau, Lytton Strachey, and others to a feverish pitch. Nijinsky *was* the faun, a wild creature temporarily trapped by society. Imagine, they said to themselves, this incredible physical specimen, given to instinct and passion, free of moral constraint . . . and they became delirious in their imaginings. Strachey sent 'a great basket of magnissime flowers' and went to bed, as he himself declared, 'dreaming of Nijinsky.'[11]

From the age of chivalry, but particularly since romanticism, woman – *das ewig Weibliche**** – had been the source of poetic inspiration and the object of lyrical worship. In the performing arts it was the diva, the prima donna, the ballerina, who was applauded and showered with flowers. But now a man, of grace and beauty, took the spotlight. This was truly revolutionary. For some it was outrageous. An aura of decadence surrounded the Ballets russes as a whole. Robert de Flers and Gaston de Cavaillet had a character in their play, *Le Bois sacré*, say, 'We're starting to become very elegant gents, to make very chic acquaintances, very rotten, very Ballets russes.'

That dance – the attempt to join mind and body in the same rhythm – became an important medium for the modern movement was natural. Although the Egyptians and Greeks had danced, Christian civilization had no place for dance, and it was not until after the Renaissance and Reformation, with their attendant secularization, that dance as an expression of imagination re-emerged. However, it was still associated almost exclusively with aristocratic court culture or, of course,

*The eternally feminine.

with pagan activities. The Protestant ethic continued to reject dance as an expression of sensuality and passion. Classical dance emerged in France and Italy but with distinct national variations: the Italians stressed virtuosity, and the French laid emphasis on the creation of a romantic mood; but even in these countries ballet had sunk by the end of the nineteenth century into a rigid formalism that left little room for individual expression. In Britain and Germany dance had disappeared into virtual oblivion.

It was from Russia that the revival came. There, among the old aristocracy and court society, the 'French style,' with imported dancers and choreographers, experienced a growing popularity in the course of the nineteenth century. The principal theater was the Mariinsky in St Petersburg. In the second half of the century, through the Marseillais Marius Petipa and the Swede Christian Johannsen, a significant attempt was launched in St Petersburg to combine the French and the Italian styles, elegance with virtuosity, emphasizing a new flow, a 'dance of the arms,' as it came to be called. Such was the beginning of the Russian school, and it was on these foundations that Diaghilev built, seeing in ballet a superior art form for expressing, through action and movement instead of persuasion and argument, the totality of the human personality, both spiritual and physical, and the essence of the nonverbal, nonrational world. One critic noted perceptively that the Russian ballet was the 'cinématograph du riche.'[12]

Diaghilev was not the first to introduce an openly erotic note to dance. There was a strong measure of sexual fantasy in Isadora Duncan's dancing and, indeed, in her success. Having read Nietzsche, this American from San Francisco decided that her art was original Dionysian art, before Apollo intellectualized emotion and turned dance from passion into style and drained it of purity and vitality. She claimed to represent spontaneity and natural expression, to capture

66

impromptu form. She wanted to 'free' both the body and the emotions of constraints and allow the two to join 'organically.' Yet she was less of an innovator than she liked to think: despite her claims, she could not escape classical Greece and the curved serpentine line that had dominated ballet since the romantics. Duncan's lusty and fertile personality was as much a creative force as her dance, and she had great success throughout Europe in the years after the turn of the century. In Germany the legend sprang up of *die heilige, göttliche Isadora.**

It was Nijinsky who brought, as *The Times* of London put it, the 'real revolution in dancing.'[13] In 1828 Carlo Blasis had written, in *The Code of Terpsichore*, 'Take care to make your arms so encircling that the points of your elbows may be imperceptible,' and the curve conquered the straight line. Invariably in classical ballet grace and charm became more important than character and interpretation. While Fokine moved back toward interpretation, Nijinsky insisted on expressiveness with a vengeance, deliberately rebelling against 'the line of beauty,' the accustomed pleasure of the eye. He took special care in his choreography to make the points of his elbows not only perceptible but inescapable.

Duncan was the instrument through which the ideas of eurhythmics, the study of rhythm, and 'aesthetic gymnastics' were popularized. Émile Jaques-Dalcroze set up an influential school for the former – first in Geneva, then in Hellerau near Dresden – and Diaghilev and Nijinsky visited it in 1912 to obtain help for *Le Sacre*. These developments corresponded with a new *Leibeskultur*, or 'body culture,' which found its greatest social resonance in Germany and Russia but surfaced elsewhere in such phenomena as 'muscular Christianity,' the Boy Scout movement, the origins of the modern

*The holy, divine Isadora.

Olympics, and, not least, the Poiret fashion revolution, which offered women freedom from corsets and a new, glittering, slouching sensuality. For the first time in a century trim bodies became fashionable, particularly in Paris. Dance, both serious and popular, seemed central to the whole trend. In 1911 every major music hall in London booked a ballerina for performance, and the implications of this provided rich material for *Punch*.

At the Crematorium the chief attraction is Frl. Rollmops, whose dancing is full of the most singular suggestiveness. In one of her measures, appropriately entitled *Liebelei*, she does some incredible things with her calves, which are made to express a wide variety of emotions – now of coaxing tenderness, now of burning passion, and in the end of contemptuous rejection . . . M. Djujitsovitch, who is to be seen at the Pandemonium, has introduced a dance which nightly holds an over-crowded house in an unparalleled grip. Attention is first riveted by a spasmodic twitching of the knee-cap; the movement then gradually spreads to other sections of the body, the dance finishing with a tremendous *tour de force* in the form of a concerted jerk of the Adam's apple and the Achilles tendon. The new Sardinian dancer at the Empyrean, Signora Rigli, created an immense *furore* at her first appearance the other evening. In the chief item of her repertoire she achieves an amazing sensation by a deft manipulation of her collar-bone, which is seen to move in a sinuous wave, culminating in a shudder that leaves the spectator clammy with a nameless terror. It has been left to Miss Truly Allright, who comes here with a big reputation from the States, to demonstrate to a British audience the subtle, yet staggering effect that can be produced in a dance bringing into play the muscles of the ears. In a wonderful 'Wag-time' number she employs those organs with irresistible charm, and the final flap invariably brings down the house. We are asked to state that owing to a slight dislocation sustained at rehearsal, Mlle Cuiboño, the 'Venezuelan Venus,' will be unable to give her famous spinal-cord dance at the Capitolium this week.[14]

Popular dance was changing rapidly as well. The turkey trot and the tango became the rage of 1912 and 1913, to the chagrin of conservative-minded establishments throughout Europe and America. Churchmen, politicians, and administrators denounced what they regarded as lewd public displays. Letter columns of newspapers and periodicals were full of comments on the subject. Boston dance halls banned the tango; certain Swiss hotels prohibited the new 'American' steps; a Prussian officer was killed by a general over the question of the propriety of the turkey trot; and the kaiser tried to forbid his army and navy officers from doing the new dances, at least when in uniform. But the rage spread, and Jean Richepin was motivated to lecture to the French Academy in October 1913 on the tango. The world of 1893, when a French manual of etiquette had declared that a respectable young man would never sit on the same settee as a young woman, seemed, twenty years later, positively medieval.

CONFRONTATION AND LIBERATION

If Diaghilev was increasingly bent on confrontation and sensation, so were his collaborators. In retrospect the preparations for Le Sacre have an almost conspiratorial air. By 1913 Stravinsky was caught up in his own importance, and with Le Sacre he had every intention of setting the musical and ballet world on its ear. His international reputation had blossomed in 1910 and 1911 with the sudden success of Firebird and Petrushka. The piano score to Le Sacre he completed in November

1912 and the orchestration finally in March 1913.

'The idea of *The Rite of Spring* came to me,' Stravinsky said later, 'while I was still composing *Firebird*. I had dreamed a scene of pagan ritual in which a chosen sacrificial virgin dances herself to death.' Asked on another occasion what he loved most about Russia, he answered: 'The violent Russian spring that seemed to begin in an hour and was like the whole earth cracking. That was the most wonderful event of every year of my childhood.'[1] And so the theme of *Le Sacre* was birth and death, Eros and Thanatos, primitive and violent, the fundamental experiences of all existence, beyond cultural context.

Although the emphasis eventually was on the positive aspects of the theme – spring, its accompanying rites, and life – the initial title Stravinsky assigned to the score was revealing and hardly affirmative: *The Victim*. And in the libretto the last tableau involves, of course, the sacrifice of the chosen maiden. The ballet ends with the enactment of a death scene in the midst of life. The usual interpretation of the ballet is that it is a celebration of life through death, and that a maiden is chosen for sacrificial death in order to honor the very qualities of fertility and life that she exemplifies. And yet in the end, because of the importance attached to death in the ballet, to the violence associated with regeneration, to the role of 'the victim,' *Le Sacre* may be regarded as a tragedy.

Whether the eventual title was original or borrowed is uncertain. The notion of regeneration and rebirth was to be found in much avant-garde activity at the turn of the century. The title of the Austrian Secessionists' journal was *Ver Sacrum*, or *Sacred Spring*. Frank Wedekind's play about the sexual problems of adolescents was called *Frühlingserwachen*, or *Spring Awakening*. Excerpts from Proust's work were published in *Le Figaro* in March 1912 with the title 'Au Seuil du printemps' ('On the Threshold of Spring').

70

Stravinsky initially discussed his brainchild with Nicholas Roerich, the painter who would eventually design the sets for the ballet, and then he put the idea for his 'primitive ballet' to Diaghilev. The latter was immediately taken by it. So too was Nijinsky when he became party to the project. Indeed, all were so excited and so concerned with the potential for fundamental innovation that they considered Fokine too conservative to serve as choreographer for the score. At the end of 1912, Stravinsky, under the impression that Fokine might nonetheless be the choreographer, wrote to his mother from Monte Carlo:

> Diaghilev and Nijinsky are mad about my new child, *Le Sacre du printemps*. The unpleasant fact is that it will have to be done by Fokine, whom I consider an exhausted artist, one who traveled his road quickly and who writes himself out with each new work. *Schéhérazade* was the high point of his achievement and, consequently, the beginning of his decline . . . New forms must be created, and the evil, the greedy, and the gifted Fokine has not even dreamed of them. At the beginning of his career he appeared to be extraordinarily progressive, but the more I knew of his work, the more I saw that in essence he was not new at all.[2]

Novelty, then, was a *sine qua non* for Stravinsky. 'I cannot . . . compose what they want from me,' he complained later to Benois, 'which would be to repeat myself.' This was Fokine's mistake as a choreographer; this was the mistake of other composers: 'That is why people write themselves out.'[3] And Stravinsky had no intention of losing his shock value.

Fokine was already upset with Diaghilev for permitting Nijinsky to choreograph *Faune*, and by the end of 1912 the rupture was complete. Nijinsky was chosen to do *Le Sacre*. That he was now intent on breaking with

71

convention far more dramatically than in *Faune* is clear. There was even an apocalyptic note to his temper. In December 1912, for instance, Nijinsky transmitted to Richard Strauss, via Hugo von Hofmannsthal, a request that Strauss compose for him 'the most unrestrained, the least dance-like music in the world.' 'To be taken by you,' Hofmannsthal wrote to Strauss, 'beyond all bounds of convention is exactly what he longs for; he is, after all, a true genius and just where the track is uncharted, there he desires to show what he can do, in a region like the one you opened up in *Elektra*.'[4]

Preparations for *Le Sacre* took place while the Ballets russes toured Europe during the winter of 1912–13, from Berlin to Budapest and Vienna, to Leipzig and Dresden, to London, and finally to Monte Carlo for rest and rehearsal. From Leipzig, Nijinsky wrote to Stravinsky, on 25 January 1913:

> Now I know what *Le Sacre du printemps* will be when everything is as we both want it: new, beautiful, and utterly different – but for the ordinary viewer a jolting and emotional experience.[5]

As the rehearsals mounted in number, Nijinsky began to have trouble with his dancers, who found his ideas incomprehensible and his style devoid of identifiable beauty. Still, though there were some initial disagreements about *tempi*, Stravinsky was full of admiration for Nijinsky's accomplishment. 'Nijinsky's choreography is incomparable,' he asserted shortly after the opening.

> Everything is as I wanted it, with very few exceptions. But we must wait a long time before the public grows accustomed to our language. Of the value of what we have already accomplished I am convinced, and this gives me the strength for further work.[6]

Pierre Monteux, the conductor at the première, termed most of the traditional music he had to conduct *la sale musique** and consequently was very excited about Stravinsky's work. In a letter of 30 March he reported to the composer:

> Yesterday I finally rehearsed all three works [*Firebird*, *Petrushka*, and *Le Sacre*]. What a pity that you could not be here, above all that you could not be present for the explosion of *Sacre*.[7]

Thus, from Diaghilev's intentions to Stravinsky's conception, Nijinsky's aims and prediction, and Monteux's sense that *Le Sacre* would be an explosive experience, an air of anticipation, provocation, and tension surrounded the creation of the ballet. There can be no doubt that a *scandale* of some sort was both intended and expected. Toward the end of the year Stravinsky wrote to his mother before she went to hear her son's latest composition for the first time in St Petersburg: 'Do not be afraid if they whistle at *Le Sacre*. That is in the order of things.'[8] This was not a recognition that came to him after the fact but an intention built into the music.

Some have argued that Russian ballet and aestheticism as a whole were basically apolitical. To do so is to ignore the social origins of art and to misconstrue the social implications of the modern revolt. Aestheticism was antipolitical in that it looked to art rather than parties and parliaments as a means of invigorating life. Yet in this very formulation of priorities it was behaving in an eminently political manner. Moreover, while it was often silent or ambiguous in its response to political movements and events, by definition it displayed a basic sympathy with progressive and even revolutionary tendencies, because aestheticism was founded squarely on the rejection of existing social codes and values. In an interview with the *New York Times* in 1916, Diaghilev proclaimed:

*Rotten music.

We were all revolutionists . . . when we were fighting for the cause of Russian art, and . . . it was only by a small chance that I escaped becoming a revolutionist with other things than color or music.[9]

The 1905 disturbances in Russia had evoked many expressions of sympathy from the *World of Art* circle. In his early response to the events Diaghilev ranged from approval to trepidation, but in October he was delighted with the tsar's manifesto promising a constitution for Russia. 'We are rejoicing,' his aunt remarked at the time. 'Yesterday we even had champagne. You could never guess who brought the manifesto . . . Seroja [little Serge; that is, Diaghilev], of all people. Wonderful.' Diaghilev even wrote a letter to the secretary of state proposing a ministry of fine arts.[10] Art and liberation, in other words, should proceed hand in hand.

But what were the social and moral implications of this quest for freedom? Despite a fascination among the avant-garde with the lower classes, with social outcasts, prostitutes, criminals, and the insane, the interest usually did not stem from a practical concern with social welfare or with a restructuring of society, but from a desire simply to eliminate restrictions on the human personality. The interest in the lower orders was thus more symbolic than practical. The search was for a 'morality without sanctions and obligations.' The Nietzschean command '*Du sollst werden, der du bist*'* was the supreme moral law. 'I am delighted at every new victory of the revolution . . .' wrote Konstantin Somov to Benois in 1905, 'knowing that it will lead us not into an abyss but into life. I hate our past too much . . . I am an individualist; the whole world revolves around me, and essentially it is no concern of mine to go outside the confines of this "I." '[11]

As it was in Max Stirner's *Das Einzige und sein*

---

*You ought to become who you are.

Eigentum * (1845), which achieved a new popularity at the end of the century, the world was telescoped here into the individualist moment: 'For me nothing is higher than myself,' said Stirner. The anarchistic and libertarian impulse, which is eminently political, is central to the modern revolt.

D.H. Lawrence was to write his openly political novel *Kangaroo* only after the war, but already his art had political connotations, if we see politics more than the formal structures of social discourse and regard it as all mediation between individual and group interests. When Anna danced, pregnant and naked, in front of her husband in *The Rainbow*, which Lawrence wrote in the years before the war and published in 1915, 'she swayed backwards and forwards, like a full ear of corn, pale in the dusky afternoon, threading before the firelight, dancing his non-existence . . . He waited obliterated.'

Despite the strange beauty of her movements, he could not understand why she was dancing, naked. ' "What are you doing?" he said gratingly. "You'll catch a cold." '[12]

The dance was Anna's art. It was the art of an Isadora Duncan that clearly inspired this passage. It was Nijinsky's art. It belonged to them and not to any husband, any lover, or any audience. Art as act erased husbands, lovers, and audiences. Art was freedom.

But the freedom had meaning only in relation to the audience. Anna's dance could have no meaning without her husband. And so, paradoxically, the negated audience was central to the art. The *acte gratuit* became a will-o'-the-wisp, and the individualistic moment became also a supremely social and hence political moment.

* *The Ego and His Own.*

Besides Venice, the city most awash with metaphorical meaning for the western world is Paris. It is a city of youth and romance, but also of experience and regret; of both exuberance and wistfulness; of bold ideas and faded dreams; of grand style and of frivolity. Many have found in the city a combination of disparities, an unrivaled completeness, and have shared William Shirer's memory of it: 'as near to paradise on this earth as any man could ever get.'[1]

Who has not imagined or recalled 'that summer in Paris' even if he or she neither has nor ever will set foot on a quai along the Seine? Harold Rosenberg, in 1940 after the fall of the city to the Germans, described Paris as 'the Holy Place of our time. The only one.'[2] He echoed the words and sentiments of Heinrich Heine, who a century earlier had called Paris 'the new Jerusalem,' and Thomas Appleton, whose idea it was that Paris is where good Americans go when they die. The suggestion in these encomia is that Paris has somehow managed to harness its discordant urban energies – its crush of humanity, its conflicts of class, its concentrations of greed and despair – and to deal with its physical problems in such a way as to produce a rich and exhilarating spiritual effect.

Starting in the middle of the last century, the city had indeed done much to encourage such an image: from the extensive improvements to the city under the guidance of Louis Napoleon's prefect of the Seine, Baron Haussmann, to the repeated organization of lavish and expensive world expositions, to the architectural additions and improvements made by people like Viollet-le-Duc, to the building of the Eiffel Tower and Sacré Coeur, to the relatively lax censorship laws, which permitted entertainment and publications that would have had little chance of survival elsewhere in Europe, and, finally, to the intentionally ambiguous morality, a morality, not found elsewhere in Europe, that tolerated a street life of absinthe, cafés, and girls.

There was, however, another side to the picture, one that became more noticeable as the century neared its end. This was the passive, lethargic, and doubtful side of Paris, Paris as object, as victim; Paris as the site of crisis, as the locus of a culture of crisis; Paris as the site of an overwhelming ennui, to which Barrès referred in 1885: 'A profound indifference engulfs us.'[3] Paris had become a cultural symbol, as Harold Rosenberg noted perceptively in his 1940 article, 'not because of its affirmative genius alone, but perhaps, on the contrary, through its passivity, which allowed it to be possessed by the searchers of every nation.' The older Oliver Wendell Holmes in 1886 found the city 'dull and dreary . . . vacuous and torpid.'[4] Three quarters of a century later a waiter told Jack Kerouac, 'Paris est pourri.'*[5]

Politically, Paris, after the great Revolution of 1789, remained a center for messianic radicalism for more than a century, until the role was usurped by Moscow in 1917. The symbol, however, was more important than the reality. The periods of genuine political tolerance in which radical elements could proselytize freely were few in France in that century, and the fate of the Revolution's ideals, of liberty, equality, and fraternity, elicited much sarcasm and scorn. In the fortnight before the première of Le Sacre Georges Clemenceau twice referred, in speeches, to the mal in French life 'that gnaws at us': the inability of the French to organize themselves in an acceptable political system.[6]

In the course of its development, Paris became not simply the ville des lumières but also a symbol of urban blight. The population became more concentrated and dense in the core area. Although the central part of the city was the most beautiful in the world, the banlieux or suburbs could lay claim to being among the most ugly.

*Paris is rotten.

Aubervilliers, Les Lilas, and Issy-les-Moulineaux, built in the last quarter of the nineteenth century to try to counter the congestion, are lyrical names for grim industrial suburbs. Slum quarters without adequate sanitation abounded – in 1850 only one house in five had water. Paris was the undisputed western capital of tramps and beggars.

All major European cities confronted similar problems in the industrial expansion of the last century, but in Paris the example of radical political action had left its mark, and social tensions surfaced twice in particularly vicious form. In the June days of 1848 and during the Commune of 1871 class hatred exploded and destroyed vast sections of the city. More people were killed in one week of street fighting in May 1871 than in the whole of the Jacobin terror, and more of the city was damaged than in any war before or after. The grand boulevards that Baron Haussmann laid out through the clogged center of the city in the 1850s and '60s to give Paris its distinctive urban elegance and cultivated airiness were said to have been designed, in part at least, to restrict the potential for barricades and to give troops both quick access from their barracks and uncluttered shooting galleries against the *classes dangereuses* in case of civil strife. Political tension was thus a constant in the life of Paris and reflected the general tug of war between past and future.

In the 1880s the horse still ruled Paris. The Étoile and the Champs-Élysées were surrounded by stables, riding schools, and the headquarters of horse vendors. The elegant gentleman, monocle attached to the rim of his top hat, carnation in his lapel, riding boots glistening, talked constantly of the Jockey Club and the horse show. Grooms relaxed in cafés in the rue de Pouthieu and the rue Marbeuf. The odor of horse manure pervaded the air, and pedestrians thought nothing of walking in the middle of the street. Yet within a few years the automobile had invaded Paris. In 1896, Hugues le Roux, a young journalist, warned the prefect of police that he would carry a pistol to deal with drivers of automobiles who threatened his and his family's safety on the street. The police, he charged, appeared totally unprepared to take any measures against the lunatic motorists who had made the streets of Paris mortally dangerous.[7] Seventy years after he first arrived in Paris in the autumn of 1904 and sat with Gabriel Astruc at the Café de la Paix, Artur Rubinstein remembered the odors of the occasion, perfume and horse scent.[8] He expressed himself with delicacy in his memoirs. Had he been frank, he might have said he recalled a mélange of fine perfume, engine exhausts, and manure. That would have expressed a little more clearly the contraries that had become so striking in Paris as it grew in the last century, contraries that were never more obvious than in the brilliant though crepuscular atmosphere of the *belle époque*.

Paris and the whole of France became increasingly absorbed in these contradictions as the century neared its end. After the stunning defeat of Louis Napoleon's Second Empire in 1870–1871 at the hands of the Prussians and the disastrous civil war fought in Paris, the nation's traditional sense of grandeur and pre-eminence in Europe was countered by an immediate memory of débâcle. A crippling sense of decline, together with a disputatious search for the roots of the malignancy, pervaded French life in the Third Republic. Enemies were sought within and without: war scares were frequent; public scandals seemed to multiply and to be accompanied by a spate of anarchist bombings, the most publicized though least costly in human life being that in the Chamber of Deputies on 9 December 1893; and the Dreyfus affair, which rent the whole country in the last decade of the century, was simply the most sensational symbol of the debility and turmoil.

In an era of imperialism France lost ground in the quest for colonies. Her foreign trade declined. As parts

of the world moved into a second stage of industrialization after 1890, France did not keep pace, and
Frenchmen, exemplifying their self-doubt, showed a
greater willingness to invest money abroad than at
home. And while the birthrate of her neighbors, particularly Germany, grew significantly, that of France
declined.

Even Paris seemed to stop developing after 1880. The
population of the city grew only because peripheral
areas were incorporated into the metropolitan
boundaries. It took more than twenty years, until 1907,
to finish Haussmann's plans for the boulevard Raspail,
and the very avenue named to honor his achievement
was left incomplete for fifty years, until the 1920s. Leth-
argy and a nagging awareness of degeneration thus confronted a legacy of *grandeur* and *gloire*. The German
ambassador to Paris sensed this in 1886; in October
Count Münster cabled Berlin: 'The wish that there may
be one day a holy war is common to every Frenchman;
but the demand for its speedy fulfilment is met with a
shake of the head.'[9]

Even as cultural arbiter to the world, a role that most
Frenchmen regarded as a permanent international
bequest and hence as their birthright, the country felt
uncertain. By the second decade of this century Paris
seemed to be far more entranced by foreign culture than
by its own: in June 1911, for example, there was a *saison
belge* at Les Bouffes, a *saison italienne* at the Châtelet, a
saison russe across the square at the Sarah Bernhardt,
and a *saison viennoise* at the Vaudeville. Although
important compositions by Charpentier, Fauré, Ravel,
Schmitt, and Debussy were accorded their first performances in the spring and summer of 1913, all the recent
stir and excitement seems to have been generated by
foreign composers and artists: Strauss, Mussorgsky,
Kuznetsova, Chaliapin, as well as the Ballets russes.
Moreover, the foreigners, the Russians in particular,
were often inclined to regard their contributions with an

80

air of superiority and even with imperious pretensions to ultimate art. 'We have shown the Parisians,' Alexandre Benois claimed after the 1909 Russian season, 'what theater should be . . . This trip was clearly a historic necessity. We are in contemporary civilization the ingredient without which it would corrode entirely.'[10]

If, however, the innovative art of foreigners elicited fascination, any native rebels, such as the Fauves, were likely to be denounced as agents of anarchy and decomposition. The widely read critic Samuel Rocheblave, for example, regretted at the time that painting in France since Courbet had lost self-control and had become polemical, political, and nothing more than spectacle. The *fin de siècle*, in his view, was a synonym for overt anarchy imported from abroad. Impressionism, which broke down color and light, and cubism, which broke down solid form, were not French styles but something approximating 'barbarism.' 'Plus d'école,' he said with a sigh, '*mais une poussière de talents; plus de corps, mais des individus.*'*[11]

If an important impulse behind experimentation in the arts at the turn of the century was a quest for liberation, a break, in aesthetic and moral terms, from central authority, from patriarchy, from bourgeois conformity, from, in short, a European tradition that had been dictated to a large extent from Paris, then it was no surprise that much of the psychological and spiritual momentum for this break came from the peripheries, geographical, social, generational, and sexual. The emphasis on youth, sensuality, homosexuality, the unconscious, the primitive, and the socially deprived originated in large part not in Paris but on the borders of traditional hegemony. The modern government was full of exiles, and the condition of exile, or the 'battle on the

---

*No school any longer, only a smattering of talent; no group any longer, only individuals.

frontiers,' as the Polish-Italian Frenchman Apollinaire described the endeavor of his cohort, became central themes of the modern mentality. The young Henry de Montherlant's first play, written in 1914 when the playwright was eighteen, was called *L'Exil*. That same year James Joyce put together the first draft of his play *Exiles*. Paris, because of its mythical associations with revolutionary ideals, became the refuge of many of these exiles, including Joyce, and thus the main setting of the modern revolt. Asked to name the great French artists of his time, Cocteau replied, Picasso, Stravinsky, and Modigliani.[12] By 1913 Paris had become, as Jacques-Émile Blanche wrote in November of that year, the *gare centrale* of Europe;[13] a center for developments but not an innovator.

The general political and economic condition of France in the *belle époque* of course provided the backdrop for the theatricality, and cultural preoccupations were related to political and strategic concerns. In both, vulnerability was the prevailing characteristic. When a Franco-Russian treaty materialized in 1893, ending a quarter century of diplomatic isolation that had been engineered largely by Otto von Bismarck, Paris erupted in jubilation verging on hysteria. Matchboxes with portraits of the tsar, Kronstadt pipes, and Neva billfolds became all the rage. Portraits of the tsar and tsarina were hung in children's rooms. Tolstoy and Dostoevsky became favorite reading.

To the interest in Russia must be added an obsession with Germany. After the defeat of 1870–1871, after the loss of the provinces of Alsace and Lorraine to the Germans, and after the added humiliation of having the German Reich proclaimed in the Hall of Mirrors at Versailles, Prussia-Germany became not simply the despised enemy but the incarnation of evil and thus the antithesis of France. Bismarck's *botte ferrée*, set on the nape of France, became the inescapable image of Hermann's relationship to Marianne. Yet in this sadistic

Mephistophelian role Prussia-Germany also obviously became the source of consuming interest, an interest expressed cautiously at first but later more openly. The treatment of Wagner is illustrative. Before the mid 1880s any regard for the German composer had to be almost surreptitious, and proposals to perform his works in Paris were met with outspoken opposition. By the 1890s, however, a Wagner wave was under way, and the pilgrimage to Bayreuth had become a fad. Wagner clearly influenced Mallarmé, Proust, and Debussy. In 1913 Wagner's centenary was celebrated in Paris with productions of *Tristan* and the whole of the Ring cycle, an extravagance that would have been unthinkable a generation earlier.

Taine had suggested in 1867 that 'the Germans are the initiators and perhaps the masters of the modern spirit.' If that idea had few takers then among Frenchmen, by the end of the century Germany had imposed herself awesomely on French consciousness, in intellectual and political circles, in business and industry, and among the military. By 1913, France, as a secure arbiter of taste, was a thing of the past. In that year, while the Germans and Russians celebrated the centenary of the first Napoleon's defeat, the French were reminded of their decline. 'In Paris, uncertainty rules,' wrote Jacques-Émile Blanche.[14] The memorable evening of 29 May 1913, at the Théâtre des Champs-Élysées was to provide a vivid expression of that uncertainty.

SCANDAL AS SUCCESS

What then was so scandalous, provocative, and surprising about *Le Sacre*?

The theme was devoid of readily identifiable moral purpose. Primitive, pre-ethical, pre-individual man was portrayed in nature. Rebirth, life, and death were

83

depicted without obvious ethical comment, without a moral 'sauce,' to borrow Jacques Rivière's typically Gallic analogy.[1] In this portrayal of the continuity of life, fundamental, brutal, and tragic, beyond individual fate, there was no suggestion of sentiment. There was only energy, exultation, and necessity. The victim was not mourned but honored. The chosen maiden joined in the rite automatically, without sign of comprehension or interpretation. She submitted to a fate that transcended her. The theme was basic and at the same time brutal. If there was any hope, it was in the energy and fertility of life, not in morality. To an audience decked out in its civilized finery, the message was jarring.

The music was equally jarring. It lacked ornamentation, moral intimation, and even, for the most part, melody. A few brief melodic lines, inspired by Russian folk tunes, did surface, but otherwise the music bore no obvious relation to the nineteenth-century tradition, even to impressionism. The laws of harmony and rhythm appeared to be violated. Instruments that have no vibrato were intentionally chosen in order to eliminate any trace of sentimentality. New sounds were created by the use of extreme registers for woodwinds and strings. The orchestra called for was immense, 120 instruments, with a high percentage of percussion, which could produce a formidable eruption of sound. With its violence, dissonance, and apparent cacophony, the music was as energetic and primitive as the theme. Debussy said of Le Sacre that it was 'an extraordinary, ferocious thing. You might say it's primitive music with every modern convenience.'[2] One critic called it 'refined Hottentot music'; another claimed that it was 'the most discordant composition ever written. Never has the cult of the wrong note been applied with such industry, zeal, and ferocity.'[3]

If the theme brought the very notion of civilization into question, and if the music underlined this challenge, then Nijinsky's choreography compounded the provocation. Every virtuosity was eliminated. There was not a single jeté, pirouette, or arabesque. Ironically, the man whose breathtaking grace and agility had been frenetically acclaimed in previous years seemed to have expunged all traces of his own achievement from his composition. Movement was reduced to heavy jumping, with both feet, and walking, in either a smooth or stomping fashion. As in all of Nijinsky's compositions, there was a basic position; this time it consisted of the feet turned inward with great exaggeration, knees bent, arms tucked in, head turned in profile as the body faced forward. In other words, the classical pose was contradicted entirely by what appeared to many as knock-kneed contortion. Nijinsky called his movements 'stylized gestures' to emphasize his departure from the flow and rhythm of classical dance, to stress the disconnections, the jaggedness, of existence. The dancers were no longer individuals but parts of the composition. Most of the movements were in groups. Since there was no melody to follow, the dancers had to follow the rhythm, but even that was extraordinarily difficult, since bar after bar had a different time signature. To compound the complexity, different groups of dancers onstage often were required to follow separate rhythms. When Diaghilev and Nijinsky visited Dalcroze at his school of eurhythmics in 1912, they had persuaded Marie Rambert to leave Hellerau and join the Ballets russes in order to assist Nijinsky in teaching rhythm to the corps de ballet. The first-night audience was not alone in finding Nijinsky's work difficult to comprehend. Many of his own dancers had left no doubt that they considered the work ugly and loathsome.

The critics were on the whole savage toward Nijinsky. Henri Quittard continued his crusade against Nijinsky's choreography, calling him a 'frustrated schoolboy' verging on lunacy.[4] Louis Laloy accused him of being 'totally devoid of ideas and even common sense.'[5]

Roerich's sets were the only element of the ballet that

did not flaunt novelty and as a result they were virtually ignored. In their use of red, green, and white in combinations suggestive of icon painting, however, they quietly complemented the sense of exoticism and Russian folk influence.

As Jacques Rivière, the most astute of contemporary commentators, pointed out, asymmetry is the essence of *Le Sacre*. The theme, the music, and the choreography were all angular and jolting. And yet, paradoxically, as we can see, the asymmetry is stylized and highly controlled. There is a powerful unity to the ballet. Implicit in the work is an ecstatic turbulence, a thick mélange of instinct, sensuality, and fate. In the words of Rivière, this is 'spring seen from the inside, with its violence, its spasms, and its fissions. We seem to be watching a drama through a microscope.'

The ballet contains and illustrates many of the essential features of the modern revolt: the overt hostility to inherited form; the fascination with primitivism and indeed with anything that contradicts the notion of civilization; the emphasis on vitalism as opposed to rationalism; the perception of existence as continuous flux and a series of relations, not as constants and absolutes; the psychological introspection accompanying the rebellion against social convention.

If these features of the ballet elicited enthusiastic appreciation from a segment of the audience, a vociferous opposition was also aroused. It demanded that art be a vision of grace, harmony, and beauty rather than an expression of idiosyncrasy or neurosis; that art be morally uplifting rather than contemptuous or indifferent to prevailing mores; that the patrons of art be respected and not intentionally insulted. Stravinsky's effort they regarded as noise, Nijinsky's as ugly parody. The opposition responded, as a result, in what it perceived as like manner. Insult would be met with insult, noise with noise, sarcasm with sarcasm.

In the next few days the response in the press was,

with few exceptions, overwhelmingly negative, not only in the daily papers but in the musical journals as well. Everyone joked about *Le Massacre du printemps*. Stravinsky's talents were acknowledged, but this time, it was said, he had gone too far with his ingenuity. 'The composer has written a score that we shall not be ready for until 1940,' noted one commentator with pre-science.[6] Nijinsky's talents too were universally recognized, but as a dancer not as a choreographer. With almost one voice he was urged to restrict himself to dancing. Marie Rambert noted that he too was 'fifty years ahead of his time.'[7]

On 2 June *Le Figaro* felt the need to editorialize on its front page about the Russian ballet company. Although a peace agreement in the Balkans was signed on 30 May, to conclude the latest round of war there, wrote Alfred Capus,

> there remain nevertheless a number of international issues that still have to be settled. Among these I have no hesitation in placing in the front rank the question of the relationship of Paris with the Russian dancers, which has reached a point of tension where anything can happen. Already the other night there was a border incident whose gravity the government should not underestimate.

This time the Russian barbarians, led by Nijinsky, 'a sort of Attila of the dance,' really went too far. They were booed and they reacted with surprise.

> It seems that they are not at all aware of the customs and practices of the country they are imposing on, and they seem ignorant of the fact that we often take energetic measures against absurd behavior.

An accord could, however, perhaps be negotiated with the Russians.

Nijinsky would have to agree not to stage any more ballets that aspire to a level of beauty inaccessible to our feeble minds, and not to produce any more three-hundred-year-old 'modern' women, or little boys feeding at breasts, or for that matter even breasts. In return for these concessions we would continue to assure him that he is the greatest dancer in the world, the most handsome of men, and we would prove this to him. We should then be at peace.

And the article concluded by pointing out that a group of Polish actors was about to arrive in Paris. They had better restrain themselves and not tell Frenchmen that the only true art is Polish art.

In front of the bust of Molière, they had better not cry: *Vive la Pologne, monsieur!*

Needless to say, Alfred Capus must have been pleased with himself when he savored his cabaret wit in print that Monday in early June.

A year later, in the midst of the 'July crisis' provoked by the assassination of the Austrian archduke, one Maurice Dupont, in an article in *La Revue Bleue*, decried the curiosity of his age, which he saw not as a sign of superior intellectual activity but as a disquieting symptom of illness: 'A healthy human being is not curious.' He saw particularly in the enthusiasm that the Russian company had generated a sign of regrettable spiritual disequilibrium. The essential character of a work like *Le Sacre* was nihilism, he charged. The work had intensity but lacked amplitude. It deadened the senses instead of elevating the soul. It was a 'Dionysian orgy dreamed of by Nietzsche and called forth by his prophetic wish to be the beacon of a world hurtling toward death.' Dupont thought, however, that there was some cause for hope, the most spectacular evidence of French sanity having been the raucous demonstration that greeted *Le Sacre*.[8]

By the time his article appeared, Dupont probably noted with relief that Gabriel Astruc had gone bankrupt. Nijinsky had married Romola de Pulszky and had been dropped as a result from Diaghilev's troupe. In short, the 'modern wave' had encountered setbacks. He might also have noted, however, that scientists were occupied with the possibility that the world might end. In the *Revue des deux mondes* Charles Nordmann wrote:

There exist in the life of societies as well as individuals hours of moral discomfort when despair and fatigue spread their leaden wings over human beings. Men then begin to dream of nothingness. The end of everything ceases to be 'undesirable' and its contemplation is in fact soothing. The recent debates among scientists on the death of the universe are perhaps the reflection of these gloomy days.[9]

II

Berlin

Wie sind zu Tänzern Bürger rings geworden.*

ALFRED WOLFENSTEIN
1914

The banging of windows and the crashing of glass are the
robust sounds of fresh life, the cries of something new-born.

ELIAS CANETTI

On the Yser Canal, where the young reserve regiments of volunteers attacked, there now lies our *ver sacrum* ... Their sacrifice
for us signifies a sacred spring for all of Germany.

FRIEDRICH MEINECKE
1914

VER SACRUM

'Germany has declared war on Russia – swimming in the
afternoon.' Such was Franz Kafka's pithy diary entry
for 2 August 1914.[1]

The days of that summer were long and full of
sunshine; the nights were mild and moonlit. That it was
a beautiful and unforgettable season is part of the lore
of that summer of 1914, part of its poignancy and mystique. Yet it is not to evoke sun and spas, sailing regattas
and somnolent afternoons – important as such imagery
is for our poetical sense of that summer before the storm
– that we begin this chapter with a reference to
weather; it is very simply because the fine days and

*How burghers everywhere have become dancers.

nights of that July and August encouraged Europeans to venture out of their homes and to display their emotions and prejudices in public, in the streets and squares of their cities and towns. The massive exhibitions of public sentiment played a crucial role in determining the fate of Europe that summer.

Had it been a wet and cold summer, like that of the previous year or the next one, would a fairground atmosphere conducive to soap-box oratory and mass hysteria have developed? Would leaders then have been prepared to declare war so readily? There is evidence that the jingoistic crowd scenes in Berlin, St Petersburg, Vienna, Paris, and London, in the last days of July and in the early days of August, pushed the political and military leadership of Europe toward confrontation. That was certainly the case in Germany. And Germany was the matrix of the storm.

After the Austrian archduke Franz Ferdinand was assassinated, together with his wife, on 28 June at Sarajevo during their imperial visit to the provinces of Bosnia and Hercegovina, it was only because of staunch German backing that the Austrian government decided to pursue an intransigent policy in dealing with Serbia, which, it was suspected, had given both moral encouragement and material support to the terrorist group that carried out the plot against the Austrian heir apparent. In Berlin, at critical stages of the decision making, large demonstrations showed the public's desire for steadfastness and commitment to an aggressive and victorious resolution of the crisis. Excitement, already high in early July, grew to fever pitch by the end of the month.

On 25 July, a Saturday, in the early evening, large crowds milled about in the streets, awaiting Serbia's answer to Austria's draconic ultimatum of the twenty-third, which made a number of demands that were clearly difficult for the Serbs to accept. The German chancellor, Bethmann Hollweg, was so unsure of the public's response to the ultimatum, and so concerned

91

that Berliners might respond negatively, that he warned the kaiser not to return just yet from his annual Norwegian cruise. A quixotic Wilhelm was deeply offended by the suggestion but presumably anxious nevertheless: 'Things get madder every minute! Now the man writes to me that I must not show myself to my subjects!'

But Bethmann had completely misjudged the public mood. A reporter for the *Tägliche Rundschau* has left us, in breathless prose, a picture of the crowds storming newspaper delivery vans for news of the Serbian response, tearing open newspapers, and reading with fierce involvement. Suddenly a cry erupts: *Et jeht los!* – a Berliner's way of saying, 'It's on!' Serbia has turned down the Austrian ultimatum! *Et jeht los!*

That is everyone's phrase in this hour. It cuts to the quick. And all of a sudden, before one is aware of its happening, a crowd has gathered. No one knows anyone else. But all are seized by one earnest emotion: War, war, and a sense of togetherness. And then a solemn and festive sound greets the evening: 'Es braust ein Ruf wie Donnerhall.'*[2]

At about 8:00 p.m. a large mass of humanity moves along Unter den Linden, Berlin's grand central boulevard, toward the Schloss, the imperial palace. At the armory there are loud cries of *Hoch Österreich*,** and at the Schloss the crowd bursts into the song 'Heil Dir im Siegerkranz.'† Another throng, thousands strong, moves to the Moltkestrasse, to the Austrian embassy, where it encamps, singing, 'Ich hatte einen Kameraden,'‡ one of the most popular of German marching songs. The Austrian ambassador, Szögyény-Marich, finally appears on a balcony and is cheered

*'A Roar Like Thunder Sounds.'
**Long Live Austria!
†'Hail to You in Victory Wreath.'
‡'I Had a Comrade.'

madly. He retires, but the singing and shouting continue, and he feels compelled to appear once again to salute the expressions of solidarity. A reporter for the *Vossische Zeitung*, a Berlin liberal paper, notes, 'German and Austrian, student and soldier, merchant and worker, all feel as one in this deadly serious hour.'[3]

After dark, at about 11:00 p.m., a large crowd gathers at the Brandenburg Gate and then moves to the Foreign Office on the Wilhelmstrasse and finally on to the War Office. Other groups collect at the Zoologischer Garten, on the Kurfürstendamm, and on the Tauentzienstrasse. The mass of mankind in front of the Schloss and another throng in front of the Reich Chancellor's Palace mill about until well after midnight.

Bethmann's secretary, Kurt Riezler, notes in his diary that Bethmann is so strongly affected by the sight of the large and enthusiastic crowds that his mood lifts perceptibly from one of foreboding, especially when he hears that similar demonstrations are taking place throughout the Reich.[4] Indeed there are even some ugly incidents, on Saturday and again on Sunday, that hint at the intensity of public emotion.

In Munich at the Café Fahrig on Saturday night the crowd becomes giddy singing patriotic songs. After midnight the band leader is told by the owners to wind things down and finally at 1:30 a.m. to stop playing. The clientèle, however, has not had enough, and when efforts are made to close the establishment for the night some of the patriots begin to break chairs and tables and to smash plate glass windows with bricks.

The next afternoon, also in Munich, a Serb expresses himself about the world situation and is quickly surrounded by a large angry crowd, which is on the point of lynching its prey when police arrive. The Serb is rescued and ushered into a local restaurant. But the crowd is baying for blood and tries to storm the restaurant. A larger detachment of police, led by the police prefect himself, has to intervene. The Serb is hidden for several hours before he is sent on his way by a side door.

In Jena, Charles Sorley, a nineteen-year-old visiting student at the university and son of the professor of moral philosophy at Cambridge, writes home to his parents on 26 July:

The drunken Verbindungen* are parading the streets shouting 'Down with the Serbs.' Every half-hour, even in secluded Jena, comes a fresh edition of the papers, each time with wilder rumours, so that one can almost hear the firing at Belgrade.[5]

The Russian naval attaché in Berlin reports on the same day, the twenty-sixth, that the main streets of the capital are so full of demonstrators proclaiming support for Austria that people who have lived in the city for over thirty years are saying that they have never witnessed such scenes.[6]

The kaiser reaches Potsdam on 27 July. He will move to his Berlin palace on the thirty-first.

The next week, on Thursday the thirtieth – one day, that is, before news of Russian mobilization reaches Berlin – excited crowds reappear, and they remain an almost permanent feature of the German capital for the next seven crucial days. On that Thursday they assemble in front of the Foreign Office on the Wilhelmstrasse, at the Kranzler-Ecke, a major intersection on Unter den Linden and the site of the famous Kranzler Café, and in front of the Schloss at the end of Unter den Linden. From Friday afternoon, the thirty-first, when the kaiser declares at 1:00 p.m. a state of *drohende Kriegsgefahr*, or imminent danger of war – which puts border patrols on alert and restricts civilian use of postal, telegraph, and rail communication – the Berlin public that pours into the streets clearly views war as inevitable. Everywhere that afternoon can be heard patriotic shouts. 'In

*Student fraternities.

94

wake of the decision that has finally been made,' notes the Berlin correspondent of a Frankfurt paper at 3:00 p.m. that Friday, 'everywhere tension has given way to jubilation.'[7] While officials insist that the declaration of *Kriegsgefahr* is by no means synonymous with a declaration of war and that the latter depends on a Russian refusal to rescind mobilization orders, the German public assumes otherwise and regards the outcome of the crisis a foregone conclusion. Housewives start a rush on grocery shops. Many store owners seize the opportunity to turn an extra penny: salt, oatmeal, and flour all go up in price markedly. In the food sections of the large department stores in midtown Berlin tinned goods are snatched up. In late afternoon, on police orders, some large stores are shut.

As the extra editions of newspapers appear that Friday afternoon with the latest information, Unter den Linden fills with humanity. Many come to await the arrival of the kaiser from Potsdam. At 2:45 the royal car appears. It has great difficulty in making its way to the imperial palace. The cheers are deafening. The kaiser's car is followed by that of the crown prince and princess and their eldest sons. They in turn are followed by the princes Eitel-Friedrich, Adalbert, August Wilhelm, Oskar, and Joachim. Then comes a line of limousines bearing imperial advisers. Every car, from first to last, is greeted with hurrahs and patriotic songs. The Reich chancellor, Bethmann Hollweg, and the chief of the general staff, Moltke, arrive for consultations, stay briefly, and leave, accompanied on both their arrival and departure by wildly enthusiastic acclaim. Other members of the royal family also gradually leave the palace, and each automobile must struggle to make its way through the excited crowd, which the *Berliner Lokal-Anzeiger* estimates at fifty thousand. All the major decision makers are confronted directly by the massive outpouring of enthusiasm from the Berlin public. None of them has ever witnessed such demonstrations before. None of them can ignore the popular mood. Aside from the cars of the dignitaries, traffic is rerouted away from Unter den Linden, and Berlin's most resplendent street – which houses the university, the Opera, the Royal Library, a number of government ministries, as well as theaters, cafés, and embassies – becomes the stage for a monumental Greek drama.

Late that night a crowd of several thousand is still gathered in front of the chancellor's residence on the Wilhelmstrasse, and shortly before midnight begins chanting for the chancellor. Bethmann finally appears and makes a brief impromptu speech. Invoking Bismarck, Wilhelm I, and the elder Moltke, he insists on Germany's peaceful intentions. However, should the enemy force a war on Germany, she will fight for her 'existence' and 'honor' to the last drop of blood: 'In the gravity of this hour I remind you of the words Prince Friedrich Karl called out to the Brandenburgers: Let your hearts beat before God and your fists upon your enemy!'[8]

The next day, Saturday, 1 August, scenes that are even more hectic and exuberant are enacted. In the morning, normally a regular end to the working week, with businesses, schools, and offices functioning until noon, things are hardly normal. The Moabit criminal courts, for example, cannot proceed as scheduled because defendants, witnesses, and even judges and lawyers simply fail to appear. In front of the royal palace a crowd estimated at anywhere from 100,000 to 300,000 gathers, spreads like a sea from the old museum and the steps of the cathedral, through the Lustgarten and across the large square to the terrace of the Schloss, and is led in a rousing sing-along by the band of the Elisabeth regiment. The regiment is in fact stuck. It was due, after the changing of the guard at the palace, to move across the square to the Lustgarten. But it was trapped by the crowd and is now unable to move. And so it leads the fervent singing. 'The enthusiasm knew no bounds,' the *Frankfurter Zeitung* correspondent cables at 1:55 p.m., 'and when as a finale the united will of the masses elicited the "Pariser Einzugsmarsch"* the enthusiasm reached its high point.'[9]

Again members of the royal family arrive at the palace in the very midst of these celebrations, as do Bethmann, the chancellor, Moltke, the army chief of staff, and Tirpitz, the naval minister. The crowds remain through the afternoon as fateful consultations take place. They sing, they chatter, they cheer. Finally, at 5:00 p.m., the kaiser signs the order for general mobilization; and an hour later, in St Petersburg, Count Pourtalès, the German ambassador, calls in the Russian foreign minister, Sazonov, to hand him a declaration of war. The momentous decisions of the last days have all been made against the backdrop of mass enthusiasm. No political leader could have resisted the popular pressures for decisive action.

At about 6:30, a cry goes up – 'We want the kaiser!' The curtains at the middle window of the palace part, the French doors open, and the kaiser and his wife appear to a thunderous welcome. Wilhelm waves. The noise, the songs, and the cheering slowly abate. Finally, the kaiser speaks. Germans are all one now, he tells the throng. All differences and divisions are forgotten. As brothers they will achieve a mighty victory. The short speech is greeted with more jubilation and more songs – 'Die Wacht am Rhein'** and the traditional battle hymn of the Protestants, 'Ein' feste Burg ist unser Gott.'†

The activity that evening, throughout the city, resembles an enormous celebration after a successful first-night performance by a cast of hundreds of thousands. Berlin has a cast party. Pubs and beer gardens are full to overflowing everywhere. Pianos, trumpets, violins, and entire bands accompany the raucous singing of

*March celebrating the entry into Paris.
**'The Watch on the Rhine.'
†'A Mighty Fortress Is Our God.'

patriotic songs, over and over, into the morning hours, when, in an alcoholic or simply emotional stupor, Berliners finally tumble, still smiling, into their feather-beds.

Almost two thousand emergency marriages are performed that Saturday and early Sunday in greater Berlin. The electric atmosphere prompts all manner of organizations and social groups to declare publicly their loyalty to the German cause. Campaigners for homosexual and women's rights, for instance, join the celebrations of nationality. The Association of German Jews in Berlin issues its declaration on Saturday, 1 August: 'That every German Jew is ready to sacrifice all the property and blood demanded by duty is self-evident,' it proclaims in one of many exuberant assertions.[10]

On Sunday morning at 11:30 an open-air inter-denominational church service takes place at the Bismarck monument in front of the Reichstag. Thousands are in attendance for this ceremony of incomparable symbolism and suggestion. The band of the Fusilier Guards plays, and the service begins with the Protestant hymn 'Niederländische Dankgebet,'* with its opening words, *Wir treten zum Beten vor Gott den Gerechten.*** The court preacher, Licentiate Döhring, leads the service, and for his sermon he takes the text 'Faithful unto death.' The war, he says, has been forced on Germany, but 'we Germans fear God yet otherwise nothing in this world.' The entire congregation then repeats the Lord's Prayer, and the service ends with the Catholic hymn, based on a fourth-century tune, 'Grosser Gott wir loben Dich.'† Protestant and Catholic are reunited in Germany. The secular crowds on previous days often sang hymns. Now, appropriately, the religious service is followed by secular songs.

*'Low Country Prayer of Thanks.'
**We come to pray before our just God.
†'Holy God, We Praise Thy Name.'

98

Church and state, too, have become one. The kaiser, aware of the importance of this kind of symbolism, attends a service at the old garrison church in Potsdam, where Frederick the Great, among other Prussian rulers, lies buried.

In early August Germans wallow in what appears to them to be the genuine synthesis of past and future, eternity embodied in the moment, and the resolution of all domestic strife – party versus party, class against class, sect against sect, church in conflict with state. Life has achieved transcendence. It has become aestheticized. Life has become a Wagnerian *Gesamtkunstwerk* in which material concerns and all mundane matters are surpassed by a spiritual life force.

Elsewhere in Germany, whether in Frankfurt am Main or Frankfurt an der Oder, in Munich, in Breslau, or in Karlsruhe, the scenes are similar. Princes are mobbed. The military is idolized. Churches are packed. Emotionally Germany has declared war by Friday, 31 July, at the latest – certainly on Russia and on France. Given the intensity of public feeling, it is inconceivable that the kaiser can, at this point, turn back. He would never survive such a failure of nerve. And of course in the next days the crucial decisions and the declarations of war follow: first against Russia, then against France, and finally against Britain.

The last major antiwar gatherings in Berlin had taken place on Tuesday, 28 July, when twenty-seven meetings were organized throughout the city by the Social Democrats, well-attended meetings, several of which culminated in marches. The *Berliner Tageblatt* estimated that seven thousand workers met at the Friedrichshain Brewery and two thousand at the Koppenstrasse. After these meetings the two groups moved together toward the Königstor, about ten thousand strong. Fifty police eventually blocked the march, and as the first rows of marchers pushed toward the police, blank shots were fired. The demonstration was quickly dispersed, with only a few skirmishes and minor injuries. Thirty-two German cities experienced similar antiwar gatherings. These were the last significant antiwar rallies.

By the critical weekend – Friday, the last day of July, and Saturday and Sunday, the first two days of August – the Social Democrats, confronted by the mobilization of the tsar's armies and hence by a heightened Russian threat, and also by renewed nationally minded demonstrations, began to rally to the nationalist cause. Some socialist leaders were themselves caught up in the orgy of emotion. Others felt that they could not swim against the tide of public sentiment. A number of deputies on the left of the party, summoned to Berlin for a caucus meeting, left their homes still adamantly opposed to the war and determined to vote against war credits, but faced repeatedly by scenes at railway stations en route of public support for war, they changed their minds. By 3 August, a day before the vote on credits in the Reichstag, the Social Democratic Party (SPD) caucus swung overwhelmingly to a prowar position. On that Monday, the *Bremer Bürger-Zeitung*, before and again during the war positioned on the left of the party, trumpeted in headlines DO YOUR DREADFUL DUTY![11] Gustav Noske said later that had the SPD caucus not approved the war credits, socialist deputies would have been trampled to death in front of the Brandenburg Gate. In sum, not only were the monarch and government influenced by the outpourings of public feeling, but virtually all opposition forces were swept up in the current as well.

Kurt Riezler ruminated, some days after, on the effect of the public emotion:

> The incomparable storm unleashed in the people has swept before it all doubting, halfhearted, and fearful minds . . . The nation surprised the skeptical statesmen.[12]

The crowds, in fact, seized the political initiative in Germany. Caution was thrown to the wind. The moment became supreme. Hours, years, indeed centuries, were reduced to moments. History had become life.

Many were never to forget the mood of those August days. Ten years later Thomas Mann would refer to those days as marking the beginning of much that was still in the process of beginning. Thirty-five years later Friedrich Meinecke, the doyen of German historians, would experience a shiver when he thought about the mood of that August, and he confessed that, despite the disasters which followed, those days were perhaps the most sublime of his life.[13]

OVERTURE

To argue that Germany was a 'belated nation' has become almost a cliché of historical writing on that country. Certainly the social and economic trappings of modernity – urbanization, industrialization, colonies, political unity – all came late to Germany in comparison with France and in particular with Britain.

In 1800, when France and Britain had at least a century or more of centralized government behind them, the German territories were still a quiltlike configuration of close to four hundred autonomous principalities, only loosely federated in an association with the paradoxical name of Holy Roman Empire of the German Nation. In a part of Swabia in an area of 729 square miles were to be found ninety states. Cities were few and hardly comparable with either Paris or London. Berlin in 1800 had a population of about 170,000 and was little more than an administrative center of Prussia. No nationally organized industry like the English cloth trade existed to develop commercial ties, no national religion to encourage religious unity. For many Germans the greatest achievement in German history was the Reformation. That a development which divided the German-speaking peoples instead of uniting them should be so regarded spoke volumes on German identity. In the early eighteenth century a bride wrote to her betrothed, 'Nothing is more plebeian than to write letters in German.' Fifty years later Frederick the Great agreed wholeheartedly. Of the German language he wrote in *De la littérature allemande*** that it was 'half-barbarous,' breaking down 'into as many different dialects as Germany has provinces.' 'Each local group,' he added with scorn, 'is convinced that its patois is the best.'[1] Even a century later, by 1850, when, in the wake of Napoleonic reform, which destroyed the Holy Roman Empire as an official structure and encouraged the beginnings of social mobility and industrialization, when Prussia had clearly begun to assert herself as the strongest and most ambitious of the German states, Berlin, though now a growing financial, commercial, and railway center, still had a population of only 400,000.

Germany, of course, had few natural boundaries apart from the sea to the north and the Alps to the southwest. Otherwise the great central European plain dominated her geographical sense of self – the broad highway for all invaders, marauders, and movements of peoples since the advent of the Germanic tribes themselves from the east in the fourth and fifth centuries. The lack of territorial, ethnic, religious, and commercial definition was a hallmark of German history, and the legacy was a tradition of regionalism, particularism, and provincialism, not to mention insecurity and mistrust. 'Germany? But where is it? I do not know how to find the country,' exclaimed the joint voice of Schiller and Goethe at the end of the eighteenth century.[2] Metternich, the Rhinelander who resettled in Austria, remarked at the Congress of Vienna that the idea of 'Germany' and of 'a German people' was an abstraction.

When political unity did finally come in the years 1866 to 1871, it came in part as the outgrowth of social

On German Literature.

102

change whose most consequential feature at the time was the development of an entrepreneurial spirit in a segment of the middle class. Equally important, the Prussian leadership recognized the power-political necessities of the European state structure, seized the initiative, and pursued a policy of conquest and centralization. New and traditional elements combined, then, to forge a German political unity, such as it was.

Yet despite a surface unity, the strong regionalist traditions in Germany could not be eradicated overnight, and consequently the German Reich that emerged under Bismarck and the Hohenzollerns on the one hand and a middle-class elite on the other was a curious constitutional amalgam of federalism and centralism, of democracy and autocracy, of provincialism papered over by 'national' necessity, of middle-class ambition and aristocratic restraint. Although a spirit of political wholeness was an aspiration in a segment of the German population, particularly within some of the middle strata, regional loyalties and a sense of diversity remained the reality, and the old elites were able to retain a good deal of their pre-eminence because they recognized the diversity – most of their privileges were, in fact, based on it – and expended considerable energy in 'managing' it.

Otto von Bismarck had presided over German unification in the 1860s. He had become Prussian prime minister in 1862 and had skillfully guided Prussia through three wars – against Denmark, Austria, and France – that culminated in the creation of a united German state in 1871. He remained chancellor of the new German Reich for almost two decades until his forced resignation in 1890. While Bismarck's conservative ideals aimed at the establishment in Germany of a harmonious, well-integrated society governed by an appreciation of Prussian traditions and institutions, the effect of his brilliance as a political tactician over thirty years was quite the opposite. In the end his tactics had perhaps a more significant impact on German development that did his goals.

With his constant need for a scapegoat, an enemy to finger – he pointed to the liberals as the source of all ills in the 1860s, to the Catholics in the 1870s, and to the socialists in the 1880s – and with his successful refrain 'The Reich is in danger,' he increased existing class tensions, religious divisions, and ideological differences. In the short run Bismarck had great success as a political manipulator; in the long run he failed strikingly to realize his ideals. His dismissal in 1890 from the chancellorship by the new emperor, Wilhelm II, was the most eloquent comment on this failure. It is one of the succulent ironies of history that Bismarck, the 'iron chancellor,' who helped to unify Germany and make it a great international power, also fragmented and weakened the country further. Germany was in many ways more divided when Bismarck left office than when he became Prussian prime minister.

His effect, then, on Germany was a paradoxical one: he helped instill in Germans a craving for national wholeness, an illusion of unity, greatness, and strength, but at the same time, by playing on the disintegrative, centrifugal tendencies in Germany in his 'divide and rule' approach to life and politics, he promoted these tendencies. The accentuation of differences rather than of similarities made the quest for wholeness all the more urgent and all the more a matter, in view of the reality, of spiritual transcendence. Lacking objective definition, the idea of Germany and Germanness became a question of imagination, myth, and inwardness – in short, of fantasy.

Now there was, of course, a well-established pattern in the German past of taking the external world, the impressions of the senses, of visible reality, and of relegating them to a position secondary in importance to the world of spirit, inner life, and 'true freedom.' In the Lutheran tradition, religion was a matter of faith rather than of good deeds or doctrine. In the German classical humanist outlook, freedom was ethical not social; *innere Freiheit*, inner freedom, was far more important than liberty and equality. For the German idealist, *Kultur* was a matter of spiritual cultivation, not external form. Germanness was, by necessity, a matter of spiritual association rather than geographical or even racial delineation. Bismarck, instead of weakening this internalization of life, this mythopoeic quality, accentuated it. Bismarck 'Prussianized' Germany and at the same time turned Germany from the reality of a geographical expression into a legend.

Yet Bismarck's political achievement – this appearance of national unity against a backdrop of deep, historically rooted schisms – was possible only because it coincided with Germany's social and economic development in the second half of the nineteenth century. That development set the stage for Bismarck's stratagems and reinforced their effect. It was characterized by overwhelming speed and a corresponding disorientation in the populace. While in Britain Charles Dickens, in *Bleak House*, could refer to 'the moving age' in which he lived, and Tennyson could speak of his era as 'an awful moment of transition,' the statistics for social and economic transformation in Germany suggest that no other country had a greater right to summon up impressions of movement and transitoriness. There appears to be a direct relationship between the assault on old fixities and the growth of new myths.

If Britain led the way in changing the mode of life on our planet from the rural agrarian to the urban industrial, Germany more than any other state took us toward our 'postindustrial' or technological world, not only in an objective sense, in that her inventors, engineers, chemists, physicists, and urban architects, among others, did more than those of any other nation to determine our modern urban and industrial landscape, but also in an experiential sense, in that she more intensively than any other 'developed' country has given evidence to the world of the psychic disorientation that rapid and wholesale environmental change may produce. The German experience lies at the heart of the 'modern experience.' Germans often used to refer to themselves as the *Herzvolk Europas*, the people at the heart of Europe. Germans are also the *Herzvolk* of modern sense and sensibility.

Iron and steel were the building materials of the new industrial age. In the early 1870s British production of iron was still four times that of Germany; its production of steel doubled Germany's. By 1914, however, German steel production equaled that of Britain, France, and Russia combined. Britain, the leading exporter of both iron and steel to the world for a century, by 1910 was importing steel from the Ruhr.

Energy use is another indicator of industrial development. In Britain coal consumption between 1861 and 1913 multiplied two and a half times; in Germany in the same period it multiplied thirteen and a half times to draw almost equal. But it was in the new industries of chemicals and electricity, which became in our century the foundations of further growth, that the German advance around the turn of the century was astonishing and at the same time suggestive of the staggering potential of the German economy.

In 1900 British output of sulfuric acid – used in petroleum refining and in the manufacture of fertilizer, explosives, textiles, and dyes, among other things – was still nearly double Germany's, but within thirteen years the relation was almost reversed: by 1913 Germany produced 1.7 million tons and Britain only 1.1 million. In dyestuffs German firms – mainly Badische Anilin, Höchst, and AGFA – controlled 90 per cent of the world market by 1900. In electrical manufacturing the developments were equally stunning. The value of German electrical production by 1913 was twice that of Britain and almost ten times that of France; Germany's exports in this area were the largest in the world, almost three times those of the United States. The value of all German exports more than tripled between 1890 and 1913.

Within little more than a generation, less than one prolonged lifetime, Germany had moved from a geographical assemblage, with limited economic ties among its parts, to become the most formidable industrial, not to mention military, power in Europe.

To achieve this required mammoth changes in demographic patterns, in social and economic organization, and in the labor force. Germany's population increased from 42.5 million in 1875 to 49 million in 1890 and 65 million in 1913. In the latter period the population of Britain, by comparison, grew from 38 to 45 million, and that of France from 37 to only 39 million. On the eve of the Great War the prospect was that Germans would soon outnumber Frenchmen two to one. In 1870 Germany's population was two-thirds rural; by 1914 that relationship had been reversed, and two thirds of all Germans lived in an urban setting. In 1871 there were only eight cities with a population of over 100,000, whereas in 1890 there were twenty-six, and by 1913, forty-eight. By then twice as many laborers worked in industry as in agriculture, and over a third of the population consisted of industrial workers and their families. The concentration of German industry was another of its striking features. By 1910 almost half of all employees worked in firms using more than fifty workers, and the capitalization of the average German company was three times that of the average British firm.

The speed of urbanization and industrialization in Germany meant that many workers were first-generation urban dwellers, confronted by all the attendant social and psychological problems that the shift from countryside to city entailed. The concentration of industry and population also produced the rapid growth of a managerial class, of service personnel, and of municipal and state bureaucracies. As Gesellschaft, or society, overwhelmed the sense of *Gemeinschaft*, or community, as speed and bigness became the dominant facts of life, work and social questions, ambition and job enjoyment became abstract notions, beyond the individual and his scale of personal reference, a matter of theory and intuition rather than experience and knowledge. The rural pre-industrial setting had been replete with its own social problems and indignities, but it is undeniable that industrialization, particularly the rapid industrialization undergone by Germany, brought with it a disturbing measure of depersonalization that material well-being could not expunge or rectify. The so-called new middle class – this enormous army of semiskilled white-collar workers involved primarily in management and service – was a sudden and direct offshoot of the later phases of industrialization and was perhaps even more prone to a sense of isolation and hence vulnerability, than the laboring classes. The concentration of industry and of commerce meant that this social group was particularly large in Germany.

Nevertheless, all sectors of German society were caught up in the momentum and the centrifugal tendencies of the age. Hence, ironically, as consolidation took place on one level – in the population, industry, and the state structure – disintegration characterized the social, political, and, perhaps most significantly, psychological realms. The upshot was a preoccupation with the administration of life, with technique, to the point where technique became a value and an aesthetic goal, not merely a means to an end.

TECHNIQUE

The cult of *Technik*, the emphasis on scientism, efficiency, and management, reached a peak in Germany in the late nineteenth century. Reinforced by the material developments and concerns of an industrializing age, it was nevertheless founded on long-standing and well-entrenched cultural and political traditions: on an awareness of weakness and diffusion and a recognition that survival was dependent on an effective management of resources both natural and human.

The survival of the Holy Roman Empire for almost a millennium was a tribute to the ability of Germans to manage and manipulate what, for at least the last two centuries of its existence, was nothing more than a skeletal construct that, in Voltaire's famous phrase, was not Holy nor Roman nor an Empire. But the history of Prussia provided the most striking example of effective management.

That history, from the time of the great elector in the seventeenth century through the career and achievements of that most Machiavellian of anti-Machiavellians, Frederick II – who wrote his tract *Anti-Machiavel* shortly before he attacked Silesia in 1740 to seize it from Austria – through the great reform period of the Napoleonic era and right up to Bismarck's famous 1862 speech to the finance committee of the Prussian lower house, in which he denounced the parliamentary efforts of the liberals and called for a policy of 'iron and blood,' the entire history of this mechanically constructed state emphasized and venerated management. Good and efficient administration was the key to survival and control. 'A well-conducted government,' Frederick II declared in his Testament of 1752, 'ought to have a system as coherent as a system of philosophy.'[1] For Frederick, the philosopher-king, means were as vital as ends. The Prussian bureaucracy was to become a model of efficiency throughout the world.

It was in large part this overwhelming emphasis on means and technique that was the basis of the nineteenth-century German accomplishment in education, which in turn was the most important single human component, as opposed to the mere availability of natural resources, of Germany's rise to industrial and military pre-eminence in Europe by 1914. The rest of Europe began introducing compulsory elementary schooling in the 1870s because in the best of cases less than half of school-age children were receiving some education, but in parts of Germany such legislation went back to the sixteenth century, and by the Napoleonic period French travelers like Madame de Staël and Victor Cousin were full of enthusiasm and praise for the extent and quality of education in the German states. Defeat, initially, at the hands of Napoleon furthered educational reforms and improvements. By the 1860s the proportion of school-age children in Prussia attending school was nearly 100 per cent, and in Saxony it was actually over 100 per cent because may foreign students and children under the age of six and over fourteen were in school.[2] If, as is often stated, the great revolution in education in the nineteenth century came at the primary school level, then Germany was by far the most advanced and revolutionary country in the world. Renan was to say that the Prussian victory over France in 1870–71 was a victory of the Prussian schoolmaster over his French counterpart.

The achievement in secondary and higher education was almost as impressive. Germany was much less prone to channeling students at an early age into areas of study; her secondary education was more diversified than elsewhere; and her universities were not only the most open and 'democratic' in Europe, they were world-renowned centers of scholarship and research. Henry Hallam said in 1844, 'No one professor at Oxford, a century since, would have thought a knowledge of German requisite for a man of letters; at present no-one can dispense with it.'[3] And some years later the historian John Seeley remarked, 'Good books are in German.'[4] Even before unification the German states were actively involved in founding and promoting institutes of learning and centers of research, and after unification the pace of state involvement was accelerated. Moreover, technical and vocational training was not left to private enterprise, as was generally the case in Britain, but remained a matter of national and state concern.

German scientific and technological accomplishment in the half century before 1914 is universally recognized, but what is less appreciated is the degree to which Einstein, Planck, Röntgen, and other internationally famous men were merely the best known of a large and active band. State encouragement of technical education and research brought forth an astonishing harvest. One example in an area of technological development that by its nature suffocates sensationalism, and is therefore perhaps all the more noteworthy, is the coal-tar industry. The six largest German firms in that industry took out, between 1886 and 1900, 948 patents; their British counterparts took out only 86.[5]

The cult of technicism and its vitalist connotations had reverberations in much of German society by the last years of the nineteenth century. In most quarters a concern with newness and inevitable change was manifest, even within the old landed aristocracy, where in the past change had usually been regarded with skepticism and chagrin. In his last novel, Der Stechlin, finished in 1898 and set in the Prussian countryside, Theodor Fontane had one of his characters, a rural pastor, say:

A new age is dawning, a better and happier age I believe. But if not a happier age, then at least an age with more oxygen in the air, an age in which one can breathe better. And the more freely one breathes, the more one lives.

Among much of the rural gentry change was now regarded as unavoidable, especially in the wake of the agricultural depression that in the second half of the 1870s had made economic survival for the landed classes complex and difficult. The important consideration was not to allow change to get out of hand; one had to control it somehow.

German conservatism moved in the Bismarckian era – with Bismarck setting the example – from a dogmatic concern with beliefs and principles to a preoccupation with interests. This new opportunism was perhaps best symbolized by the creation of the 'rye and iron' alliance, a marriage of convenience between large-scale agriculture and heavy industry, which parented Germany's turn to economic protectionism in 1879. 'Nothing could be less conservative,' argued Wilhelm von Kardorff, 'than to fight for forms which in the course of time have lost their importance.'[6]

But the rest of the German body politic was also caught up in a reformist wave by the first years of the twentieth century. This was evident in, among other things, the burgeoning of pressure groups and nationalist societies, whose membership was interested not in the preservation of the status quo but in the rejuvenation of the whole political process. Among the political parties themselves the beginnings of a distinct reorientation were noticeable. The Social Democratic Party (SPD) moved toward a more moderate position, showing a clear willingness to reject its previous negativism. The left liberals in turn showed an interest in becoming a party of social and political reform, one that would conciliate left and right, 'democracy and monarchy.' And finally, an influential segment within the Catholic Center Party also sensed that a more conciliatory attitude toward socialism was necessary and that reform should receive more emphasis in the party's program. In short, the basis for a loose democratic reform movement was laid in German politics in the years before 1914.

The elections of 1912 produced a stunning result. The three political tendencies that Bismarck at one point or another had called 'enemies of the Reich' and hence traitors – left liberals, Catholics, and socialists – won

112

two thirds of the national vote. One out of every three Germans voted for a socialist candidate, and the SPD became by far the largest political group in the Reichstag. The party thus reaffirmed its prominence as the largest socialist organization in the world and leader of the socialist international movement. Though obviously concerned about the large socialist gains, the left liberal Friedrich Naumann nevertheless remarked in the days after the elections, 'Something new has begun in Germany in these past days; an era is approaching its end; a new age has dawned.'[7]

The general impulse in Germany before 1914 was, then, starkly future-oriented. Where there was dissatisfaction or anxiety, it was to be overcome by change. The entire German setting at the *fin de siècle* was characterized by a *Flucht nach vorne*, a flight forward.

CAPITAL

The capital city of, in the first instance, the state of Prussia and then of a united Germany made all its visitors instantly aware of newness and vitality. Berlin was representative in many ways of the transformations that Germany as a whole was experiencing. In comparison to other European capitals, Berlin was a parvenu city, in its sprawling development in the second half of the nineteenth century more like New York and Chicago than its Old World counterparts. Walther Rathenau in fact called it 'Chicago on the Spree.'

Berlin's central location in Europe made her, as it did Germany in general, an immigrant center, attracting and temporarily housing transients from the eastern territories, from Russia, the Polish lands, Bohemia, and settlers heading in the other direction from France and even from Britain. This was her fate from the time of the great elector onward, and real Berliners – that is, fourth-, third-, or even second-generation inhabitants –

113

were always, it seemed, a minority. In the first half of the nineteenth century the city grew steadily as Prussia asserted herself within the German Confederation and particularly as the Zollverein, the German customs union, founded in 1832 with its headquarters in Berlin, expanded both in size and activity. Well before unification in 1871 Berlin was undeniably the financial and commercial capital of the German states, but in this role she was more a clearinghouse and communications center than the hub of German or even Prussian industry; that developed in the Ruhr heartland, in Silesia, and in parts of Saxony. Although in the second half of the century Berlin did develop important industries, appropriately the new electrical and chemical industries in particular, she remained the embodiment and symbol of technicism and management. In relation to her ballooning administrative function, especially after unification, she grew mightily in size. In 1865 her population stood at 657,000; by 1910 it was over two million, and if one included the surrounding suburbs, which were to be incorporated into 'greater Berlin' in 1920, her population was already close to four million by the eve of the war. It is estimated that about half of her new population came from the agricultural lands of eastern Prussia.

Almost every visitor to the capital of the new Reich was struck by the corresponding air of newness that permeated the city. Victor Tissot, a Swiss writer, saw it in 1875 and remarked:

Heinrich Heine speaks of the surprise and magic that Paris produces for the stranger. Berlin, too, achieves surprise, but hardly any magic. One is surprised that the heart of the new empire, the city of intellect, exudes far less of a capital's spirit than Dresden, Frankfurt, Stuttgart, or Munich. What Berlin displays to its visitors is modern and absolutely new. Everything here bears the mark of an adventure, a

114

monarchy put together out of bits and pieces . . . There is nothing less German, in the sense of the old German, than the face of Berlin . . . When you've explored these straight streets and for ten hours seen nothing but sabers, helmets, and feathers, then you understand why Berlin, in spite of the reputation that events of the last years have bestowed on it, will never be a capital like Vienna, Paris, or London.[1]

In the next decades the city was unable to rid itself of its aura of newness, this rather indelicate fragrance of the *nouveau riche*; rather, that flavor was enhanced by technological change. The liberal economist Moritz Julius Bonn, reminiscing about experiences in the German capital in the last years of the century, noted that in Berlin

everything was new and extremely clean; streets and buildings were spacious, but there was a lot of tinsel meant to look like gold . . . The place was not unlike an oil city of the American west, which had grown up overnight and, feeling its strength, insisted on displaying its wealth.[2]

Berliners, unlike the natives of other German cities and other European capitals, seemed to be fascinated by the very idea of urbanism and technology and even developed, as Friedrich Sieburg put it, a romanticism from 'railway junctions, cables, steel, and track . . . noisy elevated trains, climbing towers.' Contrary to the Parisian, who tried to retain a local and community atmosphere in his *quartier*, the Berliner enjoyed and consciously promoted his city's cosmopolitanism and sense of novelty.[3] It was this energy which was to attract, in the last prewar years, artists and intellectuals from other German cities, such as Dresden and Munich, and even from Vienna, to the more haphazard and more ebullient atmosphere of Berlin.

115

In the years before the war Berlin was able to exert as a capital city nothing near the cultural control of a Paris or London or even Vienna on its own country, but this lack of influence heightened the city's own sense of newness. Berlin was a capital created, so the argument ran, by will and imagination rather than historical momentum. Berlin was seen to represent the victory of spirit over conformity and tradition.

Berlin was then, in many respects, an improvised capital, a symbol of mechanism and even transience, but it was as well an expression of energy and dynamism, a city with its eye on the future.

KULTUR

By the turn of the century the futuristic vision entranced much of German society, even those people who decried the vulgarity of Berlin. The economy was expansionist. The population was growing at a staggering pace. After the military victories of the 1860s and 1870–71, no-one in Europe, let alone Germany, had any doubt that the Germans represented the most formidable landed military might in Europe and probably the world. By 1914 there was a consensus, both at home and abroad, that in economic and military terms Germany constituted the most powerful country in the world.

But while Germans may simply have acknowledged that their international success was the result of hard work, an excellent educational system, and a measure of military and political acumen, most were reluctant to accept such a mundane explanation of the nation's stellar performance. They dreamed of a fusion of worlds, physical and spiritual. Indeed, as the technical accomplishment grew in dimension, it was correspondingly more prone to fabulation. Necessity may have fathered invention, but invention then brought forth intention. The technical became spiritual. Efficiency became an end, not a means. And Germany herself became the expression of an elemental 'life force.' Such was the stuff of German idealism.

Thus, education as social concept was superseded by *Bildung*, or self-cultivation, which involved the nurturing of the spirit rather than of the social being. Military prowess born of geographical necessity gave way to *Macht*, or might, which was accorded a purity of being beyond conscience and stricture. And the state, as the instrument of public welfare, was replaced by *der Staat*, the idealized embodiment of the *salus populi*. Germans in the imperial era seemed particularly susceptible to secular idealist notions that ultimate reality was spiritual, and that the material world not only could but ought to be transcended by ideals.

Not surprisingly, many Germans by the end of the century came to attribute to their supposed enemies those characteristics which they so wished to surmount in themselves. Thus they could argue that Anglo-French civilization, which since the sixteenth century had gradually established a political and cultural hegemony in the world, was based on rationalism, empiricism, and utility; in other words, on externality. This was a world of form, devoid of spiritual values: it was a culture not of honesty and true freedom but of manners, superficiality, and dissimulation. Notions of liberalism and equality were in the Anglo-French ethos merely hypocritical slogans – *Lug und Trug*, lying and cheating. They masked the dictatorship of form, which was obvious in a Gallic preoccupation with *bon goût* and a British absorption in commerce. In such a context genuine freedom was not possible.

German *Kultur*, by contrast, was said to be concerned with 'inner freedom,' with authenticity, with truth rather than sham, with essence as opposed to appearance, with totality rather than the norm. German *Kultur* was a matter of 'overcoming,' a matter of reconciling the 'two souls' that resided in Faust's breast. Richard

117

Wagner's contribution to the German perception of *Kultur* in the last quarter of the nineteenth century was of particular importance. His vision of grand opera aimed not only at uniting all the arts but also at elevating his *Gesamtkunstwerk*, his total art work, to a position where it was the supreme synthesis and expression of *Kultur*, a combination of art, history, and contemporary life in total drama, where symbol and myth became the essence of existence. Even politics were subsumed into theater. Wagner's influence on German consciousness and his role in the emergence of a modern aesthetic as a whole are difficult to exaggerate. Bayreuth became a shrine to the transcendence of life and reality by art and the imagination, a place where the aesthetic moment was to encapsulate all the meaning of history and all the potential of the future. Many outside Germany as well were swept up by the Wagnerian promise: Diaghilev, Herzl, Shaw, for starters. 'When I play Wagner,' said Arthur Symons to James Joyce, 'I am in another world.'[1] In the Berlin festival of 1914, just before the outbreak of war, *Parsifal* was performed at the Royal Opera House from 31 May to 7 June, and then the entire Ring cycle was done from 9 to 13 June.

Other, more 'vulgar idealists' called for a similar aestheticization of life. Julius Langbehn, in his immensely successful *Rembrandt als Erzieher*,* urged Germans to turn away from what he saw as a preoccupation with materialistic pursuits and to become a nation of artists. Life ideally should follow art. Life should be both vision and spectacle, a panoramic art work, a quest for titanism, not a concern with codes of behavior and with morality. That was the sterility of bourgeois liberalism, said Langbehn, into which the Germans seemed to be slipping by the end of the century.

Langbehn's impact was reinforced by Houston Stewart Chamberlain, whose enormously popular

Rembrandt As Educator.

118

Grundlagen des neunzehnten Jahrhunderts* was published in 1899. Chamberlain, who derided any pretense to objectivity among historians as 'academic barbarism,' was a morose though highly talented and intriguing wayfarer in the modern odyssey into irrationalism, a striking symbol of the journey from bourgeois respectability, with prescribed world view and social values, toward narcissism and total fantasy. A sickly youth whose mother died early and whose seafaring father shunted him between relatives in France and school in England, Chamberlain matured as a 'marginal' personality, subject to nervous disorders, without country, family ties, or social niche. His father planned to send him to farm in Canada, but the venture was abandoned because of Chamberlain's poor health. He drifted via Versailles, Geneva, and Paris, where in 1883 he lost a great deal of money in financial speculation, to Germany, having taken as a first wife a woman ten years his senior and having also been swept up in the Wagner cult. Despite his demonstrated abilities as a scientist, it was to be as a servant of the Wagnerian mythos that Chamberlain found his *raison d'être*, first in Leipzig, then in Vienna, and finally in Bayreuth at the hearth of the *Gesamtkunstwerk*, where he eventually took as his second wife Wagner's daughter to complete the symbiosis. In a parallel development he was to become a proponent of a xenophobic and virulent Germanic ideology, which struck a responsive chord in the kaiser, Wilhelm II, and, after 1906, in the chief of the general staff, Helmuth von Moltke, and which would lead in the last years of Chamberlain's life to a reciprocated admiration for Adolf Hitler.

Chamberlain is an interesting character for many reasons: as an articulate racist who cannot be dismissed peremptorily as a fool; as a publicist and propagandist with prodigious influence. But from our

**Foundations of the Nineteenth Century.*

standpoint it is his flight into a self-indulgent aestheticism that is of particular significance. Confronted in 1884 by financial disaster at the age of twenty-nine, he wrote:

> I think it is my passion for Wagner which enables me to stand everything; as soon as the door of my office is closed behind me, I know it's no good fretting, so I eat a good dinner and stroll on the boulevard, thinking of the art works of the future, or I go to see one of my Wagnerian friends, or I write to one of my numerous Wagnerian correspondents.[2]

He came to believe that man could be redeemed and ennobled by art and that Wagner's art in particular could bridge man's sensuous nature and his moral purpose. History existed only as spirit and not as an objective reality; its truths could be approached only by intuition, not by a critical method. Chamberlain may have vulgarized Johann G. Droysen, Wilhelm Dilthey, Heinrich Rickert, and Wilhelm Windelband – who shifted the emphasis in historical thought from the object to the subject; in other words, from history to the historian – but he was also part of a broader cultural tendency, in an era of high industrialization, to look for answers to man's social problems not in the external world but in his soul. Correspondingly, the public view of that external world was increasingly influenced, in an age of rapidly developing communications, by these explosions of egomaniacal interpretation. 'Descartes,' wrote Chamberlain, 'pointed out that all the wise men in the world could not define the colour "white," but I need only to open my eyes to see it and it is the same with "race." '[3]

Chamberlain belonged to the group of mystical nationalists who gained ascendancy in German intellectual circles after the turn of the century and who, following Wagner, tried to spiritualize life by turning it into a quest for beauty. Like Langbehn and the poet Stefan George, who also looked on art as power, he wished to turn life into an art work, for only in such a context would man's total personality unfold. History too in the process had to become a wholly spiritual product.

The impassioned distinction that Germans began to make in the late nineteenth century between *Kultur* and *Zivilisation* was, of course, as much a reaction to the mirrored image of self as it was a response to observation of an outside world. Indeed, there was a strong, perhaps even preponderant element of self-criticism and wishful thinking in the distinction, as some of the more perceptive critics, from Schopenhauer through Burckhardt and Nietzsche, pointed out in their philosophical and historical speculations. That a Germany absorbed in *Macht* and technique should decry the English as stolid merchants and the French as Gallic buffoons, Nietzsche, for one, found profoundly ironic: the Prussian victory over France contained the seeds of defeat for German *Geist*, or spirit, he noted. *Geist* was becoming, by itself, a contradiction.[4]

If self-criticism and self-hatred were evident in German idealism, there was still an underlying optimism embedded in a metaphysical or romantic faith that Germany represented the essential dynamic of the age, that she was in the vanguard of movement and change in the world of the early twentieth century, and that she was the foremost representative of a Hegelian World Spirit – a view captured in a line of doggerel that became the main claim to posthumous fame of one Emanuel Geibel of Lübeck, a contemporary of Bismarck: *Denn am deutschen Wesen soll die Welt genesen.**

---

*By the German soul the world will be made whole.

If central to the self-image of the European avant-garde before 1914 was the idea of spirit at war, Germany as a nation best represented that idea; and if central to an emergent modern aesthetic was a questioning of what were perceived to be the prevailing standards of the nineteenth century, Germany best represented the revolt.

Her political system was an attempt to produce a synthesis of monarchy and democracy, centralism and federalism. Her universities were admired for their research. She had the largest socialist party in the world, looked to for leadership by the entire international labor movement. Her youth, women's rights, and even homosexual emancipation movements were large and active. These mushroomed in the context of a *Lebensreformbewegung*, which, as the word suggests, aimed at a reorientation not only of basic habits of living but of fundamental values in life. According to the 1907 census, 30.6 per cent of German women were gainfully employed. No other country in the world could match that figure.[1] Berlin, Munich, and Dresden were vibrant cultural centers. Picasso said in 1897 that if he had a son who wished to be an artist, he would send him to Munich to study, not to Paris.[2] In the introduction to his catalogue for his second postimpressionist exhibition, in 1912, Roger Fry, obviously identifying postimpressionism with experimentation in general in painting, wrote, 'Post-Impressionism schools are flourishing, one might almost say raging, in Switzerland, Austro-Hungary, and most of all in Germany.'[3] Strindberg, Ibsen, and Munch got a warmer reception in Germany than in their own countries. In the decorative arts and in architecture Germany was more open to experiment, more ready to accept industry and base an aesthetic on it, than either France or Britain. While, for example, the British cultural establishment was thoroughly critical of the construction of the Crystal Palace, Lothar Bucher reported in 1851 that the German popular imagination was enchanted by it: 'The impression produced on those who saw it was of such romantic beauty that reproductions of it were seen hanging on the cottage walls of remote German villages.'[4]

We have already seen how the Paris critics of the Théâtre des Champs-Élysées associated it with German experimentation and ahistoricity. The movement that German architects, craftsmen, and writers fostered 'proved strong enough,' in the judgement of one critic, 'to yield a universal style of thinking and building, and not merely some revolutionary sayings and deeds of a few individuals.'[5] In modern dance it was in Germany that Isadora Duncan and Émile Jaques-Dalcroze founded their first schools. Diaghilev naturally gravitated toward Paris in his *tournées* in the west, because after all it was the heart of western culture he wanted to conquer, but his seasons in Germany met with more ready acceptance though with equal applause. After the opening of *Faune* on 12 December 1912, in Berlin, he cabled to Astruc:

> Yesterday triumphant opening at New Royal Opera House. Faune encored. Ten calls. No protests. All Berlin present. Strauss, Hofmannsthal, Reinhardt, Nikisch, the whole Secession group, King of Portugal, ambassadors and court. Wreaths and flowers for Nijinsky. Press enthusiastic. Long article Hofmannsthal in Tageblatt. Emperor, Empress, and Princes coming to ballet Sunday. Had long talk with Emperor who was delighted and thanked the company. Huge success.[6]

Germany's essential ethos, then, before 1914 involved a search for new forms, forms conceived not in terms of laws and finiteness but in terms of symbol, metaphor, and myth. As a young student of art Emil Nolde was in

123

Paris from 1899 to 1900. He often went to the Louvre to copy pictures. One day he had almost completed a copy of Titian's *Allegory of Davalos* when a stranger behind him remarked: 'You are no Latin. One sees that from the intensity of character of your human figures.'[7] Whether the story, related by Nolde in his memoirs, is true, it represents well the German perception of self at the beginning of the century: the German, so he thought, was far more spiritual than his neighbors. 'German creativity is fundamentally different from Latin creativity,' wrote the artist Ernst Ludwig Kirchner.

> The Latin takes his forms from the object as it exists in nature. The German creates his form in fantasy, from an inner vision peculiar to himself. The forms of visible nature serve him as symbols only . . . and he seeks beauty not in appearance but in something beyond.[8]

Germany, more extensively than any other country, represented the aspirations of a national avant-garde – the desire to break out of the 'encirclement' of Anglo-French influence, the imposition of a world order by a Pax Britannica and French *civilisation*, an order codified politically as 'bourgeois liberalism.'

While in some quarters in Germany there was a feeling that *Kultur* was under attack from superficiality, caprice, and ephemera, and that steps had to be taken to consolidate it – as Langbehn and Chamberlain, among others, suggested – and while there was a good measure of anxiety in all classes, a mood that naturally concerned governments and leaders, there was still a strong sense of confidence, optimism, and mission, a belief in *die deutsche Sendung*, a Germanic mission. The feeling was widespread that the reform wave was something larger and more meaningful than any of its specific – and in some cases unacceptable – parts, and that it constituted the heart and soul of the nation. Friedrich Gundolf and Friedrich Wolters, two of the disciples of the poet Stefan George, addressed this idea when they insisted in 1912 that there was nothing immoral or abnormal in homoeroticism. 'Rather we have always believed that something essentially formative for German culture as a whole is to be found in these relations.' The vision was of a culture committed to 'heroized love.'[9]

Germany in fact had the largest homosexual emancipation movement in Europe on the eve of the First World War. August Bebel felt it necessary to make a Reichstag speech on the subject as early as 1898. Homosexuality in the kaiser's entourage was well known even before the journalist Maximilian Harden decided to expose it in 1906. Magnus Hirschfeld led the campaign in Germany to revise paragraph 175 of the civil code, and by 1914 his petition had 30,000 doctors, 750 university professors, and thousands of others as signatories. Berlin by 1914 had about forty homosexual bars and, according to police estimates, between one and two thousand male prostitutes.[10]

None of this is meant to suggest that Germans welcomed or were prepared collectively to tolerate homosexuality publicly – they were not – but the relative openness of the movement in Germany does indicate a measure of tolerance not known elsewhere. Moreover, homosexuality and tolerance of it are, as many have suggested, central to the disintegration of constants, to the emancipation of instinct, to the breakdown of 'public man,' and indeed to the whole modern aesthetic.

Sexual liberation in fin-de-siècle Germany was not limited to homosexuals. There was a new emphasis in general on Leibeskultur, or body culture, on an appreciation of the human body devoid of social taboos and restrictions; on the liberation of the body from corsets, belts, and brassieres. The youth movement, which flourished after the turn of the century, reveled in a 'return to nature' and celebrated a hardly licentious but certainly freer sexuality, which constituted part of its rebellion

125

against an older generation thought to be caught up in repression and hypocrisy. In the 1890s *Freikörperkultur*, or free body culture – a euphemism for nudism – became part of a health-fad movement that promoted macrobiotic diets, home-grown vegetables, and nature cures. In the arts the rebellion against middle-class mores was even more dramatic: from Frank Wedekind's Lulu plays, which celebrated the prostitute because she was a rebel, through Strauss's *Salomé*, who beheaded John the Baptist because he refused to satisfy her lust, to the repressed but obvious sexual undercurrent in Thomas Mann's early stories, artists used sex to express their disillusionment with contemporary values and priorities and, even more, their belief in a vital and irrepressible energy.

The sexual themes in literature and art involved a measure of violence that was more striking and sustained in Germany than elsewhere. Here again the fascination with violence represented an interest in life, in destruction as an act of creation, in illness as part of living. In Wedekind, Lulu is murdered; in Strauss, Salomé murders; in Mann, Aschenbach dies from a combination of diseased atmosphere and unfulfilled sexual craving. In early German expressionism there was a motif of violence – in theme, in form, in color – which was more intense than that to be found in either cubism or futurism. Marinetti's futurist manifestoes trumpeted the destruction of monuments and museums and the burning of libraries, and Wyndham Lewis founded a journal named *Blast* to capture his intentions, but an element of histrionic performance and even jocularity dominated these endeavors. In the German expressionists Franz Marc and August Macke the violence was less a surface manifestation and more an expression of a profound spiritual excitement, of which their appearance, bordering on schoolboy innocence and charm, gave no hint. 'Our ideas and our ideals must wear hair shirts,' wrote Marc; 'we must feed them locusts and wild honey, and not history, if we are to escape the fatigue of our European bad taste.'[11]

The fascination with primitivism, or, in another sense, the desire to establish contact with the elemental in the German spirit, reached many levels in Germany, particularly within the middle classes. The youth movement, with its urge to escape from an urban civilization of mere form and sham back into nature, was replete with such associations. It venerated Turnvater Jahn, the man who had founded gymnastic societies in the German states during the wars of liberation against Napoleon and who for a time in his own youth had lived in a cave and later had walked the streets of Berlin dressed in a bear skin. The tribal origins of the Germans were also evoked constantly at the turn of the century both in political and general discourse. In a notorious speech delivered to troops being sent to help quell the Boxer Rebellion, the kaiser called for a return to the spirit of the Huns. On 8 July 1914, the *Berliner Tageblatt*, a major Berlin daily of left-liberal persuasion, began to serialize a novel by Karl Hans Strobl entitled *So ziehen wir aus zur Hermannsschlacht.** The paper continued to publish episodes into August after the outbreak of war. The title referred to the famous battle of AD 9, when Arminius of the Cherusci tribe defeated the legions of the Roman general Varus in the forests north of modern-day Hanover. The enormous Hermann monument, which still stands in the Teutoburg Forest, had been completed in 1875. Many artists in addition to Marc and Macke found inspiration in the contemplation of the primitive. During a trip to the South Seas, Emil Nolde commented in early 1914:

> Primitive men live in nature, are one with it, and a part of the whole. I sometimes have the feeling that they are the only real human beings left and that we on the other hand are malformed puppets, artificial and full of conceit.

*So We Departed for the Hermann Battle.

He regretted the whole process of imperialism, particularly the British version: so much essence had, he felt, been destroyed and replaced only by pretense.[12]

Many people were captivated, some incensed, both at home and abroad, by the cultural effervescence in Germany. In the German middle strata there was hardly universal appreciation for the plays of Wedekind, the art of Marc and Macke, or the 'body culture' and rarefied idealism of urban youth. The working classes, needless to say, were hardly attuned to the pretensions of bourgeois bohemians. But, interestingly, none of this seemed to negate the general identification by most Germans with the ideas of newness, regeneration, and change. Foreign observers had a similar response. The Spanish-born American philosopher George Santayana was thinking primarily of Germany when he wrote:

> The spirit in which parties and nations beyond the pale of English liberty confront one another is not motherly nor brotherly nor Christian. Their valorousness and morality consist in their indomitable egotism. The liberty that they want is absolute liberty, a desire which is quite primitive.[13]

Santayana denigrated German 'egotism,' what he saw as the emphasis on private virtues and public conformism, an attitude that indicated to him the backwardness of German social and moral development. Nevertheless, despite the sarcasm and chagrin, he too sensed the vitality at the heart of German affairs: 'The German moral imagination is . . . in love with life rather than wisdom.'[14] In the early days of August 1914, H.G. Wells would speak of 'the monstrous vanity' that characterized the Germans.[15]

Igor Stravinsky was more favorably disposed. By February 1913, he had heard Strauss's *Elektra* twice and in a letter he wrote:

I am completely ecstatic. It is his best composition. Let them talk about the vulgarisms that are always present in Strauss – and to which my reply is that the more deeply one goes into German works of art, the more one sees that all of them suffer from *that* . . . Strauss's *Elektra* is a marvelous thing![16]

By 'vulgarisms' Stravinsky presumably meant the 'elemental' aspects of the work and also the challenge to the public which the work entailed. Moreover, if much of modern German art was concerned with fundamentals, the implication was that German culture as a whole, consumers as well as creators, was more attuned to experimentation and novelty. To be 'elemental' was to rebel against suffocating and stultifying norms, against meaningless conventions, against insincerity. All this was at the heart of the German interpretation of *Kultur*. If individual Germans were not always clear in their attitude toward change, the culture promoted change with a vengeance.

Nowhere was there more dramatic evidence of this than in the area of foreign relations and foreign policy goals. In her aggressive attitude toward other states and peoples, Germany showed little comprehension, especially after the turn of the century, of the anxieties, wishes and interests of allies, neutrals, or foes. Thus, British fears about German naval ambitions, French concern over German colonial claims, and Russian wariness about German postulations on the subject of a middle European customs union stretching from the North Sea to the Adriatic, and from Alsace to the borders of Russia, received little sympathy in Germany, either in the corridors of power or among the general public.

In 1896 the government openly adopted what came to be called *Weltpolitik*, or 'world policy,' in contrast to a foreign policy centered hitherto on Europe. *Weltpolitik* was not a foreign policy imposed on Germans by the machinations of a small clique of advisers surrounding the kaiser. It reflected a widespread feeling, promoted by a host of eminent intellectuals and by public associations, that Germany must either expand or decline. This shift in policy, accompanied as it was by the inauguration of a naval building program and an obstreperous pursuit of additional colonies, naturally aroused concern abroad about Germany's long-range intentions. Within Germany, however, these foreign queries were interpreted as nothing but veiled threats. Given Germany's geographical location, her recent consolidation as a nation-state, and the amalgam of insecurity and self-assertion in her make-up, it was not unnatural that Germans began to fear that a conspiracy was afoot, led by England, that perfidious Albion, to encircle and crush Germany, and in the process to crush newness, spirit, incentive, and adventure. British pretensions about free trade, an open market, and a liberal ethic were, on the world level, sheer hypocrisy – so it was argued in Germany. Britain was a country bent on retaining its international position, on arrogantly maintaining control of the seas, on dictatorially denying the right of any other nation to build a navy and to pursue an imperial policy. British pronouncements about the rule of law, about democracy and justice, were, given her foreign policy, obviously a sham. In the international context Germans were inclined to regard their country as a progressive, liberating force that would introduce a new honesty into power arrangements in the world. By contrast, Britain was, from the German point of view, the archconservative power, intent on maintaining the status quo.

Kaiser Wilhelm II, who had ascended the German throne in 1888 at the age of twenty-nine, was an appropriate representative of this burgeoning and blustering Germany. Walther Rathenau would say of him that 'never before has a symbolic individual so perfectly represented an age.'[17] Wilhelm not only embodied the contradictions and conflicts of the country he ruled; he sought a resolution of those conflicts in fantasy.

In reality he was a soft, effeminate, and highly strung man whose closest friends were homosexuals, men to whom he was drawn for the warmth and affection he could not find in the sharply circumscribed world of officialdom and the confines of traditional, male-dominated family life. Nevertheless, the image that he felt constrained to present of himself was that of the supreme war lord, the epitome of masculinity, hardness, and patriarchal resolve. Yet, although he centralized government and administration in Germany to an unprecedented degree, and although he sired seven children, he seems to have found little satisfaction in his role either as ruler or as father. Confronted by the dichotomy in himself between weakness and power, with neither extreme being acceptable, he resorted to the same behavior as that of the nation collectively – interminable play acting. Bertrand Russell had the impression that the kaiser was above all an actor.[18] Of Wilhelm's dismissal of Bismarck in 1890, Prince Bernhard von Bülow remarked that Wilhelm himself wanted to play the part of Bismarck.[19]

Wilhelm's histrionic nature, his love of pomp and circumstance, and his life of fantasy were remarked upon by many. His attention span was short; consequently, briefing reports for him had to be terse yet dramatic. His restless nature demanded constant excursions and constant titillation; he was the modern tourist as opposed to the traditional traveler. His closest friend, Prince Philipp zu Eulenburg, was a reasonably accomplished poet, musician, and composer, who regarded himself principally as an artist forced by social circumstance and parental pressure into the drab life of the civil service. Wilhelm delighted in the arts, particularly in lavish spectacle. He had a keen interest in opera and theater and repeatedly astonished professional people with his expertise. If his tastes were for the most part conventional, he at least was occasionally tolerant of experimentation, and he expressed a particular affection for the Ballets russes.

The interest of the kaiser and court in dance had some odd but revealing overtones. Not infrequently, apparently, Dietrich Count von Hülsen-Häseler, chief of the military cabinet, would attire himself in a tutu and, before the kaiser and assembled guests, usually a mixed audience though never including the empress, would perform admirable pirouettes and arabesques. One such performance was to be Hülsen's last. In 1908, at the home of Max Egon Fürst zu Fürstenberg, another close friend of Wilhelm's and an important foreign policy adviser, Hülsen danced and suddenly dropped dead of a heart attack.[20] One can perhaps all too readily dismiss such entertainment as an amusing juvenile prank, worthy of a campfire skit, but in light of the paradoxes in both the kaiser's character and the cultural dynamics of his nation, Hülsen's acclaimed performances take on considerable symbolic importance. Even setting aside the sexual implications of the Hülsen episodes, one can say that, although Wilhelm regarded art in the public domain as a means to cultivate ideals in society and particularly to educate the lower orders, in his private life and personal sensibility he was inclined to look on art in vitalistic terms.

Wilhelm was, however, interested not only in the arts; he had an insatiable appetite for new technology. In a speech in 1906 he heralded 'the century of the motor car' and forecast perceptively that the new age was 'the era of communication.'[21] He saw in himself and in his own interests an image of the German soul, where ends and means, art and technology, were one. The art historian Meier-Graefe found the kaiser a synthesis of Frederick Barbarossa and a modern American, an insight that correctly suggested that history had no integrity for Wilhelm and was little more than a plaything for a gargantuan ego. Not surprisingly

Wilhelm was excited by H.S. Chamberlain's view of history as spirit rather than objective reality, and the Kaiser Wilhelm Memorial Church, which he had erected in the center of Berlin in honor of his grandfather, together with the horrendous Siegesallee, which cut through the Tiergarten and linked the West End with Unter den Linden, displayed the totally mythical nature of his historical sense. Theodor Fontane had a response similar to that of Meier-Graefe: 'What I like about the kaiser is his complete break with the old, and what I don't like about the kaiser is this contradictory desire of his to restore the ancient.'[22]

There was a comparable tendency in the art of the period, where the themes of apocalypse and atavism were central motifs – the marriage of the primitive and the ultramodern along with the denial of history that this entailed. Although lacking in profundity, the kaiser's mind worked in a similar direction. Modern art had become event. The kaiser, too, liked to pretend that he was an event.

The Schlieffen plan, the only military strategy the Germans possessed for a two-front war, was a further fateful expression of the dominance of fantasy and of the preoccupation with the Faustian moment in German thought. The plan foresaw a rapid attack through Belgium, a sharp left wheel in the north of France, and the conquest of Paris, whereupon all resources could then be turned against Russia. The plan promised total victory in Europe on the basis of one major battle in the north of France. It was a grand scheme, a Wagnerian script, that elevated a limited tactical adventure to a total vision. The strategy was that of the gambler who sees himself as a bank director.

The man whose fate it would be to implement the Schlieffen plan, Schlieffen's successor as chief of the general staff, Helmuth von Moltke, displayed splits in his personality akin to those of the kaiser. Moltke had much more of a passion for the arts than for military matters. He painted and he played the cello. Privately he admitted, 'I live entirely in the arts.'[23] He was working on a German translation of Maeterlinck's *Pelléas et Melisande* and was said always to carry a copy of Goethe's *Faust*.

WAR AS CULTURE

In August 1914, most Germans regarded the armed conflict they were entering in spiritual terms. The war was above all an idea, not a conspiracy aimed at German territorial aggrandizement. To those who reflected on the matter, such aggrandizement was bound to be an offshoot of victory, a strategic necessity, and an accompaniment to German self-assertion, but territory was not what the war was about. Until September, the government and military had no concrete war aims, only a strategy and a vision, that of German expansion in an existential rather than a physical sense.

The idea that this was to be a 'preventive war,' to forestall the aggressive designs and ambitions of the hostile powers surrounding Germany, was certainly a part of the thinking of men like Tirpitz and Moltke. Yet these defensive considerations, while often discussed, were invariably subsumed by a grand sense of German power, whose time, it was felt, had come. The two aspects, the practical and the idealistic, were not mutually exclusive, as so many historians who have debated the war aims have implied; both were essential ingredients of the German personality on the eve of the war.

Despite sufficient evidence from the Crimean War, the American Civil War, and the Boer War that a major conflagration would involve long, drawn-out, and bitter fighting, few strategists, tacticians, or planners, German or any other, foresaw anything but a quick resolution to a future conflict. Despite a growing preoccupation by the military in the course of the nineteenth century with size and numbers, with war as a mass phenomenon, the vision everywhere was still of a war of movement, heroism, and quick decisions. Railways would get men to the front promptly; machine guns would be used in attack; mighty ships and mighty artillery would overwhelm the enemy in short order. However, although matériel was important, war was regarded, especially in Germany, as the supreme test of spirit, and, as such, a test of vitality, culture, and life. War, wrote Friedrich von Bernhardi in 1911 in a volume that was to go through six German editions in two years, was a 'life-giving principle.' It was an expression of a superior culture.[1] 'War,' wrote a contemporary of Bernhardi's, was in fact 'the price one must pay for culture.'[2] In other words, whether considered as the foundation of culture or as steppingstone to a higher plateau of creativity and spirit, war was an essential part of a nation's self-esteem and image.

At the outbreak of the war Germans were convinced, as Theodor Heuss, a staunch liberal and certainly no rabid nationalist, put it, of their 'moral superiority,' their 'moral strength,' and their 'moral right.'[3] For Conrad Haussmann, also on the liberal left, the war was a question of will: 'In Germany there is a single will in everyone, the will to assert oneself.'[4] Of course this was to be a national effort, this war, but only because it was to be an effort by every German. 'Since we have no Bismarck among us,' declared Friedrich Meinecke, 'every one of us must be a piece of Bismarck.'[5] The SPD declaration on war credits in the Reichstag on 4 August even included the mythical word *Kultur*, associated earlier by socialists with class interests but now adopted as a symbol of each German's cause. It was a question, said the socialists' statement, of protecting the fatherland, in its hour of need, against Russian despotism, of 'securing *Kultur* and the independence of our land.'[6] The SPD press spoke of defending *Kultur* and thereby 'freeing Europe'! 'Therefore,' wrote the *Chemnitzer Volksstimme*, 'we are defending in this moment all that German *Kultur* and German freedom mean against a brutal and barbaric enemy.'[7]

About the actual vote in the Reichstag on war credits the socialist deputy Eduard David wrote in his diary, 'The memory of the incredible enthusiasm of the other parties, of the government, and of the spectators, as we stood to be counted, will never leave me.' Afterward he went walking with his child along Unter den Linden. The emotional strain of that day had been such that he had to fight back his tears. 'It does me good that my child is with me. If only she wouldn't ask so many unnecessary questions.'[8] The direct questions of the child were obviously a threat to the fantasies conjured up by the day's events.

For the artist Ludwig Thoma in Munich the war was a tragedy but also an unavoidable necessity. On 1 August he was on his way to the train station, intending to go to the Tegernsee, when a crowd gathered in front of the station at the Schützenstrasse corner, and mobilization orders were read. 'Gone was the pressure,' wrote Thoma about his reactions to the situation,

> gone was the uncertainty . . . And then I was struck by the impression of how this courageous and industrious people has to purchase with its blood the right to work and to create values for mankind. And a fierce hatred for those who had disturbed the peace pushed aside any other feeling.

Germany had worked hard and successfully; the upshot was envy and jealousy among her neighbors. Thoma was outraged.[9] Similar sentiments were expressed throughout the land. For Magnus Hirschfeld, the leader of the homosexual movement and no admirer of the country's bureaucratic establishment, the war was for

136

the sake of 'honesty and sincerity' and against the 'smoking jacket culture' of Britain and France. To the argument that Britain was the home of freedom and Germany was the land of tyranny and oppression, Hirschfeld replied that Britain in the last century had damned her great poets and writers. Byron had been chased out of the country, Shelley forbidden to raise his children, and Oscar Wilde sent to prison. Lessing, Goethe, and Nietzsche had, by contrast, been greeted in their country with acclaim, not humiliation.[10]

If in Britain, France, and the United States millenarian notions were to surface in the course of the war – 'the war to end all wars' and 'the war to make the world safe for democracy' – in Germany the mood was apocalyptic from the outset. The visions in the Allied nations had a strong social and political content to them, as in Lloyd George's promise of 'homes fit for heroes.' For Germans, however, the millennium was to be, first and foremost, a spiritual matter. For Thoma the hope was that 'after the pain of this war there would be a free, beautiful, and happy Germany.'

The war, for Germany, was, then, *eine innere Notwendigkeit*, a spiritual necessity. It was a quest for authenticity, for truth, for self-fulfillment, for those values, that is, which the avant-garde had evoked prior to the war and against those features – materialism, banality, hypocrisy, tyranny – which it had attacked. The latter were associated particularly with England, and it was to be England, of course, who was to become Germany's most hated enemy after she entered the war on 4 August. *Gott strafe England* – may God punish England – became the motto even of many Germans who had been moderates before the war.

For many the war was also a deliverance – from vulgarity, constraint, and convention. Artists and intellectuals were among those most gripped by war fever. Schoolrooms and lecture halls emptied as students literally ran to the colors. On 3 August the rectors and senates of Bavarian universities issued an appeal to academic youth:

> Students! The muses are silent. The issue is battle, the battle forced on us for German *Kultur*, which is threatened by the barbarians from the east, and for German values, which the enemy in the west envies us. And so the *furor teutonicus* bursts into flame once again. The enthusiasm of the wars of liberation flares, and the holy war begins.[11]

After the rector of Kiel University appealed to students, almost the entire male student body enlisted.

The association of the war with liberation and freedom, a *Befreiungs-* or *Freiheitskampf*, was widespread. For Carl Zuckmayer the war represented 'liberation from bourgeois narrowness and pettiness'; for Franz Schauwecker it was 'a vacation from life'; for Magnus Hirschfeld the uniforms, stripes, and weapons were a sexual stimulant.[12] When the *Berliner Lokal-Anzeiger* remarked in an editorial on 31 July that the mood in Germany was one of relief, it captured what was probably majority sentiment. But the freedom was above all subjective, a liberation of the imagination. Emil Ludwig, who after the war became the scourge of those whom he considered to have been the 1914 war lords, was as caught up in the fever of August as everyone else. With an exuberance that he later clearly wanted to repress and hide – in his 1929 book *July 1914* he referred to the masses as 'the deceived' and talked about 'the collective innocence on the streets of Europe' – he wrote 'The Moral Victory,' an article that appeared in the *Berliner Tageblatt* on 5 August: 'And even if a catastrophe were to befall us such as no-one dares to imagine, the moral victory of this week could never be eradicated.'[13]

For Ludwig and many others the world seemed

138

altered all of a sudden. 'The war,' as Ernst Glaeser would put it later in his novel *Jahrgang 1902*, 'had made it beautiful.' The Faustian moment that Wagner and Diaghilev and other moderns sought to achieve in their art forms had now arrived for society as a whole. 'This war is an aesthetic pleasure without compare,' one of Glaeser's characters would say.[14] Glaeser was not inventing ideas after the fact. German letters from the front are full of associations between war and art. 'Poetry, art, philosophy, and culture are what the battle is all about,' insisted the student Rudolf Fischer.[15] Franz Marc, after he had been in the trenches for some months, still viewed the war as a question of spirit:

> Let us remain soldiers even after the war . . . for this is not a war against an eternal enemy, as the newspapers and our honorable politicians say, nor of one race against another; it is a *European civil war*, a war against the inner invisible enemy of the European spirit.[16]

Hermann Hesse made similar associations. The war, ironically, was a matter of life, not death; it was an affirmation of vitality, energy, virtue. The war was a matter of art. 'I esteem the moral values of war on the whole rather highly,' he told a friend.

> To be torn out of a dull capitalistic peace was good for many Germans and it seems to me that a genuine artist would find greater value in a nation of men who have faced death and who know the immediacy and freshness of camp life.[17]

Otto Braun, a youngster of seventeen, was fervently caught up, as he left to join his regiment, in what he regarded as an act of creation – 'the rising form of a new era' – and he prayed that he might play his part 'in helping to create this new era in the spirit of the still sleeping godhead.'[18]

In July and August 1914, Germany enacted her *Frühlingsfeier*, her rite of spring.

III

In Flanders' Fields

The scene was very dramatic, and I don't suppose will be witnessed again on a battlefield.

A private, in B Company, 2nd East Lancashire Regiment, in a letter home at the end of 1914

In a progressive country change is constant; and the question is not whether you should resist change which is inevitable, but whether that change should be carried out in deference to the manners, the customs, the laws and the traditions of the people, or whether it should be carried out in deference to abstract principles, and arbitrary and general doctrines.

BENJAMIN DISRAELI

All play means something.

J. HUIZINGA

A CORNER OF A FOREIGN FIELD

When Mrs Packer of Broadclyst in Devon received a letter from her husband in the last days of December 1914, she was probably at first unwilling to believe its contents. She knew that he was somewhere at the front

– exactly where, she was not sure because the military censor forbade the disclosure of such details in letters – and she no doubt believed that he was fighting valiantly for king and country. She had hoped that Christmas Day at least he might spend in billets rather than in the front lines, but when she began reading the letter she quickly realized that her wish had not been fulfilled.

Her husband had indeed spent Christmas at the front – as a member of A Company, 1st Battalion, Devonshire Regiment – in position near Wulverghem to the south of Ypres in Flanders. But he had spent most of the day not so much in the firing line as outside it. What a Christmas it had been! Instead of fighting the Germans, Corporal Packer, along with several hundred of his regimental, brigade, and divisional fellows in the sector and several thousands altogether along the British line in Flanders, had ventured out into no man's land between the trenches to meet and fraternize with the enemy. The Germans had appeared in equal numbers.

Packer related, in his account of this amazing day, how in return for a little tobacco he had been showered with gifts: chocolate, biscuits, cigars, cigarettes, a pair of gloves, a watch and chain, and a beard brush! A remarkable haul! A ratio of giving and receiving this was which should have shamed a child, but Packer exulted in the experience, as did many of his compatriots. 'So you see,' he told his wife in his understated way, 'I got a good Christmas present and was able to walk about safe for a few hours.' Mrs Packer was so astonished by the letter that she sent if off at once to the local newspaper, and it appeared on New Year's Day in Exeter's *Western Times*.[1]

Rifleman G.A. Farmer, whose 2nd Queen's Westminster Rifles were farther down the line that Christmas Day, could include in his letter home to Leicester a more articulate and exuberant comment: 'It was really one of the most wonderful Christmas times I have ever spent.' His family must have been flabbergasted. There was a war on, after all! Farmer continued:

> The men on both sides had the true sense of the season come over them, and with one accord they ceased fighting and took a different and brighter view of life, and we were quite as peaceful as you in good old England.[2]

For the highly literary and imaginative mind of Edward Hulse of the 2nd Scots Guards, in line farther south from Farmer, the incidents in his sector were 'absolutely astounding, and if I had seen it on a cinematograph film I should have sworn that it was faked!'[3] For Gustav Riebensahm, commanding a Westphalian regiment across from some of Hulse's Scots Guards, the impressions were similar. Fighting an urge to disbelieve what he had seen with his own eyes, he noted in his diary on Christmas Day, 'One had to look again and again to believe what was happening, given everything that had occurred earlier.'[4] Expressions of fascination, astonishment, and excitement surface in virtually every account of the fraternization that Christmas.

'This sight I will never forget in my entire life,' wrote Josef Wenzl of the 16th Reserve Infantry Regiment.[5]

'Christmas will remain engraven on the memory of many British soldiers who were in our trenches as one of the most extraordinary days of their lives,' insisted an officer of the Gordon Highlanders.[6]

'These have turned out to be the most extraordinary days we have spent out here – if not in my life,' reflected Private Oswald Tilley of the London Rifle Brigade.[7]

That Christmas truce of 1914, with its tales of camaraderie and warmth between supposedly bitter enemies in the crater-scarred territory of no man's land, that bit of ground between opposing trenches whose very name appeared to forbid such intercourse, is a remarkable chapter in the history of the First World War and indeed of all war. While the highest incidence of fraternization took place along the British-German front, there were numerous similar occurrences between the French and Germans, Russians and Germans, and Austrians and Russians. The Christmas truce of 1914 reveals much about the social values and priorities of the opposing armies and, by extension, of the nations they represented. That such massive fraternization was never to recur during the war suggests, furthermore, that it was not the 'guns of August' but subsequent events that shattered an old world. The 'Edwardian garden party' did not end suddenly on 4 August 1914, as has been claimed.[8] W.A. Quinton, of the 1st Bedfordshires, was to write a decade after the war:

> Men who joined us later were inclined to disbelieve us when we spoke of the incident, and no wonder for as the months rolled by, we who were actually there, could hardly realize that it had happened, except for [the] fact that every little detail stood out so well in our memory.[9]

R.G. Garrod, of the 20th Hussars, was one of those who consistently refused to believe that fraternization had taken place. He wrote in his memoirs that he had never actually met a soldier who had gone out into no man's land and consorted with the enemy that Christmas of 1914, and consequently his conclusion was that the Christmas truce was simply a myth,[10] like the angels that were supposed to have aided British troops in their retreat from Mons in August 1914.

Garrod's disbelief and the expressions of astonishment at the truce are of course related. To many the truce, particularly its dimensions, came as a surprise. It was a surprise not because truces in war were unusual – quite the opposite; they were normal – but because the fighting in the first five months of the war had been so bitter and intense and had taken such a high toll in

Nijinsky, photographed by Stravinsky, in Monte Carlo, 1911

Stravinsky and Nijinsky in his Petrushka costume

Diaghilev and Cocteau

Le Théâtre des Champs-Élysées

The corps de ballet in *Le Sacre du printemps*

Berlin, imperial palace, August 1, 1914. The crowd hails the kaiser.

Paris, Gare de l'Est, August 2, 1914

Petrograd, Nevsky Prospekt, August 3, 1914. The picture has been touched up in a painstaking but crude manner. Why? The head on the smallest boy in the front row clearly does not belong to the body below it.

London, Trafalgar Square, August 4, 1914

German Christmas, 1914. This picture was taken on the Eastern Front, near Darkehmen. It looks posed, but real celebrations did take place on both Eastern and Western Fronts.

Peace on earth: Christmas Day, 1914. British and Germans meet in no man's land near Armentières. Cameras were not permitted in the front lines, so pictures often had to be snapped surreptitiously. The result is evident here.

Battle ballet. The French censors would not allow this picture to be published during the war.

Christmas, 1916. British troops eat their Christmas dinner in a shell hole near Beaumont Hamel. There was no postprandial fraternization this time.

Menin Road

Menin Road by Paul Nash

Armored lookout man

Dada dancers

casualties. Moreover, from the outset propaganda played an important role in the war, and the Anglo-French campaign to portray the German as a barbarian beyond the pale, incapable of such normal human emotions as compassion and friendship, had by that first Christmas already taken effect. And finally, the attempts by various parties, including the Vatican and the American Senate, to arrange an official cease-fire for Christmas had been rejected by the belligerents. Hence, most combatants who had survived those first five grim months and, most notably, those – and they were the majority – who had come to the front recently, imbued with certain ideas about the enemy, had good reason to think that this was no conventional war and that the world was indeed in the process of being transformed by it. But what the truce revealed, by its unofficial and spontaneous nature, was how resilient certain attitudes and values were. Despite the slaughter of the early months, it was the subsequent war that began profoundly to alter those values and to hasten and spread in the west the drift to narcissism and fantasy that had been characteristic of the avant-garde and large segments of the German population before the war.

GUNS OF AUGUST

The war had begun with movement, movement of men and matériel on a scale never witnessed before in history. Across Europe approximately six million men received orders in early August and began to move. The Germans shifted their strategy, aiming at a quick knockout blow in the west, into high gear on the sixth. Over the Rhine bridges moved 550 trains a day. The Hohenzollern bridge at Cologne would bear one train every ten minutes in the early stage of the war. Within less than a week one and a half million men were amassed for the advance. The French were equally assiduous. In a fortnight over three million Frenchmen were moved about in seven thousand trains.

The Schlieffen plan, as originally conceived, was to have the features of, in Basil Liddell Hart's analogy, a revolving door. As the push increased from the Germans entering the door on one side through Belgium and the north of France, the French, who were concentrating their attack to the south, would be drawn in and would add to the momentum of the door and thus of the northern attack. As implemented by Moltke, however, the plan was modified. The push in the north was not as hard as originally intended. A nervous Moltke decided first to strengthen his left flank in the south against the French. Then when the Belgian army retreated to Antwerp, Moltke detached seven divisions from the attacking right flank to deploy them against the Belgians and prevent a breakout. And later in August he weakened the assault again by sending four divisions to counter the Russian advance into East Prussia. Then, in addition to undermining the thrust of the northern attack, he decided to allow Crown Prince Rupprecht of Bavaria, who was commanding the Sixth Army in the south, to exercise his discretion as to whether he would attack the French or, as the Schlieffen plan dictated, draw them into a trap. Rupprecht, spurred by a desire to underline the importance of the Bavarian contribution, took the initiative and decided to attack, and the French, although pushed back in the area of Morhange-Sarrebourg, were forced by Rupprecht's action to consolidate their defenses instead of venturing into a more vulnerable forward position. German particularism thus played a role in the fate of the Schlieffen plan. Once again the reality of Germany – its fragmentation and regional loyalties – undermined the vision of unity and solidarity.

The German move through Belgium was slowed by unanticipated local resistance. Then the right flank, under von Kluck, after clobbering the British at Mons,

146

turned the corner earlier than initially intended, and the weakened German advance was finally halted at the Marne in the second week of September. There followed the German retreat to the Aisne, where the Germans began entrenching themselves against the Allied pursuit, and then the mutual maneuvering to the north – the so-called race to the sea – which was an attempt by both sides to avoid being outflanked. From mid October through early November the Germans tried desperately to break through at Ypres, using great numbers of volunteers who had flocked to the colors in August, but the Allied line held despite enormous losses. After the first battle of Ypres, a battle some Germans would call 'the children's massacre,' the war of movement was for the time being over in the west. The regular armies had been decimated. Stores of ammunition, for a war that was supposed to have been concluded by the time 'the leaves fall,' had been depleted. The machine gun, intended as a weapon of attack, had proved its deadly value as the supreme weapon of defense. Moreover, the terrain of Belgium and northern France, with its innumerable villages, farms, and fences, gave the defender an advantage over the attacker. From the English Channel to the Swiss frontier a bizarre scraggy line of trench fortifications appeared, the only response conceivable by the general staffs to the unexpected deadlock.

After the defeat suffered by the Germans on the Marne, Falkenhayn succeeded Moltke, and in the wake of his failure at Ypres in October and November, he decided that the Schlieffen plan had to be scrapped. While still believing that the decisive front was in the west, he bowed to pressure from the 'easterners' – Hindenburg, Ludendorff, and Conrad – who argued that the Russian danger had to be dealt with urgently. Thus, German offensive concerns shifted to the east. The British and French military leadership meanwhile reluctantly accepted that they might, briefly, have to hold their positions until the manpower and firepower necessary for a knockout blow could be assembled.

German and French casualties had been staggering. The Germans lost a million men in the first five months. France, in the 'battle of the frontiers' of August, lost over 300,000 men in two weeks. Some regiments lost three quarters of their men in the first month. Total French losses by the end of December were comparable with the German, roughly 300,000 killed and 600,000 wounded or missing. By the end of 1914 virtually every French and German family had suffered some bereavement. Because of the appalling casualties in the early fighting, by the end of the year most of the French and German Western Front was manned by reserves.

At Mons, Le Cateau, and then especially at Ypres most of the original British Expeditionary Force (BEF) of 160,000 men had been wiped out. At Ypres alone losses amounted to 54,105. By December the Old Contemptibles, as the British regulars had dubbed themselves in response to the kaiser's reference to the BEF in early August as 'that contemptible little army,' constituted little more than a fragile skeleton for the volunteer armies. As an example of the scale of casualties, the 11th Brigade had, by 20 December only 18 per cent of its original officers left and 28 per cent of its men. Within that brigade the Somerset Light Infantry had lost 36 officers and 1153 men from other ranks, and of those who had embarked in August, so joyfully, only four officers and 266 men remained. The 7th Division, which arrived in France in October, started the Ypres affair with 400 officers and 12,000 men and ended it with 44 officers and 2336 men, a loss of over 9000 men in eighteen days. 'To you from failing hands we throw the torch . . .' By the end of the year a million British men had enlisted, and the empire as a whole now had two million men under arms. By December most of the British troops in the trenches were volunteers.[1]

For military establishments that had been convinced

that the outcome of a future war would hinge on one major battle, the stalemate in the west was impossible to accept. The previous century had been one of extraordinary technological change and movement. War, it was assumed, would reflect that movement. 'Berthelot asked me,' Major General Henry Wilson recorded in his diary on 13 September 1914, after the battle of the Marne, 'when I thought we should cross into Germany, and I replied that unless we made some serious blunder we ought to be at Elsenborn in 4 weeks. He thought 3 weeks.'[2] Kitchener, as British minister of war, had had the prescience to call for the creation of a mass British army at the very first meeting of the council of war on 5 August – 'We must be prepared,' he said, 'to put armies of millions in the field and maintain them for several years' – but his appeal met marked opposition and even cynicism within the British cabinet and general staff. Sir Edward Grey, the foreign minister, noted that Kitchener's estimate of the war's length 'seemed to most of us unlikely, if not incredible.'[3] The New Armies, though approved, were in fact initially intended to secure the peace rather than win the war.

Through November and December of 1914, and throughout 1915 and even into 1916, until the disaster of the Somme, the opinion ruled in the Entente armies that the offensive spirit was all-important and that, despite setbacks and other evidence to the contrary, one breakthrough, one decisive thrust, would move the stalled war machine. Victory would then come in weeks. By December 1914 the British staff had reluctantly agreed that that decisive thrust would have to await the arrival of the New Armies in the spring, but then the war of movement would return. The French, with a good part of their country occupied by the foreign intruder, were understandably even more resolute in retaining such beliefs. Their argument by the end of the year was that with a little patience the Allies would gradually achieve superiority in manpower, munitions, horses, money, and supplies. Then at the appropriate moment the decisive blow would be struck. 'General Joffre,' stated an outline of what officers were instructed to tell their men in early January 1915, 'has not given them [the enemy] a final blow in order to economize on French lives.'[4] The general in charge of the French Fourth Army insisted that all his commanders convince their troops that it was the Germans and not the French who were besieged.[5] Even the shortage of shells and ammunition and the intolerable physical conditions of trench warfare in the west, as winter approached with its endless rain, turning the field of battle into an impassable muddy swamp, could not alter this basic preoccupation with offense. One month, two months, three at the outside: such was the general tenor of predictions. 'As soon as we were supplied with ample artillery ammunition . . .' Douglas Haig, commanding at this point the British First Army, told the Times military correspondent on 22 January 1915, 'we could walk through the German line at several places.'[6]

In December the rain, which had been intermittent since early September, became interminable in Flanders, Artois, and Picardy. More fell there that month than in any December since 1876 – over six inches. The beautiful days of August had become the stuff of dreams. Rifle barrels clogged with mud and would not fire. In the wake of a British attack on 18–19 December, the Germans reported that most of their wounds were caused by bayonets, because their opponents' rifles were jammed.[7] Rivers flooded. In the vicinity of the River Lys the water level rose to within a foot of ground level. In the Somme sector conditions were similar. In their trenches soldiers stood in water up to their knees and on occasion sank up to their chests in mud and had to be hauled out with ropes. In a sector near La Bassée a dam burst and drowned men in their dugouts. Regimental war diaries often devoted more space in December to the war against the elements than to the battle against the human foe. Typical entries like 'mud desperate' and 'trenches impossible' only hint at the scale of misery and the problems confronting the fighting men. Water pumps, hose pipes, shovels, and pick-axes became more important than rifles or artillery as weapons. On 24 December a story spread that the Germans had turned a hose pipe on the British trenches opposite, in a sector near Béthune, in an attempt to flood them. And a few days later the command of the British 7th Division became concerned that the Germans, who were reported to have closed the sluices at Comines, might be directing water toward the British trenches.[8] Both rumors presupposed an ungentlemanly form of warfare that, so went the assumption, would not be at all out of character coming from the Germans.

In many places even high breastworks did not suffice, and troops simply had to be withdrawn to dry ground, leaving only small observation posts or patrols to muck about. Communications and lateral movement proved impossible. Effecting a relief of front-line troops often took anywhere up to eight hours, whereas normally it was accomplished within an hour or so. 'Brushwood parties' assumed greater tactical significance than reconnaissance parties, because brushwood, together with wire netting, at least afforded some protection against drowning in the mud.

The nature of casualties in December and January reflected the nature of the new war: frostbite, rheumatism, and trench foot took a far higher toll than actual combat. 'It is surprising that the whole battalion has not got pneumonia,' noted one regimental diary.[9] As the wet of December soaked through skin and bone, the British First Army reported its casualties for the second week of January as 70 officers and 2886 other ranks. Of these, 45 officers and 2320 other ranks were listed as sick. By comparison, only 11 officers and 144 men had been killed, and 14 officers and 401 men wounded.[10] One corps commander reported soberly to his superiors in early January: 'For the moment the condition of affairs resulting from the prolonged wet weather is the dominating factor in the situation.'[11] A week before Christmas, Frank Isherwood sent his greetings to his family: 'Every goodwish for a Merry Christmas. I never wish to see another if it's going to be like this.'[12] He didn't.

Exhaustion was the inevitable result of three or four days in the trenches. Percy Jones of the Queen's Westminster Rifles observed the 1st Royal Fusiliers leaving the trenches on the morning of 23 December. They were

tattered, worn, straggling, footsore, weary and looking generally broken to pieces. Hairy, unshaved, dirty-faced, and dressed in every possible variety of head-dress, the men looked like so many prehistoric savages rather than a crack regiment of the British Army.[13]

The elements had no favorites. The Germans, French, and British all suffered, and neither side had better answers to the predicament. There was, however, great curiosity about how the enemy was coping with this unexpected aspect of the war. The Germans appear to have been particularly envious of the goat or sheepskin jackets that were distributed in many parts of the British line late in the year and of the high lace-up boots the British wore, as opposed to the low rubber boots supplied to the Germans. The jackets became prizes the Germans sought in skirmishes in no man's land. One German regimental history admitted that after a British attack near Neuve Chapelle on 18 December, the 13th Regiment plundered the British dead for booty, paying particular attention to the sheepskin jackets.[14]

Looting for spoils and for mementoes to send home to prove that one had seen action was common, especially at this early stage of the war. Everyone indulged in the practice. 'On fallen Englishmen we found watches, gold, and Iron Crosses of German soldiers,' charged Gustav Riebensahm. [15] If the Germans admired British lace-up boots, the British were interested in the gumboots some Germans wore to try to cope with mud and water. To regard the opponent's gear – uniforms, coats, boots, and other equipment – as superior was natural, because nothing could be worse, it seemed, than one's own equipment, totally inadequate as it was for keeping out damp and cold. This presumably accounts for at least a good number of the reports in December and January that warned of subterfuge by an enemy reportedly dressed in one's own uniforms. 'Artillery Observation Officer in left section of 17 B[riga]de reports that enemy have men wearing kilts,' read an entry in the British 6th Division diary in mid January. [16]

And yet, despite all the evidence that successful offensive action in such conditions was impossible, the army commanders, ensconced in warm and dry quarters, consistently emphasized the need to maintain an offensive spirit, to keep aggressive instincts honed for the coming decisive battles. Sniping and night raids should go on constantly; saps, or tunnels, should be driven forward; and spirited attacks tried repeatedly. Even if nothing of substance was achieved for the moment – so went the rationale – the effect on morale was important.

The weather naturally gave sufficient cause for concern about the state of morale, but the commander of the British 2nd Corps, in an order of 4 December, referred also to a 'live and let live theory of life' that seemed to have surfaced in the front lines and that, he insisted, had to be stamped out forthwith. [17] His remark was elicited by extensive evidence of friendly interchanges by Allied and enemy troops. These incidents, which increased through November and December, provoked alarm among the 'brass hats.' To come to any private understanding, let alone to consort, with the enemy without permission was treasonous. The incidents were rarely reported in the official war diaries for fear of inciting wrath higher up, but the very fact that mention did occur with growing frequency toward the end of the year suggests that the unreported incidents were far greater in number. The practice of not firing at particular times of day, especially during meals, became common among units that had been facing each other for some time. Unofficial arrangements about sniping during a relief and about behavior while on patrol also existed. Charles Sorley described such understandings in a letter some months later: 'Without at all "fraternizing" we refrain from interfering with Brother Bosch seventy yards away, as long as he is kind to us.' He noted the tedium of daytime activity, which consisted of rebuilding trenches and censoring soldiers' letters.

> During the night a little excitement is provided by patrolling the enemy's wire. Our chief enemy is nettles and mosquitoes. All patrols – English and German – are much averse to the death and glory principle; so, on running up against one another . . . both pretend that they are Levites and the other is a good Samaritan – and pass by on the other side, no word spoken. For either side to bomb the other would be a useless violation of the unwritten laws that govern the relations of combatants permanently within a hundred yards of distance of each other, who have found out that to provide discomfort for the other is but a roundabout way of providing if for themselves.[18]

Often men in opposing trenches were within earshot of one another, and banter between the lines became natural, as did attempts at entertainment. Private Frank Devine of the 6th Gordon Highlanders related in a letter home on 21 December how one morning he had struck up the song 'O' a' the airts,' a sentimental Scottish song whose essence is love of home, and how a German opposite had replied with 'Tipperary.'

They shout to us every morning asking us over to dinner. One day they held up a bit of blackboard, and on it was written in big letters, 'When are you Englishmen going home and let us have peace.' They shout across at us that they want peace.[19]

The Bavarian 16th Reserve Infantry Regiment recorded that on 18 December, near Ypres, as fierce fighting was going on farther south, a man from the Allgäu, an alpine area in the southwest of Germany, got up on the breastworks and performed a fetching yodel for Tommy Atkins.[20] The sense of humor in the midst of the misery was often sparkling. On 10 December at about 9:00 in the morning the Saxons who were facing the 2nd Essex shouted across to say that they were fed up and that they had half-masted the German flag. A member of the Essex riposted with an offer of rum and gin. The Saxons turned down the offer with the retort that they drank only champagne in the trenches![21]

Next to the 2nd Essex the Lancashire Fusiliers struck up a deal with their opponents: they would exchange bully beef tins for helmet badges. '. . . bargain is complete,' the divisional diary recorded, 'except for the slight disagreement as to who shall come out of his trench first to fetch his share.'[22] Understandings, of course, took time to cultivate and were not always appreciated or honored by a relieving unit. Thus, the 2nd Essex got on well with the Saxons, but the Prussians who replaced the latter were described as 'a surly lot, who will not answer when spoken to.'[23]

In short, a certain amount of good feeling – understandings and private agreements – had built up between opposing trenches in the weeks before Christmas. It was to form the basis for the Christmas truce. The British command was not alone in worrying about the effect of this stalemated war on the morale of the fighting men. A week before the British orders against fraternization went out, General Falkenhayn had issued similar warnings to his officers: incidents of fraternization were to be 'investigated carefully by superiors and to be discouraged most energetically.'[24] The mounting number of incidents indicates, however, that admonitions from higher-ups had little effect.

Weather and trench conditions spurred the development of a friendly feeling between the warring parties, but the deteriorating relationship between officers and men, particularly between commanders behind the lines and men in the front lines, also contributed to the mood that produced the events of Christmas. The unproductive and apparently senseless tactics of the general staffs on the Western Front caused a good measure of disgruntlement. For example, in keeping with the emphasis on the 'offensive spirit,' and in order to make the Germans feel that they could not transfer any more troops to the Eastern Front without weakening seriously their position in the west, the British launched a major attack along the southern half of their front on 18 December. The Indian Corps was the main instrument of the attack, but about two thirds of the British line was involved in supporting thrusts. The battles went on from Le Touquet in the north to Givenchy in the south until 22 December, and from the point of view of British morale, if not strategy, the whole enterprise can be described only as a disaster.

On the evening of the eighteenth, the 7th Division attacked the Westphalians and Saxons across from them near Neuve Chapelle and Fromelles with horrendous results, losing 37 officers and 784 men. The 2nd Royal Warwickshires alone lost 320 men, including their commanding officer. In one platoon of 57 men only one lance corporal and three other men came out unscathed. The 2nd Scots Guards, who captured twenty-five yards of opposing trench but, unable to hold the advanced position, were forced to retire in the morning, lost six officers and 188 men in their action. Only one officer involved in the attack returned physically sound.

All along the line the results were similar. Any

successes that were registered were temporary. The Germans experienced the same fate. They counter-attacked at Givenchy on 20 December and made slight progress, but two days later the British riposted and cleared the Germans out of their new positions. Consequently, on the eve of Christmas, after five days of fierce fighting, the positions were virtually the same as they had been on the eighteenth, before the battle began. Such gestures of 'offensive spirit' by their opponents did impress the Germans, and they did not thin out their western forces to the degree they might have liked to, but the dreadful and futile slaughter also aroused dismay among the British troops.

On the nineteenth, the 1st Rifle Brigade and the 1st Somerset Light Infantry had attacked between Le Gheir and St Yves in midafternoon in broad daylight. An artillery barrage was to have damaged enemy barbed-wire entanglements to allow the British to walk through. But just in case parts of the wire were uncut, each man carried a straw mattress to lay over the wire![25] The Germans must have been astonished by the bizarre sight that confronted them as the attack began. Not surprisingly, the artillery had failed completely in the task assigned to it, and burdened with mattresses in addition to their normal gear, which weighed over sixty pounds, few of the British soldiers reached even the enemy wire, about 120 yards away, let alone the enemy trenches. The slaughter was outrageous. One of the officers commanding the attack, a Colonel Sutton, reported subsequently that the effort had 'proved a complete failure.' While the brigade commander behind the lines thought that the action had achieved a major objective – to keep the Germans from transferring troops to the Eastern Front – Sutton could not hide his profound sorrow and chagrin when he reported.

From the Battalion point of view the only effects of the action were of a sentimental nature: firstly, pride at

157

the gallant behaviour of the attacking companies who advanced without hesitation against an unshaken line of well-armed defenders, and secondly, grief at the loss of so many well-loved comrades, who could ill be spared.[26]

As in cases of fraternization, the official war diaries are reluctant to record evidence of disaffection, so any examples that do appear in the diaries can validly be read as mere hints of the magnitude of resentment. The querulous entry for 23 December in the 15th Brigade diary (5th Division) suggests profound emotions: 'Ordered by GOC Division to take offensive and push on by bits – but difficult to know where or how to do it.'[27]

Along the Franco-German front there were similar attacks, initiated primarily by the French in Champagne, and similar disenchantment in the wake of the high casualties and lack of tangible success. Many expressions of hostility from troops and junior officers toward the higher command were to be heard in the midst of the camaraderie in no man's land on Christmas Day. A German letter of 27 December, captured by the French, told not only of extensive fraternization but of an incident observed by the Germans some days before, when French soldiers shot their own officer because he did not want to surrender in a hopeless situation, where death would have been the only reward for bravery. They murdered their officer and then surrendered.[28]

German soldiers groused too. Young Albert Sommer recounted in his diary how his 'idiot' company commander forced men to go out on patrols on Christmas Eve to find out who was across from them. Firing broke out, and this provoked enemy artillery, thus destroying the peace of the evening. Sommer added bitterly that the commander remained behind in the trench and celebrated Christmas with drink while his men faced death.[29]

And yet, while weather, physical conditions in the

trenches, and disappointment with the conduct of the war weighed on the minds of soldiers in the front lines, these concerns are not enough to explain what happened on and around Christmas 1914. The same disheartening factors would appear later in the war, often in more brutal dimensions, but fraternization on a similar scale would never recur. There was something in the motivation and sensibility of the front-line soldier in December 1914 that was to disappear as the war progressed, a set of social values and a psychological disposition that were to be drastically altered by the course of the war.

PEACE ON EARTH

On Christmas Eve the temperature began suddenly to drop. The water-logged trenches froze. The mud became less of a problem, and that in itself lifted spirits. For Germans, Christmas Eve is the most festive part of the Christmas celebrations, and in most parts of the German line, as darkness fell, small Christmas trees, the traditional *Tannenbaum*, appeared, contravening official instructions, which forbade bringing trees into the trenches. For decorative effect many of the trees had candles, either real or makeshift.

According to reports, the French – for whom the Christmas tree was often something of a novelty – and the British were puzzled initially by the strange lighting effect across the way, and thinking that it was part of a ruse, they opened fire at many points. 'The first unusual thing happened,' noted Percy Jones, 'when we noticed about three large fires behind enemy lines. This is a place where it is generally madness to strike a match.' Then lights appeared on the enemy trenches. 'Our private opinion was that the enemy was priming themselves up for a big attack, so we commenced polishing up ammunition and rifles and getting all ready for speedy action.' Then a German voice: 'Don't shoot!' 'This was all very well,' reported Jones, 'but we had heard so many yarns about German treachery that we kept a very sharp look-out.'[1]

All the general staffs had warned their troops to be ready for a surprise attack over Christmas and New Year. The German argument was that the French and British were too soulless and materialistic to celebrate Christmas in its proper spirit. The French looked on the Germans as pagans; the British regarded them as barbarians; so normal Christian behavior was not to be expected of them on Christmas Day. Still, while gunfire made the German trees disappear here and there for some minutes, they almost invariably reappeared when the shooting subsided. The Christmas spirit was irrepressible.

After the trees had appeared, the singing began, on occasion raucous, more often quiet and sentimental. In the vast majority of cases the Germans, it seems, started the singing, and the effect on the opposing trench, as the tones began to echo across the frozen wastes of no man's land, was spellbinding. In many places 'Stille Nacht, heilige Nacht' ('Silent Night') or 'Es ist ein' Ros' entsprungen' ('Lo, How a Rose E'er Blooming') was intoned quietly in chorus. At one point across from the French a lone harmonica began in a moment of stillness to play 'Silent Night,' and the gentle, haunting tones, in the midst of complete quiet, mesmerized the French. Elsewhere, despite the cold, a German soldier played Handel's Largo on a violin.[2] In the Argonne the 130th Württembergers were treated in their front line by the concert singer Kirchhoff. The French soldiers opposite were so taken by this performance that they climbed onto their parapets. They applauded and applauded until Kirchhoff gave them an encore.[3]

Émile Marcel Décobert of the 269th French Infantry Regiment, in the line near Carency, wrote home to his parents about French soldiers singing German carols with their enemy.[4] Opposite the 1st Somerset Light Infantry the Germans brought up their regimental band and played the national anthems of both Germany and Britain, after which they gave three loud cheers and proceeded to sing 'Home, Sweet Home.' The British were most taken by such a cosmopolitan and gracious choice of program.[5]

Gradually firing ceased almost everywhere along the line that Christmas Eve. Men got up and sat on their parapets and shouted greetings across to the 'enemy.' Conversations began. Opposite the Queen's Westminster Rifles a Saxon challenged the British to come across and fetch a bottle of wine. 'One of our fellows accepted the challenge,' wrote a private in a letter home to England, 'and took over a big cake in exchange. That set the ball rolling . . .'[6]

Many officers were thinking of tactical matters when they permitted or even encouraged their men to go out to meet the enemy. They hoped, for instance, to find out who exactly was facing them and to get a good idea of enemy installations. Yet these practical considerations were usually a secondary feature of the fraternization. Most of the meetings were spontaneous initiatives that had no approval or military objective. The Christmas spirit had simply conquered the battlefield.

When dawn came the next morning, the ground was frozen solid. In some areas a sprinkling of fresh snow lay on the ground. In Flanders the sudden freeze had produced a thick fog, which began to lift only gradually under the glare of a strong sun. The sudden change in the weather brought astonishment and cheer. In comparison with the monsoon conditions of the preceding month, the day was glorious. 'A hoarfrost of magic and beauty' were the words Gustav Riebensahm used to begin his diary entry for Christmas Day. Then, shortly after stand-to, what had been isolated incidents of fraternization the night before blossomed, in many sectors, into wholesale camaraderie.

161

Soldiers moved into no man's land, or in some cases even into each other's trenches, and celebrated. Some were shy. Others were more open. They talked, sang, and exchanged stories and gifts. As the morning wore on, confidence grew. Burial parties were arranged. The 6th Gordon Highlanders and the 15th Infantry Regiment, a Westphalian unit, joined in a moving ceremony for the dead. As Scotsmen, Englishmen, Saxons, and Westphalians lined up on both sides of a communal mass grave, the Reverend J. Esslemont Adams, minister of the West United Free Church, Aberdeen, and chaplain of the 6th Gordons, read the Twenty-third Psalm in English. A theology student then read it in German: 'Der Herr ist mein Hirt: mir wird nichts mangeln. Er weidet mich auf einer grünen Aue: und führet mich zum frischen Wasser . . .'

The Lord's Prayer followed, sentence by sentence, in both languages: 'Our Father Who art in Heaven. Unser Vater in dem Himmel . . .'[7]

At many points mutual entertainment through song and hymn was normal. The second in command of the 1st Leicesters was Major A.H. Buchanan-Dunlop, in civilian life a teacher at Loretto school, in Musselburgh near Edinburgh. Shortly before Christmas he received the program of the end-of-term school concert. He rehearsed his fellow Leicesters and on Christmas Day they went out into no man's land and sang part of the school program for the Germans. The Germans replied with a selection of hymns.[8] Elsewhere, behavior was more frivolous. In front of the 3rd Rifle Brigade, 6th Division, a German juggler performing his tricks drew a large and appreciative crowd.

The main Christmas meal was dished out around noon, and the fraternizers returned to their own trenches to eat. As soon as they were done, the joviality in no man's land revived. On discovering that among their opponents was a barber who had worked in England before the war, some of the 6th Gordons asked

162

him to set up shop right there in the middle of no man's land and give them a shave and a trim. The German complied!

After the initial courtesies, a barter business sprang up. In addition to Christmas parcels from family and friends, brought in hundreds of railway cars, every British soldier had received from Princess Mary a gilt Christmas box containing, for smokers, a pipe, ten cigarettes, and some tobacco, and for nonsmokers, chocolates. Consequently, every British soldier had something to trade. The Germans and the French were in a similar position. Major von Der Aschenhauer noted that his troops were so overwhelmed by gifts from home that they hardly knew what to do with them. Percy Jones echoed sentiments on all sides when he wrote home on the twenty-fourth: 'I am keeping well, in spite of the large number of Christmas parcels received.' The surplus obviously dictated exchanges for something new and different.

The Germans appear to have had a particular affection for British bully beef, which had less fat than German meats, and for British preserves. The 10th Brigade diary reported that the Germans 'were seen to almost fight for a tin of bully.'[9] Samuel Judd, unable to comprehend what the Germans liked in old bully, came to the conclusion that they were not being fed sufficiently – 'they come up again for bully and jam!'[10] Opposite the North Staffordshire Regiment the Germans wanted to exchange cigars for bully. The Cameronians, however, got what they regarded as the best bargain in this strange market – two barrels of beer for a few tins of bully![11]

All kinds of mementoes were sought and accepted. The very least that was exchanged was signatures. Private Colin Munro of the 2nd Seaforths sent his wife in Ayr a postcard with six German signatures. Newspapers and magazines were other readily available items. An officer of the 2nd Lancashire Fusiliers exchanged

163

Punch magazine for some German cigars. He mentioned this in a letter home, and his family promptly sent it off to the *Daily Telegraph* for publication; whereupon Owen Seaman of *Punch* wrote a satirical poem about his publication's having been devalued and degraded by being traded for German cigars! Various forms of tobacco were standard items of exchange. Virtually everyone in this war, it seems, smoked. But the quest for significant memorabilia could reach worrisome proportions: on the 4th Division front, according to one report, rifles were exchanged.[12]

Was a football match actually played? Despite many rumors of a match and much mention of a contest between British and Germans, no convincing evidence exists that such an event took place. The pervasive rumors, though, tell us a great deal about the wishes and mood of the front-line troops. The possibility of a match seemed to excite British imaginations most. Numerous accounts appeared in letters home of a game elsewhere on the line. There is sufficient consistency in the story of a 3–2 score involving the Saxons – in most accounts they won; in some they lost – that a primitive game involving bully beef tins or something similar may in fact have taken place. But a full-fledged encounter with a proper ball is unlikely, if only because of the cratered terrain of no man's land.

It must be noted, however, that peace and good will did not reign everywhere along the line on Christmas Day. At the northern extremity of the British line, near St Eloi, held by the 3rd Division, sniping continued all day. The 3rd Worcesters there boasted that they had 'bagged' four enemy snipers in the morning and two in the evening.[13] In the south, near la Quinque Rue, on the 2nd Division front, the Germans launched an attack on the morning of the twenty-fourth. The 2nd Grenadier Guards lost the first line of trenches here and suffered fifty-seven casualties. On Christmas Day the mood was still bitter, and a new line of trenches had to be prepared. Nevertheless, even in these sectors Christmas passed relatively quietly.

Most of the friendly communication took place on the Anglo-German front in Belgium and northern France, where almost three quarters of the troops were involved to some degree. Elsewhere, quiet, if not open fraternization, was the norm. Fighting, even sniping, was rare on that Christmas Day. 'Almost unsettling is the effect of the extraordinary quiet along the entire front,' noted the diary of a German regiment facing the French near the Somme.[14]

If the British and the Germans were reluctant to go into detail about the incidents of fraternization in official dispatches, to French officers the subject was completely taboo. Still, evidence surfaces in numerous places – German military records, private letters and diaries – that Franco-German fraternization was extensive if less widespread and less trusting than on the Anglo-German front. Tidbits of evidence appear even in the French official war diaries; in those, for instance, of the 111th Brigade in line near Foncquevilliers, of the 69th Division near Condé sur Aisne, of the 139th Brigade in Artois, and of the 56th Brigade on the Somme. The 56th Brigade's diary entry for the twenty-fifth is matter-of-fact:

> The day is quiet. A very spontaneous truce establishes itself in the entire sector, notably at the two ends where French and German soldiers come out of their trenches in places to exchange newspapers and cigarettes.[15]

No names are mentioned, no units. Yet the records of the 12th, 15th, and 20th Bavarian regiments indicate that at least twelve French regiments were involved in open fraternization in the vicinity of Dompierre on the Somme – the 20th, 22nd, 30th, 32nd, 43rd, 52nd, 99th, 132nd, 137th, 142nd, 162nd, and 172nd. In other words, the

German documents indicate that any French mention of friendly relations barely suggests the extent of the truce.

In places the truce continued to New Year's Day. In some cases it lasted well into January, even into the second week. And then, although a semblance of war reappeared, with some sniping and artillery fire, the rest of January remained remarkably quiet. The 1st Rifle Brigade diary noted on the last day of January 1915, 'This has been a very quiet month and we have got through a lot of work owing to the enemy's disinclination to annoy us.'[16]

THE REASON WHY

Morale, though an issue, does not seem to have been the crucial motivating factor in the fraternization. Those who told the enemy that they were tired of the war usually said so as a form of salutation, an alternative to 'Hello!' which somehow did not seem appropriate as a greeting. 'Rotten affair this, isn't it?' was the gist of such a remark. What else could you say to men whom you had been trying to kill hours earlier? You couldn't apologize for shooting at the enemy; that would have been absurd. Saying that you wanted the war to end was the closest acceptable way of expressing such a sentiment.

The press at home, when it got wind of some of the snippets of conversation, made a great deal of the enemy's supposed war weariness, but the soldiers at the front, while they may have recorded these statements in their letters and in regimental accounts of conversations, did not really give much credence to them. Noting evidence of war weariness was again a way of masking the feelings of guilt occasioned by participation in the truce. One had supposedly discovered some vital information about the enemy: he was fed up with the war; his morale was breaking.

The purpose of the war seems at this stage, however, to have remained inviolate. Where a morale problem existed, it was caused more by the management of the war than by its stated purpose. The Germans in particular, sitting as they were everywhere on foreign soil, remained confident of their success. Some believed that they were a stone's throw from Paris. Others said that they had heard their fellows were in London or on the outskirts of Moscow. Victory was imminent. Captain Loder's account in the Scots Guards diary is typical:

> Their general opinion of the war was as follows. France is on her last legs and will soon have to give up. Russia has had a tremendous defeat in Poland and will soon be ready to make terms of peace. England is the nut which still has to be cracked but with France and Russia out of the way she Germany would be too powerful. The war they thought might be over by the end of January. This shows what lies are circulated amongst the German troops and the hatred which exists between Germany and England.[1]

As one commentator put it later, 'The few cases of war-weariness only threw into bolder relief the confidence of the many.'[2] What was true of the Germans was true in a quieter, less overt manner of the French and British – *On les aura!*

The soldiers do not appear to have seriously questioned the purpose of the war at this stage, yet for most the ties to family, friends, and home were extremely compelling. That large numbers of reservists were now in the line, many of them in their thirties and even forties, with wives and children, was a significant factor in bringing about fraternization. The thoughts of Christmas at home were simply overwhelming, and most men were disposed to enjoy at least one day of peace and good will. Evidence suggests that of the troops in the front lines the younger men were as a whole more aggressive and less inclined to friendly behavior. The evidence also suggests, however, that the British troops were the most active fraternizers. This begs explanation.

The terrible conditions of warfare in Flanders and the north of France obviously played an important role in making Tommy Atkins receptive to the idea of a few days of relative peace. Moreover, the military threat posed by the Germans affected the British less directly – after all, the war was being fought in Belgium and France – than their allies, so again it was easier for Tommy to be inclined to take a breather. And yet perhaps the most important reason for British participation in the Christmas truce was the positive sense of Britain's purpose in the war.

For the British this was a war not specifically to deny Germany a navy or colonies or even economic superiority, though German ambitions in these areas were clearly of grave concern. Nor was this a war simply to maintain a balance of power on the continent by not allowing any one power to gain inordinate strength, though, again, this was a long-standing British interest. No, for the British this was a war with a much broader purpose. This was a war to preserve a system of British order, national and international, that was seen to be under attack by everything that Germany and its introverted *Kultur* represented. By the beginning of the twentieth century Germany had, in the eyes of the British, replaced France as the incarnation of flux and irresponsibility in the world. Britain, on the other hand, stood for the reverse: stability and responsibility. Germany threatened not only Britain's military and economic position in the world but the whole moral basis of the Pax Britannica, which, as the British argued, had given the world a century of peace, a respite from general European war not enjoyed since the Rome of the Antonines.

The British mission, whether in the wider world, the

empire, or at home among her own populace, was principally one of extending the sense of civic virtue, of teaching both the foreigner and the uneducated Briton the rules of civilized social conduct, the rules for 'playing the game.' The British mission was to introduce 'lesser breeds,' to use Kipling's words, to 'the law.' Civilization and law, then, were virtually synonymous. Civilization was possible only if one played the game according to rules laid down by time, history, precedent, all of which amounted to the law. Civilization was a question of objective values, of external form, of behavior rather than sentiment, of duty rather than whim. 'It is only civilized beings who can combine,' wrote J.S. Mill in his essay 'Civilization.'

> All combination is compromise: it is the sacrifice of some portion of individual will for a common purpose. The savage cannot bear to sacrifice, for any purpose, the satisfaction of his individual will.[3]

While priding herself on her social and political tolerance throughout the nineteenth century, having provided refuge for the likes of Louis Napoleon, Metternich, Louis Philippe, and Marx, among others, London remained a city, and England a country, that unambiguously espoused an ethic of moderation, of rational reform, and rational restraint. The law and parliamentary institutions were the social acknowledgement of such an ethic and such behavior.

If Germany was the principal activist, and hence modernist, nation of the *fin-de-siècle* world, then Great Britain was the major conservative power. Germany's disruptive energy threatened the essence of Britain's accomplishment, which was the establishment of a measure of law and order in the world. That Britain showed on the whole comparatively little interest in the manifestations of modern culture does not require extensive documentation. Despite Virginia Woolf's later assertion that human nature changed 'on or about December 1910' and Ford Madox Ford's impression that the years 1910 to 1914 were 'like an opening world,' Britain in 1914 was on balance still thoroughly skeptical of innovative artistic endeavor. Ford complained that 'the complete absence of any art' seemed to be 'a national characteristic' of the British.[4] British music and theater were little attuned to European developments; painting and literature only slightly more so. In 1904 the National Gallery turned down the gift of a Degas. 'Painting here is kept alive, a dim little flickering flame,' wrote Walter Sickert in 1911,

> by tiny groups of devoted fanatics mostly under the age of thirty. The national taste either breaks these fanatics, or compels them to toe the line. The young English painter who loves his art, ends by major force, in producing the chocolate-box in demand.[5]

Even more strikingly than in the case of France, new impulses in the arts seemed to be imported from abroad. Whistler, whom Ruskin had accused of 'flinging a pot of paint in the public's face,' had begun the important American influence; he was followed in the early part of the century by Ezra Pound, T.S. Eliot, and Jacob Epstein.[6]

If the Germans regarded the war as a spiritual conflict, the British looked on it as a struggle to preserve social values, precisely those values and ideals which the prewar avant-garde had so bitterly attacked: notions of justice, dignity, civility, restraint, and 'progress' governed by a respect for law. For Victorians and even the mass of Edwardians, morality was an objective matter. 'Opinions alter, manners change, creeds rise and fall,' Lord Acton declared in his Cambridge inaugural lecture in 1895, 'but the moral law is written on the tablets of eternity.'[7] The roots of morality might be traced in various ways, but that men, principally through education, were becoming increasingly aware of the difference between right and wrong was not in doubt. Liberty was not permissiveness; it was an outgrowth of social knowledge and discipline. Liberty was hard work. Liberty was not the right to do as you pleased; liberty was the opportunity to do as you should. Ethics was more important than metaphysics. 'Hence,' wrote J.S. Mill, 'it is said with truth that none but a person of confirmed virtue is completely free.'[8] English liberty was a doctrine not of rights but of duties.

For Germans the focus of explanation for the war was directed inward and toward the future. Thomas Mann looked on the war as liberation from a putrefying reality. Of the old world he asked, 'Did not vermin of the mind swarm about in it like maggots? Did it not ferment and stink of the decaying matter of civilization?' For Mann this war and his art were synonymous; both amounted to a struggle for spiritual freedom.[9] For the British on the other hand the focus was social and historical.

> Be you the men you've been,
> Get you the sons your fathers got,
> And God will save the Queen.[10]

For the British the war was a practical necessity, a sentiment captured by the slogan 'business as usual.' As one soldier put it in a letter to his parents on 1 Octorber 1914:

> We are just at the beginning of the struggle I'm afraid, and every hour we should remind ourselves that it is our great privilege to save the traditions of all centuries behind us. It's a grand opportunity, and we must spare no effort to use it, for if we fail we shall curse ourselves in bitterness every year that we live, and our children will despise our memory.[11]

For the Germans this was a war to change the world; for the British this was a war to preserve a world. The Germans were propelled by a vision, the British by a legacy.

For the average British soldier there was no question of who was responsible for the war. Private Pattenden of the 1st Hants had landed in France on 23 August been thrown into battle three days later, and had then been marched about constantly so that by early September, feet swollen and blistered, he could no longer walk, only shuffle. Numbed by fatigue, thirst, and hunger, dazed by the horrors he had seen, and totally cynical about his officers, he took out his personal diary on 5 September and scribbled:

> They have told us our marches have been strategical, all lies it is nothing more or less than a complete retreat and for a fortnight we have had to flee, because we fear to be utterly outclassed and beaten and now if we are attacked . . . we could not run a dozen yards and the result would be a bloody slaughter.[12]

Yet, despite the fatigue and depression, the sense of purpose did not flag. During the battle of the Marne, Pattenden found a few moments to note:

> Oh this is awful, no-one can imagine war till they are at it, every living thing suffers by it . . . The Kaiser may be accursed for ever, may he never sleep peaceful again, the mad fiend, may he never find rest even after death . . . We must finish him, for if not, we shall never be safe.

This sense of purpose was not to be affected by the hardships of the next months, and the views at the end of December were very much the same: the Germans had to be defeated; otherwise civilization would be imperiled.

What, then, brought the British out in such large numbers around Christmas to shake hands and laugh and exchange anecdotes and mementoes with the Germans?

172

It was presumably the very same set of values that they were fighting for. Some saw the fraternization as a matter of time-honored courtesies. On a holy day one saluted one's opponent and paid one's respects. During the Peninsular War at the beginning of the preceding century the French and British armies had become so friendly one Christmas that staff officers chanced upon one large group sitting around the same fires, sharing rations and playing cards. The French apparently came to refer to the British as *nos amis les ennemis.** This notion of probity and decorum, of playing the game – leaving the enemy in peace on the holiest of holy days – was a central part of the British sense of 'fair play.' The opponent was still an opponent rather than an enemy; only the implications of his effort were hated.

Of course, exceptions to the rule – some very striking ones – did arise. In some sectors of the front the British, as we have noted, actually initiated action on Christmas Day. Moreover, the Admiralty sent out seaplanes on Christmas morning to bomb the Zeppelin sheds at Cuxhaven – a raid that was a complete failure because of dense fog. Yet generally the day was characterized by restraint, repose, and reflection.

The sporting imagery of British social discourse has often been remarked upon. In the Victorian era the British did become obsessed with games, and translated the sporting ethic into guidelines for social intercourse as a whole. Sport, in Thomas Arnold's vision at Rugby, where games first became an integral part of the education program, would give a young man the body of a Greek and the soul of a Christian knight. The games cult spread from the public schools to the universities and then farther. In the second half of the nineteenth century football, rugby, and cricket became not simply pastimes but passions for the British. Coal miners, mill workers, and the laboring classes in general were

*Our friends the enemy.

particularly attracted to football, or soccer, because all that was required was an object for kicking. The middle and upper classes developed a predilection for cricket, which, with its bucolic associations, proved to be a most apt vehicle for transposing many of the myths of Merrie England to the modern industrial landscape and also to the empire. Yet both games appealed to society at large. The Clarendon Commission of 1864 insisted that

> the cricket and football pitches . . . are not merely places of amusement; they help to form some of the most valuable social qualities and manly virtues, and they hold, like the classroom and boarding house, a distinct and important place in public school education.[13]

In the 1870s and 1880s schools began to hire professionals as coaches. At Marlborough cricket came to rival classics for the attention of both masters and boys; at Radley the playing fields received as much devotion as chapel. The headmaster of Loretto, H.H. Almond, insisted in 1893 that football would be 'productive of scarcely anything but good.' It would provide 'an education in that spirit of chivalry, fairness and good temper.'[14]

Sports, then, were to serve both a moral and a physical purpose; they would encourage self-reliance and team spirit; they would build up the individual and integrate him into the group. 'Athleticism is no unimportant bulwark of the constitution,' mused Charles Box, a cricket writer, in 1888. It 'has no sympathy with Nihilism, Communism, nor any other "ism" that points to national disorder.'[15] On the contrary, sport developed pluck, determination, and public spirit; sport, as *The Times* put it on the Monday after the English football final of 1899, was of great value 'in the battles of life.'[16]

By the end of the century the sports cult had reached

all segments of society. Every conversation one heard during a walk around an industrial town in the evening seemed to involve a 'piece of football criticism or prophecy.' By Edward's reign crowds of 100,000 attended football finals at Crystal Palace. Interest in sports even over-shadowed interest in politics for a great many. G.K. Chesterton quipped in 1904 that the cricketer C.B. Fry 'represents us much better than Mr Chamberlain.' And a cartoon in *Punch* before the war showed a working-man pointing to his member of Parliament – MPs began to be paid in 1911 – and saying, 'The likes of hus . . .'as to pay him £400 a year. It makes me that wild to think as we could 'ave two first-class 'arf-backs for the same money.'[17]

Probably the most famous poem of the late Victorian and Edwardian era was Sir Henry Newbolt's 'Vitaï Lampada,' written in 1898:

> There's a breathless hush in the Close tonight—
>   Ten to make and the match to win—
> A bumping pitch and a blinding light,
>   An hour to play and the last man in.
> And it's not for the sake of a ribboned coat,
>   Or the selfish hope of a season's fame,
> But his Captain's hand on his shoulder smote—
>   'Play up! play up! and play the game!'

The next stanza transported the sporting mentality, along with the playing fields of Eton, to the outposts of empire.

> The sand of the desert is sodden red—
>   Red with the wreck of a square that broke;
> The Gatling's jammed and the Colonel dead,
>   And the regiment blind with dust and smoke;
> The river of death has brimmed his banks,
>   And England's far, and Honour a name;

But the voice of a schoolboy rallies the ranks:
  'Play up! play up! and play the game!'

'Play the game!' That's what life is about. Decency, fortitude, grit, civilization, Christianity, commerce, all blend into one – the game!

When Kipling, in his most bitter mood, frustrated by the war in South Africa and then by the death of friends like Cecil Rhodes, vented his spleen in that extraordinary about-face, 'The Islanders,' in 1902, he could find no imagery more appropriate for the scorn he felt toward the British than that of sports:

> . . . ye contented your souls
> With the flannelled fools at the wicket or the muddied
>   oafs at the goals.

At the end of July 1914, Henry James, anxious that 'some awful brutal justice' might make the British pay for years of 'materialized stupidity and vulgarity,' was reminded of Kipling's lines. James wrote:

> If anything very bad does happen to the country, there isn't anything like the French intelligence to react – with the flannelled fool at the wicket, the muddied oaf and tutti quanti, representing so much of our *preferred* intelligence.[18]

If the cynicism expressed by Kipling and James was not shared by many in Britain, the metaphors used to capture the essence of British character were. Rupert Brooke, that aesthete's aesthete, also resorted to sports imagery in his celebration of the British response to the war when it broke, likening youthful soldiers to 'swimmers into cleanness leaping.'[19]

In this spirit the British entered the war and in this spirit they continued it for some time. It was certainly in this spirit that most of the British participants joined in the Christmas truce. The war was a game, deadly earnest, to be sure, but a game nevertheless – 'all great fun,' as Rupert Brooke and so many others kept saying in their letters home.[20]

One letter reporting the events of Christmas on the 6th Gordons' front related how a hare suddenly burst into view:

> All at once Germans came scurrying from their trenches and British from theirs, and a marvellous thing happened. It was all like a football match, the hare being the football, the grey tunicked Germans the one side, and the kilted 'Jocks' the other. The game was won by the German who captured the prize. But more was secured than a hare – a sudden friendship had been struck up, the truce of God had been called, and for the rest of Christmas Day not a shot was fired along our section.[21]

Here the sporting spirit is credited with producing the truce, and of course the suggestion is that were all men to play the game properly, there would be no war. Some of the Germans who had spent time in England – and there were a surprising number of them – clearly had acquired the British passion. Lance Corporal Hines of the Queen's Westminster Rifles reported that one German said to him in broken English, 'Good morning, sir; I live at Alexander Road, Hornsey, and I would see Woolwich Arsenal play Tottenham to-morrow.'[22]

Jerome K. Jerome, author of the enormously successful *Three Men in a Boat*, took the line that the sporting spirit was the essence of civilization and called on the Germans to treat the war as 'The Greatest Game of All':

> Come, gentlemen, let us make an honourable contest of it, that shall leave as little bitterness behind it as may be. Let us see if we cannot make a fine game of it that we shall be all the better for having played out to

the end. From which we shall all come back home cleaner minded, clearer seeing, made kinder to one another by suffering. Come, gentlemen, you believed that God has called upon you to spread German culture through the lands. You are ready to die for your faith. And we believe God has a use for the thing called England. Well, let us fight it out. There seems no other way. You for St Michael and we for St George; and God be with us both.

But do not let us lose our common humanity in the struggle. That were the worst defeat of all: the only defeat that would really matter, that would really be lasting.

Let us call it a game. After all, what else is it?[23]

As Jerome was suggesting, the spirit of the game was the important thing. Winning or losing was secondary. If the spirit was right, the game would be a victory for everybody. In this very spirit, a British artillerist in a letter home described what he called 'the greatest sight.' It involved a single German Taube aircraft being chased by sixteen French and British planes. The most exciting part for the British gunner was that the German got away! 'And we gave him a cheer, for the odds were against him, and he must have been a great chap.' This letter was printed in Edinburgh's *Scotsman* in early January.

As the war dragged on such sentiments would fade. If they did appear on occasion, they certainly never found their way into the letter columns of newspapers. Though there were incidents later of officers trying to rouse their men to bravery by dribbling footballs across no man's land during an attack – the most famous example was that of Captain W.P. Nevill at the Somme in 1916 – these were isolated cases. Nevill, who was killed instantly within moments of kick-off on 1 July 1916, was remembered by one of his fellows as 'the battalion buffoon.'[24] Roland D. Mountfort, who survived the fruitless

178

attack on Pozières on the first day of the Somme offensive with only a shoulder wound, recounted the events of the day to his mother and felt it necessary to add, 'We didn't dribble footballs, neither did we say "This way to Berlin, boys" nor any of the phrases employed weekly in the "News of the World." '[25] As the war continued, the sporting spirit, if not the sporting vocabulary, which was so ingrained, would subside, but at Christmas 1914 that spirit was still strong.

The sporting cult could of course be taken to extremes, and then it could backfire. In Magdeburg five British officers who were prisoners of war were sentenced shortly after Christmas to eight days' imprisonment for playing football with loaves of black bread. To the British, when they learned of the incident through the press, the behavior of their soldiers represented the indomitable spirit of Tommy Atkins; to the Germans, such antics were the height of insolence and, coming as they did from soldiers, even more disreputable than schoolboy bun-throwing and other such pranks.[26]

Gustav Riebensahm also felt that the sporting fetish reflected badly on the British. On 26 December he wrote in his diary:

The English are said to have told the 53rd Regiment they are exceedingly thankful for the truce because they simply had to play football again. The whole business is becoming ridiculous and must come to an end. I arranged with the 55th Regiment that the truce will end this evening.

Not only the Germans but the French scoffed at British attitudes at times. The British simply did not take anything seriously. 'They consider the war a sport,' complained Louis Mairet. They are 'too calm and inclined to a who-gives-a-damn attitude.'[27] Even after the war the French were to recall the British sporting spirit with anger and were to refer to it as an expression of *l'égoïsme anglais*.[28]

Not surprisingly, sporting organizations were important in recruiting volunteers. By the end of 1914 over half a million volunteers had come forward through such organizations.[29] Even a Footballers Battalion, known officially as the 17th Battalion Middlesex Regiment, or 'the Die Hards,' was formed. Football stars were to set an example for British youth. The history of the 17th Middlesex provides an insight into the fate of the British sporting spirit in this war. Initially the battalion was kept in England to play exhibition matches around the country and to drum up recruits with appeals at half time to the patriotism of the spectators, but in November 1915 the unit was sent to France to play regiments there. The War Office had decided that the morale of the troops on the Western Front needed boosting. In France the battalion did receive some combat training, but at first it spent most of its time playing football. However, in June 1916, because of manpower needs but also to serve yet again as an example, the unit was finally sent into action at Vimy Ridge. Casualties there and later at Beaumont Hamel on the Somme were extremely high, and these decimated the battalion. In December 1916, in the final of the Divisional Football Cup, the 17th Middlesex, who usually trounced their opponents by scores in double figures, managed to beat 34th Brigade by a score of only 2-1, an indication of the toll on football talent the war had by now taken. In February 1918 the battalion was finally disbanded. At any given time earlier, over two hundred footballers had belonged to the battalion; now only about thirty remained.[30]

Many British soldiers with set views about the Germans, acquired largely from a press that had been strongly anti-German even before the war, would have regarded Jerome K. Jerome's appeal to a mutual sportsmanship as utterly futile. The German, portrayed as an insensitive, regimented brute, was incapable of playing the game. After all, even the Germans admitted – so claimed a Sheffield paper before 1914 – that what football did for the British, compulsory military service achieved for the Germans.[31] For the two peoples each activity was 'the school of the nation.'

Given such an outlook, the British approached fraternization with a mixture of condescension and moral purpose. They would show the Germans what civility meant and what trust involved. The first actual encounter with the Germans produced a variety of responses, many of them expressing great surprise. Someone like Edward Hulse would continue to voice a muffled disdain for the Germans; others found the reality of the enemy an exhilarating revelation. W.R.M. Percy of the London Rifles could hardly restrain his enthusiasm. 'They were really magnificent in the whole thing,' he wrote of the foe, 'and jolly good sorts. I now have a very different opinion of the German.'[32] Of his encounter with the Saxons Percy Jones commented:

I spoke to and shook hands with scores of the enemy. They looked very fit, well uniformed and shod, but very young. They seemed uncommonly cheerful and friendly, and gave us a royal welcome. Most of them seemed a very good class of fellows and appear, by the autographs we obtained, to be students at Leipzig ... Altogether we had a great day with our enemies, and parted with much hand-shaking and mutual good wishes. They assured us again and again that they would shoot high if we would but we had no opportunity of putting them to the test, as we are now at Houplines opposite the Prussians.[33]

From his own experience Private Dalling of the 1st Somerset Light Infantry concluded, 'They are not all so black as they are sometimes painted.' In the account he sent home Dalling repeatedly used words like 'honourable' and 'gentlemanly.'[34] Captain Loder of the Scots Guards had the impression that the civilizing mission involved in fraternization had made progress: 'Both sides have played the game,' he wrote in the battalion diary, 'and I know that this Regiment [he was referring to Riebensahm's 15th] anyhow has learnt to trust an Englishman's word.'[35] Lance Corporal Hines of the Queen's Westminster Rifles had a similar response. He was sorry to be relieved on Boxing Day, 'as we might have still further improved our good relations with the enemy.'[36] In view of this remark and presumably similar sentiments among French soldiers involved in fraternization, the comment of a French propaganda manual published in 1915 takes on particular irony. Designed for home consumption, the manual played down the dangers of trench warfare and pointed to its comforts and pleasures, and in this context remarked that the *poilus* were reluctant to go on leave after their Christmas celebrations in 1914 because they had had such a good time at the front.[37]

In other cases the British civilizing mission obviously met with setbacks, setbacks associated primarily with Prussian units. The Saxons blamed the Prussians in several areas for breaking the truce by firing on the unsuspecting enemy. Opposite the Queen's Westminster Rifles the Saxons pointed out that they did not trust the Prussians, who, as the report in the Rifles' regimental diary put it, would not 'play fair' in the same situation. Opposite the North Staffordshires the Saxons warned that the Prussians to the right were 'nasty fellows.' On Boxing Day one of the Saxon officers paid his respects to his counterpart with the North Staffs and requested politely that the British soldiers be made to keep their heads down after midday: 'We are Saxons; you are Anglo-Saxons; word of a gentleman is for us as for you.'[38] Here was evidence that at least some of the Germans knew how to play the game.

But others did not, and they had to be taught the rules of civility as if they were schoolchildren. The *Daily Mail* printed an extraordinary letter on the last day of the year relating an account of a snowball fight between British and German trenches at a point where they were only fifty yards apart. It supposedly all started after a burly German tied a flag to the end of his rifle, waved it about above his trench, and, having attracted attention, shouted in stentorian voice, 'Vas you as fed up vid za war as we vas?' 'This led up to much chaff,' the *Daily Mail* letter recounted, 'the dinging of tobacco and chocolate at one another, and ended up with a snowball match.' Relations, however, 'became a bit strained' when a German 'put a stone in a snowball and hit a Tommy in the eye with it.' Of course, in keeping with this schoolboy atmosphere, tearful protests and complaints followed, and finally the culprit apologized, 'so all was well again.'[39]

VICTORIAN SYNTHESIS

What we are suggesting here is that there was a frame of mind common to the Victorian and Edwardian eras. Of course, neither age was one of certitude, the latter much less so than the former, but both were ages seeking certitude. For all our attention to the movement and moral questioning that abounded – and our view of the Edwardian age in particular has been dominated recently by this sense of transition – we should not lose sight of the craving for fixities, the belief that experience should be subservient to order, that bridged the eras. That inimitable Victorian Samuel Smiles summed up the urge pithily: 'A place for everything, and everything in its place.' This was an urge that was no less strong in Britain after the turn of the century than before. Smiles's guidebook to moral rectitude and success, *Self-Help*, published in 1859, had sold over a quarter million copies by 1900.

This frame of mind naturally involved a social code, a combination of social and ethical values. This code was not immutable, and to describe it as 'bourgeois' or 'Victorian' or 'Edwardian' is to reduce it to a catchword that distorts. Yet to deny the existence of a prevailing social code or morality, which in one way or another involved the majority of citizens, regardless of class or station, to deny that experience was compartmentalized into categories and priorities of good and bad and right and wrong, is equally to distort. The social code was like an atom with its components in constant motion and in an ever-changing relationship to one another, but it did, despite many prominent exceptions and anomalies, exist. Indeed, the exceptions and anomalies actually reinforced the power of the code by making the public more aware of the need for propriety.[1]

Without going back to the Roman conquest or the battlefield of Hastings, one can assert that the insular reality of Great Britain, the gradual centralization, especially in the seventeenth and eighteenth centuries, of political authority, the availability of moderately good channels of communication by sea and a network of navigable rivers, and the importance of London as a center of political, economic, and cultural authority, all this encouraged the emergence of a national sense of identity. As the systems of communication improved – with the advent of the railway, the telegraph, the steamship – and as urbanization proceeded, that sense of identity was passed on to wider segments of the population. But perhaps the most important influence in the development of a vision of social order based on commonly accepted values was the growth of Protestantism and of Bible reading, especially in the wake of the great revival in the early nineteenth century. By the end of that century a shared vision of social order was widely in place.

This vision and its accompanying values were not imposed through social imperialism but grew out of the religious environment and, where this did not suffice, out of improved economic and social conditions. It is generally accepted that by the end of the Victorian era, most of the British population no longer had to struggle simply to subsist. A measure of comfort, however small, had been achieved in most cases. Consumption of meat instead of bread, of milk and eggs instead of just potatoes, was rising. In recent years, before the turn of the century, there had been a steady rise in real wages, a decline in family size, a drop in the consumption of alcohol, and the beginnings of social welfare provisions. Archdeacon Wilson, headmaster of Clifton College, remarked in a speech to the Working Men's Club of St Agnes in 1893:

> Possibly a future historian writing the history of the English people in this period will think much less of the legislative and even of the commercial and scientific progress of the period than of the remarkable social movement by which there has been an effort made, by a thousand agencies, to bring about unity of feeling between different classes, and to wage war against conditions of life which earlier generations seem to have tolerated.[2]

As Robert Roberts has argued in his memoir of working-class life in Salford, values associated primarily with the middle classes had, by the eve of the First World War, permeated the lower orders, which wished for, according to Roberts, 'nothing more than to be "respectful and respected" in the eyes of men.'[3] Respectability was perhaps the key feature of the moral and social climate of this period in Britain. Whether one was respectable was more important as a criterion of social acceptability than wealth or power. Prudence, earnestness, and moral fervor were necessary signals of respectability, and following the preachments of evangelicalism and utilitarianism, of John Wesley, Jeremy Bentham, and J.S. Mill, duty came to be included in the category of pleasure and virtue in that of happiness.

185

Of course an Edwardian sense of crisis existed that was fueled by suffragette activity, labor unrest, opposition to the role of the aristocracy in the legislative process, and concern regarding the future of Ireland. In the agitation surrounding each of these problems many saw a challenge to the rule of law. Any reference in Britain to war in the summer of 1914 was thought to be a reference to the possibility of civil strife in Ireland, not to British involvement on the continent. In late Victorian and Edwardian writing a sense of decline permeates the literary imagination. As a young boy trying out his pen, J.B. Priestley wrote poetry about disaster and annihilation without understanding why: 'Tonight I think the world is dying.'[4] Moreover, a considerable amount of intellectual excitement was created in Britain by the likes of G.B. Shaw and H.G. Wells, not to mention the titillation caused by the Aubrey Beardsleys and Oscar Wildes. But despite the premonition of doom and despite a measure of artistic and intellectual effervescence, conformity, complacency and even smugness were far more firmly established in Britain than in France, let alone Germany, Italy, Austria-Hungary, or Russia. In values and judgements on issues of decency, the family, social and political order, and religion, the Edwardians were extensions of the Victorians. That there was a greater threat of change and a stronger sense of challenge afoot in the later era, that was the difference.

After the start of the new century that threat of change came to be identified primarily with Germany. Germany represented the new, the different, the dangerous. In this role she had replaced France. The spate of invasion stories centering on the Germans that became great literary and theatrical hits in the first decade of this century – notably the play *An Englishman's Home* by Major Guy du Maurier – is evidence of this fear of change and the identification of this change with Germany.

A parable, related in *The New Statesman* in 1913, told

of a passenger, on an express train that had made an unexpected stop at a suburban station, who decided that he would descend from the train. 'You can't get off here,' said the conductor to the passenger, who was already standing on the platform. 'But,' came the reply, 'I *have* got off.' 'The train doesn't stop here,' insisted the conductor. 'But,' said the former passenger, 'it *has* stopped.'[5] The critic and poet Gerald Gould used this story to illustrate his point about the privileged position of the artist in relation to morality, but an equally important point that might have been drawn from the story is that the rebel's fellow passengers failed to comprehend, much less follow, his initiative. That interpretation of the parable certainly applied to the British public.

IS THERE HONEY STILL FOR TEA?

At the end of July 1914, Rupert Brooke, alarmed by the heightening European crisis, wrote to his friend Edward Marsh, 'And I'm anxious that England may act rightly.' But what did it mean to 'act rightly'? Another letter, a few days later, in which Brooke described an outing into the countryside, hinted in a general way at his own response to this question:

I'm a Warwickshire man. Don't talk to me of Dartmoor or Snowdon or the Thames or the lakes. I know the *heart* of England. It has a hedgy, warm bountiful dimpled air. Baby fields run up and down the little hills, and all the roads wiggle with pleasure. There's a spirit of rare homeliness about the houses and the countryside, earthy, uneccentric yet elusive, fresh, meadowy, gaily gentle . . . Of California the other States in America have this proverb: 'Flowers without scent, birds without song, men without honour, and women without virtue' – and at least three of the four sections of this proverb I know very well to be true. But Warwickshire is the exact opposite of that. Here the flowers smell of heaven; there are no such larks as ours, and no such nightingales; the men pay more than they owe; and the women have very great and wonderful virtue, and that, mind you, by no means through the mere absence of trial. In Warwickshire there are butterflies all the year round and a full moon every night . . . Shakespeare and I are Warwickshire yokels. What a country!'[1]

Aware of his sentimentality he went on to say, 'This is nonsense,' and yet when it came to locating some of the ingredients encapsulated in perhaps his most famous lines of poetry – his reference to

> . . . some corner of a foreign field
> That is for ever England

– it clearly was not nonsense.

This England was one of honor and virtue and duty in which an aristocratic and middle-class view of the world had merged, in which empire and sport, honesty and social stability, were all part of an indivisible whole. This was a society for which the German adventure was a revolutionary threat, a threat to security, prosperity, and integrity. It was a threat to the Wessex landscape of Hardy's novels, to the Shropshire lad of A.E. Housman's imagination, and to Mr Badger of Kenneth Grahame's *The Wind in the Willows*, who had built his house on the remains of an ancient civilization.

> . . . oh! yet
> Stands the Church clock at ten to three?
> And is there honey still for tea?

Those lines from 'The Old Vicarage, Grantchester' Rupert Brooke had, ironically, written in Berlin in a café in May 1912. He was to die during the 1915 Gallipoli campaign on St George's Day, the day on which both Shakespeare and Wordsworth had died.

From the start for Britain the war had nothing to do with territory, either in the Balkans or in Belgium. The invasion of France was a much more serious strategic threat to the British than the invasion of Belgium and yet, publicly, it was over 'poor little Belgium' that the British government declared war and mobilized sentiment. From the start this was for the British a war about values, about civilization, about sportsmanship, and especially about the relationship of the future to the past. As Lloyd George put it in his Queen's Hall speech of 19 September 1914:

> We have been living in a sheltered valley for generations. We have been too comfortable and too indulgent . . . and the stern hand of Fate has scourged us to an elevation where we can see the great everlasting things that matter for a nation – the great peaks we had forgotten, of Honour, Duty, Patriotism, and, clad in glittering white, the great pinnacle of Sacrifice pointing like a rugged finger to Heaven.[2]

A segment of the population, particularly the young, looked on the war as an adventure to be welcomed, and their reason for supporting the war was not dissimilar to that of the Germans: the war was a pathway to the future, to progress, to revolution, to change. A certain millenarianism was in the air in Britain as well. An element of this is to be seen in Rupert Brooke, Herbert Read, Charles Sorley, and other young aesthetes. But for most people in Britain this was a war to preserve and restore.

Such then was the British background to the Christmas truce. From a practical standpoint there was good reason to postpone the war until the pitch became playable again, but, what was more significant, it was the broader ideal – that the British gentleman must show his mettle – that brought the British over the top into no man's land.

But why did the Germans join in such large numbers? What must be noted first of all about German participation is that it was highest among non-Prussians, among Bavarians and Saxons in particular. We have seen the tension that existed between these men and the Prussians. The Bavarian and Saxon soldiers came from territories with a strong regional identity, for whom, as in the case of the British, history was not subservient to a vision of the future, as it was for so many Prussians. While Prussian regiments also joined in fraternization, they seem not to have been involved as extensively or enthusiastically as non-Prussian units. The German quest for modernity was led by Prussia. The Christmas truce of 1914 was, by contrast, a celebration of history and tradition.

At home in all belligerent countries the news of the fraternization was greeted with mixed feelings. The British were by far the most open about it. The press in Britain freely published letters describing the events. The *Daily Mail* even published, on 5 January 1915, two pictures showing a French and German soldier filling buckets together at a well and then walking to their respective trenches. The headline at the top of the page read EXCLUSIVE PHOTOGRAPHS OF THE UNOFFICIAL TRUCE. Some editors, by paying correspondents for letters describing trench life, may in fact have contributed to a measure of hyperbole and in some cases outright invention. Newspapers certainly editorialized on the significance of the truce, and clergymen in Britain discussed its implications from their pulpits. The conclusion drawn in most quarters was that the war must regrettably go on. The German challenge must be met. The war revolved not around territorial questions but around values: one simply could not yield to German egotism.

The French, by contrast, muzzled all mention of fraternization. The press was not allowed to print any accounts of the events, not even from foreign papers. Instead, a new degree of stridency appeared in the French press over the Christmas period. Maurice Donnay of the Académie française submitted an article over Christmas to *Le Figaro* which appeared on the front page on the last day of 1914. It was entitled 'La Sainte Haine' ('Sacred Hate'). An article on the day before began with the words 'No German can open his mouth or take up his pen without lying.' How out of touch with events of the war the home front in France was becoming was indicated by the booklet *La Vie de tranchée*,* published some months later. In its portrait of life in the trenches it included an anecdote about Anglo-German relations in the front line. The British, it claimed, loved to sing in chorus in the trenches at night. The Germans were supposedly enthralled by this entertainment and would shout *wunderbar schön!*

And then these pigs they want to sing too, and you should hear the sounds that greet them: dogs, cats, tigers . . . and their voices are drowned out, with lots of vigorous cries of 'Shut up!' as well.

Incensed by the insult, the Germans start firing. The English, in turn, laugh themselves sick. That's how nights at the front are spent, claimed *La Vie de tranchée* – in good fun![3] It was the same mentality that both produced this type of fiction and claimed at the same time that every German was a liar.

The German authorities allowed the national press to talk about the truce for a few days. The socialist organ *Vorwärts* was intrigued by the subject and published the most information on it. The Berlin liberal press also carried the odd item. But suddenly the military

Trench Life.

authorities forbade any further mention of the subject.

Strict orders went out to troops in all armies that a recurrence of such incidents would have drastic repercussions; and since headquarters in each army pursued the matter for a time, seeking names and all available information, soldiers did become wary of further contacts with the enemy. Nonetheless, sporadic incidents of fraternization continued to occur throughout 1915. And in November and December of that year there were truces, although active fraternization at Christmas was limited to a very few cases, the most publicized being one involving the Scots Guards yet again. By then the mood was changing. 'How many Christmases the war may last,' Walter H. Page, American ambassador to the Court of St James's, noted in a dispatch, 'nobody's wise enough to know.'[4]

In 1916 the incidents of fraternization dwindled to a handful, and in 1917 and 1918, despite mutinies in the French armies when remarks such as 'We must make peace with the Germans and attack the British' were heard,[5] fraternization on the Western Front was negligible. The enemy became increasingly an abstraction as the nature of the war changed. The gentleman too became an abstraction. And the hero lost his name: he became the nameless, faceless unknown soldier.

The regimental history of the 6th Cheshires includes this laconic sentence: 'On the 2nd September 1918, in our attack from Locon, we re-took the trenches in which we spent Christmas Day, 1914.'[6] Presumably the author discovered this only later. It is doubtful that anybody in the regiment in 1918 had been in those trenches earlier, at Christmas 1914, or, what is even more significant, could have recognized them again four years later. The world had changed greatly in the meantime.

Act Two

IV

Rites of War

O Weissdorn mit den roten Beern,
was wird der Frühling uns beschern?*

RICHARD DEHMEL
'Der Frontsoldat,' Christmas 1914

... But many there stood still
To face the stark, blank sky beyond the ridge,
Knowing their feet had come to the end of the world.

WILFRED OWEN
'Spring Offensive'

Often during the scientific, chemical 'cubist' warfare, on nights
made terrible by air raids, I have thought of the *Sacre* . . .

JACQUES-ÉMILE BLANCHE

BATTLE BALLET

The artillery barrage is deafening. When the air is still,
the din can be heard faintly in London and Paris. Sometimes the pounding lasts for days. In June 1916 at the
Somme it continues for seven days and nights. Field
artillery, medium artillery, and heavy howitzers. The
fifteen-inch-caliber gun of the British can fire a shell of
fourteen hundred pounds. 'Big Bertha' of the Germans,
with a caliber of seventeen inches, can project a missile
weighing over a ton. At Verdun in 1916 the Germans
bring in thirteen of these twenty-ton monsters. Each is

*O hawthorn with your berry red,
What will spring bring instead?

195

moved into position by nine tractors; a crane is required to insert the shell. The impact of this shell annihilates buildings; it shatters windows in a two-mile radius. In August 1914 these huge machines of war had demolished the purportedly impregnable forts of Liège. As the Krupp guns 'walked' their shells toward the final target, Belgian defenders inside the forts went mad.

For concentrated attack there is usually one field gun for every ten yards under fire, and one heavy – six-inch caliber and up – for every twenty yards. When the huge shells burst, they ravage the earth with their violence, hurling trees, rock, mud, torsos, and other debris hundreds of feet into the air. Craters the size of swimming pools remain. When a lull comes and the rains return, men bathe in these cavernous holes. The small and medium shells, which make up most of the barrage, are less sensational in their effect. But to the soldier they too can mean annihilation without trace. 'A signaller had just stepped out,' wrote a medical officer of the 2nd Royal Welch Fusiliers, 'when a shell burst on him, leaving not a vestige that could be seen anywhere near.' The same officer described another image of shellfire:

Two men suddenly rose into the air vertically, fifteen feet perhaps, amid a spout of soil 150 yards ahead. They rose and fell with the easy, graceful poise of acrobats. A rifle, revolving slowly, rose high above them before, still revolving, it fell.[1]

Defenders huddle either in 'funk holes' burrowed out of the forward side of the trench, or in dugouts, often fifteen to twenty feet underground, perhaps five paces square and about six feet high. The heavier shells not only demolish trenches; they can bring the wooden support beams, corrugated iron, and wire netting of the dugouts tumbling down and at the very least rearrange the earth above so as to obstruct exits. Acetylene lights and candles flicker. Larger concussions extinguish them altogether. A respite, will it come? Yes. Finally. But then the muted voice of a sentry, who has survived in a forward sap, is heard to shout 'Gas!' There is a wild scramble to find masks, to tug and pull to get them on; and the ordeal mounts as gas fumes begin slowly to mix with darkness and smoke. At last there is stillness, apart from muffled breathing, some rasping, coughing, and traces of weeping.

Will the cycle begin again? Is the attack on its way? Have the sentries survived? Are the periscopes manned? For when the attack comes, there will be a 'race for the parapet,' up the dugout steps, should that still be possible, into the trenches, if they are still there, to fix bayonets, to assemble machine guns, to locate grenades, and if time permits, to man mortars, flame throwers, and other sundry weapons of this war of 'troglodytes.'[2] One must reach the parapet before the enemy arrives!

On the other side of no man's land men wait. Faces assembled at scaling ladders are drawn and ashen. The tot of navy rum or *Schnaps* or *pinard*, which has been distributed a few minutes earlier, can dull the senses but not reverse the flow of blood. Equipment has been checked. Picks and shovels, bags for sand, Verey lights, wire. A load of over sixty pounds rests on each man's back. Along with personal kit there is a water bottle, rations, a gas mask, field dressings, mess tins, ammunition. Some men carry hand grenades and trench mortar bombs. 'Carrying your house on your back is no joke,' wrote Peter McGregor, a choirmaster from Edinburgh.[3] Officers travel more lightly, the British with swagger sticks to indicate commands, for a voice is unlikely to be heard above the tumult, with a pistol in lieu of a rifle, and without most of the other more cumbersome gear. Conversation at this point is almost insignificant. A few men chatter nervously. Some exchange final wishes. Some whisper prayers. Watches of platoon leaders are now synchronized.

Zero. A shrill whistle. The wave of a cap. Men clamber up ladders. Many are clumsy – because of the load, from fear, or by nature. Over the top! Physical nakedness is the first sensation. The body is now exposed, tense, expectant, awaiting direct violence upon it. Even if one is to follow the 'creeping barrage' – the practice by 1917 – of one's own artillery toward the enemy trenches, that first moment of exposure reduces him to innocence. 'A man who stepped out of the trenches at that moment and lived through has never in all the ensuing years faced such a climax,' wrote a survivor.[4]

Then the advance. Slow and faltering, because of the load, because of the terrain, and because of the tactics of the attack. The Germans and French are more innovative, often rushing forward in groups. The British are more systematic. A man every two or three yards, platoons abreast, a second wave twenty yards back. Heads are bowed, by the weight of the pack and by the instinctual effort to shrink the target presented to the enemy.

The cratered honeycomb of no man's land quickly breaks down any planned order. Men slip and fall. The line becomes straggly. Some get up and continue. Others cannot. In the mud of Passchendaele in 1917 some men drown in the huge, sewerlike craters filled with slime that comes of rain, earth, and decomposition. Some now begin to hear the bullets. Some note the stench, an overpowering odor, emanating from corpses the barrage has churned up. Some are hit. The race for the parapet has been lost. The field is now being swept by machine guns, pocketed by mortar fire, and scoured by rifle bullets.

More men fall. Some cry out. Most are silent. The wounded rarely feel pain initially. Officers try to keep the line together. But these men in the limbo of no man's land, these 'wanderers between two worlds,' need little encouragement, for isolation in this situation means fear. Only in the group is there any emotional safety, any

198

comfort. Indeed, the attackers are inclined to bunch, to herd together for mutual protection.

Has the artillery managed to cut the wire, as promised? Rarely, with any kind of consistency. Breathless, on the brink of exhaustion, men look for gaps in the wire. The disappointment is overwhelming. The gaps are few, if any. The enemy fire has become withering. Only a handful of men reach the wire. They pitch their grenades. They fire their rifles. A few get through to the enemy trench, but bayonet combat is uncommon. Most of the officers leading the attack have been hit. Communication has ceased. The second wave experiences the same fate as the first. The third wave then decides that the attack has failed. Another whistle, this time a faltering one, signals retreat. Survivors stumble back. Some are disoriented and head in a lateral direction. Wounded men crawl. Some huddle in shell holes. The enemy artillery open up, wreaking havoc on the retreat, but at least this time there is no counterattack. A remnant of the attacking unit returns.

The wounded in no man's land are left to their fate until nightfall. Then an attempt will be made to bring them in. They try to stifle their rising agony. Moans bring down a torrent of bullets. And at last a tortured stillness falls on the battlefield.

THEMES

The illusion of the knockout blow continued to dominate strategic thinking throughout 1915, particularly in Britain and France, despite shortages of munitions and of adequately trained troops. British and French attacks in Artois, Picardy, and Champagne, German attacks in Flanders, and even the British vision of a breakthrough against the Turks in the Dardanelles, were all based on the dream of the 'gap,' the sudden parting of the enemy front, as if it were the Red Sea confronted by the faith of

Moses, and the subsequent charge to victory.

Only the abysmal Allied failures of Second Ypres, Gallipoli, Neuve Chapelle, Festubert, Arras, and Loos forced a reconsideration of the approach, but even then it was not so much active as reactive thinking that gradually changed the view of the military planners. It was the German attack on Verdun, in February 1916, with an intensity and firepower unprecedented in warfare that definitively changed attitudes. The year 1916 saw the advent and acceptance by both sides of a new war, the intentional war of attrition, which would swallow up millions of men, not under the pretext that quick victory was in the offing provided one could clear a major hurdle but because the decision had been made that only by wearing down the enemy could one win this war. Everywhere industry was mobilized, the work force reorganized, food rationing applied or planned, taxation readjusted. The war, in short, became an all-consuming enterprise. It became 'total.' Charles Sorley termed attrition 'that last resort of paralyzed strategy.'[1]

Behind Falkenhayn's decision to concentrate German offensive power on Verdun lay a number of motives and considerations. He was always a 'westerner' in that he believed that the decisive battle in the war would take place in the west. While he agreed to place more effort on the Eastern Front in 1915 in the attempt to defeat Russia, by December of that year he had concluded that, contrary to expectations, Russia would not be broken quickly. By contrast, France was on the edge of collapse, and she might use the salient around Verdun, which constituted an advanced French position in relation to the rest of the Western Front, as a point from which to launch a last desperate offensive. That danger had to be forestalled. Moreover, a strong German attack would wear down the French completely and would also force the British to counterattack to the north. This would cause Britain to sustain enormous casualties and push her, too, toward exhaustion.

At Verdun General Falkenhayn assembled, along with his troops, 1220 pieces of artillery for an assault on a front of roughly eight miles. He estimated that for every two lives his armies lost, the French would lose five. That was the essence of attrition. Somehow, however, the French managed to survive the opening barrage and the initial attacks, and the battle then settled down to an atrocious mutual punishment. By November the French were to lose half a million men in this salient. Under such pressure they had to ask the British to take up the slack. The British response was to mount the great offensive on the Somme in July 1916, in which 60,000 men were lost on the very first day and another half million by November. Despite these Allied losses, Falkenhayn's mathematics had failed him. In the two battles of Verdun and the Somme the Germans lost about 800,000 men, slightly less than the French and the British.

Ypres and the surrounding salient in Flanders continued to be pounded during 1916 and then fought over tenaciously again in 1917, at Passchendaele or Third Ypres, and so one can add Ypres to Verdun and the Somme to produce a trinity of horror. General Falkenhayn called this *Stellungskrieg*, position warfare. 'The first principle of position warfare,' he wrote, 'must be to yield not one foot of ground; and if it be lost to retake it immediately by counterattack, even to the use of the last man.'[2] Both sides adopted the same rules. 'Whole regiments gambled away eternity for ten yards of wasteland' – that was the judgement of Ivan Goll.[3] For Ernst Jünger, after the Somme the war and life in general had changed complexion:

Here chivalry disappeared for always. Like all noble and personal feelings it had to give way to the new tempo of battle and to the rule of the machine. Here the new Europe revealed itself for the first time in combat.[4]

For over two years the belligerents on the Western Front hammered at each other in battles, if that old word is appropriate for this new warfare, that cost millions of men their lives but moved the front line at most a mile or so in either direction. If the war in the west can be divided into four periods – the opening battles of movement, the consolidation of 1915, the war of attrition of 1916–17, and the dénouement of 1918 with its renewed movement – then the situation of 1916–17 constitutes the longest and most consistent period.

The battles of Verdun, the Somme, and Ypres embody the logic, the meaning, the essence of the Great War. Two of every three French *poilus* were funneled through Verdun in 1916; most British soldiers saw action at the Somme or Ypres or both; and most German units were in Flanders or at Verdun at some point. These also constituted the crucial battle areas of the war. And the standard imagery that we have of the Great War – the deafening, enervating artillery barrages, the attacks in which long lines of men moved forward as if in slow motion over a moonscape of craters and mud, only to confront machine guns, uncut barbed wire, and grenades – comes from these battles rather than those of the first or last year of the war.

This middle part of the war reversed all traditional notions of warfare. Defense was turned into offense, a process that Joffre, unaware of the implications of his own idea, had earlier called a 'victorious resistance.'[5] The gulf between technology and strategy meant that the attacker, regardless of numbers, was far more vulnerable than the defender, notwithstanding the effect on nerves of preparatory barrages. Despite the dramatic effects of heavy artillery at Liège, Verdun, the Somme, and Passchendaele, rarely was there sufficient firepower to destroy the enemy lines. As a result, defenders almost invariably won the 'race for the parapet.'[6] This meant that the attacker faced a far greater risk of defeat than the defender. The attacks of 1914 and

1915 decimated all the armies, and at the end of 1915 the stalemate was complete. In 1916 while the Germans and French were battering each other at Verdun, the attacking British lost at the Somme. In 1917 the French lost on the Chemin des Dames, to the point where their armies mutinied. The British lost at Passchendaele. In 1918 the Germans defeated themselves in their final desperate attempt to break through. Exhaustion, in the wake of that attack, led to their final retreat.

The victimized crowd of attackers in no man's land – a scene dramatically opposed to the hearty revelries between the lines at Christmas 1914 – has become one of the supreme images of the war. Attackers moved forward usually without seeking cover and were mowed down in rows, with the mechanical efficiency of a scythe, like so many blades of grass. 'We were very surprised to see them walking,' wrote a German machine gunner of his experience of a British attack at the Somme.

> The officers went in front. I noticed one of them walking calmly, carrying a walking stick. When we started firing we just had to load and reload. They went down in their hundreds. You didn't have to aim, we just fired into them.[7]

A Frenchman described the effects of his machine gunners more laconically: 'The Germans fell like cardboard soldiers.'[8] Herbert Read recalled seeing German soldiers falling like shooting-gallery targets.[9] Here the hero became the victim and the victim the hero. The attacker became the representative of a world, the nineteenth-century world, which was demolished by this war.

If the attacker was the representative of a world in its death throes, the defender, either the dogged, frightened defender or the resilient, cocky repeller, became the symbol of a new world dawning. Since full-scale attacks were the exception rather than the rule, most of trench life consisted of a form of defense, of a constant and wearisome struggle to defend 'existence,' to survive the conditions that were primordial at best. Words like *poilu* or *Frontschwein*, the hairy one and the front pig, referring to the dirty, mud-caked, bearded French soldier and his German counterpart, became terms of affection in their respective countries by 1916, not the terms of abuse they might have been in an earlier age of colorful and heroic military engagements. In this existence the assault on the senses was total. 'Our master is our daily misery,' wrote a Frenchman.[10]

The whole landscape of the Western Front became surrealistic before the term *surrealism* was invented by the soldier-poet Guillaume Apollinaire, in his program notes for the Diaghilev production of *Parade* in 1917, on which Stravinsky, Satie, Picasso, and Cocteau collaborated. A panorama of devastation confronted the soldiers in the major battle zones. Trees had been reduced to charred stumps; charred stumps were in turn erected – as observation posts – to look like despoiled trees. Mud was ubiquitous. 'Sunset and sunrise are blasphemous,' wrote Paul Nash, who served in the Ypres salient, was invalided home, and then returned to Flanders as a war artist:

> . . . only the black rain out of the bruised and swollen clouds . . . is fit atmosphere in such a land. The rain drives on, the stinking mud becomes more evilly yellow, the shell-holes fill up with green-white water, the roads and tracks are covered in inches of slime, the black dying trees ooze and sweat and the shells never cease . . . they plunge into the grave which is this land . . . It is unspeakable, godless, hopeless.[11]

A French aviator, looking down on the Verdun landscape after a rainfall, was reminded of 'the humid skin of a monstrous toad.'[12] The most inarticulate diaries of common front soldiers who experienced Verdun or the Somme or Ypres manage to transmit at least a sense of the physical misery of this warfare.

A tour of trench duty consisted normally of three or four days and nights in the front line, followed by the same length of time in support trenches, followed in turn by a similar period in reserve. Only in reserve was it possible, as Herbert Read put it, 'to be civilized – to wash and change and write letters.'[13] Otherwise each man was a savage. Before the mutinies of 1917, the French command was frequently lax about the proper organization of leaves and rest periods. A tour could last for over a month, and sometimes even for more than two months.

Dirt and filth were, of course, constant companions in the trenches. The enveloping dirt was so depressing that men in midwinter sometimes braved the cold and took baths in shell holes. These were often full because of the persistent rain. 'A life so frightfully bestial . . . Even pigs are better off!' Such was the comment of Louis Mairet.[14] Soldiers debated about whether the mud of Ypres or the Somme was worse. Of Ypres in 1917 one Englishman wrote:

It was not war. It was more like a mud lark if it had not been for the machine guns and shelling. One dragged about everywhere. The tenacious mud pulled one's puttees down and would have pulled boots and socks and legs off if they had not been properly fixed.[15]

On taking over a flooded trench a Frenchman quipped, 'It'll be all right so long as the U-boats don't torpedo us.'[16]

'Never was there a climate as this of Flanders,' wrote J.W. Harvey in a letter,

and I hope my objurgation against this rain, rain, rain, will not be deleted as censorable matter! I suppose the continual firing may be in part to blame; yet I feel I shall look with far greater clemency in future upon our own proverbial English weather in comparing it with this.[17]

Such comparisons were inevitable. 'I always thought France was the land of sunshine,' remarked Peter McGregor with genuine innocence in June 1916, 'but it has been very cold and showery.' Four days later the news to his wife, Jen, was 'It rains here like a blooming tap.'[18] Edward Thomas even wrote a poem on the subject, 'Rain': 'Rain, midnight rain, nothing but the wild rain.' The rain had dissolved all love, all meaning

> . . . except the love of death,
> If love it be for what is perfect and
> Cannot, the tempest tells me, disappoint.[19]

Soaked through and freezing, Ernst Jünger decided that 'no artillery fire could break man's resistance so thoroughly as wet and cold.'[20] No amount of clothing – wool socks, vests, jerkins – or even added newspapers, wrapped around various parts of the body, helped. Winter nights seemed impossibly long, and dawn was the coldest moment of the day. 'We don't think of death,' wrote a Frenchman in the winter of early 1915. 'But it's the cold, the terrible cold! It seems to me at the moment that my blood is full of blocks of ice. Oh, I wish they'd attack, because that would warm us up a little.'[21] In the next winter, in Artois, coffee and even wine froze in November. 'Weather for polar bears,' Marc Boasson commented in a letter. 'Before you can have a drink, you have to chip away the ice. The meat is frozen solid, the potatoes are bonded by ice, and even the hand grenades are welded together in their cases.'[22] In the severe winter of 1916–1917 hot tea froze within minutes, and bread, bully beef, and sausage turned to chunks of ice. In a poem titled 'Exposure,' Wilfred Owen evoked shriveled hands, puckered foreheads, and eyes of ice.[23]

In such conditions food could not be enjoyed, and the strain of battle reduced appetites further. The irregular hours for meals, the unreliability of supply lines, the lack of vegetables, the sameness of the meat diet – all this destroyed any possibility of pleasure. When Siegfried Sassoon returned to the Somme from home leave in the spring of 1916, he brought with him a smoked salmon to share with his men, but as he stumbled and splashed up a communication trench known as Canterbury Avenue he reflected that 'smoked salmon wasn't much of an antidote for people who had been putting up with all that shell-fire.'[24]

The weather, then, had a great deal to do with a soldier's spirits. A sudden lifting of cloud and the appearance of sun could raise morale. 'Splendid weather,' exulted Charles Delvert in the midst of the Verdun battle in March 1916. 'This life has its charm. It's like camping out. You wander through the trenches; the air is fresh, the sun brilliant. Gay little clouds flit across the blue sky.'[25] But such weather was very much the exception in the war, and such a lyrical outburst was also very much the exception in Charles Delvert's diary.

The trenches were infested with vermin. Flies, mites, nits, fleas, mosquitoes, and beetles were bothersome, but lice and rats were the major irritants. Lice laid their eggs in the seams of garments and multiplied at a terrifying rate. The louse was so fertile, said the *poilu*, that one born in the morning was a grandmother by evening. The battle against them was unwinnable. Soldiers tried to crush them with their thumb nails, burn them with candle flames, drive them out with powders and pomades sent from home, but to little avail. 'The only way is to heave a few Rum Jars at them,' quipped one Tommy.[26] The biggest of them were given names: Kaiser, Kronprinz, Hindenburg. Only field laundry service and hot baths had any effect, and then just briefly. Roger Campana found these pests more ferocious than the 'vampires of the Congo or Polynesia . . . If Mr Magpie had had a chance to get to know them, he would have cited them as an example for all Frenchmen.' Campana's only consolation was the rumor that the lice in German trenches were bigger![27]

Rats the size of cats were reported in the trenches, although they existed in even larger numbers around rest quarters. They were attracted by food left lying about and by decomposing corpses. They chewed up haversacks and gnawed through ration bags. In his section of the line, Roland Mountfort wrote to his mother, the rats'

> greatest feat was to kill and devour five kittens nearly three weeks old that the trench cat was rearing in one of the dugouts. I don't know why they haven't done it before unless they were waiting in order to get a better meal.[28]

The battle against the rats was as serious at times as that against the human enemy. To Percy Jones the rats became an obsession. 'I am . . . addicted to rat-hunting,' he admitted in his diary. He went after them every night with pickhandles and spades.

> We sometimes go a bit too far. For instance the night before last four of us were in full cry after a rat between our front line trenches and chased him right up to the second line where a sentry nearly shot us, imagining us to be Germans!

Jones's obsession followed him to rest billets a fortnight later. Near the canal in Ypres he participated in a veritable massacre:

> We had a great battle last night and killed nearly a hundred, excluding many that must have been stoned while swimming. The raft party ran out of ammunition and had to come ashore for more bricks.[29]

The only effective instrument against rats and other pests was gas. A gas attack would clear the trenches of vermin for a time.

It was at night that much of the work in the trenches was done. The normal bourgeois approach to time and to the clock was reversed. As darkness fell, armies of troglodytes emerged from their holes, like the very vermin they despised, and scurried about their tasks: wiring parties went out into no man's land; trench fortifications were repaired and extended as the Western Front became a vast, intricate anthill; vicious little raids, comparable to mosquito bites on the body of the collective enemy, were carried out. And even if one had no specific task to fulfill, sleep was impossible. Delvert described a night in the trenches in January 1916:

> Lights out. Now the rats and the lice are the masters of the house. You can hear the rats nibbling, running, jumping, rushing from plank to plank, emitting their little squeals behind the dugout's corrugated metal. It's a noisy swarming activity that just won't stop. At any moment I expect one to land on my nose. And then it's the lice and fleas that begin to devour me. Absolutely impossible to get any shuteye. Toward midnight I begin to doze off. A terrible racket makes me jump. Artillery fire, the crackling of rifle and machine-gun fire. The Boches must be attacking Mont Têtu again. The charivari seems to quiet down about 1:30. At 2:15 it starts up again, this time with a frightful violence. Everything shakes. Our artillery thunders away without pause. At 3:00 the cannon shots become more spread out and slowly things quiet down. I doze off so as to get up at six. The rats and the lice get up too: waking to life is also waking to misery.[30]

After a couple of days and nights of this relentless bombardment of the senses, men easily became disoriented, sluggish, even apathetic. 'I felt I would barter my soul for a few hours of uninterrupted slumber,' noted one.[31] 'What kills is the absence of sleep,' wrote Delvert.[32] When relief finally came, the battalion moved off to rest quarters. Wilfred Owen:

> Bent double, like old beggars under sacks,
> Knock-kneed, coughing like hags, we cursed through sludge,
> Till on the haunting flares we turned our backs,
> And towards our distant rest began to trudge.
> Men marched asleep . . . [33]

The odor of decomposition – masked only by the almost equally intolerable reek of chloride of lime – and clouds of flies attracted by the carrion were other inescapable curses. Limbs and torsos were churned up again and again by the shelling. Working parties digging or repairing trenches repeatedly uncovered corpses in all stages of decay and mutilation. Most of the time they simply shoveled them out of the way. Fragments of bodies did find their way, however, into sandbags. If those burst, they could divulge their contents in a manner so horrific that black humor became the only defense against hysteria. In the Ypres salient at one point men being relieved all filed past an arm protruding from the side of the trench and shook hands with it – 'Tata, Jack.' Those effecting the relief did the same on arrival – ''ello, Jack.'[34] An artillery gunner captain, F.H.T. Tatham, described to his mother another situation so grotesque that it was almost humorous:

> There has always been a horrid smell at our O.P.* in the trenches, which creosote has failed to remove. I found today that it is decomposed remains in a sandbag against which we leaned to use the periscope. I

*Observation post.

believe the unfortunate corpse may have been there six months – the rats don't usually leave them alone, so it was probably a dirty German. Having disturbed it it stinks more than ever – full of maggots. The offending sandbag has been drowned in creosote and thrown far away – but they evidently couldn't get what was left of Fritz into one sandbag, and I fear to eradicate the evil would mean a fall in the parapet, so am in rather a dilemma.[35]

The Australian J.A. Raws sent home an equally 'rum' tale. At work with a digging party at Pozières at the end of July 1916, he was subjected to, as he put it, 'a tornado of bursting shells.' He was buried twice. The second time, after struggling free, he saw a body, half buried, nearby. Thinking it a comrade who had just suffered the same fate as himself, he stumbled over to help the man out. He tugged and lifted. Suddenly, blood spouted all over Raws, and the head came off in his hands. 'The horror was indescribable,' he wrote.[36] His brother had been killed three days earlier, and Raws himself would be killed on his next tour. A Frenchman at Verdun noted: 'We all had on us the stench of dead bodies. The bread we ate, the stagnant water we drank, everything we touched had a rotten smell.'[37]

Mutilation was a daily spectacle in some sectors. At Fresnoy on the Somme a house with German soldiers quartered in it received a direct hit. Ernst Jünger ran to help.

We grabbed the limbs sticking out of the rubble and pulled the corpses out. One was missing its head, and the neck sat on the torso like a large bloody fungus. On another shattered bones protruded from the stump of an arm, and the uniform was sodden with blood from a huge chest wound. On a third the innards flowed forth from a body that had been slit open. As we were pulling this one out, a splintered board that had stuck

211

in the terrible wound gave resistance, making gruesome sounds.

On another occasion Jünger was witness to a machine gun duel.

Suddenly our master marksman collapsed, shot through the head. Although his brains were running down his face to his chin, he was still fully conscious as we carried him to an adjoining tunnel.[38]

After his dugout had been hit by a shell, Roger Campana took a photograph of a comrade's body in order to prove to a friend what a near miss he had lived through. The body was 'laid open from the shoulders to the haunches like a quartered carcass in a butcher's window.'[39] Delvert recorded with greater precision the death of a colleague:

The death of Jégoud was atrocious. He was on the first steps of the dugout when a shell (probably an Austrian 130) burst. His face was burned; one splinter entered his skull behind the ear; another slit open his stomach, broke his spine, and in the bloody mess one saw his spinal cord gliding about. His right leg was completely crushed above the knee. The most hideous part of it all was that he continued to live for four or five minutes.[40]

The Verdun of César Méléra included this scene and observation:

Horses and mules buried. A fetid mud sometimes reaches your ankle, disgorging an awful smell and a heavy opaque air. He who has not seen the wounded emitting their death rattle on the field of battle, without cares, drinking their urine to appease their thirst . . . has seen nothing of war.[41]

Men were threatened not solely by enemy fire but by their own artillery, too, when it fired short. General Percin estimated that seventy-five thousand French troops were killed or wounded by their own artillery.[42] Jean Giraudoux noted ironically to Paul Morand, 'I belong to the French regiment that has killed the most English.'[43] Short shelling was caused by poor communication, human error, damp ammunition, or wind conditions, and invariably created bad blood between troops in the front lines and staff officers and the artillery regiments. Its incidence appears to have increased in general proportion to the increase in shelling as the war progressed.[44]

The front, in short, was, in Siegfried Sassoon's words, 'rotten with dead.'[45] A month before his own death Louis Mairet reflected on the subject:

Death! that word which booms like the echo of sea caverns, striking and restriking in dark and unseen depths. Between this war and the last, we did not die: we ended. Neatly, in the shelter of a room, in the warmth of a bed. Now we die. It is the wet death, the muddy death, death dripping with blood, death by drowning, death by sucking under, death in the slaughterhouse. The bodies lie frozen in the earth which gradually sucks them in. The luckiest depart, wrapped in canvas from a tent, to sleep in the nearest cemetery.[46]

Can one exaggerate the horrors of trench life? Many have supposedly done so and been reprimanded by others for producing in their accounts nothing other than 'mud and blood' sensationalism. Some veterans of the Great War never experienced an attack; some never even saw the enemy, despite lengthy front-line duty; a few survived the whole war without more than a few scratches. Some parts of the front were indeed very quiet. Some men never lost their sense of romance and adventure. Some never lost their sense of humor. Thus, to concentrate on the horror of Verdun, the Somme, and Ypres, say the critics, is to distort the reality of the war. Even in these sectors, which were not, they claim, the norm, massive artillery bombardments and attacks were rare. Most of the time men were occupied by the humdrum problems of trench existence and essentially by boredom.

Part of the problem in this debate is a matter of definition and semantics. What sort of experience does one classify under 'horror' and what constitutes 'boredom'? Cannot one man's horror be another man's boredom, and vice versa? If one insists that horror is the sensation aroused solely by the *unexpected* contradiction of values and conditions that bestow meaning on life, and that in turn boredom is the inevitable upshot of routine, even of routine slaughter, then the question can never be resolved, because no sense of horror, even one caused by this war, can remain constant. After several weeks of frontline experience there was little that could shock. Men became immunized, rather rapidly, to the brutality and obscenity. They had to if they were to survive. As Fritz Kreisler, violinist and Austrian infantryman, put it:

A certain fierceness arises in you, an absolute indifference to anything the world holds except your duty of fighting. You are eating a crust of bread, and a man is shot dead in the trench next to you. You look calmly at him for a moment, and then go on eating your bread. Why not? There is nothing to be done. In the end you talk of your own death with as little excitement as you would of a luncheon engagement.[47]

And John W. Harvey, a Quaker from Leeds who was with the Friends' Ambulance Unit, wrote from Ypres, 'I am having a wearing time amid sights that would be too full of horrors and pity to bear but for human nature's capacity to get hardened by familiarity to anything.'[48]

Hence, even horror can turn to routine and bring on ennui – the sense that one has seen it all before and that existence no longer holds any surprises. 'There is nothing left in your mind,'continued Kreisler, 'but the fact that hordes of men to whom you belong are fighting against other hordes, and your side must win.'[49]

Even when things seemed quiet, the casualties continued to accumulate – from sniper activity, from random artillery fire designed to keep the enemy on edge, and from accidents. It was this attrition, precisely when nothing of any consequence seemed to be happening, that horrified some soldiers the most. Death seemed totally without purpose. In the war diaries of army units there is often a terrible irony lodged in the terse one-line reports for the day's activity: 'All quiet. Three casualties.' As the anguished American ambassador put it in a letter from London, 'When there's "nothing to report" from France, that means the regular 5,000 casualties that happen every day.'[50]

The dichotomy set up in the 'horror versus boredom' debate is a false one. What is crucial is the broader significance of the 1916–1917 phase of the war, its relationship to previous forms of warfare, to expectations and values; and here it is hard to deny that the 'front' experience of 1916–1917 was indeed a 'frontier' experience, an experience of something that was, in its implications, completely new. Of course soldiers continued to classify sensations according to previously existing categories – this was an instinctive reaction – but the actual experience as a whole was crucial, and that, in its broader context, was novel.

With time the former categories and the accepted relationship of the war to previous history wore thin and collapsed. The rate of this deterioration varied among

215

the belligerents and among people, depending on the resilience and resonance of existing values, but everywhere, even if only in the postwar period, in the cauldron where purpose, memory, and outcome brewed together, the validity of former categories disintegrated.

TRANSVALUATION

The Germans had been, even before the war, the most readily inclined of the leading nations to question the norms and values of nineteenth-century liberal bourgeois society, to elevate the moment beyond the grasp of the law, and to look to the dynamics of immediate experience, as opposed to those of tradition and history, for inspiration. In the war they concentrated from the start on the idea of 'victory,' on a Dionysian vitalism, which meant that the moment of conquest would proffer, of and by itself, an exciting range of opportunities, primarily spiritual and life-enhancing and only secondarily territorial and material. Territorial war aims, to which so much of the literature on the German war effort has been devoted, were never more than hazy expressions of ebullience or hysteria born of war weariness. The war-aim issue was never anything more than a political device that reflected the fortunes of the front. The front dictated war aims, not the other way around.

That it was the Germans who were the first to begin to reverse the rules of warfare by recognizing the importance of defense and then by implementing officially the idea of attrition – exhausting the enemy through self-sacrifice instead of 'defeating' him by dashing enterprise – was no accident. Germany had been the country most willing to question western social, cultural, and political norms before the war, most willing to promote the breakdown of old certainties and the advent of new possibilities. As a corollary, the Germans were less reluctant to stretch the rules of warfare. They were

216

less reticent to break with international conventions associated by them with a rule of law imposed by Anglo-French hegemony and regarded by them as prejudicial to German interests.

The idea of attrition was in the short term the upshot of a particular military situation, a response to the unexpected stalemate that resulted from the failure of the Schlieffen plan in 1914 and then continued through the next year. But it was also an indication of the willingness of the German military and the civilian leadership to translate the emotional involvement of the nation, so evident in the early days of the war, into military strategy. The army, which in the Prussian tradition had been regarded as 'the school of the nation,' was to become that for all Germans. 'Total war' was the means by which this could be achieved. Now the soldier and civilian would no longer be distinguishable. A war of attrition would involve the commitment of the entire nation.

Such an idea did not spring up overnight. Many of the activities of the prewar Pan-German movement, of the Navy League, the colonial societies and other radical nationalist organizations, were prompted by the aim of revitalizing German society through military principles and virtues. And interestingly, much of this popular form of militarism stemmed from non-Junker elements, from new social types in the military, men like Ludendorff and Bauer, and from white-collar elements – the so-called new middle class – in the nationalist leagues. Total war was an ideal not of the aristocratic Junkers – of the Schlieffens and the Moltkes – but of the new Germany. Erich Ludendorff, commoner, son of a businessman, careerist, man of action rather than reflection, was a supreme symbol of this new Germany. He, like the modern impulse he represented, came from the periphery – from his place of birth in a one-story house in the midst of an orchard in Kruszewnia in the eastern Prussian province of Posen. By July 1917

217

Ludendorff held more power than anyone else in Germany. To Ludendorff and to the new Germany, all political questions, all economic questions, all cultural questions, were in the end military questions.

Now, attrition was to be merely an offshoot of such thinking. It could not have grown had there not been a consistent buildup toward 'totality.' This called for the breakdown of the distinction between soldiers and civilians and the rejection of accepted morality in warfare. The treatment of civilians in Belgium by the occupying German forces and the reliance on new methods of warfare – especially the use of gas and inventions such as flame throwers, and the introduction of unrestricted submarine warfare – were the most important steps, until attrition, in the advent of total war.

How the changing social and physical landscape of Europe would affect future war was an issue that had concerned statesman and politicians and legal experts across the continent in the decades before 1914. Would one be able to distinguish readily between soldiers and civilians? At the beginning of the nineteenth century the Spanish response to the Napoleonic invasion, the resort to guerrilla warfare, had pointed to future problems. Then the Franco-Prussian War of 1870–71 revealed dramatically that Napoleon's experience in Spain sixty years earlier was but a mild taste of what was in store if war enveloped Europe's most populated areas. Between the battle of Sedan in September 1870 and the armistice in the spring of 1871, all the problems surrounding the relationship between civilians and soldiers in war came to the surface. The Germans bombarded Strasbourg, Péronne, Soissons, firing into civilian neighborhoods, arguing all the time, however, that civilians and military were assisting each other and that therefore little distinction could be made between the two. Terror was also applied in occupied areas: civilian houses were burned, hostages shot, and fines levied.

Between 1871 and 1914 international legal discussions

concentrated on defining the duties and rights of military invaders on the one hand and civilian defenders on the other. In these exchanges the Germans generally insisted on the right to requisition and to demand docility from a population under occupation. They were not alone in this, but they were virtually alone in positing an extreme version of the argument – the idea of *Kriegsverrat*. According to this view, the disruption of the war effort by civilians in occupied territory is as treasonous as disruption by one's own nationals.[1]

The German occupation of Belgium was consistent with this position, and while as a whole certainly not as monstrous as Allied propaganda made it out to be, the occupation policy was nevertheless draconic. If babies were not systematically snatched from mothers' arms and smashed against brick walls, if nuns were not deliberately sought out for sodomy, rape, and slaughter, if old people were not made to crawl on all fours before being riddled with bullets, considerable numbers of hostages were shot, including women and children and octogenarians. Louvain was razed, together with its library, founded in 1426, with its 280,000 volumes and its priceless collection of incunabula and medieval manuscripts. *Schrecklichkeit*, or frightfulness, was pronounced official policy in the occupied areas, initially in Belgium and then in France and Russia. The term *furor teutonicus* was used by Germans with pride.

The treatment of civilians became incontrovertible evidence to the Entente powers of German inhumanity; 'poor little Belgium' and 'crucified Belgium' were the principal rallying cries in the mobilization of British prowar sentiment. The fate of Louvain and its library was regarded as a symbol of German barbarism, of a Teutonic hostility to history and to western civilization as a whole, to its artifacts, its accomplishments, and its values. To the library at Louvain were soon added the cathedral at Rheims, bombed first on 20 September –

'the most hideous crime ever perpetrated against the mind of man,' asserted Henry James[2] – the Cloth Hall at Ypres, and eventually the cathedral at Albert. The Germans claimed that the towers of these structures were being used for observation and optical telegraphy and that they had no option but to bomb them, regardless of the adverse publicity the action would create. Soon, however, they undermined their own reasoning by attacking civilians and historical monuments far beyond immediate battle perimeters. On 11 October two Taubes reached Paris and dropped twenty-two bombs, killing three and wounding nineteen citizens. Notre Dame Cathedral was also scratched. This was looked upon by the Entente powers as an undeniable and unacceptable broadening of the forms of warfare. Then in December 1914 the war was taken to the civilians of England when the northern English port of Hartlepool and the seaside resorts of Scarborough and Whitby were shelled from the sea. In 1915 Zeppelin raids on London and Paris began, and by early 1916 these raids were being undertaken as far north as Lancashire.

The young, talented, and already greatly respected historian Friedrich Meinecke wrote in the early months of the war that what the foreigner calls brutality in German behavior, the German himself must call simply honesty. After all, if the cathedral at Rheims was being used by French observers, it had to be bombed. It was as simple as that. For the French and the British to call the German a barbarian in these circumstances was pure hypocrisy.[3] Meinecke was relatively moderate. Another German historian expressed similar ideas in shriller tones:

Better that a thousand church towers fall than that one German soldier should fall as a result of these towers. Let's not have any whining from humanists and aesthetes among ourselves. We have to assert ourselves. Those are such simple truths that it becomes tedious to have to repeat them to people who don't wish to hear.[4]

Rather than such unequivocal assertions about the pre-eminence of life force over history, one might have expected from Meinecke and his confrère, given their professions, a greater respect for the dependence of the individual and the nation on their historical context. Yet the emphasis in their comments is on the Dionysian act of self-assertion. In the course of the war, thirty-five of forty-three holders of chairs of history in German universities were to aver that Germany had become involved in the war only because she had been attacked.[5]

A frequently observed alternative to the denial of history was denial that acts of destruction had occurred. In October 1914 a manifesto appeared, addressed to 'the world of culture' and signed by ninety-three German intellectuals. Among the signatories were such luminaries as the theologian Adolf von Harnack, the writer Hermann Sudermann, the composer Engelbert Humperdinck, the scientist Wilhelm Röntgen, and the playwright Gerhart Hauptmann. 'It is not true,' they insisted, 'that we have criminally violated the neutrality of Belgium . . . It is not true that our troops have acted brutally in Louvain.'[6] Wish, fantasy, and illusion increasingly would become dictators over reality as the war – and as the century – advanced. In this process Germany led the way. Men should 'open their hearts to humanity only as long as it cannot hurt them,' said Ernst Jünger. Such egoism and lust for sensation played a role, Jünger was prepared to admit, in the advent of the war.

An interest in the gruesome was of course part of the complex of desires that dragged us so irresistibly into the war. A period of law and order as long as the one our generation had behind it brought a real craving for the extraordinary.[7]

Were the French and British justified in becoming so agitated about German methods of warfare? After all, the British themselves had denounced – as the Germans were now doing to the Belgians – the 'unsporting' tactics of the Boers when the latter resorted to hit-and-run raids and civilian resistance in the South African war at the turn of the century, and the British military had felt forced to set up detention centers in which women and children, as well as men, were incarcerated in harsh conditions. Wits who charged Britain with hypocritical behavior savored the saying 'Britain rules the waves and therefore Britain waives the rules.' Moreover, there is evidence that French soldiers committed 'atrocities' in occupied territory early in the war,[8] and as a result one can rightly wonder how the French would have behaved had the war been fought largely on German soil. A few days after mobilization, Louis Pergaud, a teacher and a former pacifist, wrote, 'It is necessary and it is urgent that we eradicate to the last stone and to the last individual this race of vipers that is the Prussian race.'[9]

Nonetheless, the evidence as it stands shows overwhelmingly that the Germans denied international standards most systematically – in part out of a sense of necessity, viewing these standards as injurious to their immediate welfare, but also in large part because they, the Germans, were simply less disposed to abide by rules they considered alien and historic and hence not applicable either to themselves or to the colossal significance of the moment. The Germans were to berate themselves after the war by claiming that their propaganda effort had been far inferior to that of the Allies, but the truth of the matter was that the Allies did have more substance behind their claims against the Germans than the Germans had against their enemies. The Germans' appeal to 'honesty,' 'openness,' and 'truthfulness' had a romantic and idealistic ring; it was an appeal to internal, private virtues. The Allies' appeal was a social, ethical, and historical one; it was to external, public values.

Henri Bergson accused the Germans in December 1914 of having made their barbarism 'scientific,'[10] and Henry James referred in January 1915 to the 'baseness of demonism' that lay behind the destruction of Ypres,[11] but the first systematic use of asphyxiating gas on the Western Front by the Germans, on 22 April 1915, at Langemarck near Ypres, against French and Canadian troops, removed any doubts in the Allied populations about the satanic nature of the German threat and about German 'guilt.' That event in the spring of 1915 was the most spectacular act in what Pierre Miquel has called 'the terrorist war.'[12]

The Hague Declaration of 1899 and the Hague Convention of 1907 had forbidden the use of 'poison or poisonous weapons' in warfare. Although the French and British were buying liquid chlorine as early as September 1914, and though the French in particular had been working on gas munitions for some time prior to April 1915, the fact remains that the Germans were the first to use gas extensively and methodically. The chemist Fritz Haber, later a Nobel laureate for his prewar work on ammonia synthesis, had had the idea in the autumn of 1914 that the use of chlorine would allow the Germans to regain the initiative in the war and, despite munition and manpower shortages, bring it to a victorious end. The Germans' allegations that the Allies were using poison gas in their shells, as opposed to relatively harmless and nontoxic irritants that both Germans and French had already used – these allegations they could not document; and their claim that the Hague agreements did not extend to the diffusion of cloud gas, only to use of projectiles emitting gas, was mere obfuscation.

Some commentators at the time and some historians subsequently have argued that an unwarranted to-do has been made about the use of gas. Gas, they argue, was actually more humane than shelling, because it resulted in fewer casualties, even after killer gas was introduced.[13] Such an argument is specious. Gas was certainly not used because it was more humane but because it compounded the horrors to which the front soldier was subjected. It was not used instead of artillery; it was used in addition to artillery. As a British artillery man himself put it in May 1915, after the Germans had taken Hill 60, a strategic point near Ypres, with the help of gas:

If we are not going to meet disaster at every turn we must use something of the sort ourselves. These humanitarians claim that it is more merciful to asphyxiate a man than to blow him up with high explosive shell. That is their pleasant way of trying to appear before the world at large. In reality – having turned on the gas they bayonet everyone who has been too overcome by the fumes to move and then turn their high explosives on to the wretched crowd of people who remain struggling for breath. Words fail to describe one's feelings about the whole thing.[14]

Soldiers, even seasoned veterans, on all sides never got used to the idea of gas. Indeed, some of the Germans directly involved in the development of poison gas considered it an 'unchivalrous' and 'repugnant' weapon.[15] Crown Prince Rupprecht of Bavaria, commander of the Sixth Army, tried to prevent its use, claiming that the enemy would respond in like manner, but he was overruled. Ironically, it was his Sixth Army that was to be the object of the first major British gas attack, at Loos in September 1915. Even though it quickly became a standard part of the arsenal on both sides and deadlier forms were introduced as the war progressed, soldiers continued to associate gas with improper methods of fighting. 'I shall never forget the sights I saw by Ypres after the first gas attacks,' asserted Lieutenant Colonel G.W.G. Hughes of the medical corps.

Men lying all along the side of the road between Poperinghe and Ypres, exhausted, gasping, frothing yellow mucus from their mouths, their faces blue and distressed. It was dreadful, and so little could be done for them. I have seen no description in any book or paper that exaggerated or even approached in realization of the horror, the awfulness of these gassed cases. One came away from seeing or treating them longing to be able to go straight away at the Germans and to throttle them, to pay them out in some sort of way for their devilishness. Better for a sudden death than this awful agony.[16]

Victims of gas, once seen, tortured the mind far more, it seems, than soldiers mutilated by shells:

> In all my dreams, before my helpless sight,
> He plunges at me, guttering, choking, drowning.[17]

Soldiers were of course intensely superstitious, and British troops came to feel that using gas would bring bad luck.[18] The home front in Britain and France thought the Germans had put themselves beyond the pale by resorting to gas. Domestic opinion was outraged, and when the *Daily Mail* asked the women of Britain to make a million small cotton-wool pad respirators, according to specifications set out in the paper, for the emergency of late April, the army was inundated with donations. Several thousands of these were immediately sent to France and issued to the troops as a stop-gap measure. The technology of gas warfare developed quickly: from chlorine to phosgene and mustard gases. Mustard was the most deadly, and once again it was the Germans who introduced it. Respirators became accordingly more sophisticated, with face covers made of rubberized fabric and eyepieces of nonsplintering glass. The men hated the masks. Breathing was difficult at best, and vision and mobility were restricted.

Surrounded by masked men during a phosgene attack at Verdun, Pierre de Mazenod was reminded of a 'carnival of death.'[19] For many, gas took the war into the realm of the unreal, the make-believe. When men donned their masks they lost all sign of humanity, and with their long snouts, large glass eyes, and slow movements, they became figures of fantasy, closer in their angular features to the creations of Picasso and Braque than to soldiers of tradition. Dorgelès called the gas mask 'this pig snout which represented the war's true face.'[20] British comment on the German gas attacks included the following:

> With use by the Germans of poison gas the war took a more bitter turn and horror followed horror until the soldier of civilization had to rise to a height of courage putting altogether in the shade that of the Knights of old, who went out to fight loathly dragons which breathed fire and mephitic vapours. In this mortal struggle with a race of scientific orang-outangs, it requires a shutting of the eyes to externals and a looking inward to see the nimbus shining from the brow of the soldier . . . But how more splendid than that of any beplumed, caparisoned soldier of old, is his courage as he rides, or squats in mud or dust, swathed in his chemical bandages so that all human likeness is lost, awaiting not only shot and shell and steel, but *flammenwerfer*, asphyxiating gas, lachrymatory gas, stink gas, and other instruments of German warfare![21]

It is not surprising that when the 'Anti-Gas Establishment' of the Royal Engineers got together for a reunion ten years after the war, one of the sketches in a comedy program made reference to the Russian ballet. Both gas and the Russian dancers were regarded as the height of 'newness,' as expressions of a sense of the modern that far exceeded what was considered acceptable by most of society. Lieutenant Colonel Henry S. Raper, CBE, FRS, Cavalier Crown of Italy, was presented on the anniversary program in the following way:

Raperski Presents his famous Russian Ballet, 'Dialysis.' *Argument:* – The scene is laid in a woodland glade in which the three beautiful sisters, Chlorine, Bromine and Iodine, are discovered wandering. Sodium, a notorious bad character, approaches and beguiles them by presenting each with an electron for their rings. Too late they discover what has happened and they are about to crystallize out in despair, when they are precipitated by Argentum and thus saved from their awful doom. The last scene depicts Sodium, who has now become an Ion, in Brownian motion.[22]

Given the outcry in Britain when gas was first used, it is interesting to look at the introductory paragraphs of the Holland report on chemical warfare published in 1919. The report begins:

That gas is a legitimate weapon in war the Committee have no shadow of doubt and that it will be used in the future they consider may be taken as a foregone conclusion, for history shows that in no case has a weapon which has proved successful in war ever been abandoned by Nations fighting for existence.[23]

Twenty years later, at the outbreak of the next war, everyone in Britain would receive a gas mask. The 'cubist war' had spread to the entire nation.

The flame thrower was another weapon the Germans introduced first; it was a part of their arsenal from late 1914. The Allies said that it contravened the Hague agreements, which forbade the use of 'arms, projectiles and materials calculated to cause unnecessary suffering' and insisted, moreover, that 'belligerents have not an unlimited right as to the choice of means of injuring

227

an enemy.' The flame thrower consisted of a cylinder of oil and a steel tube from which the oil was projected at high pressure. Here was a weapon that, like gas, was not terribly effective in the long term – it was most useful for incinerating the inhabitants of pillboxes or dugouts – but that instilled appalling fear in its potential victims. For Mairet the *Flammenwerfer* was the supreme 'symbol of this merciless war, a glowing vision of this century of madness.'[24] The French and the British did not relish using the flame thrower to the same degree as the Germans: they felt that if there was any resistance from the trenches being attacked, then the man carrying the flame thrower was likely to be hit, would become a human torch, and would represent more of a danger than a help to his own troops. If there was little resistance to an attack, then the flame thrower was hardly necessary. The French did retain the *lance-flammes* for mopping-up operations after a first assault wave had succeeded.

Among other innovations of trench warfare that the Germans were the first to apply methodically were trench mortars and sniping. *Minenwerfer*, or Minnies, as they were called by the British with ironic affection, appeared as early as September 1914 on the Chemin des Dames and elsewhere. The French hated them, calling them 'coal scuttles' or 'stovepipes.' Snipers, too, with their telescopic sights, were loathed – sometimes even those on one's own side – as unsporting types.

The British and the French were much slower in introducing new ideas of warfare – trench mortars, gas, or tanks. From the start there was a reluctance to accept the reality of trench warfare: 'I don't know what's to be done,' said Kitchener; 'this isn't war.'[25] Trench warfare of course was blamed on the Germans; they were the first to resort to this 'unmanly' form of fighting. General Cherfils accused the Boche of behaving like a 'cowering mole,' refusing an honest and virile fight *à la loyale*.[26] But beyond denunciations of the Germans, little inspired and innovative thinking appeared. After the Somme battle had dragged on for three months without any sign of breakthrough, General Robertson could still describe tanks as 'a somewhat desperate innovation.'[27]

Tanks were about the only Allied invention of significance in the war of the trenches. Yet their premature use, in insufficient numbers, on 15 September 1916, on the Somme, wasted the important weapon of surprise. Surprise was regarded by the Victorian world as somehow unethical. Surprise belonged to the immoral world of the gambler and *flâneur*. Success had to be the upshot of hard work and effort, not chance and surprise. And so the tank was not to be conceived of as a secret weapon but rather as an offspring of British determination and commitment. As far as Haig was concerned, the tank was always to remain subordinate to infantry assault. In the end men, not machines, would win this war – men 'playing the game.'

If tanks were accepted reluctantly as a necessary part of the game by the Allies, the German use of submarines to attack all shipping within a designated zone was regarded by the French and British from the start as another manifestation of German barbarism. The Germans had always attached more importance to the symbolism of their war fleet than to its practical use. In October 1912 Bethmann Hollweg, for instance, told Lord Granville, a senior officer in the British embassy in Berlin, that Germany required her fleet 'not merely for the purpose of defending her commerce, but for the general purpose of her greatness.'[28] When the war broke out, British naval superiority was evident from the start, and by the end of 1914 Britain had firm control over home waters and had applied an effective blockade against German shipping in the North Sea and English Channel; in addition, she had done considerable damage to the German battle fleet on the seas. The kaiser was reluctant to risk the rest of his prize fleet, to have his symbols shattered, so with the exception of some hit-and-run raids on the east coast of England and the battle of Jutland in 1916, the German fleet remained in harbor behind its minefields. Deprived of the use of this status symbol, the German naval authorities shifted the emphasis to a newer weapon of naval warfare, one that was more 'modern' in its effect, involving secrecy, surprise, and sudden destruction, the submarine. In their emphasis on submarines the Germans once again changed traditional patterns of strategic thinking. The naval fleet should have been backed by the submarines, but the reverse occurred: the submarine became the principal German weapon in the sea war, and the surface navy was relegated to a position of support. On land the Germans resorted to an underground war; on the high seas their approach was the same.

In February 1915 they announced the establishment of a 'war zone' around Great Britain in which all shipping, merchant or otherwise, would be attacked without regard for the safety of crews and passengers. Again the Germans argued that the British had led the way in the breakdown of law on the seas and that they were simply responding to the British blockade of their country. Britain had refused to ratify the Declaration of London of 1909, which attempted to establish a code of law for naval warfare, and she continued to interpret contentious questions about, for example, the nature of contraband to her own advantage; hence, so the argument went, Germany had no alternative but to adopt countermeasures, brutal though these might appear.

In this case there certainly was some merit to the argument. Yet it is the nature of the German response that is of interest here. By resorting to unrestricted submarine warfare, and again refusing to make distinctions between soldiers and civilians, neutrals and belligerents, the Germans took the war, with much greater drama and élan than did the British with the blockade, into the realm of total war. *Schrecklichkeit* was applied on the seas. In March 1915 the passenger ship *Falaba* was hit by a torpedo that was fired while lifeboats were being launched. Over a hundred lives were lost. On 7 May the British liner *Lusitania* was torpedoed off the coast of Ireland, with a loss of 1198 lives, including 120 Americans, out of over 2000 passengers and crew. In a display of xenophobic fervor a medal was struck in Germany to commemorate this 'victory' on the seas. Coming as it did within a few days of the first use of gas, the sinking of the *Lusitania* brought down the wrath of the neutral world on Germany. Josiah Royce, a professor at Harvard, had up until that point refrained from mentioning the war in his classes. But when he learned of the fate of the *Lusitania*, he could no longer restrain himself. 'I should be a poor professor of philosophy, and in particular of moral philosophy, if I left my class in the least doubt as to how to view such things,' and he went on to refer to 'these newest expressions of the infamies of Prussian warfare' and 'this new experiment upon human nature.'[29] Royce's reaction was representative of the American response.

In the Entente countries the sinking of the *Lusitania* was followed by moral indignation and a flood to the colors. William Gregson, a twenty-five-year-old teacher at Arnold House, a grammar school in Blackpool, whose diary hitherto had contained more entries about school life and football than about the war, was clearly influenced by the event. On Sunday, 9 May he wrote in his diary, 'Lusitania's loss still hangs like a cloud over us and brings forth more than usually fiery sermon from Rigby at Matins.' Within a fortnight Gregson had decided to join up.[30]

The Germans continued their tactics through the summer, attacking unsuccessfully a large Cunard liner on 9 July and then sinking the White Star liner *Arabic* on 19 August. It was clear that opinion against them was mounting and that submarine warfare was not having the desired economic effect on Britain, and in September 1915 the attacks were called off.

231

However, as Falkenhayn developed his view of *Stellungskrieg* – set forth most completely by him in a memorandum of December 1915 – he included, in his wider version of the nature of the new war, the energetic pursuit of unrestricted submarine warfare. Both were essential ingredients of total war. Falkenhayn was to be unsuccessful in convincing the civilian authorities and the kaiser on the subject of the U-boat war through 1916. But the realization, after the battle of Jutland, that Germany had little chance of toppling British naval supremacy and the similar lack of progress in the land war in 1916 finally convinced the kaiser and Bethmann Hollweg that a new campaign of submarine warfare was the only possible way to achieve victory. Despite the likelihood that such a campaign would result in American entry into the war, the Germans believed they could bring Britain to her knees before American power could be felt in Europe.

If tonnage sunk is the criterion of success, this time the campaign in its early stages held definite promise, at least until the end of the summer of 1917, when the British introduced an effective convoy system. The worst repercussion for the Germans was, however, the entry of the United States into the war in April. The submarine war was to be continued to the end, but by July 1918 the turning point had come, because by then the British were producing more tonnage of new shipping every month than the Germans were sinking.

In the air, as we have noted, the Germans also took the initiative in expanding the boundaries of combat. Thus, at every level, in the war on land, at sea, and in the sky, it was the Germans who usually tried the most novel methods first. It was they who most blatantly stretched international standards of behavior and morality. In all these areas and aspects of warfare, the year 1916 assumed great importance. Many of the new ideas were first tried out in 1915 – gas, submarine warfare – so that year becomes in retrospect a transitional year; but 1916 saw the advent and acceptance of the new war in its most spectacular dimensions. Many were aware that momentous changes were afoot. Georges Blachon published two articles in early 1916 in the *Revue des deux mondes* entitled 'La Guerre nouvelle' and 'La Guerre qui se transforme sous nos yeux.'*

In methods, tactics, and instruments of war, Germany took the initiative in 1914. The war was to bring a revolution in the European spirit and, as a corollary, in the European state structure. Germany was the revolutionary power of Europe. Located in the center of the continent, she set out to become the leader of Europe, the heart of Europe, as she put it. Germany not only represented the idea of revolution in this war; she backed the forces of revolution everywhere, whatever their ultimate goals. She helped Roger Casement and the Irish nationalists in their struggle against Britain, and she shipped Lenin back to Russia from Switzerland to foment revolution in Petrograd. What was important above all for Germans was the overthrow of the old structures. That was the whole point of the war. Once that had been achieved, the revolutionary dynamic would proceed to erect new structures valid for the new situation.

*'The New War' and 'The War That Is Changing Before Our Eyes.'

233

V

Reason in Madness

O God, our help in ages past,
Our hope for years to come.

ISAAC WATTS

I think no permanent change of importance has been made by
the War in the character, customs and habits of the people.

MICHAEL MACDONAGH
1916

I'm going back to Blighty, which
    I left to strafe the 'Un;
I've fought in bloody battles,
    and I've 'ad a 'eap of fun;
But now me flipper's busted,
    and I think me dooty's done,
And I'll kiss me gel in Blighty in the mawnin'.

Christmas card verse,
British Red Cross Society, 1917

THEIRS WAS NOT TO REASON WHY

Schoolteachers, coal miners, bank clerks, poultry farmers; gentry, urban middle class, laborers, and peasantry – in the midst of the fury, what kept them in the
trenches? What sustained them on the edge of no man's
land, that strip of territory which death ruled with an
iron fist? What made them go over the top, in long rows
that, despite the noise, terrain, terror, and confusion,
remained remarkably orderly? What sustained them in
constant confrontation with death or its symbols, in
attack and counterattack; in defense or on fatigues or

on marches; in summer and winter; in the fire line, in support, in reserve, at rest, and, perhaps the supreme test, on leave?

We are talking here not of professional armies but of mass armies, of volunteers and conscripts, such as the world had not seen before, and we are talking not about military systems in which obedience was achieved by the knout or the noose or the bed of Procrustes. Desertion was still punishable by death, and courts-martial were active in this war, but the incidence of insubordination and sedition was minuscule in relation to the numbers of men under arms and in view of the conditions they had to brave. The question of what kept men going in this hell of the Western Front is central to an understanding of the war and its significance.

What becomes clear from the diaries and letters of front soldiers is that in front-line service, particularly in action but in routine duty as well, the senses became so dulled by the myriad assaults on them that each man tended after a short while to live according to reflexes. He functioned instinctively. Of course self-preservation was an important instinct, but even more important, considering the situation the soldier found himself in, were the firm rules of behavior the military laid out and especially the social norms that constituted the broader context of the military. Reflexes and instincts were in large part prescribed by the soldier's society.

Of an attack Alan Thomas wrote afterward: 'The noise, the smoke, the smell of gunpowder, the rat-tat of rifle and machine gun fire combined to numb the senses. I was aware of myself and others going forward, but of little else.'[1] Thomas may have been unaware of why he was going forward, but going forward he was, loyally, dutifully, honorably, for many reasons; and most of these reasons were positive, not negative. 'The cause,' with its multitude of interpretations – personal, familial, and national – was a far more significant factor in determining behavior than the threat of punishment.

For Patrick McGill of the London Irish, going over the top meant that 'the moment had come when it was unwise to think.'[2] Time and even place ceased to matter. The immediate task at hand – getting through one's own wire, negotiating the scarred terrain, observing the signals of the platoon leader, coping with the weight of one's pack – was all-consuming. In this situation the soldier functioned according to rules drummed in through training but also according to a whole code of values instilled by his society, education, and upbringing.

That reflex response should have determined behavior in situations of extreme danger is perfectly understandable. The documentary material contains frequent references to a state similar to anaesthetization. Here is Alexander Aitken describing an attack at Goose Alley on the Somme in September 1916:

I passed through the smoke . . . In an attack such as this, under deadly fire, one is as powerless as a man gripping strongly charged electrodes, powerless to do anything but go mechanically on; the final shield from death removed, the will is fixed like the last thought taken into an anaesthetic, which is the first thought taken out of it. Only safety, or the shock of a wound will destroy such auto-hypnosis. At the same time all normal emotion is numbed entirely.[3]

Yet other accounts suggest that for many this state approaching narcosis became a constant condition of prolonged life in the trenches. After a soldier had been at the front for about three weeks a distinct change was noticed in him: his reactions generally became dulled, his face showed less expression, his eyes lost their sparkle. The German student Hugo Steinthal remarked on the insensitivity the soldier developed that allowed him to survive mentally in this hell. After being relieved from a particularly wearying stint in the trenches, he wrote home:

> Whoever has been in these trenches for as long as our infantry, and whoever has not lost his sanity in these hellish attacks, must at least have lost feeling for a lot of things. Too much of the horrific, too much of the incredible has been thrown at our poor chaps. To me it's unbelievable that all that can be tolerated. Our poor little brain simply can't take it all in.[4]

Marc Boasson referred to the *automatisme anethésiant* that the trench experience induced.[5] Fritz Kreisler remarked on the 'strange psychological, almost hypnotic, state of mind' one lapsed into.[6] General Pétain saw innocent youths entering the 'furnace of Verdun' for the first time feigning lightheartedness and indifference. When the survivors came out they had expressions 'frozen by a vision of terror.'[7] Shell shock or neurasthenia was the term eventually applied to extreme cases of this condition, but army staffs and medical officers were slow to admit to such a condition. Lieutenant Colonel Jack of the 2nd West Yorkshires noted in his diary in November 1916 the case of one of his officers who had served with the battalion in France since November 1914 and who now was clearly suffering from nervous exhaustion:

> I . . . reported him to Higher Command as worn out, and requested that he be sent home for a change from battles. The curious reply came that there was no such thing as a soldier being 'worn out' and my application was refused.[8]

237

If the military was reluctant to recognize shell shock, the civilians had no inkling whatsoever of the condition. Garfield Powell, incensed during the Somme offensive by the platitudinous rubbish spouted by politicians, suggested they all be required to spend a week in the trenches:

> Shell shock! Do they know what it means? Men become like weak children, crying and waving their arms madly, clinging to the nearest man and praying not to be left alone.[9]

That many, perhaps even the majority of front-line troops in major battle areas suffered from some degree of shell shock may not be a wild hypothesis. As the French soldier-poet Charles Vidrac put it:

> . . . the man who has tripped
> Between death's legs and then
> Recovers himself and breathes again,
> Can only laugh or only weep:
> He has not the heart to mourn.

Even if a man thought he was functioning normally, life in the line demanded so much menial work – repairing trenches, digging new latrines, going on wiring parties, standing sentry duty, cleaning equipment, hunting rats and lice – that he rarely had time or energy to contemplate meaning and purpose in the war. Officers censoring letters found the task excruciatingly dull because of the mundane contents of virtually all letters. Material concerns – references to meals, cigarettes, clothes, equipment, and a host of such irritants as weather and vermin – dominated; emotions rarely transcended trite sentimentality; and the war as a whole was usually described in platitudes. Even a sensitive observer like Roland Dorgelès admitted that 'the most profound impressions came to me later, with some distance. On the spot, I attended to small matters and this detail often prevented me from judging the whole.'[10]

Preoccupied in the trenches by the mass of details – 'crushed,' as André Bridoux put it, 'by the necessity of the hour'[11] – and denied precise information about the course of the war on other fronts, men found it difficult to assemble a coherent picture of the war as a whole. This is one of the reasons that a novel like Henri Barbusse's Le Feu was passed around and read so eagerly when it appeared in 1916. Men craved some wider vision of the war. Most went through the war like blind men.

André Gide visited a medical station at Braffye as the wounded from a battle were being brought in, in the hope of getting some authentic reactions from those who could still speak about the encounter. He was stunned to hear survivors spouting the same clichés contained in newspaper reports of the battle. 'None of them could provide the slightest original reaction,' he complained. It was as if the soldiers had read the articles that were to be printed about the battle before they went into it.[12] The war, it seemed, was run on the basis of assumptions, on reflex responses that were engendered by a code of values and ideas, not solely about the war itself but about civilization in general. At the Somme the Reverend Walker gave communion to a badly wounded man:

> After the blessing his hands went together, eyes closed and he said 'Gentle Jesus meek and mild, look upon a little child etc' – God bless father, mother, grandfather, and make me a good boy – then the Lord's Prayer.[13]

If dying soldiers resorted to rituals taught them at bedside in childhood, those who were threatened by annihilation that day, the next day, or the next week responded in an equally fundamental fashion. Life came to be looked on as a reprieve. Nothing else. Men stopped asking questions, deliberately. They ceased to interpret. 'Just as he tried to delouse himself as regularly as possible,' said Jacques Rivière,

> so the combatant took care to kill in himself, one by one, as soon as they appeared, before he was bitten, every one of his feelings. Now he clearly saw that feelings were vermin, and that there was nothing to do but to treat them as such.[14]

The war had become so monumental in significance, like an unknowable, indefinable godhead, that words and ideas were useless. Gabriel Chevallier: 'Never have I felt myself so empty of thoughts.'[15] Charles Delvert: 'One's intellect is numb. You don't think anymore. Your head is like lead.'[16] Dillon Lawson: 'The inevitable conclusion that one comes to out here is that it is worse than useless to think about things.'[17]

Among British and German troops there was, with the exception of some relatively minor incidents, almost absolute loyalty to the very end. Disagreements, cases of insubordination, even the mutiny by labor companies at the British base camp at Étaples in 1917, should not be overblown. Put in the broad context of the massive mobilization of millions of fighting men and the gargantuan industrial and bureaucratic substructure created to fight the war, the incidence of indiscipline was low. In the French lines widespread mutinies did occur in 1917, after the disastrous and totally futile offensives in April of that year on the Chemin des Dames. Yet studies of the mutinies have shown that they were hardly inspired by fundamental doubts about the purpose of the war but, rather, by basic grievances focusing on such matters as regularity of leave, the quality of food, inadequate recreational facilities in rear positions, the cost of *pinard*, the lack of tobacco, and so forth. The French administration of the war effort had broken down and that upset morale, not vice versa.

If the war was reduced, certainly by 1916, to reflex responses, then the assumptions of the civilizations and cultures fighting the war were all-important. And here the crucial catchword for those assumptions was 'duty' or *devoir* or *Pflicht*. After the gloss of heroism had worn off in the first month of the war, and as the war settled into the enervating phase of attrition, the concept of duty became the linchpin to the effort. As long as the word retained any semblance of meaning, spoken or unspoken, the war would continue. As long as soldiers could somehow relate their reflexes and instinctive behavior in moments of reflection to an underlying sense of responsibility, they would continue to fight, despite horror, weariness, and even despondency.[18]

A good deal of the literature of and on the war, beginning with works like Barbusse's *Le Feu* and the war poetry of Siegfried Sassoon, Wilfred Owen, Robert Graves, and Herbert Read, through the 'literature of disenchantment' of the 1920s, to some of the recent analyses of soldiers' sensibility, places great stress on the emerging sense of irony, disillusionment, and alienation among front soldiers. This sense of deracination and marginality in relation to the existing social order and its values is important, and we shall return to the issue, but what deserves emphasis in the context of the war is that, despite the growing dissatisfaction, the war continued, and it continued for one reason: the soldier was willing to keep fighting. Just why he kept going has to be explained, and that matter has often been ignored.

Only in Russia did the front collapse. Here was a society that was still relatively backward and that had not developed the means, economic, social, and moral, to fight a long war. Socialization, through education and other institutions of state, had not gone far enough in Russia. Industry was not sufficiently extensive or modern to provide adequate munitions or supplies, and shortages of matériel plagued the tsar's armies throughout the war. Most of the Russian soldiers, like most of the Russian population, were illiterate peasants whose inspiration for fighting was simply loyalty to the tsar. Their attitude toward life was more basic than that of soldiers of urban, industrialized, and literate societies; it was devoid of social trappings and ideological accoutrements. Their morale as a result was worse. In two and a half years the Russians suffered five and a half million casualties. The troops were constantly short of ammunition, the civilian population of food; the transport system was in chaos; and the government was divided. The terrible winter of 1916–17, with its mass starvation, completed the collapse. By the spring of 1917 the Russian people had had enough. That year witnessed two revolutions, in March and November, with the Bolsheviks engineering the latter. By March 1918 the Treaty of Brest-Litovsk had been signed with the Germans, and Russia was out of the war.

Elsewhere, the Russian example did spark murmurs of sympathy in the second half of 1917, but on the whole morale held. What, then, did 'duty' mean, and how did that meaning change in the course of the war?

DUTY

In the world view of the nineteenth-century middle class, progress, which in the end constituted the essence of history, was a product of moral continence and secular ambition, an amalgam of a sense of destiny and a belief in individual effort. Implicit in this general outlook was the idea that a reconciliation, if not a complete identification, between public need and individual wish was possible and desirable. For a man like Samuel Smiles, notions of collective progress on the one hand and of individual honor, industry, and happiness on the other were all tied together: 'Honourable industry travels the same road with duty; and Providence has closely linked both with happiness.'[1]

Yet we see here that for Smiles industry and duty were only 'closely linked' with happiness. They did not overlap. If a state of supreme well-being did not necessarily result from the performance of duty, a strong sense of personal satisfaction would. In the ideal moral code of the nineteenth-century middle class, the goal of individual effort was always social harmony, the commonweal, the public good. In the end the interests of the individual, which were to be protected and furthered by the state, were nevertheless subservient to the public good; personal restraint was the hallmark of respectability; and the idea of service to the public, or duty, became the great achievement of this class.

As the institutions and instruments of state developed in the nineteenth century and gradually came under public control, it was the middle class that staffed and ran schools, hospitals, treasury boards, public utilities, and colonial services, let alone, increasingly, government as well. And in the private sector, too, banks, insurance companies, and industrial corporations profited from middle-class enterprise and ambition. Even armies came to be, by the end of the century, predominantly middle-class institutions, from the officers down through the ranks. Only the general staffs remained in the grip of the old aristocracy, though even here class control was no longer solid.

In 1914 in France, Britain, and Germany, it was primarily the middle class, imbued with ideas of service and duty, that went to war. This was the first middle-class war in history. If previous wars were wars of dynasticism, of feudal and aristocratic interests, of princely rivalries, then the First World War was the first great war of the bourgeoisie. It is therefore hardly surprising that the values of this middle class should have become the dominant values of the war, determining not only the behavior of individual soldiers but the whole organization and even strategy and tactics of the war. Its very extent – it was of course called the Great War – was a reflection of the nineteenth-century middle-class preoccupation with growth, gain, achievement, and size. Machines, empires, armies, bureaucracies, bridges, ships, all grew in size in the nineteenth century, this maximalist century; and Dreadnought and Big Bertha were the telling names Europeans applied to their most awesome weapons on the eve of the war, this maximalist war.

King George's message to the parting BEF in August 1914 was 'I have implicit confidence in you, my soldiers. Duty is your watchword, and I know your duty will be nobly done.' When Kitchener pointed his finger at the British public in the famous recruiting poster – 'Your Country Needs You' – the corresponding slogan the piercing stare was meant to evoke was 'Do Your Duty.' Of the 'first hundred thousand,' Ian Hay wrote in his immensely popular and vibrant celebration of the BEF:

> Within their hearts be writ
> This single-line memorial:—
> He did his duty – and his bit![2]

In the effervescence that accompanied the opening months of the war, the notion of duty, on all sides, had a grandiloquent ring, sounding of a glorious defense of the home country against ignoble and perfidious foreign aggression. Duty and adventure were one.

In Britain and France duty was associated with honor and loyalty and a fight for civilized and civilizing values, such as justice and dignity and freedom from tyranny. These were proclaimed loudly, indeed vociferously, in, as Anthony Powell later put it, 'great rolling phrases.'[3] The raucous appeal to duty undoubtedly had its effect on many, but others joined actively in the war effort

244

after making sober and reasoned decisions based on a Socratic argument. E.L. Woodward, who was to become a distinguished historian, had gone down from Oxford in 1913 and then spent a year in Paris. He joined up at the outbreak of the war not because he wished to fight German 'barbarism' but because he felt that if one has in general benefited from the laws of one's country, one is not morally entitled to reject those laws if they suddenly do not suit.[4] An Australian major, B.B Leane, who was to be killed in action in 1917, confided comparable though less articulate sentiments in his diary in April 1915: 'I trust that I will come through alright, but it is impossible to say, and I must do my duty whatever it is.'[5] In France there were similar appeals and arguments but of course with an added note of urgency, since France was directly under attack and occupation.

In both Britain and France duty was initially associated with patriotism, and the loud patriotism had a strong historical flavor. The achievements of these two countries over the centuries had an objective reality, a tangible appeal, a visibility discernible on any map of the world, and in many of the governmental and legal institutions of the world – in parliaments, cabinets, judicial systems. History, in fact, provided the substance of the British and French identity, and that identity had an external essence. Hence duty was not an abstract notion at the beginning of the war. It was a practical imperative. 'I suppose at no time did one live so much with a consciousness of the past,' wrote a Welsh veteran of the war, David Jones.[6] Individual happiness, self-realization, and even individual purpose were not, as a rule, motivating factors, though admittedly there were some, especially in the intellectual and artistic community, whose enthusiasm for the war was prompted by such self-interest. The war, for most Britons and Frenchmen, was a stage in the march of civilization, in the continuation of progress, both of which were based on what were seen as concrete

245

historical foundations. 'I am intimately convinced, in my soul as a gentleman, that I am fighting for civilization,' wrote Louis Mairet at Easter 1915 before going into his first attack. 'I understand very well what my duty is; I shall not fail . . . I am not at all a warrior; but I shall become one of necessity.'[7]

As the war bogged down into stalemate and attrition, the notions of duty and *devoir* began to lose their aggressive and confident overtones. Before his death in July 1915 in the Artois, Jean-Marc Bernard wrote a poem that included these lines:

> *Nous sommes si privés d'espoir,*
> *La paix est toujours si lointaine*
> *Que, parfois, nous savons à peine*
> *Où se trouve notre devoir.**[8]

Percy Jones, reflecting on what had been achieved in 1915, got 'cold shivers' when he looked at a map and saw 'how far the Germans must be driven back.'[9] And Charles Sorley was convinced by September 1915 that the line he defended was impregnable: 'The line can now never be bent backwards where we are; but I wonder if it can or ever will bend forward.'[10] At home Vera Brittain noted in early 1916 that the pessimists now mentioned that the war might last for ten years.[11]

In the letters and diaries of front soldiers, both volunteers and conscripts, there is less and less mention, as the war drags on, of the overall purpose of the war, the defense of civilization, and more and more reference to the individual's limited social horizons – his family, comrades, and regiment. While one of the great fears of soldiers was that they might break under stress, that they might lose self-control, and their legs or nerve

---

*We are so without hope,
Peace is still so far away
That sometimes we hardly know
Where to find our duty.

might fail them in an emergency, it is surprising how little attention is devoted overall to the self, the spiritual self, to discussions of personal emotions, such as courage, fear, hope, or anger. Nor is there much mention of religion, even among chaplains. Personal diaries become reserved about emotions and ideals. Garfield Powell found the 'whole damned show' of the Somme

> so impersonal that one cannot . . . feel any personal emotion . . . when in the thick of things. Hope, revenge, anger, contempt: any of these would be a sustaining emotion in action but very few experience them, I believe.[12]

The focus of attention is on externals – material needs and deprivations, the welfare of fellows, the mood of the home front. Abel Ferry, who earlier in the war had exuded idealism, could write from the front in May 1916: 'Idealism is dupery. The world belongs to those who don't believe in ideas.'[13] General Pétain noted of the soldiers at Verdun that 'determination' had become their main characteristic and motive too: 'an inflexible desire to defend their families and their goods against the invader.'[14] It was real concerns rather than sublime principles that kept men going.

In the soldier's immediate surroundings, his regiment became the focus of duty. An intense sense of comradeship was one of the strongest sentiments generated by the war. 'I don't want you to think we are unhappy,' wrote a morose Herbert Read from the front line in April 1918; 'we have comradeship in our troubles and that makes all the difference.'[15] The core of this comradeship was a feeling of responsibility toward and utter dependence on one's fellows. It was an intense sense of belonging.

Soldiers, interestingly, appear to have been concerned that the home front might crack. Consequently, propaganda flowed in two directions. Not only did the home front – the press in its editorials, clergymen in their sermons, teachers in their lessons, for instance – paint a rosy picture of the war; soldiers were inclined to hide the gruesome reality of the war from their loved ones at home. The military censor encouraged this; also, the language and metaphors appropriate to describe the unexpected new experience were lacking; and there was a desire to spare loved ones concern and anguish. It seems clear that as the war progressed the spirit of the home front became much poorer than that of the fighting front. Frank Isherwood complained to his wife as early as January 1915 about the 'depressing letters' everybody, except apparently her, wrote. His brother, for instance, seemed 'to have lost his faith in his country and God and everything else. Even the Pope is in disgrace!! It is just these people who have suffered nothing who make the most fuss.' In another letter he remarked that the king had said 'that the only cheerful faces he had seen for the last six months were in France.'[16] The situation at home deteriorated as the years and war dragged on: 'We really are fighting for something worth having,' Dick Stokes felt compelled to write to his parents in August 1917. A few months later, after his father had given further sign of flagging morale at home, Stokes responded, 'You say something must crack – it won't be the British Army! whatever else it is!!'[17]

As the focus of duty narrowed, the earlier élan gave way to resignation and stoicism. Percy Jones was a young journalist before the war and an enthusiastic volunteer in 1914. His diary entry for 26 June 1916, concerns preparations for the Somme offensive:

General Snow and his staff are busy telling us that we shall have practically no casualties because all the Germans will have been killed by our artillery barrage. There is nothing like the truth! . . . Nearly all the boys have no faith in the carefully drawn up plans of

248

attack and consolidation, but they are all determined to go on until something stops them . . . Our duty is plain enough – to go on until something stops us.[18]

Of Jones's platoon of Queen's Westminster Rifles one man survived 1 July 1916, without being wounded or killed. E. Russell-Jones, a lieutenant, expressed in his diary thoughts like Jones's before the start of the attack on 1 July – 'a very few minutes before the start of what is to be the beginning of the end of German Culture':

War is a curious business, and very well for those who like it, but I must say I am no lover of the game. At the moment I feel pretty rotten and hate myself for it, for when one has such splendid fellows under one as I have, one feels one's deficiencies very much, but here we are and we've all got to see it through now, so all there is to do is stick it to the end as well as possible.[19]

By 1917 duty and *devoir* began gradually to disappear from the active vocabulary of front soldiers. Many more of these men were now conscripts. In Britain compulsory service had been introduced in January 1916. What perhaps deserves more emphasis, however, than the lapsing of conscious affirmation of the war – something that is understandable, given that the war was now well into its third year without end in sight and given the continuation of tactics that promised no success – is the soldiers' willingness, despite fatigue and despondency, to 'carry on,' to 'stick it to the end.' Thus, of three thousand letters written by men of the French 36th Infantry Regiment, a regiment involved in the mutinies after the disaster on the Chemin des Dames, only four hundred, or 13 per cent, were retained by the postal control because they expressed some sympathy with the mutinies. The vast majority did not even mention the insubordination.[20] What is remarkable here is not the evidence of mutiny but the restraint and loyalty of most of the troops.

In some respects, the likelihood of insubordination was actually magnified by the old commanders, who were suspicious of the new armies. Haig did not trust the new soldiers:

> They came forward under compulsion and they will depart the Army with relief. Men of this stamp are not satisfied with remaining quiet, they come from a class which like to air real or fancied grievances, and their teaching in this respect is a regrettable antidote to the spirit of devotion and duty of earlier troops.[21]

The commander of the French Third Army in June 1917, General Humbert, estimated that of every hundred French soldiers at the time fifty were loyal, thirty-five were doubtful, and fifteen were bad. Humbert called for resolute action by courts-martial against the shirkers.[22] In view of such assumptions, what is striking is how loyally the soldiers, old and new, performed, against all expectations of the high commands. If unbounded public school enthusiasm disappeared from the ranks, this was owing less to the modest change in the social complexion of the British and French armies – in Britain, under conscription, the working class was now more likely to be kept at home because of the needs of industry – than it was to the nature of the war itself.

Moreover, the decrease in mentions of duty was an indication of the growing difficulty soldiers faced in verbalizing their experiences and sentiments; it had less to do with the disappearance of the concept of duty. Wilfred Owen could now say, for instance, that he 'heard music in the silentness of duty.'[23] By the summer of 1918, in the wake of the massive German offensive and partial breakthrough, Haig and many of his generals, along with the journalists and politicians who visited the front in a despondent mood, were encouraged and more optimistic because of the resilience of the troops.

By 1916 the war appeared to have developed its own rationale, devoid of interpretation in traditional terms – 'It is ridiculous to talk about reason when unreason holds sway,' wrote Louis Mairet – but the clouding of previous clarity did not mean that the war was not to be continued. 'Despite everything, it is necessary that the struggle continue,' said Mairet, 'until the end of one of the two parties.'[24] Implicit in such a statement is the idea that the war had developed a momentum of its own, but there is also the stoical acceptance, despite confusion and horror, of the need to remain loyal to the original cause. The sentiment is still 'our country, right or wrong,' even if the concept of country had narrowed to one's regiment, one's family, and one's friends. The Scotsman Peter McGregor, whom we have encountered before, was killed by a shell while working in a reserve trench in September 1916. The death lacked any vestige of heroism, as did virtually all deaths in this stage of the war. The letters of condolence to the widow from, among others, the captain of B Company, 14th Argyll and Sutherland Highlanders, and from the platoon sergeant, stressed McGregor's good humor, 'cheerfulness and grit.' The chaplain who officiated at the burial also wrote:

We prayed . . . We gave thanks that your husband had heard and answered the call of duty and that God had seen him fit to lay down his life in his country's service. That must be your comfort now. You will console yourself with our Lord's words – words repeated over your husband's grave – 'Greater love hath no man than this that a man lay down his life for his friends!'[25]

Duty is mentioned here, service to country, but the emphasis is on the immediate circle of fellow soldiers.

Naturally, if purpose was no longer as obvious to the combatant as at the start, and if the war had to continue, then it had to be fought on the strength of 'eternal verities,' inner resources one had acquired from one's culture and society. A sensitive friend of Vera Brittain's who was worried that he might not pass the test of courage in the front lines in an emergency wrote: 'I tell you it is a positive curse to have a temperament out here. The ideal thing to be is a typical Englishman.'[26] And to be a typical Englishman meant, of course, that one repressed inner feelings, stiffened one's upper lip, and functioned according to form. What was vital was what the British used to call 'bottom,' stability of character, staying power, integrity. In this primitive existence, courage and morality tended to be equated. The courageous were inevitably 'the good,' 'the good' inevitably the courageous. Morality, then, was essentially a matter of external behavior, of decorum. Among those who couldn't stick it were usually the hard drinkers and the womanizers. 'In the trenches your sins found you out,' said one soldier.[27] Among both British and French troops, by 1917, there was no talk about glory and gallantry, fewer references specifically to duty, but a great deal of talk about holding out, about determination, commitment, grit, about sticking it.

It is often said in the literature of the war that men no longer made war; war was made on men. Given the overpowering technology of warfare – the machine guns, the artillery, and the gas – the individual soldier was overwhelmed by a sense of vulnerability and helplessness. César Méléra, who had sailed around the world before the war, said at Verdun that this form of warfare marked 'the bankruptcy of war, the bankruptcy of the art of war; the factory is killing art.'[28] But despite the loss of individuality, soldiers kept on fighting.

252

They did not mutiny, for the most part, or desert en masse. Men still made this war – not only generals but miserable foot soldiers. The literature on the war is lacking in balance. It concentrates for the most part on the negative repercussions of the war, not on the positive instincts that fired it for over four years. Even Herbert Read, who admired Nietzsche and was given to anarchistic leanings even before the war, could write in a letter in July 1917, 'I begin to realize that quite the most important thing in life is to possess the vague qualities of, and be upon every occasion, a "gentleman."'[29] This is exactly what the British claimed they were fighting for, the unwritten laws of civilized behavior. That a free spirit like Read should come round to this view shows how strong the unspoken motivation was.

That motivation, in the case of every soldier, regardless of nationality, was rooted in the social order and values of his respective country. And for all the misuse to which the word *bourgeois* had been subjected – by cynics, political partisans, and angry youths – it still has applicability to the nineteenth-century order as it developed in western Europe and to the cultural components of this order. As an adjective, the word has applicability, moreover, to the manner in which the 1914–18 war was fought. This was the civil war of the European middle class above all else. Though we no longer find it easy, in our stratified pluralistic societies, to define *bourgeois* or *middle class* in contemporary terms, the European of the turn of the century did not have such difficulty and the terms had a reality, in social organization but particularly in a reservoir of virtues. While material well-being, education, career, and social affiliations were important determinants of status and respect, the willing adherence to a code of values and compliance with certain forms of behavior were the key to membership in bourgeois society. Values were the glue that held class and society together.

Britain was the society in which those values we identify with the middle class had penetrated farthest. The lay religion of progress, the concern with utility, success, and decorum, the worship of industriousness, perseverance, and moral commitment, the veneration, above all, of socially motivated effort and service – these elements were at the core of British achievement in the world, and they lay also at the center of British conduct of the war. France, too, despite a measure of turmoil, was governed in large part by a similar code of values on the eve of the war, bequeathed by the idealism of the Revolution, by the shifts in power that had accompanied the 'bourgeois monarchy' of Louis Philippe, by the economic upsurge under the Second Empire of Louis Napoleon, and by the gradual though admittedly patchy achievements of the republican parliamentary order after 1871. Much of France adhered to a positivist ethic of accomplishment through effort. 'The bourgeoisie is essentially an effort,' insisted the French bourgeois René Johannet.[30] The Great War was essentially an effort too. 'The worst horror of this war,' remarked Benjamin Crémieux later – he was an infantryman throughout the war and was wounded three times – 'was that the men who made it were able to do so with the same conscience as any other work.'[31]

How were bourgeois values inculcated? In a discussion of the requisites for social stability, John Stuart Mill gave principal emphasis to the need for 'a system of education, beginning with infancy and continued through life, of which, whatever else it might include, one main and incessant ingredient was restraining discipline.'[32] The key to stability was the subordination of individual interests and whims to the needs and ends of society. Although formal schooling was only a modest part of Mill's wider vision of education, western Europe had achieved through the institution of compulsory primary education almost universal literacy by the end of the century, and it is generally agreed that

254

secular schooling, which was inclined to play down religious training and stress civics and national history, was a major instrument in developing national pride and loyalty. Socialization was also furthered in the second half of the century by a newspaper press that became available and geared to a mass reading public. Compulsory military service, the idea of a 'nation in arms,' a cry harking back to the revolutionary wars at the end of the eighteenth century, this, too, made a contribution in France to the socialization process. But most important in the process was the general breakdown of individual self-sufficiency in a mass industrial society, in which the division of employment and labor became the hallmark, and in which the individual came to be enveloped by the institutions and instruments of the state – the schoolteacher, the tax official, the gendarme, or the justice of the peace. The arm of the state was becoming longer and longer and more embracing, and the agents of that state were essentially middle class, whether of a higher or lower echelon. They embodied the middle-class notion of virtue. Thus, most soldiers functioned within the bourgeois world, but so too, of course, did most strategists and military leaders. The Channel ferry that bore George Sherston (Siegfried Sassoon) to France 'was happily named Victoria.'[33]

The military leadership of the First World War has received a very critical press ever since. Some military historians, in defense of the commanders of the war, have argued that there was no alternative to trench warfare on the Western Front, and rather than being the product of a failure in imagination, as is usually claimed, trench warfare constituted a reasonable way of trying to deal with the tremendous technological and scientific advances in warfare. This may well be true. Trench warfare may indeed have been inescapable. But it is not inconsistent with such a view to go on and argue that, once the belligerents were locked in stalemate on

255

the Western Front, the very methodicalness of Anglo-French strategic and tactical thinking, the general unwillingness to take even calculated risks, the suspicious attitude toward ingenuity, and moral inhibitions about surprise tactics, all were consistent with a frame of mind and rigid outlook on life that we can characterize as bourgeois. The very promotion of Douglas Haig to chief of the British general staff contains symbolic value: here was a man whose entire life and demeanor were the epitome of middle-class values and ambitions. Dour, religious, dedicated, hard-working, emotionally repressed, and yet a model of honor, achievement, and respectability, he is a symbol of an age – probably every major city in the Commonwealth has a school named after him. And yet he also represents the tragedy of an age.[34]

General Joffre, the French chief of staff – until he was relieved in 1916 – though far less abstemious, was nevertheless a Gallic version of Haig. Each displayed confident persistence and sangfroid. To the minister of war, Gallieni, who was concerned about the German buildup at Verdun in December 1915, Joffre replied arrogantly, 'Nothing justifies the fears that have been expressed.'[35] He would on one occasion describe his tactics by saying, '*Je les grignote*' (I keep nibbling at them), a telling image.[36]

Haig and Joffre were merely surface manifestations of a general condition. Other staff officers reinforced their influence and views. The commander of the French Tenth Army in Artois in 1915 was Colonel Maud'huy, who three years earlier had declared to his assembled regiment: 'Many men salute correctly, very rare are those who salute beautifully . . . One could say that the salute is the hallmark of education.'[37] This is the voice and sentiment of the aristocrat-dandy, enamored of blue and red uniforms and the *attaque à outrance*, preferably on steeds. But the preoccupation with form and decorum, evident in Maud'huy, was also an aristocratic bequest to the bourgeoisie, who then claimed to put substance to the form. In an attack, formation was absolutely essential, insisted a French company captain:

> In general one is tempted to use, in an advance, the enemy's approach routes and trenches. Even if these permit you to approach the enemy with surprise and without losses, they nevertheless disrupt the company and attack formation. Moreover, when the shooting begins and you have to get out into the open, it will be difficult to do so.[38]

The logic here exemplifies a particular frame of mind. Even if you can occupy the enemy trench by chicanery, do not. Chicanery will get you in trouble! The British were perhaps even more consistent in implementing such attitudes. The German 15th Reserve Regiment's diary has this to say of the British attack at Loos in September 1915:

> Ten ranks of extended line could clearly be distinguished, each one estimated at more than a thousand men, and offering such a target as had never been seen before, or even thought possible. Never had the machine-gunners such straightforward work to do nor done it so effectively.[39]

The weight of their packs prevented the soldiers from running or jumping or diving into shell holes for cover. But no-one ever seriously considered removing the packs from soldiers' backs to allow at least the first assault wave greater maneuverability and an opportunity to exercise surreptitiousness and imagination. The backpack thus became a symbol of the social and cultural baggage each soldier carried with him into battle. Robert Graves, who experienced Loos that September, wrote a poem in memory of Captain A.L Samson, who was killed near Cuinchy:

We found the little captain at the head;
His men lay well aligned,
. . . they died well;
They charged in line, and in the same line fell.[40]

Method, order, system: they would be the key to success. Perseverance en masse. The 1st Australian Division was thrown in at Pozières on the Somme in mid
July 1916 repeatedly to attack a high ridge. The Austra-
lians came out on 4 September, having suffered 23,000
casualties. The Australian *Official History* could not
hide its disdain and anger afterward:

> To throw the several parts of an army corps, brigade
> after brigade . . . twenty times in succession against
> one of the strongest points in the enemy's defence,
> may certainly be described as 'methodical,' but the
> claim that it was economic is entirely unjustified.[41]

The trouble was that the determination and grit of a
unit had come to be measured by the number of casualties. Officers whose companies incurred light casualties were suspect, so they pressed their attacks with
appropriate vigor.

Men knew that slaughter would be in store for them
when they went over the top. How did they react? 'I
hope to play the game and if I don't add much lustre to
it I will certainly not tarnish it,' wrote a young British
volunteer before the Somme.[42] 'To be able to comport
oneself correctly in the face of death,' that, said a
French sergeant before an attack at Verdun, that was
the most important thing.[43] This preoccupation with
correct response in the face of danger is reflected in
the documents over and over again. Courage was not
a matter of inspiration; it was a matter of moral
reserves, and every man hoped that he possessed them
in sufficient measure. And so 'play the game' and
'comport themselves correctly' they did, by the million.

After enemy shells had scattered a British attack, 'we carried on like a crowd moving off a cricket field,' reported Wilfred Owen.[44]

Rumors of desertion were rampant, but among the British they appeared for the most part to remain rumors. 'How we enjoy trying to believe these rumours,' commented T.S. Hope. 'The only disturbing factor is we can never find an eye-witness to any of them.'[45] Similarly, during the French mutinies in May and June 1917, the letters of soldiers frequently mentioned reports of officers having been killed by their own men, but none of the correspondents seems to have witnessed such an incident.[46]

In September 1917 the journalist Michael MacDonagh was at London's Clapham Junction station, where he observed two trains as they drew up on opposite sides of the platform. One contained Tommies bound for the front and the other German prisoners of war. The Germans laughed and shouted 'Kamerad,' and the Tommies responded by throwing the Germans chocolate and tobacco. 'Many people,' reflected MacDonagh initially, 'say the War will never end. I often wonder whether it may not be brought to a finish by the rank and file on both sides deciding to lay down their arms and go home.' But then he thought better of such a vision: 'Impossible! The sense of duty – a tremendous force – forbids it.'[47]

Jean Norton Cru showed after the war that among the French the liberal professions had suffered by far the highest number of casualties in the front lines.[48] The same was probably true of the German and British armies. In Britain, enlistment was highest among men in the professions and in commercial and clerical occupations.[49] What does that suggest? A lack of practical thinking and expertise on the part of lawyers, teachers, and architects? A touch of naïveté may have been a minor factor in the casualty rate, but it is certainly not a full explanation. Middle-class professional men were most caught up, it seems, in the purpose of the war, in the notions of duty and service, notions that continued to have residual meaning for them even when that meaning could no longer be articulated with precision. On 11 November 1918, the day of the Armistice, Henri Berr, the French historian, wrote the concluding sentences of an introduction to a book about the war. Of his nation's victory he said, 'France is experiencing the satisfaction felt by a good worker who has completed an honorable job.'[50] That is the language and morality of the *bon bourgeois*. That is the language and morality of *devoir*. All the horror, all the suffering, all the cost are equated with a good worker's completion of a job!

Two French doctors, Louis Huot and Paul Voivenel, concluded in July 1918 a study of the psychology of the *poilu*. They argued that, contrary to the postulations of Gustave Le Bon, who had stressed the effect of environment on the individual, the French soldier's psychic constitution had not been fundamentally changed by the war experience. The *poilu*, they claimed, had remained true to himself, his nation, and his 'race.'[51] The psychologists were both right and wrong. The soldier had been sustained by social values in which he genuinely believed, but, as we shall see, those values had been subjected to such grievous attack in the course of the war that his attitudes toward society, civilization, and history were indeed irreparably altered.

The recourse to residual values brought Britain and France through the war, but the inherent conflict between those values and the brutal reality of modern warfare was bound to undermine the values. To the grieving parents of Louis Mairet, who was killed in April 1917, a French general wrote about 'the beauty of duty so nobly done.'[52] Hundreds of thousands of wives and parents received letters expressing such sentiments. How long would these phrases sustain a generation of widows, orphans, and cripples?

In 1919 in a rector's address to undergraduates at St Andrews University, Douglas Haig continued to articulate the purpose of the war in the old lofty terms, terms that indeed had motivated soldiers of the Entente throughout the war, terms that, however, were also very much rooted in a bourgeois ethic of the nineteenth century:

In every stage of the great struggle from which we have at length emerged victorious, our courage was heightened and our resolve made stronger by the conviction that we were fighting, not only for ourselves and for our own Empire, but for a world ideal in which God was with us. We were doing battle for a higher form of civilization, in which man's duty to his neighbour finds a place more important than his duty to himself, against an Empire built up and made great by the sword, efficient indeed, but with an efficiency unredeemed by any sense of chivalry or of moral responsibility towards the weak.[53]

That was one way of explaining the essence of the Anglo-French war effort. A decade later F. Scott Fitzgerald put the same idea in different language and more comprehensive terms. Dick Diver, the hero of *Tender Is the Night*, is touring the Somme battlefields and says:

This western front business couldn't be done again, not for a long time. The young men think they could do it but they couldn't. They could fight the first Marne again but not this. This took religion and years of plenty and tremendous sureties and the exact relation that existed between the classes . . . You had to have a whole-souled sentimental equipment going back further than you could remember. You had to remember Christmas, and postcards of the Crown Prince and his fiancée, and little cafés in

Valence and beer gardens in Unter den Linden and weddings at the *mairie*, and going to the Derby, and your grandfather's whiskers . . . This kind of battle was invented by Lewis Carroll and Jules Verne and whoever wrote *Undine*, and country deacons bowling and *marraines* in Marseilles and girls seduced in the back lanes of Württemberg and Westphalia. Why, this was a love battle – there was a century of middle-class love spent here . . . All my beautiful lovely safe world blew itself up here with a great gust of high-explosive love.[54]

VI

Sacred Dance

... where the object is creation and production, there is the province of Art; where the object is investigation and knowledge, Science holds sway. After all this it results of itself that it is more fitting to say Art of War than Science of War.

KARL VON CLAUSEWITZ

Wir werden solchen Frühling, bald verschattet,
Nie wieder auf der weiten Welt erleben.*

ERNST BLASS

WAR GOD

In Germany before the war a substantial gulf existed between social, economic, and political reality and cultural ideals. The German attempt to resolve this duality led them to a *Drang nach vorne*, a 'push forward,' an effort of will and exploration that, many Germans hoped, would lead to a spiritual, albeit secular, transcendence of material concerns and limitations. *Geist* and *Macht*, spirit and might, would be reconciled in a state of surreal harmony, of Dionysian activity together with Apollonian tranquillity, in which means and ends, object and subject, would be fused. Archaism and modernity would become one. Technological innovation and industrial progress would, in a grand synthesis, combine with a spirit of pastoral simplicity. Society and

*Such a spring, soon in shadows,
Never again shall we experience in the entire world.

263

culture would no longer be conflicting realms but an indissoluble whole.

In the jubilation of August 1914 Germans genuinely believed that this goal had been achieved, that the conditions of war had in fact brought about a condition of peace, of 'overcoming.' Conflicts and differences had been set aside, and Germans had finally achieved that unity, spiritual and physical, which Bismarck had tried, but in the end failed, to bring about. 'Among the most beautiful things that the war brought,' wrote one commentator, 'is the fact that we no longer have a rabble.'[1] Mobilization was uplifting: the mob disappeared and only Germans remained, a nation of spiritual aristocrats.

For Friedrich Naumann, Max Weber, and others on the moderate left, the spirit of August amounted to a realization of the *sozialen Volksstaat*, the people's state, in which the political left and right, the worker and the bourgeois, cooperated voluntarily and productively. And not only were Germans resident in Germany united; they were fused inseparably now with the various racial minorities within Germany's boundaries and with their brothers in Austria. Ernst Toller, who was to become an irrepressible opponent of the military and political establishment, was as caught up in the orgy of nationalism in 1914 as everyone else. 'The nation recognizes no races anymore; all speak one language, all defend one mother, Deutschland.'[2]

The euphoria of those August days was millenarian. 'Victory' had already been won, by the very eruption, the very enunciation, of the 'ideas of August.' Victory on the battlefield would be a mere formality. It was inevitable, an inevitable byproduct of the German act of national self-assertion. 'We will conquer!' insisted a student of law from Leipzig on 7 August. 'With such a powerful will to victory nothing else is possible.'[3] Six weeks later he was dead.

The mood of August was, as we suggested earlier,

essentially aesthetic. Form had been used and then transcended, by a supreme act of creative will, to achieve beauty of, so it was thought, a lasting and ultimate nature. 'German morals and German customs speak to us like newly discovered sources of everything beautiful,' wrote a Bonn professor.[4] And a 'magical power' for the future was what another commentator called Germany's spiritual unity and idealism.[5] The poet Rainer Maria Rilke and many others bowed in humble and awed obeisance to the 'War God.'

> Und wir? Glühen in Eines zusammen,
> In ein neues Geschöpf, das er tödlich belebt.*[6]

Invigoration by death: such was Germany's 'rite of spring.'

The German concept of *Pflicht*, or duty, was filled with this idealism. If British duty and French *devoir* were rooted in a sense of history as foundation and building block, German *Pflicht* was anchored to a view of history as myth, as poetic justification of the present and future.

Doubts about the validity of history, about the ability of historians to produce objective accounts of the past, had of course penetrated the cultural climate of the entire western world before the war. Historians themselves, in the second half of the nineteenth century, were skeptical about the drift of western civilization; they posited as an alternative to materialism and standardization a renewed emphasis on spirituality and 'inner experience.' But in Germany by the end of the century the process was much farther advanced than elsewhere. Early in the nineteenth century Schopenhauer had defined history as 'the long, difficult and confused dream of mankind,' and derided all pretensions to objectivity and universality.[7] He did not

*And we? We glow as One,
A new creature invigorated by death.

265

receive much attention during his lifetime, but in the second half of the century his star began to rise. In 1870 an admirer of Schopenhauer's, the historian Jacob Burckhardt, who, though Swiss, was trained in Berlin and exerted his greatest influence on German colleagues, wrote, 'If anything lasting is to be created it can only be through an overwhelmingly powerful effort of real poetry.' Poetry, he said in agreement with Aristotle, is more profound than history.[8] In Burckhardt, history and art moved together. Theodor Mommsen, the historian of Rome, who earlier in his career had had positivistic inclinations, was following a similar path by 1874 when he suggested in his rector's address to the University of Berlin that 'the writer of history is perhaps closer to the artist than to the scholar.'[9] The effect of the so-called Prussian school of historians, among them Johann G. Droysen, Heinrich von Sybel, and Heinrich von Treitschke, and of social and historical thinkers like Wilhelm Dilthey and the neo-Kantians was to contribute significantly to the German tendency to search for answers to man's problems not in the outside world but in one's imagination. History was, in short, more a matter of the present than of the past and of intuition rather than of rational analysis. Nietzsche's tirades against objectivity became increasingly popular after his death in 1900; and, as we have seen, widely read cultural critics like Julius Langbehn and Houston Stewart Chamberlain called for the complete aestheticization of life. History's truths could be approached only intuitively, not by a critical method. History was art, not science. German thinkers were in the vanguard of the reorientation – or dismantling – of nineteenth-century historical thought, in the revolt against empiricism and positivism, and in the reaction to a social, political, and cultural order identified with western liberalism and materialism and with a long-standing Anglo-French hegemony in the world.

German patriotic fervor in 1914 did include historical

associations – with the wars of unification of Bismarck, the 'wars of liberation' against Napoleon, the rise to power within Europe of Prussia under the Hohenzollerns, especially under Frederick the Great, the rebellion of Luther against the church of Rome, the adventures of Frederick Barbarossa and Otto the Great, the missionary endeavors of the Teutonic Knights, and even the victory of Arminius in AD 9. Nevertheless, the very newness of the German nation-state, the paucity of evidence of German influence in the world on secular institutions of law and government; the fact that the German historical bequest to the world was largely spiritual, in music, philosophy, and theology; all this gave the German version of history and of nationalism in 1914 a strongly idealistic content, and, by comparison with Britain and France, a version devoted much more to a heralding of the future than to an understanding of the past. In 1889, on the very edge of his mental collapse, Nietzsche told Burckhardt that he was 'every name in history.'[10] Of his band of men at the front, Gerhart Pastors used similar language in April 1915: 'Luther, Bismarck, Dürer, Goethe – a whole heaven of stars lights up in us.'[11] And for Wilhelm Klemm the war was a 'fantastic reality.'[12] In other words, history, poetry, dream, and the individual moment were all combined into one exhilarating sensation.

As a corollary, German *Pflicht* involved more than a defense of the fatherland, more than an adherence to a social code of service; it contained a strong subjective ingredient consisting of personal honor and will. Honor, here, was more than blind obedience to the rules of behavior, more than loyalty to tradition; it involved personal inspiration and initiative. The individual was not just a particle within a utilitarian association called society; the truly German individual *was* the nation, the embodiment of community. And the nation, in turn, was simply 'a higher human being,' as one writer put it.[13] The nation had been telescoped into the dynamic individual.

This was in line with the thinking of Schopenhauer and Nietzsche: the world did not exist except as one's own creation. The nation was a creation of one's imagination, a poetic truth, an ethical, not a social construct.

Will was linked with honor. Will was the means by which honor was enacted. Will was a creative, not a repressive force. It was synonymous with an aggressive, inspired implementation of the code of duty. To the criticism of Germany's enemies and of her own political left before the war that the country was an *Obrigkeitsstaat*, a hierarchical state, in which blind obedience was the only value, one writer responded, with a bow to Rousseau, that the weaker a person is, the more he commands; the stronger he is, the more he obeys.[14] Germany had become a nation of Titans. Gerhard Anschütz, a professor of law inclined to the political left who would play an important role in drafting a democratic constitution for Germany after the war, could write in 1915, 'The word *militarism*, which is being used throughout the world as a swear word against us, let it be for us a badge of honor.'[15] The young soldier Walter Harich echoed these sentiments when he wrote that the German comprehension of what a military order meant was exactly what gave Germany the upper hand in this struggle: 'We know full well that we are fighting for the German idea in the world, that we are defending German feeling against Asiatic barbarism and Latin indifference.'[16]

'Do more than your duty' was the regimental motto of the 24th Brandenburgers, and that captured the idea of personal initiative complementing communal dictate. 'Things go beyond mere strength here,' wrote Walter Harich from the front lines; 'here the impossible is made possible.'[17] What convention considers unlikely, the creative will of the individual soldier renders likely. The impossible is made possible by a spiritual transcendence of mere obligation, mere performance, mere duty – a duty that in Anglo-French culture is nothing other than a selfishly utilitarian function. From the start of the war the phrase *die heilige Pflicht*, sacred duty, was standard currency. On his way to the front by train in September 1914, reveling in the sunny and serene Eifel landscape around Trier and in the desolate gray of a rain-soaked Lorraine, the young law student Franz Blumenfeld was provoked to denounce war as something 'dreadful, unworthy of human beings, stupid, outmoded, and in every sense destructive,' but at the very same time he exulted in the idea of sacrifice and personal commitment: 'For the decisive issue is surely always one's readiness to sacrifice and not the object of the sacrifice.'[18] Here war as reality, as a product of history and the external relations between states and peoples, is denounced and lamented, but as idea, inspiration, and means, it is applauded.

While every belligerent state was inclined to use its past cultural accomplishments to buttress present resolve, in Germany that process went a step farther. History lost its integrity and independence as past achievement and became a handmaiden of the present, the voracious, all-consuming present. As soon as Fritz Klatt awoke on 28 August 1914, he was aware, he claimed, of the meaning of that day. It was Goethe's birthday. He immediately picked up Goethe's *West-östlicher Divan*, a collection of poetry; as he pointed out in a letter, the volume 'really and honestly lay right beside my pistol.'[19] As the association of Goethe with an instrument of death indicates, war as the apotheosis of German cultural endeavor was another central theme in the German concept of *Pflicht*. War is not only the supreme challenge for culture; the willingness to wage war to prove superiority should be the goal of any culture. War and true culture, as opposed to false culture, thus become synonymous.

In October 1914, young Hans Fleischer was near Blâmont on the edge of the Vosges Mountains. On a day in rest quarters he went for a stroll and came across a château, that of Baron de Turckheim, in a state of almost total devastation. A priceless library, paintings, furniture, and paneling had all been smashed. But in one corner of the ruin Fleischer found a grand piano, a Steinway to boot, untouched by the war's rage, and under the piano he found some scores. What did he choose? A piano version of Wagner's *Die Walküre*. He sat down, played, and sang – energetically, he wrote – the *Lied von Liebe und Lenz*. And then he left. 'I had been at home, made German music, and now once again I could return to the war.'[20] But what makes the scene so poignant is that the young man had not left the war. There it was, surrounding him. The piano, the music, the ruins, the war, all blended into one sensation. Hence it was so exquisite and memorable. Goethe, Wagner, and everyone else in the pantheon of German culture had become a war lord. When Romain Rolland, in an open letter to Gerhart Hauptmann, asked, 'Are you the grandsons of Goethe or Attila?' the answer was bound to be 'Both!'

Despite the initial confidence, the 'inevitable' victory on the battlefield did not come. It did not come in 1914 nor in 1915. The rhapsodic mood of the first days and weeks of the war could not possibly be maintained. The danger existed that cleavages between a spiritual essence, attained in August, and a debilitating reality, represented by material concerns both at the front and at home, would return. The reality of trench life as well as issues of wages, prices, and the organization of the war effort at home, all threatened the sublime spiritual achievement. By 1915 rifts had reappeared on the home front as more and more members of the Social Democratic Party began to raise questions about war aims and political reforms. The conduct of the war – the resort to gas and to unrestricted use of submarines – introduced more problems. Was this war really a defensive war forced on Germany, as the general staff and government claimed?

The response of the political and military leadership

to this threat to the nation's unity was to intensify the war effort, to match the initial spiritual totality of the war with a material totality. By 1916 the less aggressive, more pensive and conscience-ridden political leadership, symbolized by the chancellor, Bethmann Hollweg, was under attack and by mid 1917 it had been pushed aside. In July 1917 Germany became, to all intents and purposes, a totalitarian state under the control of her military. Even the kaiser had become little more than a puppet ruler, responding to the demands of the high command in the persons of Generals Hindenburg and Ludendorff. All the while, as military stalemate continued in the west, as casualties mounted into millions, as kitchens emptied not only of sons but even of pots and pans for making bullets, as food shortages became more and more serious, as hardship was piled on hardship, the myth of victory was further embellished by the reality, not just the idea, of sacrifice, self-denial, and fate. Death took on a creative function. Death became invigorating. War now held moral value of its own, without regard to foresight or hindsight. War became total.

As the prospect of real victory became more remote, given the decimation of German manhood, the effectiveness of the British economic blockade, the entrance of the United States into the war in April 1917, and the growth of domestic opposition to the war, the paeans to the myth of victory became more strident – and unrealistic. The lists of territorial war aims emanating from nationalist organizations and even from government circles began to lose all trace of reason and moderation. Were the Pan-Germans or the Fatherland Party, the latter newly created in September 1917, to have their way, a future Germany would stretch from the Urals to the Atlantic, from the North Sea to the Adriatic. As the German front in the west finally crumbled in the late summer and autumn of 1918, Walther Rathenau, the Prussian Jew with a curious mixture of romantic and democratic inclinations who had been the superbly efficient mastermind behind Germany's mobilization of raw materials, called for a *levé en masse*, a nationwide stand against the foreign invader, recalling the suicidal fight to the end of the Münster Anabaptists in the sixteenth century. The jubilation of August 1914 had turned to impassioned resolve in the middle years of the war, and then passed into hysteria. The path involved a continuation of the German journey inward.

And yet, despite all the evidence of disintegration, the effort of integration remained the defining characteristic of the German war of 1914–18, right up until the hour of Armistice, 11:00 a.m. on 11 November 1918. The overall orientation remained positive throughout. In the midst of death the emphasis was on regeneration, rebirth, life, 'experience.' 'I see death and call out to life' were the words of Alfons Akenbrand, who died at Souchez on 25 April 1915, aged twenty-one.[21] Only with an awareness of such metaphysics can one comprehend how the Germans continued to fight the war. They were outnumbered from the start. They fought on two fronts. They buttressed and subsidized the Austrian and Turkish efforts. Their mobilization of men and matériel was extraordinary. They managed to knock Russia out of the war. They staved off an Allied assault that, after April 1917, included American economic and, in 1918, military might. In the summer of 1918 they came close, once again, to victory.

An act of faith not dissimilar in some respects to that which fueled the Anglo-French effort sustained the Germans. In the end, however, the differences between faiths were more striking than the similarities. The Anglo-French faith had a rational foundation; the German faith was built on idealism and romanticism. The Anglo-French faith was social; the German, metaphysical. The German effort had been prepared by many of the same instruments of socialization as the

Anglo-French – religion, education, military service, and other forms of state involvement in the private sphere. But the nature of German industrialization – its lateness, relative speed, and highly concentrated form – meant that many of the social norms and values accompanying commercial and industrial enterprise had not penetrated very far into the German social being and were, in fact, looked on with suspicion. German capitalism was, to borrow a later historian's adjective, 'devalued.'[22] In Britain, John Stuart Mill had seen in the 'division of employments – the accomplishment of the combined labour of several, of tasks which could not be achieved by any number of persons singly . . . the great school of cooperation.'[23] That 'school of cooperation' had come late to Germany. The German achievement of spiritual unity, in 1914 and throughout the war – an achievement supported by most of the socialists for most of the war – was founded, as a result, more on private virtues than public values, on an effort of imagination rather than social reality. After he had been at the front for over a year, first in France and then against the Serbs, Gerhart Pastors had not lost an iota of his passionate commitment. From the banks of the Save River he wrote home in October 1915 of his fervent desire to get at the Serbs: 'We have this physical urge to get at the Serbs face to face and to put our fists in their faces. If the order to move our position forward comes tonight, we'll feel as if we're going to heaven.' Battle he still identified with heaven, with salvation, with a state of transcendence. In 1916, in an edition of student war letters that he prepared for publication, Philipp Witkop chose this brutal-idealistic passage, which associated fists smashing into faces with heaven, to end his volume.[24]

Britain quickly became Germany's principal enemy. She was the nation of commerce and dissimulation, of *Händler* rather than *Helden*, of bourgeois businessmen rather than heroes. Because, like a businessman out for

273

personal gain, she had not placed all her cards on the table from the start in the July crisis, because she had declared neither her neutrality nor her support of France at the outset, she was accused of being responsible for the war. She was guilty, the argument implied, of inaction when she should have acted. Here was reasoning worthy of the modern aesthetic. The victim, not the murderer, is guilty. Inaction and contemplation are by definition impure, suggesting deviousness, calculation, and dishonesty. Action is by contrast liberating, action is life, and he who acts therefore cannot be blamed. With Nietzschean heroics the Sermon on the Mount is negated. 'Not who is guilty but what is guilty, that must be established,' insisted Magnus Hirschfeld. Britain was the foremost representative of a life-denying order that Germany had to break out of – a world that stifled true enjoyment, inspiration, and spirit.[25]

Many German professors who had had ties to England before the war took the unexpected British involvement as a personal slight and interpreted it as a damning comment on western culture as a whole. The theologian Adolf von Harnack never got over the blow.[26] Belgium, so he and others concluded bitterly, was used by Britain simply as a pretext to strike at Germany. Britain, this *Krämer-Nation*, this 'nation of shopkeepers,' was simply out to destroy her economic rival. How else could one possibly explain her involvement? In a 'poem' evoking the imagined death of Edward Grey, the British foreign minister, and his terrible fate before the judgement seat, Friedrich Jacobsen would decry England's war 'for booty and filthy lucre.'[27] On New Year's Eve of 1914, the officers and first battalion of the 15th Bavarian Infantry Regiment were gathered in regimental headquarters, and as the clock struck midnight, although they were facing the French near Dompierre, they greeted the new year with the shout *Gott strafe England.**[28]

*May God punish England.

274

Since the German rationale for the war was from the outset less specific than that of the French and British, the German interpretation of the war's continuation was correspondingly cloaked in mystical and romantic notions. A common theme was that the war represented ultimate experience and that, despite the horror and apparent waste, by total surrender to the energy of the war, by fusion of the German essence with the reality of war, a higher, more sublime form of national existence would ensue. Hence the war was both education and revelation. In the words of the soldier Ernst Wurche,

> If the meaning and goal of human life is to get beyond the mere form of existence, then we've achieved a lot already in life, and regardless of our fate today or tomorrow, we know more than hundred-year-olds and philosophers. No-one has seen more masks drop, more vileness, cowardice, weakness, selfishness, conceit, no-one has seen more virtue and silent nobility of spirit than we. We have little more to ask of life: it has revealed more to us than others, and beyond that there is no human claim – we shall wait patiently to see what it demands of us. If it demands everything, it has after all given everything, and so a balance is struck.[29]

If at its start the war was synonymous for many Germans with beauty, its ever-increasing fury was regarded by many as merely an intensification of its aesthetic meaning. In other words, as its destruction mounted, the war continued to be spiritualized, or internalized, proportionately. After several weeks of rain, mud, artillery bombardments, and French attacks, the 'good' side of the war had become even clearer to Gerhart Pastors:

> You become strong. This life sweeps away violently all weakness and sentimentality. You are put in chains, robbed of self-determination, practiced in suffering, practiced in self-restraint and self-discipline. But first

and foremost: you turn inward. The only way you can tolerate this existence, these horrors, this murder, is if your spirit is planted in higher spheres. You are *forced* into self-determination, you *have* to come to terms with death. You reach, to find a counterweight for the ghastly reality, for that which is most noble and highest.[30]

The word *self* is the motif that runs through this passage. As the external violence mounted, a man searched with greater urgency for peace in his self, in his soul.

As the myth of inevitable victory fragmented, the fragments became new, even larger, even brighter, myths. In a prolific spasm, illusion gave birth to a host of illusions. Horror was turned into spiritual fulfillment. War became peace. Death, life. Annihilation, freedom. Machine, poetry. Amorality, truth. Over eighteen thousand church bells and innumerable organ pipes were donated to the war effort, to be melted down and used for arms and ammunition.[31] As the assault on the physical and social fixities of the nineteenth-century bourgeois world was intensified, the resulting sensation was one of growing liberation from constraint, frontiers, forms. The promotion of this liberation continued to be the most important component of *Pflicht*. This association of death with life was a re-enactment, writ large, of the sacrificial sequence of *Le Sacre du printemps*.

CONGREGATION

To cite the letters of idealistic students and other intellectuals is to invite the complaint that a minority of the population – the sector most engaged in the war intellectually – is being offered as representative of the nation as a whole. What about German working-class men? Farm laborers? What about the majority of the fighting men?

Sources for their views are, of course, less readily

available. These men rarely kept diaries, and no-one seems to have been interested, or at any rate successful, in collecting or assembling their letters after the war. The main German military archives were, moreover, destroyed by Allied bombing in the Second World War, and the records of postal censorship seem to have disappeared as well. Thus, there is only scattered and usually indirect evidence for the attitudes of non-intellectuals toward the war.

The relatively low incidence of military insubordination is, however, one piece of evidence that suggests, in a general way, that morale held and that working-class and peasant soldiers functioned in the context of the values described above. The following table enumerates cases of insubordination and misdemeanors, which were investigated but not necessarily tried by military courts, in the 4th Bavarian Infantry Division. The division spent most of the war on the Western Front. The misdeeds and offenses included absence without permission, desertion, cowardice, espionage, intentional injury to self, suicide, misuse of weapons, disobedience, abuse of

NUMBER OF INVESTIGATIONS[1]

	1914	1915	1916	1917	1918
January		63	12	47	87
February		26	18	41	59
March		33	23	46	70
April		40	27	42	47
May		20	22	54	80
June		24	14	52	112
July		23	20	82	118
August	17	32	32	48	103
September	12	25	72	77	115
October	29	27	80	47	136
November	20	46	59	86	91
December	65	31	37	153	47

authority, property damage, treason, acts against the postal law, criminal acts, and a variety of other misdemeanors.

The months that stand out are December 1914 and January 1915; September through November 1916; July, September, November, and December 1917; and with the exception of April, all of 1918. The first period coincides with the fraternization of 1914; the second with the failure of the Verdun offensive and the toll taken by the battle of the Somme; and the third and fourth reflect the general debilitation and test of morale as prospects for victory receded. That April 1918 saw a drop in the figures is to be explained by the initial successes of the Lundendorff offensive that spring. One sees that the figures increased as the war dragged on, but what should be emphasized is that the figures for insurbordination never became excessive.

In the German army, as in all armies, the usual grousing was heard, about provisions, food, equipment, strategy, and the creature comforts accorded to officers. In August 1917, for instance, an artillery battery complained, in a report that was to reach the supreme command, 'that the staff officers possess better horses for recreational riding than the troops for fighting.' The divisional command was incensed at this 'unmilitary' remark and issued instructions that such comments be avoided in future.[2] Orders were also distributed that summer that soldiers who had legitimate complaints about conditions and treatment were to make these complaints through proper channels and not merely grumble.[3] The French and British military archives are full of this kind of evidence as well; it suggests minor problems with morale – perfectly understandable, given the nature of this war – but hardly a major erosion of purpose.

That the general approach to the war described above was not just the property of intellectuals or adventurers – men like Ernst Jünger, who before the

278

war had run away from home and joined the French Foreign Legion, or Ernst Wurche or Walter Flex – is indicated further by a popular novel of Reinhold Eichacker's that went into its second printing in 1916. *Briefe an das Leben: Von der Seele des Schützengrabens und von den Schützengräben der Seele** is an unbearably treacly tale of a soldier who goes off to the war deeply in love with the young woman he had married twelve months earlier. After a year in the trenches he comes home unexpectedly to find his wife in the arms of another man. Without so much as a word, he turns on his heel and rushes back to the front, only to learn shortly that his wife has taken her own life. After lengthy rumination on the meaning of life and war he finds his peace with her and also with the prospect of death. His final consolation is that he will be reunited with her in eternity. In this story, as in so much of the German war effort, the meaning of life is to be found only in death.

Needless to say, German soldiers, like those of other nations, suffered from fatigue, depression, and trauma. They too found themselves fighting the war on instinct and inner resources, but for the German those inner resources had a predominantly metaphysical form, in contrast to the social and historical values that motivated the average Englishman and Frenchman. The war was a struggle of will and energy rather than material means; it was to perpetuate the 'spirit of 1914,' to realize *eine grosse Idee*, a grand ideal.

At the end came what appeared to be, for many, an absolute void – defeat. Rudolf Binding knew, by July 1918, that 'we are finished. My thoughts oppress me. How are we to recover ourselves? *Kultur*, as it will be known after the war, will be of no use; mankind itself will probably be of still less use.'[4] An opponent, David Ghilchik, aware in October that the end was approaching

---

**Letters to Life: From the Soul of the Trenches and the Trenches of the Soul.*

for the Germans, remarked, 'I would not be a German now for anything.'[5]

Yet even the void was somehow capable, as we shall see, of manipulation and permutation. One could indeed, as it turned out, revel spiritually in the void. From defeat would come the idea of 'the stab in the back,' the notion that Germany had not been defeated at the front in honorable combat with the foe but had been laid low by calumny abroad and treachery at home. The nation most recently enraptured with newness, with experiment and a rejection of old forms, would project, in a supreme feat of mental acrobatics, her own revolt on to her perceived foes, without and within. The traitor would become the betrayed, the rebel would become the victim, the defeated would become the conqueror, as in Dada anti-art would become art.

Back in October 1914, on the evening of the day Antwerp fell to the Germans, a grand dinner party was held at the Esplanade in Berlin. Decorum dictated that dress at society functions should remain modest, in keeping with the gravity of the hour. Women would avoid wearing, for instance, décolletée dresses. But on this evening one lady arrived with an extremely transparent and low-cut dress, appropriate for a gala ball at the height of the social season.

'You are very smart tonight, madame,' someone remarked.

'Yes,' was the reply. 'I put this on to celebrate the fall of Antwerp; but wait until you see the dress I am keeping for the day when England is beaten!'[6]

We have no record of what the lady in question wore in defeat, but if the way Josephine Baker was received in Berlin at the end of the war gives any clue, then the victory costume hinted at here – the emperor's clothes – would have been just as appropriate in defeat.

Are these valid generalizations? Exceptions to them are not difficult to find. General disaffection and opposition to the war did mount in Germany as the struggle progressed. In 1916 food riots broke out in parts of the country. In April of that year Catholic religious authorities in Bavaria were told by their bishop that countering disaffection with the war was their most important duty.[7] Over the next two years, especially during the bitter winters, there was to be no shortage of disaffection.

The initial political home of the skeptics was in a minority wing of the SPD. In April 1917, however, the Independent Social Democratic Party (USPD) was founded on opposition to the war. It housed both political moderates like the prewar revisionist leader Eduard Bernstein and radicals like Rosa Luxemburg and Karl Liebknecht. In January 1918 a wave of strikes swept over the munitions industries, led by radical shop stewards opposed to the war and bent on extensive social and political reform. The recent success of the Bolsheviks in Russia was greatly admired in these quarters. At the front some signs of weariness and frustration surfaced in late 1917 and in 1918 as pacifist tracts reached certain sectors and as cases of insubordination increased. But the number of people involved in any of these activities was small.[8] Most of the strikes were instigated by economic rather than political reasons, above all by the terrible food shortages. The army remained loyal.

Among moderate elements at home, the war, by 1917 at the latest, had become an existential riddle. By then for Max Weber it had 'exhausted itself spiritually.' For Gustav Radbruch, a professor of legal philosophy, it had taken on the appearance, by contrast, of 'something ghostlike,' a blind and overwhelming monstrosity. Both victory and defeat would be evils, with the former only slightly the lesser of the two. Only in religion, he felt, was a kind of peace to be found in the midst of this horrendous crisis.[9] By 1917, for Hans Delbrück, Ernst Troeltsch, Adolf von Harnack, and Friedrich Meinecke, the war threatened to destroy all traces of European

281

culture. The future, whose promise had been so dazzling in August 1914, now seemed to offer only darkness, a blackness without compare. In a letter to his wife in February 1918, after the strikes and disturbances of the previous month, Delbrück admitted that he was terrified by the future. He wondered if after all the *sadness* some terrible *tragedy* might still be in store for Germany. 'If the whole thing is not at an end soon, it's going to become gruesome.'[10]

And yet, despite all these premonitions and doubts, morale – and resolve to continue – held, even during the retreat in the autumn of 1918. Danger of a complete breakdown never existed, certainly not among the soldiers. When a breakdown did come, it was modest in scale and it came in the navy, which had sat in port for most of the war. In 1917 a mutiny of sorts had occurred in Wilhelmshaven among sailors protesting their treatment, dreadful rations, lack of leave, and close quarters. In the last days of October and in early November 1918, sailors mutinied in the ports of Kiel and Wilhelmshaven, and the disturbances then spread rapidly through Germany as news of the impending Armistice broke. The army at the front, however, remained loyal to the end. Only behind the lines, in Germany, did relatively small numbers of soldiers join in the so-called revolution of 1918.

Disillusionment with and alienation from the national effort were thus never rampant in Germany during the war. Where they existed, they were more prevalent among the civilian population than the fighting men. The language and literature of disillusionment would be on the whole a postwar phenomenon – everywhere.

VII

Journey to the Interior

Though we observe the Higher Law
And though we have our quarrel just,
Were I permitted to withdraw
You wouldn't see my arse for dust.

A soldier's verse

One deserts the realm of the here and now to transfer one's
activity into the realm of the yonder where total affirmation is
possible. Abstraction.

PAUL KLEE

*Schiller, poète moyen, n'offre point d'intérêt pour un
étranger. Même en paix, la bonne règle déconseille
d'importer ce qu'on possède. Nous avons Casimir Delavigne,
Ponsard, de Bornier. Que ferions-nous de Schiller?**

JOSÉPHIN PÉLADAN
1917

WAR AS ART

From its start, the war was a stimulus to the imagination. Probably no other four years in history have produced as much testimony on public events. Artists, poets, writers, clergymen, historians, philosophers, among others, all participated fully in the human drama being enacted.

---

*Schiller, a mediocre poet, offers nothing of interest to the foreigner. Even in peacetime the rule of thumb is to avoid importing what one already has. We have Casimir Delavigne, Ponsard, de Bornier. Why do we need Schiller?

Most intellectuals, notwithstanding proud declamations of independence and rational decision making, responded to ingrained national loyalties and conducted themselves accordingly. If they were not able to enlist because of age or health, they joined the effort in other ways, as propagandists, war artists, ambulance drivers, or orderlies. But beyond the loyalty to king and country, which with few exceptions was foremost, the war exerted a singular fascination by its very monumentality and, as it progressed, its staggering ineffability. Even the introvert Marcel Proust, who composed his great *roman fleuve*, *À la recherche du temps perdu*, at night in the cloistered embrace of a cork-lined room, was spellbound by the spectacle: 'As people used to live in God, I live in the war.'[1] Edmund Gosse observed Henry James closely during the war. James apparently used to look out across the English Channel toward the faint sound of artillery. 'The anguish of his execration,' wrote Gosse,

> became almost the howl of some animal, of a lion of the forest with the arrow in his flank, when the Germans wrecked Rheims cathedral. He gazed and gazed over the sea southeast and fancied that he saw the flicker of the flames. He ate and drank, he talked and walked and thought, he slept and waked and lived and breathed only the War. His friends grew anxious, the tension was beyond what his natural powers, transfigured as they were, would be expected to endure.[2]

Even those who, like D.H. Lawrence, tried to keep a critical distance from events soon found themselves, owing to the paranoia in society, which cast suspicion on anyone who remained aloof, embroiled in the crisis.

Most radical imaginations, whether of a political or aesthetic bent, were engrossed from the outset. The war offered extremes of emotion and effort – Dorgelès called the trenches 'this huge confessional'[3] – as well as sights, sounds, and images that bore no relation to the staid Edwardian or even the febrile Wilhelmian world. The war thus acted as a veritable exhortation to the revolutionary renewal for which the prewar avant-garde had striven. 'The European war signifies a violent historical crisis, the beginning of a new epoch,' insisted Lenin in late 1914.[4] For political radicals on the left, the tension between what was viewed as an outdated social order and the war's irrepressible dynamic was – despite the pity, sadness, and horror that accompanied this tension – propitious: the war would issue in revolution. For many radicals in the arts the tension was positively delicious. Jacques-Émile Blanche and his Parisian coterie of friends who had promoted the Ballets russes were thrilled by the sight of Zeppelins over the French capital. They imagined whales or sharks in the sky or 'the monster Fafner, waddling along with his giant body of aluminium and gutta-percha, darting electric rays from his beacon eyes over the sleeping Ile de la Cité.' Misia Sert likened the war to a Berlin Secessionist poster. 'These props of terror belong in the theatre,' commented Blanche.[5] The inclination here was to regard the war as a form of art, as a superior representation of life: only when mankind recognized that salvation lay in aesthetic values, in the symbolism of life and death, and not in sterile social norms, would the horror and sadness have meaning and be overcome. As evocation, as an instrument of change, the war had a positive purpose – that was the judgement of many artists, at least early on.

The most radical artistic response to the war came from a group of people who made a complete break with traditional loyalties and gathered in neutral Zürich in 1915 to found there the Dada idea – if one can speak of this nihilistic manifestation as an idea. The cohort had an international flavor but its core was German. Among the protagonists were Hugo Ball, Richard Huelsenbeck, Hans Richter, Hans Arp, and the Rumanian Tristan

Tzara. In histrionic and epigrammatic barbs against the orgy of self-destruction Europe was involved in, they denied all meaning, even their own. The only sense was nonsense, the only art anti-art. *Bevor Dada da war, war Dada da* – before Dada was there was Dada there. Richard Huelsenbeck encouraged the 'aimless of the world' to unite.[6]

Despite the purported anguish and rage, Dada seemed to revel in the war: 'The war is our brothel' wrote Hugo Ball.[7] Dada's own orgy of denial was a spiritual counterpart to the war itself. In rejecting cause and effect, past and future, and all meaning except the roll of the dice, Dada frolicked in a narcissism that had a German tone and, though vociferously denying meaning, it nonetheless looked on the war as the essence of meaning. Dada's nihilistic games were war games of the mind.

The confusion and ambiguity inherent in finding destruction evocative some artists and intellectuals did find intolerable, and their creative impulse was silenced. After a poetic outburst celebrating the advent of the war, Rilke was reduced, by the horror, to silent consternation at the inability of the European intelligentsia to stop the slaughter. Henry James produced nothing of note in the last years before his death. Rudyard Kipling, who lost his son to the war, was to write little other than a regimental history of the Irish Guards, to which his son had belonged. Of the dilemma facing the artist, John Galsworthy said in 1915, 'With the work of his hands, the words of his lips, his thoughts and the feelings of his heart, [the artist] identifies himself with this war drama, yet in the very depths of him he recoils.'[8]

As the war's meaning began to be enveloped in a fog of existential questioning, the integrity of the 'real' world, the visible and ordered world, was undermined. As the war called into question the rational connections of the prewar world – the nexus, that is, of cause and effect – the meaning of civilization as tangible achievement was assaulted, as was the nineteenth-century view that all history represented progress. And as the external world collapsed in ruins, the only redoubt of integrity became the individual personality. David Jones looked on the Somme offensive as the last great action of the old world. Until then, the old customs and attitudes still held. What came after, he called 'the Break': 'The whole of the past, as far as I can make out, is down the drain.'[9] Similarly, Joyce's Stephen Dedalus was provoked to remark, in words reminiscent of Schopenhauer, that 'history is a nightmare from which I am trying to awake.'[10] As the past went down the drain, the I became all-important.

While most soldiers retained their sense of duty, some began to express themselves about the other aspect of their dichotomous predicament – their feeling of alienation, marginality, and, at the same time, novelty; that is, the idea that the world was in the throes of destruction, which now seemed irreversible, but was also in the process of renewal, which seemed inevitable. In this latter process lay a reality of astounding implications: the soldier represented a creative force. As an agent of both destruction and regeneration, of death and rebirth, the soldier inclined to see himself as a 'frontier' personality, as a paladin of change and new life. He was a traveler who had journeyed, on order, to the limits of existence, and there on the periphery he 'lived' in a unique way, on the edge of no man's land, on the margin of normal categories.

Yet he was also called upon to cross no man's land. That was in fact his supreme calling. That was the essence of victory. As the purpose of the war became more abstract, less amenable to conventional imagery, the meaning of victory, the consequences, that is, of successfully crossing the murderous tract separating the enemies became correspondingly abstract. For sustenance the soldier was thrown upon his own imagination. The war became increasingly a matter of individual interpretative power.

Contrary to the conclusions of observers behind the lines, psychologists and journalists alike, that the war experience had not changed the essential character of their respective nations, the front-line soldier who had experienced battle was convinced that he had changed in a very fundamental, if indescribable, way. After his first tour of the trenches in June 1916 Peter McGregor reported to his wife:

> I am all right – just the same as ever – but no – that can never be. The four days we were in the trenches has turned me upside down. No man can experience such things and come out the same.'[11]

Rudolf Fischer, on the other side, had a similar comment: 'No-one comes out of this war the same.'[12] And Marc Boasson, after taking part in attacks in Artois in September 1915 and at Verdun in June 1916, admitted in a letter home:

> I've changed terribly. I didn't want to tell you about the frightful weariness that the war has produced in me, but you force me to. I feel crushed, diminished.[13]

Diminished in what sense? As a social and moral being, he pointed out in later letters. He was less concerned about the possibility of mutiny and revolution, by himself and his fellows – that would at least be an expression of energy, life, and social conscience – than about the resignation and lassitude, 'this inexhaustible docility.' 'It seems to me,' he wrote, 'that we are passing through a very serious moral crisis, not openly apparent, without cries, without visible manifestations, but grave because of its depth.'[14] Boasson was hinting at a widespread retreat, away from an external world, which on the surface was left intact, inward into a private world of spirit.

Traditional authority had abandoned the soldier to his own fate. Leadership, in its conventional sense, had failed. Moreover, the home front did not understand the nature of the soldier's *via dolorosa*. The only social reality that could support the soldier was 'the comradeship of the trenches.' In this situation, as a young German volunteer remarked, one became an instinctive socialist. Yet the soldier's 'socialism' lacked any kind of ideological precision or practicality. It was largely sentimental and negative, yet it was surprisingly akin to the 'socialism' of the artistic avant-garde. This socialism was of the 'man is good' variety, accompanied by a rejection of form and organization and involving a projection of self – humble, anxious, and meek – in the midst of devastation, into a credo. The impulse was essentially self-pitying and at the same time anarchical. Man was victim but also rebellious survivor. Bureaucrats, politicians, brass hats, journalists, and war profiteers – those on the outside who fed like jackals on the carnage and misery – were despised. They were the true enemy, scavengers feeding and fattening themselves on death and destruction.

Sandor Ferenczi, who treated psychoneurotic soldiers in Budapest during the war, confirmed that soldiers confronted by overwhelming material force and personal helplessness withdrew into themselves. 'Libido withdraws from the object into the ego, enhancing self-love and reducing object love to the point of indifference.'[15] Many of his patients admitted sexual impotence or greatly reduced sexual interest.

The soldier became then not just the harbinger but the very agent of the modern aesthetic, the progenitor of destruction but also the embodiment of the future. Any hope for that future resided exclusively in the individual imagination. 'I have decided,' wrote Georges Bernanos in September 1915, 'that my epitaph will consist only of these two lines. Here lies a man who fought and died for his personal satisfaction and to enrage those who did not fight and die!'[16]

For a traditionalist like Louis Mairet, the destruction of moral perspective, the internalization of the external world, the disappearance of rationalism as a social and cultural solder, meant that art, too, was dead. As his unit was being relieved in March 1917, the ritual that normally accompanied such a changeover was still intact. 'Departure. Music, sound of brass, sparkle of bayonets. The flag, somber silhouette, fabric of *gloire*.' The countryside, Mairet noted, had the color of a wash drawing. Desperately he looked for a positive meaning to the whole, the ritual and the natural environment. In the collective interpretation of such symbols, in a form accessible to all, resided the traditional purpose of art, art as knowledge and not just energy. But for his fellow soldiers all interest in an overriding meaning had disappeared. They were immersed in themselves, exclusively: '. . . Each one sees in everything but a development of his own personal preoccupations.' A hill, striking because of its abrupt contours, leads an officer to remark, 'That's an impregnable position.' Farther on, a large plain opens up: 'That would make a good airfield.' An area of level grass provokes an excited remark: 'What a great football pitch!' And Mairet concludes sadly, 'Poetry is dead.'[17] What he meant, of course, was that traditional poetry was dead.

The horror the soldier encountered had, after a time, little interpretative potential except in very personal terms. Unlike Mairet, some saw in this situation not the death of art but the birth of a new aesthetic. For Robert Graves the sight of human brains spattered on a comrade's cap became 'a poetical figment.'[18] The sound of a morning artillery barrage made Wyn Griffith think of music, not a music of conventional melodies and harmonies, but a new music, the antithesis of all customary composition.[19] Jacques-Émile Blanche claimed that air raids on Paris made him think specifically of Stravinsky's *Le Sacre*.[20] Graves, Griffith, and Blanche were making similar associations. They connected the sights and sounds of war with art. Art became, in fact, the only available correlative of this war; naturally not an art following previous rules, but an art in which the rules of composition were abandoned, in which provocation became the goal, and in which art became an event, an experience. As the war lost external meaning, it became above all an experience. In the process, life and art moved together.

Some soldiers began to find, as Percy Jones noted on seeing Ypres in late 1915, 'something horribly fascinating about such appalling devastation.' Photographs, he said, could not do justice to the reality. Two months later he was still spellbound by this vision of 'the end of the world': 'The fascination of Ypres grows upon me, and I am still searching for a house that has not had a direct hit from a shell.'[21] J.W.Gamble, who was there at the same time, had an almost identical response.

> On Saturday . . . I took advantage of the temporary calm, and had another look around Ypres. It is really a wonderful sight – weird, grotesque, and desolate of course – but most interesting. I expect the place will be flooded with sight-seers and tourists after the war, and they will be amazed by what they see. The ancient ruins of Pompeii and such places will be simply out of it.[22]

Ypres, despite its contemporaneity, had surpassed Pompeii, in Gamble's mind, as a monument of ruined civilization. Its scale of symbolism was incomparable. And yet in both Jones and Gamble there is an obvious exhilaration in being witness to such colossal destruction. When Garfield Powell wrote in in his diary on 28 August 1916, 'We have now moved to the land of our dreams, Ypres,' the tone was intentionally sardonic but the choice of cliché was most telling.[23] For David Jones, too, the 'wasteland' of the trenches became 'a place of enchantment.'[24] And Canon F.G. Scott, a Canadian, when he came across the corpse of a young boy covered with a coating of yellow mud, immediately thought of 'a statue made of bronze. He had a beautiful face, with finely shaped head covered with close, curling hair, and looked more like some work of art than a human being.'[25]

Harry Crosby, from Boston, one of the large number of young Americans who volunteered for ambulance service in France, found in the furnace of Verdun in 1917 an escape, paradoxically, from death. He shuddered when he thought about

> the horrors of Boston and particularly of Boston virgins who are brought up among sexless surroundings, who wear canvas drawers and flat-heeled shoes and tortoise-shelled glasses and who, once they are married, bear a child punctually every nine months for five or six years and then retire to end their days at the Chilton Club. Christ, what a narrow escape.

Verdun had 'Death's hand . . . written over it all.' But for that very reason he found it 'acts as a magnet.'[26] The war, despite its destruction or, indeed, owing to its pervasive horror, had become an evocative force, a stimulus not to social creativity but to personal imagination and inwardness, an avenue to a new and vital realm of activity.

ART AS FORM

Nonetheless, the inwardness, if it was not silence, literal and figurative, produced a quandary. How was one to assemble and order the experience of the war, even for oneself alone? Traditional modes of expression – words, pictures, even music – were clearly inadequate in this situation.

'Confronted by the spectacle of a scientific struggle in

which Progress is used to return to Barbarism, and by the spectacle of a civilization turning against itself to destroy itself, reason cannot cope,' wrote Louis Mairet.[1] For the artist Paul Nash the normal tools of his craft were insufficient: 'No pen or drawing can convey this country,' he remarked to his wife about the landscape of Flanders.[2] The rejection of traditional form in art seemed to be the only honest response. Nash and many of the other official British war artists, most of whom had had traditional training and came from conventional backgrounds and from a prewar cultural environment that was generally hostile to artistic innovation, turned increasingly to experimental modes of composition. They met with some opposition but mostly acclaim.

Even in official circles, there was a reluctant recognition by 1917 that the war had ushered in a new era, one that called for a new sensibility. C.R.W. Nevinson was one of a small coterie of British artists who had rebelled before the war against a traditional academic approach to composition; he had gone off to Paris to associate with cubists and futurists and to share a studio there with Modigliani. 'Heavy, powerful motor-cars rushing through the crowded streets of our cities,' he had written in 1913,

> dancers reflected in the fairy ambience of light and colour, aeroplanes flying above the heads of an excited throng . . . These sources of emotion satisfy our sense of the lyric and dramatic universe, better than two pears and an apple.[3]

When war came, Nevinson, plagued by ill health, which precluded his enlisting, but 'pursued,' as he put it, 'by the urge to do something, to be "in" the war,' joined first the Red Cross, to serve at Dunkirk, and then the Royal Army Medical Corps. Rheumatic fever, however, invalided him out of the army in January 1916. Then in June 1917, despite his radical artistic past, he was hired as

293

an 'official artist of the British army.' Initially he felt compelled to restrain his natural creative instincts. But his employers in the Department of Information noticed that his work suffered as a result. After seeing Nevinson's latest paintings, T. Derrick, an official at Wellington House, where the British propaganda effort was coordinated, noted in October 1917, in a memorandum to Charles Masterman, in charge of the literature and art section of the department:

> I will tell him that I have reason to believe that his own unrestrained savage self can appear in subsequent work, without giving offence in official quarters. I believe that this is so. And that his restrained, decorous, official self is valued rather less highly; instead of – as I think he fancied – more highly.[4]

Masterman agreed and gave Nevinson free rein. Nevinson did subsequently run into trouble with General Headquarters and the War Office, particularly with his painting *The Paths of Glory*, which was thought to endanger morale by depicting dead men at the front and by having so bitterly ironical a title, and *A Group of Soldiers*, which was considered 'too ugly' and, according to the War Office, offered the Germans possible 'evidence of British degeneration.' But the rest of his pictures – although horror, not heroism, was the keynote – met with approval and even enthusiasm. In January 1918 the National War Museum, forerunner of the Imperial War Museum, even purchased *The Paths of Glory* for £50 and *A Group of Soldiers* for £100, recognizing their significance as documents of the war. In March 1918, Lord Beaverbrook, the newspaper magnate and newly appointed minister of information, formally opened an exhibition of Nevinson's works at the Leicester Galleries on Leicester Square, even though Nevinson insisted on including the following vitriolic passage in his foreword to the catalogue:

I have no illusions about the public, for, owing chiefly to our Press, our loathsome tradition-loving Public Schools and our antiquity-stinking Universities, the average Englishman is not merely suspicious of the new in all intellectual and artistic experiment, but he is mentally trained to be so unsportsmanlike as to try and kill every new endeavour in embryo, especially if it shows signs of developing a future health and strength.[5]

All but four of the paintings were sold. In 1919 the *Daily Express*, Beaverbrook's organ, would approvingly refer to Nevinson as 'the famous futurist artist.'[6]

In general, then, a distinct flexibility was shown by the authorities in artistic matters. This did not escape the critics. One critic congratulated those in control of official art for

possessing the salutary eclecticism to choose their interpreters of the war not alone from the approved precincts of the Royal Academy Schools and Burlington House, but also from the Slade and the so-called rebel art centres of Camden Town where freedom alike of idea and expression flourish unabashed.[7]

British sensibility as a whole had traveled a long way since the postimpressionist exhibition at the Grafton Street Galleries in 1911.

A mounting suspicion among intellectuals toward language, toward the implications of the 'great rolling phrases,' was another response to the war. Honor, Glory, Patriotism, Sacrifice, began to lose their capital letters. E.E. Cummings, who served in an American ambulance unit with the French, retreated, in the wake of his war experience, from capitals not only in his poetry but in his own name: he became e.e. cummings. 'There are grand words that don't sound the same today as in 1914,' exclaimed Roland Dorgelès after the war.[8]

Traditional language and vocabulary were grossly inadequate, it seemed, to describe the trench experience. Words like *courage*, let alone *glory* and *heroism*, with their classical and romantic connotations, simply had no place in any accounts of what made soldiers stay and function in the trenches. Even basic descriptive nouns, like *attack*, *counterattack*, *sortie*, *wound*, and *shelling*, had lost all power to capture reality. In October 1916 John Masefield illustrated the problem when, on a visit to the Somme, he sent home some of his impressions of the front. 'To say that the ground is "ploughed up" with shells is to talk like a child.' And about the mud – 'to call it mud would be misleading.'

> It was not like any mud I've ever seen. It was a kind of stagnant river, too thick to flow, yet too wet to stand, and it had a kind of glisten and shine on it like reddish cheese, but it was not solid at all and you left no tracks in it, they all closed over, and you went in over your boots at every step and sometimes up to your calves. Down below it there was a solid footing, and as you went slopping along the army went slopping along by your side, and splashed you from head to foot.[9]

Thus:

> . . . Words strain,
> Crack and sometimes break, under the burden,
> Under the tension, slip, slide, perish,
> Decay with imprecision, will not stay in place,
> Will not stay still.

So T.S. Eliot would write later.[10] It was as if words had become like the mud on the Somme.

Of course the home front remained mired in euphemisms, and most soldiers too continued to talk about having 'a rough time of it,' having 'a near go,' being involved in 'a show' that was 'ripping fun' and 'jolly good sport.' Dick Stokes was at Vimy Ridge for its capture in April 1917: 'It's a great war . . . It was a grand show and very successful.' In November he was in the Ypres salient when he heard about the attack at Cambrai: 'I wish they'd send us down there, it sounds great fun.' By October 1918 his language had not changed: 'Just back after a jolly and very exciting week strafing bosches. Absolutely safe and sound but covered in bug bites.'[11] Of course, Stokes, like most of his fellows, never realized that his accounts, which associated 'strafing bosches' and 'bug bites,' were positively absurd.

J.W. Gamble, in a similar manner, described a scene after a gas attack near Ypres in December 1915 which belongs in a play by Pirandello or Ionesco.

> I had just been bandaging up a couple of wounded when one of them called my attention to a couple of big rats which were staggering about on their hind-legs as if drunk. It really was one of the funniest sights imaginable. One usually only gets glimpses of rats as they scuttle rapidly by (during the day), but these two were right out in the open, and their antics were too quaint. They were half-gassed of course, but strangely enough it was one of the things I remembered best after the show was over.[12]

Gamble does not seem to have been aware of the incongruity of the scene when he wrote these lines. Shortly before he was killed, in May 1916, he did, however, write a brief essay on the contrast between the peace and power of nature and the storm and ineffectiveness of war. An intelligent man, as his correspondence indicates, his sensibility clearly became sharper as the war, and his own experience of it, deepened. He, too, before he died, had become a traveler on the journey inward. Other sensitive spirits began to turn away

297

from vague generalities of expression, from euphemism, some even from adjectives, and to look for clear images and powerful understatement. Language, then, was gradually robbed of its social meaning and became a highly personal and poetic instrument. The extreme example of the metamorphosis was again the phonetic and onomatopoeic 'non-sense' concocted by Dada. In the process, irony, which is one expression of sensibility at odds with its surroundings, became for many the rhetorical mode and mood.

In a war in which men buried themselves so as to live, in which soldiers went fishing with bombs, in which Senegalese troops at first ate the grease sent to lubricate trucks, in which a dead carrier pigeon was decorated with the Légion d'honneur, in which the British commander in chief declared, on 30 June 1916, the day before the 'big push' at the Somme, that 'the wire has never before been so well cut,' in which, on 20 March 1918, the eve of the last mighty German offensive, a French general remarked, 'More and more confirmation is coming in for the opinion that the Boche will not attack';[13] in such a war and such a world the jackal of Kilimanjaro and the sniggering footman of Prufrock appeared to be the only suitable inhabitants. Humor became bitter and black, and *Monty Python* would never have lived in the last quarter of this century had its forebears not gone through that 'great war.'

Near Béthune, at the end of November 1914, Brigadier P. Mortimer recorded in his diary:

Our chief anxiety seems to be to clear German corpses from in front of our trenches – as the latter are becoming untenable through stench. Men are being offered rewards and promotion for going out and burning them and many gallant deeds are being performed. One man in the 2/39th after disposing of 3 corpses out in the open and 50 yards from the

German trenches – was shot dead in the fourth attempt – cold blooded pluck.[14]

Mortimer made the entry, without further comment, obviously in all seriousness. How long would it be before men sensed the horrible ironies of a world in which gallantry was called upon to fight corpses, in which the living died trying to destroy the already dead? Basil Liddell Hart's 9th Battalion of the King's Own Yorkshire Light Infantry marched up to the battle of the Somme, in July 1916, eight hundred strong, singing 'Pack Up Your Troubles in Your Old Kit-Bag.' A few days later seventy men and four officers marched back. Again they sang 'Pack Up Your Troubles'![15].

But by then the ironies had begun to sink in. By then 'Auld Lang Syne' had been accorded lyrics befitting a Dada song. 'We're here because we're here because we're here because we're here,' sang the British soldier. And to the tune of 'Take It to the Lord in Prayer' Tommy warbled:

> When this blasted war is over,
> No more soldiering for me.
> When I get my civvy clothes on,
> Oh, how happy I shall be!
> No more church parades on Sunday,
> No more asking for a pass,
> I shall tell the Sergeant-Major
> To stick his passes up his arse.

A conversation overheard in the trenches in March 1916 went as follows:

'Say Bill, when's this war goin' to end?'

'Ah dunno: when there's no more o' Belgium to put into sandbags.'[16]

On 12 February 1916, in an old bombed-out printing house off the main square, near the Cloth Hall, in Ypres, appeared the first issue of the *Wipers Times*, famous precursor of the 'New Church' Times, the Kemmel Times, the Somme Times, the B.E.F. Times, and, finally, in November 1918, the 'Better Times.' The humor was, with scarce exception, black. In addition to letters to the editor, mimicking the London Times, about sightings of the first cuckoo of the season, there were advertisements.

Building Land for Sale.
Build that House on Hill 60
Bright – Breezy
& Invigorating.
Commands an excellent view of historic
town of Ypres. For particulars of sale
apply: – BOSCH & CO. MENIN.[17]

And in the Somme Times, at the end of July 1916, was to be found a questionnaire:

Are you a victim to Optimism?
You don't know?
Then ask yourself the following questions.

1. Do you suffer from cheerfulness?
2. Do you wake up in the morning feeling that all is going well for the allies?
3. Do you sometimes think that the war will end within the next twelve months?
4. Do you believe good news in preference to bad?
5. Do you consider our leaders are competent to conduct the war to a successful issue?

If your answer is 'Yes' to any one of these questions then you are in the clutches of that dread disease. We can cure you.
Two days spent at our establishment will effectually eradicate all traces of it from your system.
Do not hesitate – apply for terms at once to:—

Mssrs. Walthorpe, Foxley, Nelmes and Co.
Telephone 72: 'Grumblestones'
Telegrams: 'Grouse'[18]

As Louis Mairet sensed and regretted, much of the irony voiced by soldiers was 'false.' 'An illness is ravaging the current generation: false irony,' he charged in early 1916. 'The worst thing is that it brings with it an insensibility, or rather its pretense, which is even more dreadful.'[19] The introduction to a 1918 reprint of the *Wipers Times* also felt compelled to point out that 'the hilarity was more often hysterical than natural.' Private David Ghilchik certainly agreed. 'Funny thing, dear,' he told his wife in a letter from the Italian front, where he was serving as a truck driver in August 1918, 'but I seem to have lost the capacity to laugh.'[20] Yet if much of the humor was forced, its very appeal for many suggests that it did strike a chord. The undercurrent represented by irony during the war would become a floodtide in the postwar world.

For some, however, unable to laugh, the inwardness was accompanied by silence. Dada might scream about nothingness, but some men found even the urge to scream stifled by awe or the totality of incomprehension. 'War . . . is a silent teacher and he who learns becomes silent too,' wrote Rudolf Binding.[21] 'The reality surpasses all literature, all painting, all imagination,' insisted another survivor.[22] One combatant who did not survive, Marc Boasson, was overwhelmed by pessimism: 'Nothing is being created, everything is being lost.' He complained of being asphyxiated spiritually by the war, as if poison gas existed for the soul as well. Humanism, after three centuries of agony, was in its death throes.

The intellectual and moral regression of the world can be avoided as little as an absolute baseness of thought, which will be enveloped in technical

301

perfection and practical skills encouraging illusion. The misery that will follow the war will bring with it a prodigious industrialization, a multiplication of useful improvements. All human activity will turn toward practical ends . . . Unbiased culture has had its day. Mankind is giving way to human matériel according to the expression the war has already made familiar. The Renaissance is bankrupt. The German factory is absorbing the world.[23]

The 'German factory' is here equated with 'technical perfection and practical skills encouraging illusion.'

If the past had become a fiction and if all was indeed flux, then perhaps the cinema, some witnesses felt, was the only appropriate vehicle for capturing the movement to the abyss. It is striking how often references to the cinema appear in the letters, diaries, and reminiscences of soldiers. The newness of the medium and the excitement aroused by its development are part of the explanation for the frequent references, but there does seem to have been a genuine feeling among some participants that what was happening belonged somehow on the screen rather than in life. A member of the French 360th Infantry Regiment witnessed an attack by a neighboring battalion near Arras in May 1915. The men left their trenches, ran toward the wire, and were cut down by machine-gun fire. The observer and his men, standing in their trenches, craned their necks to watch the action – 'one might as well have been in the cinema.'[24] A British soldier who experienced Gommecourt in 1916 wrote afterward, 'The other men were like figures on a cinematograph screen – an old film that flickered violently – everybody in a desperate hurry . . .'[25]

The war assaulted moral standards as rudely as it did aesthetic forms. That the slaughter of masses of men by any conceivable method was turned into routine, into duty, into moral purpose, was merely the crudest of assaults on a moral order that claimed to be rooted in a Judaeo-Christian ethic. Although Kitchener sent off the BEF with a warning to avoid the women and wine of France, it was not long before army chiefs on all sides began to make arrangements for the basic sexual needs of masses of men – of course, for the sake of morale! In the nineteenth-century world morals and morale were thought to be indistinguishable; the Great War wrought havoc on their partnership and threatened to make them mutually exclusive. For large numbers of people, probably for most, they remained connected, as we saw earlier, but for a growing proportion of men morale was associated with the repudiation of morality, or at least with a loosening of the moral code.

When facing mortal danger and imminent death, armies and soldiers throughout history have considered themselves privileged citizens in relation to, among other things, morality. The very democratization of war between 1914 and 1918 meant that millions of men assumed these privileges. For an innocent organist and choirmaster from Edinburgh like Peter McGregor, even training camp, near Plymouth, was a new and titillating world. On a Sunday in September 1915 he went into Plymouth. 'I had quite a good time,' he reported in a letter to his wife, who probably had a fit when she read what followed.

We discovered a tea shop where I had fried fish. But that is not all. I was buying a packet of cigarettes at a tobacconist's and asked him if he knew of any place where we could have tea – and he told of this place. Well it was a French place and no mistake, there

303

were ladies beautifully dressed and painted – they smoked cigarettes and laughed at the men in the place. There were Argylls and sailors. Oh my, you could get anything you wanted, the food was good and well served. The waiter was French. It was a regular bad place. I have never been in a place like it before. I was all right. Don't be alarmed at your old husband – he is quite safe. I ate such a lot that my belt wouldn't meet. Fried fish and chipped potatoes is very good and tea in a cup at a table with white cloth and spoons, etc. But the company! oh my! the ladies simply floored me and the way they went on. We were waiting at the lavatory door and thought a man would come out, but it was two ladies, well that's all. I fled out of the place.[1]

In a couple of months the shock had worn off for McGregor, but the novelty of his new life remained. In late November he was in Guildford: 'We had tea in a small tea room, officers galore with their women folk, it seems to me soldiers wherever they go manage to pick up women. Our men are no sooner in a place than you see them with girls.'[2]

On the Western Front brothels were soon regular appurtenances of base camps and of larger towns serving as rest quarters. Men would queue up, as at the latrines, the only difference being that the military police ensured order. An eighteen-year-old, Bert Chaney, noticed early in the war, a long queue of soldiers standing in two-by-two order.

Thinking there might be a concert or cinema . . . I asked what was going on. 'A bit of grumble and grunt,' I was told, 'only costs two francs.' Puzzled, I asked what that meant. 'Cor blimey, lad. Didn't they learn you anything at all where you came from?' They thought me a proper mug. Fancy a lad like me, and a Cockney at that, not knowing what that meant – and didn't I know what a red lamp stood for? These places, I was told, were not for young lads like me, but for married men who were missing their wives.[3]

In the British army 27 per cent of all diseases that warranted hospitalization were classified as venereal, and in the course of the war 416,891 men were treated for VD.[4]

On the home front morality loosened its corsets and belts too. Prostitution increased strikingly. In Paris, of 3907 girls arrested in 1914–15, over half were found to have venereal disease. Most of the girls were novices; many came from occupied areas.[5] There were some attempts to restrict the activity of the girls, but the public generally turned a blind eye. Casual relationships between women and soldiers also became more common. The British music hall song 'There's a Girl for Every Soldier' set the tone everywhere. Who knew if Tommy would come home again? Let him enjoy himself while he could. The growing independence of women, as they were brought into the labor force by the absence of men, meant that the moral constraints of the home and paternal authority slackened. More women now had their own lodgings in which to entertain men friends. If the assault on a fixed moral code was well under way before 1914, the war acted like a battering ram. Morality and sex became not a matter of social dictate but more and more of individual conscience.

Frederic Manning noted that soldiers' moods seemed to swing 'between the extremes of a sticky sentimentalism and a rank obscenity.'[6] Perhaps this has always been the case with soldiers. One of the first things that struck Percy Jones when he joined up in 1914 was the cursing by his fellows – 'Swearing seems to be natural to soldiers, like long hair to artists and check suits to golfers.'[7] But the soldiers of the Great War seem to have felt a special need to harp on scatology. The imagery of defecation became a pronounced motif. Surprising this is surely not. Millions of men died, and as they died they did not 'go west,' as the British euphemism put it; instead they 'kicked the bucket,' full of excrement. When the 'great release' came, it came from the bowels primarily. 'War is so beautiful in books but in reality it stinks of shit and rotting flesh,' complained Charles Delvert.[8]

The British home front associated anality with Germany. A 1917 compilation of alleged war crimes accused the Germans of 'disgusting' as well as brutal behavior. 'In houses robbed by them they leave, by way of visiting cards, excrement in beds, on tables, and in cupboards.'[9] But the soldiers at the front had a different outlook. Living in the midst of death and decay wrought by inhuman machines, the men found a symbolic innocence in human filth. The artillery behind the lines might, as Humphrey Cobb claimed in his novel based on the war, have had the enemy's latrines registered[10] – bourgeois culture does not permit men to defecate – but soldiers actually in the firing lines often looked differently on their opponents' plight. Philippe Girardet was occupying an observation post in September 1915 when he saw a fellow Frenchman get out of his trench, unarmed, take a few steps back into a field, undo his trousers, and squat. The Germans must have seen the *poilu*, said Girardet, because there was nothing obscuring their vision. Yet they did nothing. The *fantassin* took his time, got up, readjusted everything carefully, and returned to his trench unharmed.[11]

The latrine motif is a recurrent one in diaries, memoirs, and especially the imaginative literature of the war. For Thomas Boyd the trenches were 'gigantic latrines built for monsters'; for T. Fredenburgh the entire landscape of war was 'a yellow, pestilent muckheap'; and E.E. Cummings's *The Enormous Room* is replete with symbols of defecation:

Whistling joyfully to myself, I took three steps which brought me to the door end. The door was massively

made, all of iron and steel . . . It delighted me. The can
excited my curiosity . . . At the bottom reposefully lay
a new human turd.[12]

Erich Maria Remarque's *All Quiet on the Western Front*
has numerous references to latrines and defecation;
they would lead offended critics to call his novel the
foremost example of the 'lavatory school' of German
war literature.

The resort to sexual and defecatory imagery was a
long-standing tradition among the avant-garde.
Nietzsche identified bad odor with the heroic. Alfred
Jarry's *Ubu Roi* (1886), filled with crude language and
ferocity, began with the word *Merdre*.* Joyce's Bloom in
Ulysses revels in the quality of his fart. Again on this
level the war turned the revolt of small artistic coteries
into a mass phenomenon.

AVANT-GARDE

All soldiers craved leave. Many of course enjoyed it to
the hilt. Coming home as a seasoned veteran brought a
sudden and welcome respectability. Roland Mountfort
had worked for the Prudential Life Insurance Company
in London before the war, and when he revisited the
office in July 1916 he was, in his words,

> dragged all over the place, even to the Asst. Managers,
> quite exalted persons before whom I should have
> stood and trembled in the old days, but with whom in
> my new position I had quite a familiar conversation.[1]

French soldiers mutinied in 1917 in part because equi-
table arrangements for *permissions*, or leaves, had broken down.

*He added an extra *r* to *merde*. Hence the translation might be 'shitt.'

Yet some soldiers, on coming home, found the life they had once known exasperating and depressing. When he was invalided home in August 1916 Robert Graves felt conversation with even his parents was 'all but impossible.' Asked in December whether he would like a few more months of home service, he said no.[2] Such an experience was not uncommon. Louis Mairet, on home leave in March 1916, was shocked to find people living their lives as if nothing out of the ordinary were occurring. He was especially upset by those who, when told about some of the appalling conditions at the front and about the tenacity of the enemy, yawned and complained about the price of veal.[3] An English soldier, asked by a friend whether he had told his wife about the front while on leave, replied:

> I didn't get a chance, she was so busy tellin' me all the news about Mrs Bally's cat killin' Mrs Smith's bird, and Mrs Cramp's sister's new dress, and how Jimmy Murphy's dog chewed up Annie Allen's doll.[4]

A common feeling among soldiers was that their experience at the front had created an insurmountable barrier between them and civilians. Communication with home was no longer possible. People simply could not understand what the soldiers had been through, and the soldiers themselves could not articulate their experience appropriately. Ernst Jünger was disgusted by the 'phrases, washed in lye, about heroes and heroic death' that he heard at home. Soldiers did not need this kind of thanks, he protested. They wanted some 'sympathy.'[5] But was a genuine sympathy, based on understanding, possible?

For those who pretended to understand, but did not, was reserved the soldiers' most venomous hatred. Journalists who wrote about the war instead of fighting it stood in a category by themselves. To Marc Boasson, journalists were 'idiots.'[6] With their stupid, lying accounts of battle, with their denigration of the enemy, they were devaluing the French effort, achieving the reverse of what they were trying to do. 'The newspapers give me epileptic seizures,' wrote another French soldier. 'If they ever erect a statue to the Press, I insist that this goddess be given duck's feet, the stomach of an ostrich, the brain of a goose, and the snout of a pig.'[7]

Next in line for contempt were the armchair strategists. They, too, nauseated the soldier. 'You feel an inextinguishable hatred for the potbellied bourgeois, soft and well-groomed, who by lamplight discusses military operations in a peremptory tone of voice, surrounded by his admiring family,' wrote Charles Delvert. That fat, despicable bourgeois, M. Prudhomme, had absolutely no inkling – *pas même le soupçon* – about what was going on in the trenches.[8]

And yet let us beware of exaggeration. Even Delvert, with his bitterness toward journalists and pear-shaped amateur strategists, could admit that reading matter from home was essential to sanity in the front line. The glossy *Vie Parisienne*, full of sketched pinups – the photographed ones belonged to the Second World War – was the most popular magazine in the French trenches, 'with the little women in corsets and in Gerda Wegener knickers.' During bombardments the little blonde 'with the big eyes and voluptuous paleness languishes in her chair to my right and reminds me that beyond the lines life goes on.' But as he is thinking and writing, the sarcasm suddenly surfaces again, and Delvert concludes the passage, 'We really are under the Directory,' a reference to the interregnum after the Revolution and before Napoleon, when – as the radical interpretation of France's history charged – the best of France was at the front fighting the enemy and the worst was at home governing, if that is the word, the country.[9]

Letters from home were often painful because of their naïveté. The ironies jumped out at the soldier: 'Try not to get wounded!' or 'We are having a hard time, too!' 'My

God! From what?!' was Delvert's response.[10] The soldier's sensation, on reading such comments from home, was often one of complete isolation. The troops might as well have been on the moon. They lived and fought in a place beyond understanding, beyond imagination, even beyond feeling. 'The Army fights on its own' was Garfield Powell's conclusion during the Somme offensive. Powell hoped that, given the number of British soldiers involved in the fighting at the Somme and given the extra effort required of the home front to equip the armies, there might be some change, but he admitted that hope was slight: 'While Englishmen are the cold, calculating selfish race they have always been and while idealism is non-existent and discouraged we are always on the brink of national disaster.'[11] The words could have been written by a German propagandist.

Some soldiers, so overcome by the sense of isolation, felt more hatred and disdain for the civilians at home than for the enemy. Such sentiments surfaced frequently during the French mutinies. Here was the stuff of revolution, and the French military and political authorities quivered in May and June of 1917 at the thought that France might be on the brink of total collapse and upheaval. Even Siegfried Sassoon toyed with the vision of turning the guns around.[12]

Overwhelmed by the sense of being alone – a feeling that the term 'lost generation' would capture after the war – some soldiers came to look on their isolated fraternity as hallowed. Cut off from the home front, cut off even from prewar militarism, for which they had nothing but scorn – 'satin dolmans, mustaches of bellicose cats, souls of mean-spirited bureaucrats'[13] – their admiration for the wartime army had no bounds. Pierre Drieu la Rochelle, Herbert Read, Siegfried Sassoon, Ernst Jünger, and Robert Graves were all of the same mind, but they were merely the articulate representatives of a group that included virtually all volunteers once they became seasoned veterans.

The tone of utterance varied – nostalgia could be found mixed with defiance – but all agreed that the war experience, the experience of the 'real war' in the trenches, marked men off from the rest of society. This was, as the German phrase put it, a *Schicksalsgemeinschaft*, a community of fate. All were in agreement that for them an epoch was over, a world had ended. The moment, the intensity of the moment, was all that was certain; and in varying degrees, despite the pervasive horror and mutilation, despite twinges of sorrow and regret, the experience was exhilarating. Most soldiers who underwent action did not regret the experience, their bitterness about the official conduct of the war notwithstanding.

Men like Drieu and Jünger positively reveled in it. Both glorified the war as a manifestation of Force. Drieu even thanked the enemy for dragging France out of her torpor and up to solemn affirmation – 'a solemnity in our life that we had no longer expected.' He had no regrets whatever.

> *Quand cesserons-nous de pleurer*
> *l'écroulement des vieux temples?**

History was not in the past; history was a magical dream that motivated men to action in the present.[14]

In the trenches social barriers broke down as intellectuals became dependent on working-class men and aristocrats on crop farmers. 'It was in the war that I learned about men,' confessed André Bridoux; 'before that my social kind hid from me human kind.' One became, in the war, 'naked, that is to say mankind viewed from the point of view of nature and not from the point of view of social classification.'[15] Marc Boasson, who discussed Zola, Wagner, Brueghel, and Jansenism in

*When will we stop mourning
The collapse of the old temples?

311

correspondence with his wife, also told her of his great affection for 'my *poilus*. They are tired and gentle.' He rhapsodized about their simplicity, their language, their sense of humor, and their instinctive good sense.[16]

The regiment was the axial unit for this spirit of comradeship, and regimental pride seemed capable of surviving any disaster. In fact, disasters welded men together. Robert Graves noted that men were more interested in and learned more about their regiment's history than about the fighting on the other fronts in the war or even about the causes of the war.[17] After a three-week stint in the line and some 'fetid' action, a weary Herbert Read reflected:

> It would be a nightmare to any individual. But we create among ourselves a wonderful comradeship which I think would overcome any horror or hardship. It is this comradeship which alone makes the Army tolerable to me. To create a bond between yourself and a body of men and a bond that will hold at the critical moment, that is work worthy of any man and when done an achievement to be proud of.

Like Boasson, Read went on to praise

> the 'simple soul.' He is the only man you can put your money on in a tight corner. Bombast and swank carry a man nowhere out here. In England they are everything. Nor is the intellect not a few of us used to be so proud of of much avail. It's a pallid thing in the presence of a stout heart.[18]

A French soldier said that the comradeship of the trenches was 'the most tender human experience' that he had ever enjoyed. A British soldier, thinking about his fellows, confessed to his diary 'a strength of pure affection which I have never felt for anyone else.' Many waxed lyrical on this subject. For the philosopher-writer Émile Chartier, who went by the pen name Alain, the war was 'a poem to friendship.' 'My strapping brutes,' he wrote, 'will get themselves killed, not on account of any academic rhetoric, but for "old man Chartier." '[19]

In postwar literature, many male characters would prefer the companionship of men to that of women whose affections they found trite and sentimental. 'The war,' said Henri de Montherlant, 'was the only place where you could love men passionately.'[20] Herbert Read was intoxicated by this atmosphere of fraternity. Despite his hatred of the army as an institution, by May 1918 he was considering staying on once the war was over: 'I like its manliness, the courage it demands, the fellowship it gives.'[21] And after the war G.L. Dickinson received a letter from a young officer who managed to capture a whole range of important sentiments in one passage.

I should not stress too much the horror of the war to those who actually took part in it. I know my experiences were with an exceptionally united and successful body of men, and that to many the war was plain hell. But there was, to many of us, very much on the other side. Nor was this a joy in the actual fighting, nor a fascination with tawdry romance. There were greater things. You may say we were spiritually drugged and pathetically deluded. But never before or since have we found them. There was an exaltation, in those days of comradeship and dedication, that would have come in few other ways. And so, to those of us who had ridden with Don Quixote and Rupert Brooke on either hand, the Line is sacred ground, for there we saw the vision splendid.[22]

The spiritual bond forged between men in the isolation of the trenches was, however, not all that resilient outside the battle zone when men were forced

313

to confront the complexities of the 'real' world. The intensity of feeling and companionship belonged to a singular time and place. That explains why some soldiers were keen to get back to the trenches, from leave and even from rest quarters. Herbert Read, on leave in England, missed an attack his regiment was involved in: 'I feel a little shamed of having escaped it all. There is always a regret in not having shared dangers with friends. Perhaps one is jealous of their experiences.'[23]

If soldiers in the ranks, unable to compose a coherent picture of the war as a whole, were perplexed by the general situation, the general staffs, unable to devise any successful strategic or tactical approach, were equally baffled. Some, like Haig and Fayolle, turned to religion for sustenance. 'I am convinced that God will save France once again,' Fayolle confided to his diary in February 1918, 'but He'll have to get involved directly.'[24] The war seemed to have passed long ago from human hands. For some commanders repeated disasters could never be explained in terms of material or personal inadequacy: failures were projected on to others, particularly secret agents and related forces of darkness. Conspiracy theories flourished. When mutinies infected their armies in 1917, a large number of French generals were convinced that the troubles stemmed ultimately not from their own maladministration of the war, but from sinister undercover forces – *agents provocateurs* and occult organizations in the pay of Germany. Any peculiarity became suspect. One soldier came under scrutiny as a possible agent of revolution because his letters indicated that he had a knowledge of English and German.[25] Had Pétain not been admirably levelheaded in trying to rectify the administrative injustices that plagued the existence of the *poilu*; had the French armies collapsed; had the French not been on the 'winning' side in the war; it is more than likely that they would have experienced a version of the witch hunt for saboteurs that Germany underwent in the 1920s and '30s.

314

In Britain there was a similar undercurrent of paranoia. On the fourth anniversary of the outbreak of the war Richard Stokes could still write, 'I wish to goodness they'd intern all these alien blighters.'[26]

The war entailed a 'journey inward' for soldiers, but a parallel journey was taken by civilians at home. Censorship and propaganda played the major role in this process, blurring, as was their purpose, the reality of the war. The home front never knew with any precision how the war was progressing. Defeats were presented as victories, stalemate as tactical maneuvering. Truth became falsehood, falsehood truth. As euphemism became the official order of the day, language was turned upside down and inside out. Atrocity stories were invented, and real atrocities buried. The intention of war leaders, civilian and military, was of course to bolster morale, to give the impression, within and without, of societies wholeheartedly dedicated to the 'cause.' Newspapers were forbidden to publish pictures of dead soldiers or, often, to print stories about train wrecks and industrial accidents. However, anything to boost morale was encouraged. Early in the war stories circulated in the French press about German weapons that would not fire, shrapnel that fell like harmless rain, bullets that were not dangerous because they passed through flesh without tearing it. Looking at the German arsenal, 'our footsloggers burst out laughing,' insisted *L'Intransigeant*.[27] The same publication had carried his headline on 4 August 1914: TODAY'S WARS ARE LESS MURDEROUS THAN THOSE OF EARLIER TIMES. As the war continued, this *bourrage de crâne*, as the French soldiers labeled the propaganda, did not let up. 'Our soldiers don't give a fig for poison gas,' wrote *L'Écho de Paris* on 16 December 1916. 'Among the many victims of gas,' reported the *Petit Journal* on 24 August 1917, 'there is hardly a single death.'

Soldiers were discouraged from keeping diaries, and personal cameras were not permitted in the front lines, for fear that evidence of one's military plans and preparations might fall into enemy hands. Such reasoning was normal. But as the war continued, an equally important reason for such proscriptions was the fear that bad news, in documented form, might reach home and upset morale. Censors vetted all letters sent from the front. Some incoming mail was examined too. 'We are afflicted with a censorship of frightful conscientiousness,' complained John Harvey, not sure if even those remarks would reach their destination;

> and I gather that previous letters of mine have suffered severely at his hands . . . If you were to see all the forbidding list of the things we may not say, you would feel that it is a task of some exertion to think out a letter that will not be expunged and detained.[28]

The power of the censor to intervene in discourse and emotion, both at home and at the front, is evidenced by a pithy and, for the human beings involved, powerful example. 'One of our officers censoring,' wrote John Walker, 'noticed 2 letters to 2 girls from 1 man – love letters and calculated to elicit parcels. He put Ethel's letter in Meg's envelope and vice-versa.'[29] Curiously, that little tale got through.

The effect of such tampering by officialdom – whether on a grand scale or affecting merely an Ethel or a Meg – was to unleash imaginations, fears, neuroses. Denied factual knowledge, people naturally turned inward. Myths, some of astounding magnitude, were spawned: the angels who protected the British retreat at Mons; the legions of Russians who, destined for the Western Front, traveled 'with snow on their boots' from Archangel to Scotland and then in hundreds of closed speeding train carriages to the Channel ports; the Canadian crucified, literally, by the Germans. Moreover, amidst the enforced silence, traitors, spies, and enemies were thought to be hiding under every bed.

The boundaries between truth and falsehood became so blurred that official denials of rumors were regarded as attempts to mislead the enemy. Henry James, for example, was completely taken in by the story about Russian troops destined for the Western Front. In early September 1914, he sent Edith Wharton in the United States a picture clipped from the *Daily Mail* of 1 September, showing soldiers who looked like Russians, disembarking at Ostend: 'If they are not straight out of the historic, or even fictive, pages of Tolstoy, I will eat the biggest pair of moujik boots in the collection!' For James the picture was 'a regular gem of evidence.' Yet several days later the War Office denied the reports. James, however, was skeptical:

> There remains an extraordinary residuum of fact to be accounted for: it being indisputable by too much convergence of testimony that trains upon trains of troops seen in the light of day, and not recognized by innumerable watchers and wonderers as English, were pouring down from the north and to the east during the end of last week and the beginning of this. It seems difficult that there should have been that amount of variously scattered hallucination, misconception, fantastication or whatever – yet I chuck up the sponge![30]

Others, however, did not 'chuck up the sponge' as readily and continued to believe in the Russian transport even after a second denial was issued in mid September. What was the origin of the story? One theory was that it started when a dealer in provisions received a telegram from Russia stating, 'Two hundred thousand Russians are being dispatched via Archangel.' The message referred not to soldiers but to eggs. Whatever the origins, people clearly were desperate for some comfort and were prepared to accept the wildest tales.

Living on tenterhooks, people invented succor, but

they also imagined danger. In all belligerent countries bizarre stories circulated throughout the war about agents who wrecked trains by overpowering signalmen, sentries, or guards; spies who signaled with lights to ships and submarines; traitors who used carrier pigeons to pass messages to the enemy. There were windmills that turned when the enemy was approaching, or stood still when conditions were thought to be favorable for attack. Even bad weather was blamed on the conjuring tricks of the enemy. And when news reached London in June 1915 that Kitchener had drowned after his ship went down in the North Sea, a rumor quickly spread that the report was a fabrication intended to confuse the Germans. Kitchener was supposedly alive and well and traveling to Russia by a different route.

If the British were encouraged to believe that Germans crushed the skulls of Belgian and French babies with their jackboots, that the kaiser was personally involved in torturing three-year-olds in satanic rituals, and that corpses were recycled in Germany to produce fats, oils, and pig fodder, the Germans were told that Gurkha and Sikh troops crept across no man's land at night, slipped into German trenches, slit German throats, and then drank the blood of their victims, and that the Senegalese fighting with the French were cannibals.

The press led the propaganda effort, but churchmen, educators, artists, musicians, and authors buttressed it. All the belligerents were involved in the creation of myth and the distortion of reality. Reality, a sense of proportion, and reason – these were the major casualties of the war. The world became a figment of imagination rather than imagination being a figment of the world. German rationale for the war had a metaphysical orientation from the start; the Allied argument initially was more practical – defense against the German attack. But as the war continued, as the immediate provocations – the

Austrian attack on Serbia and the German invasion of Belgium – paled to insignificance, as even civilized values lost their sheen in the face of endless slaughter, the rhetoric of the Allies became at times indistinguishable from that of the Germans.

'Kill Germans! Kill them!' bellowed the Right Reverend A.F. Winnington-Ingram, bishop of London:

> ... not for the sake of killing, but to save the world ... kill the good as well as the bad ... kill the young men as well as the old ... kill those who have shown kindness to our wounded as well as those fiends who crucified the Canadian sergeant ... As I have said a thousand times, I look upon it as a war for purity, I look upon everybody who dies in it as a martyr.[31]

Clergymen dressed Jesus in khaki and had him firing machine guns. The war became one not of justice but of righteousness. To kill Germans was to purge the world of the Antichrist, the great beast from the abyss, and to herald the New Jerusalem. At the Madison Avenue Baptist Church in New York the Reverend Charles Aubrey Eaton attacked Woodrow Wilson for not avenging the *Lusitania*. It had to be done 'if it took ten million men, if our cities were laid in the dust and we were set back a hundred years.'[32] Not since the wars of religion of the seventeenth century, and perhaps even the crusades, had men of the cloth encouraged killing for the greater glory of God with such enthusiasm.

Propaganda, both of a positive and negative nature, evoked extremes of emotion: passionate hatred and unrealistic visions of the future. In the process, as hopes became apocalyptic, the past was pushed aside, by many ruthlessly. And for many in the Allied camp, as for the Germans, the struggle became a war to attain utopia, not a war to preserve achievement. The balance for many had shifted. The future was now glorified, not the past; but the future was a figment of imagination, a matter of desperate wish rather than constructive planning. When the war finally ended, Isadora Duncan, in Paris, had the feeling that 'for the moment we were all poets.'[33]

While the differences between Anglo-French and German motivations, which we stressed earlier, remained distinct for soldiers and civilians during the entire war, the sensibilities of the British and French had moved toward the German. Appropriately, on the vary day the Germans first used gas at Ypres, 22 April 1915, Louis Mairet, unaware of the new development, urged an eye-for-an-eye, tooth-for-a-tooth ethic: 'It is through savagery that we shall defeat the savages.'[34] After the war General Sir Ian Hamilton, who had commanded the ill-fated Dardanelles enterprise, admitted, 'The war has forced us to crib from the enemy.'[35] He was referring principally to army organization and discipline, but his point was just as valid on the broader social and cultural level. The western nations moved in the course of the war toward stronger social control but also toward a new spiritual liberality. Within this paradox, as the social and cultural realms seemed to split away from each other, would lie the essence of the modern experience.

Socially, the state tightened its grip on each person during the war. Labor and the economy were regimented, taxation was increased, international trade was disrupted, passports were introduced for travelers, rationing was imposed, and the state became involved even in art patronage. The Leviathan envisaged by Hobbes became reality. Spiritually and morally, however, soldiers and civilians in the Great War moved, by parallel routes, away from an external world – too horrible to endure – into a visionary landscape. This imagined landscape created by the war was bound to fade when the war was over, and with its disappearance, modernism, which in its prewar form was a culture of hope, a vision of synthesis, would turn to a culture of nightmare and denial. Robert Graves would speak of the 'inward scream' the war provoked, 'the duty to run mad.'[36] The Great War was to be the axis on which the modern world turned.

On 11 November 1918, at a hospital near Étaples, an officer in the Scottish medical corps signed an order that was posted in the wards: 'To celebrate the conclusion of hostilities every patient will be allowed an extra piece of bread and jam with his tea.'[37]

René Hemery, an officer with the 48th French Infantry Regiment, was in St Dizier on the Marne that day when the Armistice was finally signed a little north in Compiègne. In St Dizier, as elsewhere in the victor nations, the churchbells pealed and the streets filled with singing and dancing crowds. But Hemery, like most veterans, found it difficult to indulge in any form of celebration, and as dusk fell, he walked in search of better air toward the edge of town, where stood a small cemetery. As he approached the burial ground he heard sobbing. He moved closer. And finally he could see figures. One was a little boy playing with a flag, a Tricolor. The other was a woman, on her knees, forehead to the ground, overcome with grief. Clutching his 'emblem of glory,' as Hemery described the flag in his diary, the child suddenly shouted: '*Papa, c'est la Victoire!*'[38]

> Now all roads lead to France
> And heavy is the tread
> Of the living; but the dead
> Returning lightly dance.[39]

Act Three

VIII

Night Dancer

Tu avais dansé toute cette nuit,
Et tu es parti, dans l'aube inquiète,
Comme Alan Seeger, moins enfant que lui,
Mais aussi poète!*

MAURICE ROSTAND
May 1927

There can be no question of art as soon as the idea of
establishing a record enters in.

ANDRÉ GIDE
1910

'That corpse you planted last year in your garden,
'Has it begun to sprout? Will it bloom this year?
'Or has the sudden frost disturbed its bed?'

T.S. ELIOT
The Waste Land, 1922

Ohne Scham und ohne Schande
Penn'ich mit der ganzen Bande,
Nicht nur mit dem Einzelherrn.
Hemmungslos ist jetzt modern.**

Song sung by ILSE BOIS,
cabaret artist

*You had danced all that night,
And you departed at anxious dawn,
Like Alan Seeger, less of a child than he,
But also a poet!
**Without shame and without pang
I sleep with the whole gang,
Not just with a single gent.
Without restraint is the modern bent.

Saturday, 21 May 1927. Paris.

The morning newspapers predict that he might arrive, should he arrive at all, sometime after nine in the evening. *Le Temps* chooses the earlier hour. *Le Matin* reckons on 1:00 or 2:00 a.m. on Sunday. The cafés of Montmartre and Montparnasse are abuzz with excited conversations all day. Yet pessimism dominates. By early evening the roads to Le Bourget, which lies fifteen kilometers north of central Paris, are clogged. The first modern traffic jam is in the making. By 9:00 p.m. traffic is at a complete standstill, and even the special buses, which depart from the place de l'Opéra every few minutes that evening, packed with customers, have come to a halt. Only those on bicycles or on foot can make any progress past the jammed vehicles, many of which have now been abandoned at the sides of the various access roads as their former passengers hurry in droves toward the lights of Le Bourget.

The Paris correspondent of a German paper, the *Deutsche Tageszeitung*, finds traffic at the porte de la Villette so bad by 8:00 p.m. that he has to walk the rest of the way, roughly eight or nine kilometers. Isadora Duncan, on her way to dinner at Chantilly, eighteen kilometers farther north, is trapped in the traffic, gives up her plans for the evening, and joins the curious throng, the size of which no Paris stadium and not even London's Wembley, completed a few years earlier to seat 100,000, could accommodate. Many of the journalists sent to cover the spectacle never arrive and eventually submit secondhand reports, filled with inaccuracy and rumor. Even those reporters who make it have difficulty in moving about the crowd, in getting admitted to the field itself with their press passes, and in observing the central events. Estimates of the crowd that reaches Le Bourget will go as high as a million; most will be in the range of 150,000 to 200,000.

Montmartre, the highest point in Paris, from which one hopes to see at least the lights of Le Bourget, is like an anthill in commotion by 9:30. In the place du Tertre, next to Sacré Coeur, the crush of humanity is such that movement is almost impossible. At the place de l'Opéra, a crowd, estimated by one journalist at ten thousand, mills about expectantly. On the grand boulevards, throughout the city, traffic grinds to a halt. In some cafés telegrams begin to be posted after 9:30. In some theaters performances are interrupted with news bulletins.

At Le Bourget the densely packed crowd presses against the fences surrounding the field. Lights, red and green, flash, and acetylene searchlights hiss as they scan the sky. A cool southwesterly wind is blowing. From time to time parts of the crowd break into song. Harry Crosby, veteran of Verdun and now an American expatriate living in Paris, has arrived early, around 8:00 p.m. with his wife, Caresse, and a group of friends. The event excites Crosby as little else has done since the war. It is now 10:20 p.m.

And suddenly unmistakably the sound of an aeroplane (dead silence) and then to our left a white flash against the black night (blackness) and another flash (like a shark darting through water). Then nothing. No sound. Suspense. And again a sound, this time somewhere off towards the right . . . Then sharp swift in the gold glare of the searchlights a small white hawk of a plane swoops hawk-like down and across the field – C'est lui, Lindbergh, LINDBERGH! and there is pandemonium wild animals let loose and a stampede towards the plane and C and I hanging on to each other running people ahead running people all round us running and the crowd behind stampeding like buffalo and a pushing and a shoving and where is he where is he Lindbergh where is he and the extraordinary impression I had of hands thousands of hands

327

weaving like maggots over the silver wings of the Spirit of Saint-Louis and it seems as if all the hands in the world are touching or trying to touch the new Christ and that the new Cross is the Plane and knives slash at the fuselage hands multiply hands everywhere scratching tearing and it is almost midnight when we begin the slow journey back to Paris.[1]

The 'new Christ' had arrived! Despite all odds. Alone. Completely alone. From the New World to the Old. From Roosevelt Field in New York to Le Bourget in Paris. He had left behind even the gray kitten, Patsy, which some reports claimed he was taking with him. The trip would have been too dangerous for her was the explanation attributed to the hero. That comment enhanced, it was felt, the magnificent simplicity, the true heroism of the man. He had no special instruments on the plane, not even a radio, only a magnetic compass.

Parisians craved to see him. They wanted to acclaim him, touch him, hoist him on their shoulders, worship him. They trampled the iron gates and barbed-wire fences of the airport; they trampled each other. The Paris correspondent of the *Daily Mail*, presumably in a state like that of the people he was describing, cabled his paper:

Thousands of people fought among themselves and struggled with burly policemen to get near Lindbergh and shake his hand. Women who had sworn to kiss him had their fur cloaks torn to shreds and emerged from the fray with their hats gone, their hair dishevelled and their dresses tattered and torn.[2]

Ten people were taken to hospital, a woman and child in serious condition. People attacked the plane, seeking mementoes. Hands pulled and ripped the canvas of the wings; pocket knives were used, to greater effect. The initiative of local officials and some admirers saved

328

the flyer. A car sped out to the plane, and Lindbergh was rescued, by pilots and soldiers using rifle butts to clear a path. He was quickly given a French military tunic to wear as a disguise and whisked off to an outlying hangar, where the official greetings took place. To distract the crowd, imposters were lifted on to shoulders, and the throng worshiped the decoys.[3] A father raised his child so that the little boy could see, and the mob acclaimed the child. In the darkness Lindbergh had become Everyman, and Everyman had become Lindbergh.

In the days that followed, Lindbergh was fêted like no one else in previous history, not kings or queens, statesmen or churchmen. Overnight he had become the most famous man ever. Overnight! A day before he was 'the flying fool' and 'Lucky Lindy' to his mates, an airmail pilot and reserve captain in the American air force, a youthful adventurer whose audience consisted usually of pigeons or nighthawks. Now he was LINDBERGH! – *homme de rêve, homme oiseau*, a modern Icarus who, unlike his mythical forebear, had dispelled tragedy. Congratulations poured in to the US embassy in Paris and to the State Department in Washington from around the world, from monarchs and heads of state as well as ordinary people. In Paris American flags flew everywhere, even from that bastion of Gallic introspection and sangfroid, the Quai d'Orsay, which in the past had reserved the honor for visiting heads of state.

Everyone seemed to want to write odes to Lindbergh. They named drinks after him and baptized their children with his name. Charles Augustus Lindbergh. The middle name bespoke the imperial accomplishment. The crowds that saluted him were endless – probably half a million on Thursday afternoon, the twenty-sixth, as his motorcade made its way from the American embassy, where he had been staying, along the avenue d'Iéna, the rue Pierre-Charron, the Champs-Élysées, the place de la Concorde, and the rue de Rivoli, to the Hôtel de Ville –

and their enthusiasm was relentless. Omnipresent hands reached toward him yet again, threw flowers and waved handkerchiefs and hats. For a week Paris indulged in what was probably the most extraordinary outpouring of emotion she had ever displayed. And that for an American from Little Falls, Minnesota, whose tousled blue-eyed fairness and ill-fitting suits made him look even younger than his twenty-five years and the very antithesis of carefully cultivated Gallic *grandeur* and *gloire*.

Officialdom tried to keep pace with public sentiment. A phalanx of graybeards vied with each other to bestow honor after honor on the young American. Virtually every pillar of the French establishment saluted him and praised him. The French president, Doumergue, pinned the cross of the Légion d'honneur on his chest, the first time an American had received such an honor. National and municipal officials lined up to fête him – Briand, Poincaré, Painlevé, Doumer, Godin, Bouju, Chiappe. He lunched with Blériot, the first man to fly the English Channel back in 1909. He was received by Marshals Joffre and Foch. The French ambassador to Washington, Paul Claudel, poet-diplomat, stalwart of classical French sensibility, who had returned to Europe on home leave in April, proposed a toast to Lindbergh's mother.

And in symbolic gestures, in an obvious attempt to Gallicize him and claim him as one of their own, two Paris restaurants offered to feed him and a tailor proposed to dress him gratis for the rest of his life; then, in a delightful prank, a student at the École normale rang the press and proclaimed him an honorary *élève* of the institution, which was a traditional steppingstone to the upper echelons of the French administrative hierarchy.

France of course had not had a monarchy since 1870, so for recognition from the supreme symbols of Europe's historicity, its monarchies, Lindbergh had to go either south or north. The decision was made for him. He had to proceed north, to the courts of the Allied nations that had not wavered in the war – to Brussels and to London. On Saturday, 28 May, Lindbergh flew a patched-up Spirit of St Louis to Brussels, where King Albert decorated him with the Knighthood of the Order of Leopold, and on the next day, Sunday, the twenty-ninth, he went to London.

There at Croydon airfield the reception was even more frenzied and carnivalesque than at Le Bourget a week earlier. People began arriving at the field in mid-morning and by afternoon a crowd estimated by many at over 100,000 had assembled. All around the perimeter of the field, blankets had been spread on the grass, and people picnicked festively. Air trips for the hardy and solvent were offered at five shillings a ride, and five planes did a booming business throughout the day. Just after four o'clock one of these planes came to grief before the eyes of horrified onlookers. As it was coming in to land, its engine appeared to stall and the plane nose-dived to the ground, smashing its undercarriage. Although the four passengers were not seriously hurt, the accident brought home to the spectators, as if on cue, the danger and immensity of Lindbergh's accomplishment.

As Lindbergh's plane was finally sighted, a few minutes before 6:00 p.m, all British self-possession dissolved, and the mass of humanity went berserk, breaking through heavy wooden barriers, wire fences, and police cordons – which, reinforced in the wake of the Le Bourget episode, were thought to be adequate to restrain the mob – trampling each other and rushing on to the runway. Seeing the crowd streaming toward him, Lindbergh had to abort his first attempt to land for fear that he would plow into the sea of welcomers. On the second approach he brought the plane down farther afield and began to taxi toward the Imperial Airways control tower, but the crowd was not to be denied. It quickly surrounded the plane and made progress impossible. Lindbergh, mindful of the damage his plane had suffered at Le Bourget, struggled to keep people off, pushing and shoving, but to no avail. Hands, hands, and more hands. They tugged at the plane, pulled at his clothes, grabbed his helmet. An eyewitness:

> The police repeatedly charged the crowd to try and clear a space around the machine, and the yells and cheers of the people were mingled with the frantic blowing of police whistles. Cars continually sounding their horns attempted to drive through the mob to the rescue.[4]

The ruse that had worked at night at Le Bourget – a decoy wearing a flying helmet – failed to deceive the daytime crowd at Croydon. In the crush people fainted. Ten were taken to local hospitals. About fifty people had climbed on to the roof of a ramshackle building outside the airfield, but the roof gave way and some fell through, though none suffered serious injury.

Finally, Lindbergh was rescued. When he mounted the control tower to greet the crowd, it broke spontaneously into its traditional song of acceptance and approval, 'For He's a Jolly Good Fellow!' After a brief ceremony in which the American admitted that his reception at Croydon, while welcome, was even more harrowing than the one at Le Bourget, he climbed with Ambassador Houghton into the embassy limousine, but the crush of admirers was such that two windows in the car were broken and, as he removed jutting fragments of glass from a pane, Lindbergh was cut slightly. The *Berliner Tageblatt*'s London correspondent reported:

> I have witnessed the British potential for enthusiasm at the opening of Wembley, at the Cup Final, at the boat race, and on the return of Allan Cobham from Australia. But the reception given Lindbergh yesterday overshadows all of this.[5]

In the London program Lindbergh was received by King George at Buckingham Palace and awarded the Air Force Cross. Lady Astor, who was American by birth, was his hostess at the House of Commons. He was a guest of the Prince of Wales at the Derby Eve Ball and of the Earl of Lonsdale at the Epsom Derby.

After his London visit Lindbergh returned briefly to Paris and then sailed from Cherbourg for New York. There on 13 June he was subjected to the inevitable parade up Broadway, during which an estimated four and a half million Americans came out to cheer him and treated their returning hero to eighteen hundred tons of ticker tape. In Washington President Coolidge bestowed the Distinguished Flying Cross on him. Lindbergh was home. His travail as 'the last hero' had, however, only begun.

STAR

What nerve had Lindbergh struck in the sensibility of the western world? He was literally worshiped and adored. People sought relics from his person and his plane as if he were some new god. He was revered more openly in 1927 than were the American astronauts who walked on the moon in 1969. His sudden and fabulous fame, overnight, has not been matched.

Did the achievement warrant the extraordinary response? Or was Lindbergh filling some desperate need? Was he perhaps a creation of a spectacle-craving public? Or was he a creation, as some liked to think, of a sensation-hungry press, which he came shortly so to abhor, which he would blame for the kidnaping and murder of his first child, and which he would try to escape by moving to England for a time in the 1930s?

His feat cannot, of course, be denied. Others had flown the Atlantic before him several times since John Alcock and Arthur Whitten Brown first made the northern crossing from Newfoundland to Ireland in June 1919. But no-one had ever tried to make the crossing alone, and without a radio. The achievement required either stunning audacity or mind-boggling insensitivity, and Lindbergh's character, as it was revealed, suggested that, though he was certainly stubborn, he was anything but insensitive.

He demonstrated quickly that he was in fact a superb diplomat. During his fortnight in Europe in 1927, despite the fatigue that gradually overwhelmed him, despite the strain of the social whirl to which he was subjected, he positively charmed the professional diplomats, statesmen, monarchs, and other officials who greeted him. The youth seemed unable to make a wrong step. Myron T. Herrick, the American ambassador in Paris – an old hand who since 1920 was on his second tour as ambassador to Paris, having been there the first time at the outbreak of war in 1914 – was dazzled by Lindbergh's poise. His impromptu speeches could not have been bettered by a training manual for diplomats, and Herrick's telegrams home sang Lindbergh's praises with limitless admiration, referring to his 'divine genius and simple courage' and calling him an 'ambassador without portfolio.' The comparisons Herrick made, in his public speeches, of Lindbergh with Joan of Arc, Lafayette, and even a biblical David sound strained in retrospect, but they were delivered, it appears, without a trace of cant. No statesman, no politician, not even Woodrow Wilson – such was the implication – had ever done as much for the American image in Europe. 'Did one ever see such an ambassador?' Herrick asked rhetorically.[1] Ernest Hemingway commented: 'Isn't it fine what the American embassy's doing for Lindbergh. It's as if they'd caught an angel that talks like Coolidge.'[2]

The Paris and London press corps, no novices when it came to dealing with visiting dignitaries, agreed with official opinion. They were, without exception, unreserved in heaping praise on the performance of

Lindbergh as public personality. 'Lindbergh is doing more for the rapprochement of nations than all the diplomats,' remarked an exultant Ère nouvelle.[3] The conservative right was as charmed as the socialist and communist left. And the liberal press was ecstatic.

The conservative Times of London was enchanted by Lindbergh's behavior at Buckingham Palace, particularly by his gentle gesture to the little toddler Princess Elizabeth, who had been brought down by her nurse to witness his arrival. 'Captain Lindbergh walked across to her, took her hand, and patted her cheek.' As he left, Lindbergh once again remembered the princess, went over to the little girl, and shook her hand in farewell.[4]

The French communist organ L'Humanité was scathing about the antics of officialdom. LINDBERGH, VICTIM OF OFFICIALS, THE EAGLE DEVOURED BY DWARFS, BIRD MAN LINDBERGH TRAPPED IN PARLIAMENTARY CESSPOOL – these were some of its headlines during Lindbergh's week in Paris. But for Lindbergh himself and for the enthusiastic crowds there was not one sarcastic word. On the contrary, 'In Lindbergh we greet A MAN, of the very best stamp,' judged the paper.[5]

At his press conference Lindbergh was, of course, assisted by American officials. In Paris, Herrick fielded some of the more difficult questions, but throughout Lindbergh maintained his poise, even if at times, as Waverley Root, on the staff of the Paris edition of the Chicago Tribune, claimed, he appeared uncertain. When Hank Wales, the gruff, cigar-smoking, former police reporter in New York and now the chief Paris correspondent for the Tribune, abruptly asked, 'Say, Lindy, did you have a crapper in that plane?' – both Herrick and Lindbergh remained composed and simply skirted the indelicate question.[6]

Europe and America went into a tizzy over Lindbergh in 1927. On his return to New York the London Observer's headline for the story included the words THE UNSPOILT HERO.[7]

335

Was Lindbergh in any sense a creation of the press? The press was at its apogee in the 1920s. Never before or since have there been as many newspapers or as many readers of the printed word. The press was the source of news, information, and entertainment. Every European capital had dozens of newspapers. Many editors, moreover, did judge the Lindbergh flight to be the biggest news story since the war.

But though it played an important role in informing the world of Lindbergh's feat and the acclaim it met, the press can scarcely be charged with creating the American's renown. At most one can say that the printed word and the paucity of pictorial evidence encouraged some people to venture forth to the airfields and into the streets to try to catch a glimpse of the modern hero. On the whole the press followed the excitement rather than created it. Waverley Root has pointed out how unprepared, in fact, the professionals were – the diplomats, the airport officials, the police, and the journalists.[8] Before Lindbergh's departure from New York there was scant mention in the European press of the impending venture. The sensational story blossomed in people's minds before it reached the front pages, while Lindbergh was over the Atlantic.

The acclaim, then, has to be put into a broader context if its dimensions are to be appreciated. Lindbergh, through his achievement and character, seemed to satisfy two worlds, one in the throes of decline and the other in the process of emergence. The one was a world of values, of decorum, of positive accomplishment, of grace. It was a world that had room and ready recognition for individual achievement based on effort, preparation, courage, staying power. It was a world in which man used the machine and technology to conquer nature, in which means were subordinate to ends. It was a world of positive values, revolving around family, religion, nature, and the good and moral life. It was a world whose values had sustained the French and British armies in the war.

For this world, what a hero Lindbergh was! Home-spun

to the core. He was solicitous about mothers, children, animals. He did not drink or smoke or even dance. Milk and water were his potions. When he arrived at Le Bourget and was taken to safety, he was offered coffee and wine. He asked for water. In its social column, 'The Talk of London,' the *Daily Express* gossiped, on 31 May, about the Derby Eve Ball that evening at the Albert Hall. 'Many women, I hear,' the reporter bubbled, 'are going with the express purpose of dancing with him. Should they succeed in doing so, they will no doubt pick up some useful hints as to the very latest steps from across the Atlantic.' The embarrassment that ensued from the gaffe leaped from between the lines of the same reporter's column a few days later: 'Captain Lindbergh did not dance, which must have been a disappointment to many [especially to the reporter!], but he made an amusing speech.'[9]

Lindbergh rejected all the monetary and material rewards and temptations that were dangled before him: not only clothes, meals, but houses and enormous sums of money offered for appearances in film, on stage, on radio, or in advertisements. One correspondent estimated that within two days of the flight Lindbergh had been offered in the vicinity of $650,000. The conservative world adored him for his restraint. He was even associated indirectly with the taming or toning down at least of some of the more disreputable manifestations of the modern scene. At the Derby Ball, 'the dancing,' commented one observer, 'was unusually sedate, and nineteen out of twenty men wore white ties.' Dresses, of course, were long, and they were not suited to the standard frenzied version of the Charleston. 'But it is an adaptable dance,' continued our observer. 'Two Indians last night in full English evening dress were dancing the flat Charleston very beautifully and quietly, and they made a perfect picture.'[10] Here was the old world adapting itself to the new age, and Lindbergh was interpreted as a model for the old order in meeting and overcoming the challenges of the modern age. Therefore monarchs, patriarchs, and all officialdom honored the young American.

The modern sensibility, however, was equally exhilarated. It was enchanted above all by the *deed*. Lindbergh had not swum the Atlantic nor rowed across it nor catapulted over it. He had flown! Man and machine had become one in this act of daring. The purpose was immaterial. The act was everything. It almost captured Gide's prewar vision of an *acte gratuit*, a perfectly free act, devoid of meaning other than its own inherent energy and accomplishment. And Lindbergh had been alone on his flight, completely alone, free of civilization and its constraints, in communion with the oceans and the stars, the winds and the rains. He flew for no-one, not even for mankind. He flew for himself. That was the greatest audacity – to fly for himself. That he was young, that he was unmarried, without even a girlfriend, that he was handsome – all that magnified the enchantment. He was not the creation of an old world; he was a harbinger of a new dawn.

Romanticism in the previous century had associated the artist with flight, with the free-soaring bird, Icarus, the lark – with a transcendence of the real world. In the second half of the century Nietzsche, among others, had been fascinated by the idea of flight. The closing passage of *The Dawn of Day* he had entitled 'We Aeronauts of the Intellect.' At the turn of the century other moderns, too, were captivated by the idea and then by the reality of flight. The airplane caught Kafka's attention in 1909; it figured in Marinetti's futurist manifesto of the same year. Robert Delaunay paid homage to Blériot's Channel crossing in a painting. In 1912 the Grand Palais in Paris put on the exhibition 'Aerial Locomotion.' Léger, Brancusi, and Duchamp visited it. To the others Duchamp remarked: 'Painting is finished. Who could do better than that propeller? Could *you* make that?'[11] Lindbergh, in short, had become the

Nietzschean 'aeronaut' who had fulfilled a personal passion, who had flown not into the setting sun but into the morning.

Harry Crosby idolized him. So did Maurice Rostand, son of Edmond, the playwright and the creator of *Cyrano*. Maurice, wan and drawn, always attired in black and white, with high-heeled shoes and long locks, penned a poem to Lindbergh, thirteen stanzas long, which he dated *21 mai 1927, onze heures du soir*. Since Lindbergh did not arrive until 10:22, that meant, as Janet Flanner pointed out in her 'Letter from Paris' for *The New Yorker*, that Rostand must have composed a line a minute and hence must have been 'almost as speedy as The Spirit of St Louis.' Anna, Comtesse de Noailles, poetess of stature and patroness of Diaghilev and the Ballets russes, referred to Lindbergh as an *enfant sublime*.[12]

And so it went. The moderns were as entranced as the ancients. Both adopted this Homeric individual from small-town, midwestern America as one of their own. In their enthusiasm, however, both sides talked past each other. Nor could anyone really explain with conviction why Lindbergh had excited imaginations and yearnings to such a degree. But if we look beyond the immediate excitement, we see a motif that recurs again and again – in Lindbergh's itinerary, in the language of reporters and commentators, and in other events that framed Lindbergh's conquest of Europe; a motif that no one discussed at length at the time, but that runs through the entire cultural landscape like a black thread. The war.

LEST WE FORGET

Officially, the war had ended eight and a half years earlier, on November 11 1918. Civilians, here and there, had celebrated with a few victory parties. Soldiers had by and large felt little emotion. The end had come, as for

T.S. Eliot's 'Hollow Men,' 'not with a bang but a whimper.'

A rancorous and bitterly debated peace treaty had been presented to the Germans in the form of an ultimatum. In Germany, the new democratic and republican government – elected in the wake of disturbances that had beset the country in November and December 1918, and had induced the kaiser to abdicate – collapsed when confronted with the treaty; but the makeshift replacement government saw no alternative other than acceptance of the Versailles terms. The 'hunger blockade' of the country by the British fleet had been tightened at the end of the war. The Rhine was closed off, and British, American, and French troops occupied bridgeheads across it, at Cologne, Coblenz, and Mainz respectively. Starvation and social breakdown threatened. No-one, on any side, was satisfied with the treaty, which tried to accommodate the idealism of Woodrow Wilson, the vengefulness of Georges Clemenceau, and the pragmatism of David Lloyd George. The Germans considered the terms too harsh; the Allied populations, too mild. Germany was saddled with a guilt for the war which she refused morally to accept. But what could she do? The *levée en masse* that Walther Rathenau's apocalyptic imagination had conjured up in the last days of the war as a defense against foreign intrusion on hallowed German soil was, by the summer of 1919, not only impractical but impossible.

On 14 July 1919, Bastille Day, Paris manufactured an official 'victory' parade. Its size was grand; its emotions were not. America refused to ratify the treaty and even to embrace Woodrow Wilson's political offspring, the League of Nations. The United States retreated into isolationism and abandoned Europe to her wheelchair.

The gargantuan effort, especially the emotional intensity, of the war could not possibly be sustained in effecting the peace, and Europe slumped into a monumental melancholy. The homes promised its heroes

340

remained fictional palaces, and the utopian social dreams evoked by wartime rhetoric were brutally erased by inflation, unemployment, and widespread deprivation, not to mention an influenza epidemic that ravaged the world in 1918–19 and killed more people than the war itself. Disillusionment was the inevitable upshot of the peace.

Faced by the horrendous idea that the war might not have been worth the effort, people simply buried the thought for a time. And if one was to bury that thought, one also had to bury the war. So be it. The war was buried. Robert Graves and T.E. Lawrence had an agreement at Oxford that they would not discuss the war. Edmund Blunden tried to write his memoirs in the immediate aftermath and found that he simply could not. And so, after composing a fragment, he stopped. One mourned loved ones, but avoided thinking about the object for which one had paid such a price. Nine million dead. Twenty-one million wounded. Economies in ruins. Godless Bolshevism in Russia and threatening central Europe. Civil strife in Russia, Germany, Hungary, Poland, Ireland, Italy – everywhere, it seemed. Turkey and Greece at war. The middle east inflamed. 'Lest we forget' was intoned on every conceivable occasion, but forget was exactly what everyone wanted to do.

Veterans' organizations had been founded, but relatively few veterans wanted to join. Employers were encouraged to hire former soldiers, but many found them a poor risk. The incidence of unemployment among ex-servicemen was pitifully high. When the Soviet diplomat Ilya Ehrenburg arrived in Berlin in the autumn of 1921, he found that people were clearly trying to repress the war, even though the scars of war were everywhere. He saw, as he put it, 'catastrophe . . . presented as a well-ordered existence,' and noted that

the artificial limbs of war-cripples did not creak, empty sleeves were pinned up with safety-pins. Men

341

whose faces had been scorched by flame-throwers wore large black spectacles. The lost war took care to camouflage itself as it roamed the streets.[1]

In the victor states the masquerade was no less elaborate. They had won, yes, but what had they won?

The repudiation of the war's political stewards and military politicos came quickly. Wilson, Lloyd George, Clemenceau, Orlando, Ludendorff, Hindenburg, they were all soon forced into frustrated retirement or opposition. (Hindenburg was to be the exception when he was coaxed out of retirement in 1925 and elected to the presidency of the German republic.) Everywhere the left gained ground. In Britain the Liberal Party was decimated, and in 1924 for the first time the Labour Party, whose meteoric rise was as swift as the stunning demise of the Liberals, formed a government. In France in the same year a center-left coalition took office. In Germany the Social Democrats were the largest party by far in the decade after the war and the Communist Party, founded in December 1918, also gained strength.

The growth of the left was a reflection of a desire for radical change in the wake of what was regarded as the bankruptcy of the old order. The effect of this upsurge on the left was to reinforce the noticeable shift of conservatism toward a more extreme position on the right, a 'new conservatism.' The shift was, however, not simply a reaction against the left; it was propelled by a recognition that conservatism had to do more now than conserve: the task was not to conserve but to rebuild. The right, too, had to engage in radical reform if the world was to be set aright.

Political polarization, which was to be the hallmark of the interwar era everywhere, confirmed the disappearance of a normality everyone craved but no-one knew how to effect. The war was the critical stimulant in the political sphere, not social issues nor economic problems. They, while visible and acute, were still subordinate to one question: What did the war really mean? That was the pivotal question behind all political activity, indeed all activity in the aftermath that was called peace. But few tackled the issue directly. The war 'took care to camouflage itself' as it roamed not only the streets but the corridors of power.

Official histories of the war as a whole and regimental and service histories of its separate parts poured from the presses in the early 1920s, but after formal notices and commemorative niceties in appropriate journals, they went on to shelves in libraries and in the homes of ex-servicemen or the bereaved, either unread or, if read, undiscussed. The Germans established a legislative committee in August 1919 to examine the causes of their defeat, and the committee sat longer than the war had lasted, so long, in fact, that it was forgotten by the public and, for much of the time, by the press.

Cenotaphs were erected, cemeteries prepared, headstones manufactured. Between 1920 and 1923 British shipments of headstones to France reached four thousand a week. On 11 November 1920, the unknown soldier was borne from France and buried at Westminster Abbey, and within two days 100,000 wreaths had been laid at the cenotaph in Whitehall. Year after year, on every possible occasion, not just on Armistice Day, the rituals and solemn phrases were repeated. To some they may have brought a measure of solace, but what did the ritual and rhetoric really mean, especially in relation to the postwar world? The old catchwords – freedom, dignity, justice – simply rang hollow. Even arguments relating to what had been averted by the war, as opposed to what had been achieved, offered little sustenance in relation to the sacrifice. Best not to ask such questions. Commemorate, yes; think, no.

This disequilibrium between the experience of the war and the subsequent response to it meant that the war, in its most important sense, as a social, political, and, foremost, existential problem, was relegated to the realm of the unconscious or, more precisely, to that of the consciously repressed. Assigning the crucial issue of the day to either neurosis or simply ignorance, in the true sense of the latter word, confirmed the journey, begun during the war, of western society as a whole – no longer merely groups of intellectuals or some segments of the population or even just one country – toward the edge of a gulf between individual consciousness and tangible problems. Old authority and traditional values no longer had credibility. Yet no new authority and no new values had emerged in their stead.

Not surprisingly, the act of repression, individual or collective, conscious or unconscious, of the most conse-quential events of the age called forth the very opposite: the denial of repression. As people became less able to answer the fundamental question of the meaning of life – and the war posed that question brutally in nine mil-lion cases – they insisted all the more stridently that the meaning lay in life itself, in the act of living, in the vitality of the moment. The twenties, as a result, witnessed a hedonism and narcissism of remarkable pro-portions. Freudian psychology was eagerly grasped as a justification for this denial of repression, and it became thoroughly unfashionable to be 'repressed.' The senses and the instincts were indulged, and self-interest became, more than ever before, the motivation for behavior. The growth of political radicalism was only one manifestation of this development. The rituals of public life were still rooted in the positivistic certainties of the previous century, but the backdrop to the play acting consisted of nightmare and hallucination. 'The war had knocked the ball-room floor from under middle-class English life,' recalled Stephen Spender. 'People resembled dancers suspended in mid-air yet miracu-lously able to pretend that they were still dancing.'[2]

More than a few historians have objected that recent generations remember not the twenties but merely the dreams of the twenties. Far too much attention, they claim, has been devoted to urban exhibitionists, the 'sweet young things,' the rarefied dandyism of *Sonnenkinder*, the antics and tantrums of Dadaists, surrealists, and expressionists; and the reality of unemployment, of urban *ressentiment*, of rural anxiety, or, by contrast, of largely successful efforts on the part of middle-class entrepreneurs to regroup and rebuild have been ignored. Life went on in the twenties, so the argument runs, as it always had, with the humdrum problems of work, wages, food, family welfare, and personal ambition preoccupying people, who had no time for grandiose schemes of political and cultural renewal. If politics drifted to the extremes, this was – so these critics argue – for immediate reasons, not visionary ones.

Such criticism has its point, and it has led to some excellent analyses of the social and economic foundations of political activity. But the recent wave of social history has failed to exorcise successfully the demons, debutantes, and dreams of the twenties. A profound sense of spiritual crisis was the hallmark of that decade; it affected rural laborers, large landowners, industrialists, factory workers, shop clerks, and urban intellectuals. It affected young as well as old, female as well as male. The economic débâcles and social insecurity merely underlined and intensified what was primarily a crisis of values brought on by the war and particularly the aftermath of the war, when the peace clearly failed to meet the expectations enunciated by the leaders during the war. 'The storm has died away,' said Paul Valéry in a lecture at Zürich in 1922, 'and still we are restless, uneasy, as if the storm were about to break. Almost all the affairs of men remain in a terrible uncertainty.' He spoke about all the things that had been injured by the war: economic relations, international affairs, and individual lives. 'But among all these injured things,' he stated, 'is the mind. The mind has indeed been cruelly wounded . . . It doubts itself profoundly.'[3]

The inevitable partner of that doubt was flight, a flight from reality. If newness had been a strong German concern prior to 1914 and during the war, it became a universal preoccupation in the west after the war, accepted by socialists and conservatives, atheists and fundamentalists, hedonists and realists. The craving for newness was rooted in what was regarded by radicals as the bankruptcy of history and by moderates as at least the derailment of history. Even among those who wallowed in nostalgia for a prewar golden age, there was a basic recognition that any salvage attempt would require an enormous effort at reconstruction. But the devastation was so wide and the task of reconstruction so staggering that notions of how this was to be accomplished dissolved often into daydream and wishful thinking.

The fads and madcap behavior of the younger generation of the twenties were motivated largely by cynicism about convention in all its forms and particularly about the moralistic idealism that had kept busy the slaughterhouse that was the Western Front. Whether the activity was socially circumscribed, like the frantic treasure-hunt parties of the 'bright young things' in London's Mayfair, or more widespread like the nudist cult, or still more general, like the yo-yo craze or the new interest in travel or the fascination with film stars, it would be foolish to try to explain such preoccupations solely in terms of more leisure time with the advent of the eight- or nine-hour work day. Intrinsic to the activity was the celebration of life, not in a social or group sense, but as individual assertion *against* social norms and mores. The inspiration was anarchic. When Josephine Baker made her Paris debut in 1925 at the Théâtre des Champs-Élysées, her waist ringed with bananas, carried onstage upside down doing splits, she was symbolizing the extravagance not just of urban bohemianism

346

but of a western culture that as a whole had lost its moorings. For some that 'liberation' was exciting, for others disquieting, but the culture as a whole was adrift.

It has become customary to argue that since the wailing of the saxophone, the frenetic steps of the Charleston, the syncopated rhythms of jazz, and the figure of the gin-swilling flapper were principally urban phenomena, the countryside remained unaffected and rooted still in traditional customs. But improved train and bus services, the spread of the cinema to the small town, and the advent of radio meant that the barriers between urban and rural culture began to break down. Moreover, veterans, when they returned from the wars, returned not just to cities but to farms and villages; and indeed now that they had seen 'Paree,' it was difficult to keep them in check. When these young 'heroes' went on binges in local taverns, broke windows and chairs, assaulted girls, or caused an incipient scandal, the invariable response of the citizenry was to hush up the outrage, to show tolerance, and to say: 'These are our war heroes. We must be lenient and try to understand.' While the economic crises of the twenties came in waves – tidal waves, to be sure – to the cities, the countryside was depressed through the entire decade and never truly participated in the modest boom of the middle of the decade. Plagued by lack of credit, obsolescence of machinery and techniques, and disruption of markets, farmers struggled to survive, and many did not.

A byproduct of this mood was a sense of transitoriness. Whether in fashion, architecture, or the tableaux of Piet Mondrian, curves were abandoned in favor of straight lines, lines that suggested movement, a new simplicity, and a new beginning. Women were liberated from high-neck, ankle-length dresses; these gave way to 'glad rags' and the 'boyish look.' For the first time in history breasts were looked upon as a blemish and the brassiere became a flattener rather than booster. The

347

natural shape of the waist was eliminated and belts were slung around the hips. Since the slightest suggestion of a curve was derided as evidence of nutritional incontinence, dieting became fashionable. Buttocks, too, disappeared. As opulence was associated with decadence, Coco Chanel introduced the 'poor look' of dignified chic – *le luxe dans le simplicité*: simple wool suits with cardigan jackets and plain or pleated skirts. Short hair had appeared before the war – Irene Castle adopted it in New York and Isadora Duncan shortened her hair as she shortened her skirts – but it became, in the form of bobbed or 'shingled' hair, a part of the boyish look of the twenties. Of Iris Storm and her shingled hair Michael Arlen wrote in *The Green Hat*:

> Her hair was thick and tawny . . . It was like a boy's hair, swept back from her forehead . . . Above her neck her hair died a very manly death, a more manly death than 'bobbed' hair was ever known to die.[4]

Was the metaphor of hair dying 'a very manly death' accidental? The imagery and vocabulary of war permeated all forms of culture in the twenties. The world was still on its death binge.

In architecture and design a new 'international style' began to take hold in the twenties which emphasized not only straight lines but a general honesty in the use of materials; by employing glass and lacquer, the style suggested, through transparency and reflection, that the barriers between man and nature, subject and object, were less rigid than the old order had insisted.

In the quest for a new fluency and harmony was involved a profound rebellion against an older generation, against the fathers who had led their sons to slaughter. The cult of youth came to first bloom in the twenties. Literature, film, advertising, and even the politics of the era were dominated by this youth worship. Patricide and the act of moral reclamation that the murder of the father entailed fascinated the new literary generation. Only the young were genuinely human; the old were invariably ugly, venal, and hypocritical. In Aldous Huxley's *Point Counter Point* Lucy Tantamount calls the older generation 'aliens':

> What makes the old such an Arab tea party is their ideas. I simply cannot believe that thick arteries will ever make me believe in God and morals and all the rest of it. I came out of the chrysalis during the War, when the bottom had been knocked out of everything. I don't see how our grandchildren could possibly knock it out more thoroughly than it was knocked then.[5]

Robert Musil in *Young Törless*, Hermann Hesse in *Demian*, and Henri de Montherlant in *La Relève du matin* were among those who turned to the depiction of childhood to conjure up Rousseau-like visions of noble innocence subjected to the trickery and deceit of adult civilization. Paul Klee found inspiration for his surrealistic canvases in the primitive automatist daubings of children. An older generation, sad and guilty about the slaughter of youth in the war, said little to protest. 'A flimsy crew, these moderns,' was H.G. Wells's mild response.[6] Still, while regarded as a flimsy crew by some, the young rebels were wooed and coddled by most, particularly by political parties, which scrambled to build up youth organizations and fell over each other to attract young members. Radicalism had most success in this effort. The youth of the twenties was inclined to dismiss conventional politics with scorn. For Christopher Isherwood and his friends at Cambridge 'politics' was a 'withering word' and the activity was 'automatically dismissed as boring and vile.'[7]

However, in the general rejection of ornamentation, figurative and literal, and in the emphasis on a new simplicity, the culture of the twenties was not so much

349

establishing new value systems as decrying the old. The emphasis was on dis-establishment, on the one hand to simplify function and on the other hand to liberate creativity, but the two areas of effort – despite the hopes and aspirations and qualified success of some groups, like the Bauhaus school – were not usually reconciled. The old dichotomy, so prevalent in nineteenth-century German thought, between *Geist* and *Macht* had now become a striking feature of western culture in general, but with an even greater intensity and emotional commitment to the constituent parts than was evident in prewar Germany.

And yet the heightened emphasis on spirituality, inwardness, and the unconscious, so evident in the public's fascination with Freudian psychology, mysticism, fundamentalist evangelism, and the sentimentalism of American cinema – Ilya Ehrenburg listed twenty-two films with *Love* in their title in 1927[8] – could not hide the profound doubt that surrounded even the new stage of subjectivism. If in Einstein's atom molecules were in constant motion and matter was only energy, then in Freud's psyche the components were also undergoing constant mutation. Sanity and reason were psychological and philosophical constructs of a bygone age of fixity and faith. The faith was gone and, along with it, the fixity. Movement, melancholy, and neurosis remained. Isherwood spoke of 'the vast freak museum of our neurotic generation.'[9]

ITINERARY AND SYMBOL

After his arrival at Le Bourget and the ensuing ceremonies, Lindbergh left at around 12:30 a.m. in a car that traveled without lights initially and followed a roundabout route into Paris, via Dugny and St Denis, instead of the direct road through Aubervilliers. He was scheduled to stay at one of the city's grand hotels, the

Majestic, near the Étoile, so the car, after proceeding appropriately along the rue Lafayette and then passing the Madeleine, headed along the Champs-Élysées from the place de la Concorde. Midway along this great avenue the car stopped at the Claridge Hotel, where several bouquets of flowers were purchased – roses and cornflowers.[1]

The car then continued up the Champs and pulled up at the Arc de Triomphe, where Lindbergh got out and placed the flowers at the tomb of the unknown soldier. Thus his first official act in Paris, at one o'clock in the morning, was to pay homage to the dead of the war. As the car then proceeded toward the small side street that is the rue Dumont d'Urville, a stone's throw from the Étoile, the mammoth crowd gathered in front of the Majestic and spilling over on to the avenue Kléber made it clear that Lindbergh would have no peace in a hotel, and he was taken to the American embassy.

In Brussels the following Saturday the same routine was followed. On his way from the airport to the US embassy, before he had even changed clothes, Lindbergh laid a wreath at the tomb of the unknown soldier in the Belgian capital. On the morning of Monday, his first full day in London, he attended a cere-mony commemorating the war dead at St Margaret's, Westminster, and then went to pay his respects at the grave of the unknown soldier at Westminster Abbey. In all three capitals he was received and applauded by veterans' organizations. Officials took special care to present to Lindbergh representatives of war cripples and the blind. In Brussels, during his visit to the Hôtel de Ville, he was also greeted by the Vieux Volontaires de la Grande Guerre, those who, despite having been over fifty at the time, managed, by hook or crook, to fight in the war. Veterans' organizations from around the world sent Lindbergh telegrams of congratu-lation. Even German groups joined in.

The speeches and other public pronouncements

honoring Lindbergh in Paris, Brussels, and London were full of references to the war, to Franco- and Anglo-American amity, to the American flyers of the Lafayette Escadrille, and to the American contribution in general to the Allied war effort. Ambassador Herrick made mystical comparisons of Lindbergh's flight with the achievement on the Marne: a sublime destiny governed both victories. And Maurice Rostand, in his ode to Lindbergh, declared that the flyer's visit to the tombs of the fallen had been preordained.

In 1927, in fact, the ritualistic commemoration of the war reached a peak as numbers of war memorials, large and small, national and regimental, regional and municipal, at Douaumont, Tannenberg, Passchendaele, Ypres, as well as cemeteries throughout Belgium and France, and in towns and cities in all the belligerent countries were unveiled. On 24 May the *Scotsman* of Edinburgh, for example, published two pictures on the same page, one of Ambassador Herrick congratulating Lindbergh and the other of the dedication of the Seaforth Regiment's war memorial at Fampoux near Arras. In the *Daily Herald* of 31 May, at the bottom of a column recounting Lindbergh's previous day in London, a small item announced, 'One hundred war widows, orphans and ex-Service men of Great Britain are to visit the war cemeteries in Belgium next month.'

There was no commentary on the connections between these events – between Lindbergh's flight and the war. Indeed, there was no obvious connection. Yet without the war, the Lindbergh phenomenon cannot be understood. Although he had not participated in it, the war gave Lindbergh's accomplishment its extraordinary dimensions. Without the war the feat would of course have been celebrated, but mature responsible public figures would not have resorted to hyperbole, such as that of Mackenzie King, the Canadian prime minister, who called Lindbergh's flight 'the greatest individual achievement in the history of the world.' Nor would the general public have been as delirious in its acclaim.

War followed Lindbergh everywhere – not only past war but future war. Naturally, the military was especially interested in Lindbergh's flight. Behind the remark of a General Girod, who presided over the army subcommittee of the French Chamber of Deputies, that Lindbergh's flight was 'the most audacious act ever seen in all the centuries' was a recognition of the military potential of the achievement.[2] The critics of the military, however, summoned up visions of a war from the air in which gas bombs would rain down on civilians. Letters to newspaper editors revealed that the public was intensely concerned about this frightening implication of progress in aviation. Yet other commentators took the outpouring of public emotion for Lindbergh to indicate that humanity rather than the military was the chief beneficiary of the trans-Atlantic flight. The Paris paper *Populaire* called Lindbergh's accomplishment 'the most enormous deed of pacifistic heroism in history.'[3] At any rate war provided the context for judgement here.

If millions of war dead surrounded Lindbergh during his visit to Europe, contemporary death, especially the high fatality rate among flyers, also surrounded him. He himself had survived two incidents in previous years in which he had had to parachute to safety. One of the factors contributing to the emotional French response to Lindbergh was the disappearance, less than a forthnight earlier, of two French war aces, Charles Nungesser and François Coli, who had left Paris on 8 May in an attempt to fly to New York. They had disappeared without trace. The excitement, expectations, and tension generated by that venture and its fate were transferred to Lindbergh. One of his first acts on Sunday morning, the day after his arrival, was to visit Nungesser's mother in the boulevard du Temple to express to her his hope that the two war heroes might yet be found alive. Two British flyers, Carr and Gilman, who left for Karachi on Friday, 20 May, the same day Lindbergh took off from New York, in an attempt to break the long-distance nonstop record, were forced to ditch near the Persian port of Bandar Abbas two days later. They survived, as did the Italian aviator de Pinedo, who, in the middle of Lindbergh's week in Paris, disappeared about 240 kilometers from the Azores on his flight from Newfoundland to Portugal and was picked alive from the ocean a week later by a passing ship.

On 27 and 28 May, seven pilots were killed in air crashes, including four in an air show in Augusta, Georgia. Near Chartres a military plane caught fire during a demonstration: its two occupants jumped; one descended safely, but the other was killed when his parachute failed to open. In the first week of June there were at least ten deaths in flying accidents at Essen, Warnemünde, Leipzig, and Bournemouth. At the English city in an air meet two British pilots were killed before thousands of spectators when the wings of their planes touched in a turn and the two machines plunged to earth and exploded in flames. And several weeks later, when Lindbergh visited Ottawa on his tour around North America, one of the twelve US army planes escorting him crashed on landing, killing its pilot. These incidents made the hazards of flying clear to everyone. Thus, death, commemorated or contemporary, stalked Lindbergh wherever he went and made his accomplishment – which amounted to an affirmation of life in the midst of death – all the more notable and gave it its metaphoric meaning. The *Manchester Guardian* hoped that this positive significance would triumph, but the very need to articulate the hope had as its general context a mood of doubt, anxiety, and insecurity:

It is time that flying ceased to be chequered by the needless daring that attends pure record-breaking, and it is to be hoped that the admiration rightly evoked by Lindbergh's courage and endurance will not add to the already too numerous plans to do or outdo what he has done.[4]

As the rituals of an old world surrounded the achievement of the new, the mood was one of melancholy and regret, accompanied by a tremulous and anxious excitement. Flight has always possessed an enormous symbolism for man; during the war that symbolism was heightened. The air ace was the object of limitless envy among infantry, mired in mud and seeming helplessness. Soldiers looked up from their trenches and saw in the air a purity of combat that the ground war had lost. The 'knights of the sky' were engaged in a conflict in which individual effort still counted, romantic notions of honor, glory, heroism, and chivalry were still intact. In the air, war still had meaning. Flyers were the 'aristocracy of war' – 'the resurrection of our personality,' as one writer put it.[5] Flying was associated with freedom and independence, an escape from the horrendous collective slaughter of a war of matériel. In the air war one could maintain values, including respect for one's enemy, values that lay at the foundation of civilization and that the war on the ground appeared to be negating. The most significant technological achievement of the modern world was thus also seen as a means of affirming traditional values.

Through the postwar decade flying retained these associations. The accolades received by Lindbergh seemed to resurrect a whole vocabulary. The enthusiasm with which the French used words like *héros*, *gloire*, *victoire*, and *chevalier* to describe Lindbergh and his feat suggested that they craved to use this language unequivocally once again. The *Daily Express* noted a similar need in the British public:

Serving the hero is so splendid and comforting that it is in itself one of the major joys of life. Millions discovered this during the war. They found opportunities for cherishing some soldier or sailor or airman, and were made glad by that service. They obtained also a part in the sacrifice which the man was offering, and felt that they were united with him. We have an abiding need of heroes to lift us above the common ways of our life.[6]

That last phrase, 'the common ways of our life,' or, in its French version, *notre médiocre condition humaine*, cropped up constantly in the commentary on both sides of the English Channel. Lindbergh became a symbol of the desire for a reaffirmation of values but at the same time of the profound dissatisfaction with contemporary existence. Correspondingly, the fascination with flight was an indication of a yearning to escape the banality of an age, an age that had lost its faith.

Paul Claudel was aware of the illusions that surrounded the official welcome for Lindbergh. His diary entry for 23 May is cryptic but suggestive:

At the Am[erican] emb[assy] I shake hands with the young Charles Lindbergh, slim, pink, blond, timid. *Unam omnium rempublicam agnoscimus, mundum* (Tertullian).* Profound disgust with glory and all these nauseating compliments.[7]

Lindbergh without question represented a major achievement, but he also became a poetical figment of a world turned inward. Pierre Godin, president of the Paris Municipal Council, virtually said as much at the reception at the Hôtel de Ville:

We think much less, sir, of honoring you than of honoring ourselves through you. You are one of these men whose example will preserve humanity if it is ever tempted to doubt its greatness and to despair of

*We recognize only one state, the universe.

its future. You are one of these men in whom a great nation recognizes the image of its ideals.[8]

Godin's remarks must be read above all as a statement of doubt about humanity rather than affirmation, of pleading rather than promise. Senator Dherbécourt, president of the Conseil général de la Seine, called Lindbergh's accomplishment 'one that only the mind of a poet could have conceived and one also whose magnificence only enthusiastic verse could sufficiently exalt.' And the prefect of the police, Chiappe, referred to 'the incomparable beauty' of Lindbergh's feat.[9] The language of these public officials is that of longing, a yearning to aestheticize the world, to turn life into poetry. The Langbehns and the Chamberlains of prewar Germany had talked and written in exactly the same spirit.

The poets chimed in with parallel sentiments. Lindbergh, 'beautiful firstborn of Sagittarius . . . vanquisher of the void,' had conquered death!

> Tu fus celui par qui les hommes
> Soudain voient luire un jour plus beau.
> Hors des ténèbres où nous sommes
> L'aigle enfin chasse le corbeau! . . .
> Oh! nous vivons un temps auguste,
> Car ils sont nés, les jours nouveaux!
> La mort n'est rien!*

'Death is nothing!' So wrote Alexandre Guinle in his 'Ode to Charles A. Lindbergh.'[10] On Saturday, 28 May, Le Figaro published three poems in its literary supplement, by Pierre de Regnier, Maurice Levaillant,

---

*You were the one through whom men
Suddenly see a more beautiful day dawning.
Out of the darkness we are in
The eagle finally chases the raven! . . .
Oh! we are living in an august time,
For it is born, the new age!
Death is nothing!

357

and André David. Levaillant referred to Lindbergh as 'the man-Titan'; David called him 'poet of the blue . . . creator of a new myth.' And in the *Journal des débats politiques et littéraires* Marcel Berger called Lindbergh's feat 'a work of art' because it was 'beautiful in itself.'[11] The German poet Ivan Goll, living in Paris, published an ecstatic ode in the *Berliner Tageblatt* on 25 May. The key to Lindbergh was that his goal was 'in himself.' Paris lay in his own mind, the mind of a happy youngster who had never read a line of Kant, and whose imagination was not buried among the ruins of Egypt or throttled in the sad corridors of universities. The theme in all this commentary and reaction is that of a revival of imagination – 'the blond smile of your youth blinds us like the searchlights of Roosevelt Field' – in the midst of a ruined civilization, of a revival of individual will and spirit. That alone would lift Europe out of its pessimism and doldrums. Yet the tone throughout is one of regret rather than hope. Individualism has lost its social dimension; truth is not to be found in a social reality but in the individual imagination, in Dionysian energy and will. The acclaim for Lindbergh was an encomium for a bygone age of social individualism and at the same time a recognition, even if unconscious, that in the modern world the individual was alone, in permanent flight, devoid of footing, devoid even of the sentimental reassurance of a kitten.

Man had been set loose. Freedom was no longer a matter of being at liberty to do what is morally right and ethically responsible. Freedom had become a personal matter, a responsibility above all to oneself. The modern impulse before the war had possessed a strong measure of optimism, springing from a bourgeois religion of meliorism. The optimism had not disappeared entirely by the twenties, but it was now more wish than confident prediction. Its landscape was one of destruction and desolation, not simply the barrenness that the avant-garde had so despised before the war.

The Lindbergh episode revealed that the prewar form of modernism, with its positive urge, had shifted to America. Europe recognized this. Lindbergh was constantly referred to as a symbol of the 'high courage and dash of young America,' as a representative of America's unrestrained energy. That energy – so obvious in the cultural artifacts, forms, and personalities that America exported, whether they were Hollywood's epics or slapstick comedies; ragtime, jazz, or the Charleston; bobbed, cigarette-smoking, gin-swilling flappers; exotic sensualists like Josephine Baker; or hard-living expatriates like Ernest Hemingway and F. Scott Fitzgerald – that unrelenting and unrepentant energy was unavoidable. It was loud and brash. Most moderns were enchanted.

Maurice Ravel introduced a teasing fox-trot rhythm into his *L' Enfant et les sortilèges*; Francis Poulenc produced a *Rhapsodie nègre*; and Georges Auric and Igor Stravinsky both composed works entitled *Rag-Time*. The 'one-step' and the 'two-step' appeared on the stage of the Folies Bergères. In London's Mayfair the 'bright young things' of the twenties adopted an American accent, and in the wake of Lindbergh's stay 'flying visits' here and there became a part of their style. In Paris, the flat drawl of Josephine Baker's Americanized French, usually so abhorrent to Gallic sensibility, was suddenly all the rage. Nancy Cunard's favorite night spot in Paris was the Plantation, with its murals of Mississippi steamboats and 'darkies.'

But the glittering American dream also enthralled the working classes of Europe, who saw in every rags-to-riches story the happy ending of their own lives. To the critics who claimed that America represented nothing more than crude materialism devoid of spiritual values, her defenders responded that that was a superficial judgement which missed the whole point of America.

America's meaning, first and foremost, was spiritual. Wall Street, said Fernand Léger, was the symbol of 'audacious America, which always acts and never turns to look behind.' New York and Moscow, he said, were the centers of modern activity. Paris had become simply an observer.[1]

According to another Frenchman, Lucien Romier, America stood for youth, vibrancy, enterprise, and magnanimity. 'The United States seems to be today,' he insisted in 1927,

> the only great country whose citizens declare incessantly their love for the society to which they belong, work together enthusiastically for its betterment, and, in a world made pessimistic to the core by social problems, reveal themselves to be optimists on social issues.

America, he continued, had successfully 'deproletarianized' its masses: 'American democracy uplifts the masses with its moralism, but European democracies saturate their people with intellectualism.' And, with many others, Romier pointed to the dominance of women in the American family. The lack of fear toward men, the rejection of patriarchy, was eminently modern and liberating, he argued.[2]

For Henry W. Nevinson, Londoner, novelist, and father of the painter C.R.W. Nevinson, even the glitter and materialism of America signified imagination and drive. On leaving New York he wrote:

> Goodbye to the heaven-piled offices, so clean, so warm, where lovely stenographers, with silk stockings and powdered faces, sit leisurely at work or converse in charming ease! . . . I am going to an ancient city of mean and moldering streets, of ignoble coverts for mankind, extended monotonously over many miles; of grimy smoke clinging closer than a blanket;

of smudgy typists who know little of silk or powder, and less of leisure and charming ease . . . Goodbye to central heating and radiators, fit symbols of the hearts they warm! Goodbye to frequent and well-appointed bathrooms, glory to the plumber's art! . . . Goodbye to the long stream of motors – 'limousines' or 'flivvers'! . . . Goodbye America! I am going home.[3]

Whether they admired or despised the ebullience of America, many agreed that the future of mankind lay on that continent. The Americans, said the British writer Mary Borden,

> should be watched by everyone interested in the future of mankind, for the scaffolding of the world of the future is reared against the sky of America, and a rough map of it is spread over that continent and its voice is pounding and screaming out the news of what is to come to pass on the earth.[4]

Some moderns were nevertheless torn by these prospects. Ivan Goll praised Lindbergh, yet he was not sure that America could provide a panacea for Europe. 'Certainly, Europe is dying of senility, of the "eurocoque." But your pill "Americoon," ' he told the Americans, 'has nothing in it but bicarbonate of soda.'[5] Diaghilev revealed similar ambivalence. 'America will have a lot to say in the art of the future,' he admitted in 1926.

> Already her influence is to be felt everywhere – in painting, the theatre, and music. French composers have picked up the jazz idiom, and America has had her say even in the old and conservative institution of ballet.[6]

But he would also become very irritated by American vulgarity. In August 1926, in Venice, he was in a bitchy mood:

We have stopped in the Hôtel des Bains because the din at the Excelsior makes life impossible. The whole of Venice is up in arms against Cole Porter because of his jazz and his Negroes. He has started an idiotic nightclub on a boat moored opposite the Salute, and now the Grand Canal is swarming with the very same Negroes who have made us all flee from London and Paris. They are teaching the 'Charleston' on the Lido beach! It's dreadful. The gondoliers are threatening to massacre all the elderly American women here.[7]

The traditionalists frowned, complained, and sighed about the 'Americanization' of Europe. America, like its films, was all brilliant energy and no substance. The nation was a gross contradiction in terms, they said. Against the mindless patriotism of Americans should be set the physical disunity of the country; against the architectural grandeur of New York, that city's incredible filth; against the prudery and puritanism of America, her criminality and indecent sexuality; against the humanism of her ideals, her racism and lynchings; against the piety of her religion, the burlesque of her Bible-thumping evangelists. The adjectives and similes that the British and French had reserved for Germans during the war were now redirected at Americans. In the eyes of many an Englishman, Margaret Halsey noted, Americans 'are running neck and neck with the anthropoid apes.'[8]

Many felt that Europe, especially its youth, was adopting the worst side of America. At a conference of the National Association of Boys Clubs, held in Britain in June 1927, one speaker after another bemoaned the American influence. 'American hustle and bustle has come over here,' said one.

A tremendous desire for stunts, excitement, and change has come over our youth, and the great problem is how to make the inside attraction of clubs

362

greater than the outside attractions of the cinema, dance hall, music hall, and the girls.

He advocated physical recreation and studies in music, literature, and art! Moreover, he urged the clubs to ban the latest American dances. Youth should dance, he said in all seriousness, on 'Park-Lane lines' and not in the manner to be observed currently 'in the district of the Elephant and Castle.'[9]

Nevertheless, the fascination continued, indeed mounted, and America's influence on a war-torn and vulnerable Europe, doubting itself, was not to be denied. 'Our impression is that we have been colonized,' remarked a Frenchman.[10]

Everywhere there was a natural skepticism about Americanization, but in the end it was in Germany that the least resistance was shown. There the self-doubt was most profound, and America capitalized on this doubt, both figuratively and literally. American energy was welcomed, as was American money, public and private. By 1923 the German economy was reeling from an inflationary spiral whose proportions no society had ever experienced before. By the summer of that year the German mark had become completely valueless. Following the example of the Dawes loan in 1924, American investors penetrated the German economy. At the same time the American film magnates began to spread their tentacles and exerted a greater influence in Germany than elsewhere in Europe, buying into German companies, purchasing cinemas, and making films there for the German market. Writers like Hemingway had more success in Germany than elsewhere, apart from home.[11] Probably the only American experiment Germany did not follow in the 1920s was Prohibition. 'Germany today is a kind of America,' wrote Hermann Hesse. 'One has to swim and bustle around in it to keep from drowning. If one can do that one is all right.'[12] Many Germans, often with hesitation and a bad

363

conscience, were willing to declare by 1927 that they felt much closer to the United States than to France or Britain. Thomas Mann, like Hesse, was not sure that this was a good thing, but it did seem to be a feature of German life. Even the monuments of German culture seemed to have been subjected to Americanization, protested Mann: 'I know for certain that Bayreuth today is more a concern of the gentleman from San Francisco than of the German spirit and its future.'[13].

ASSOCIATIONS

On 26 May, on the Thursday evening of the week Lindbergh spent in Paris, a gala was organized for him at, of all places, the Théâtre des Champs-Élysées on the avenue Montaigne. On his arrival at the theater that, as we recall, one critic had claimed was built in a Zeppelin style, Lindbergh was greeted at the entrance by Marshal Franchet d'Espérey, who had been one of France's more successful generals in the Great War and who now acted as chairman of the airmen's welfare fund. The audience for the gala consisted of French air aces, past and present, and the program consisted of speeches and readings acclaiming Lindbergh and the conquest of the air in general. In this event, the modern hero, the war, and the modern aesthetic were symbolically fused.

On the following evening, Friday, 27 May, Diaghilev began his new Paris season. It marked the twentieth anniversary of the founding of his ballet company. The venue was, however, not the Théâtre des Champs-Élysées but the Sarah Bernhardt theater at Châtelet. Ten performances were scheduled, running through 9 June. On the opening night the program consisted of *The Triumph of Neptune*, an 'English' ballet that had had a successful première in London in the previous December, with music by Gerald Berners, libretto by

Sacheverell Sitwell, and choreography by Diaghilev's most recent discovery, George Balanchine; *La Chatte*, a new ballet, with music by Henri Sauguet, décor by Naum Gabo, and choreography, specifically for Olga Spessivtseva, by, again, Balanchine; and finally a revived *Oiseau de feu*, with Stravinsky himself conducting, with sets and costumes by Goncharova and Larionov, the Russian futurists, and choreography by Fokine.

The Paris press paid little attention to the new season, despite the anniversary it marked, and there were few reviews. Lindbergh dominated everyone's attention. That he, the very incarnation of the 'firebird,' should now be fêted at the Théâtre des Champs-Élysées, and by an audience of flyers, was a telling indication of how the world had turned. The Russian ballet was old hat. America was new. Lindbergh stood on the stage that Josephine Baker and La Revue Nègre had conquered some months earlier. (When Lindbergh landed, Mademoiselle Ba-kair, still the darling of Parisian night life, stopped her show at the Folies to announce the arrival of her fellow American.) Nevertheless, *Le Figaro*, which had been so vitriolic in its denunciation of *Le Sacre* in 1913, did, appropriately, carry an assessment of the opening night in 1927. Of Diaghilev, P.B. Ghéusi wrote:

This Russian animator has been the Antoine of modern choreographic art. His quiet tenacity, his mystical faith in his own success, which the perverse demon of theater did not sell him cheaply, the smiling fanaticism of his art, much more personal than Slav – all this has brought about a whole new school of thought, which has now been accepted by both the public and professional world.

Stravinsky, too, was flattered by Ghéusi.[1] How Paris and the western world had changed since 1913!

Pavlova was on tour in Stockholm at the end of May.

Chaliapin was in Vienna. The critics hardly noticed them. Those that did were kind. Chaliapin's voice had become smaller since the early days, said one, but the artist in him had grown.[2]

And Nijinsky? What had happened to him? At his last recital, in early 1919, before he was committed to a sanatorium, he had attempted, in front of a small private audience in St Moritz, to capture the war in dance. 'Now I will dance you the war,' he announced, 'with its suffering, with its destruction, with its death.'[3] In his diary of those days he identified himself, as Nietzsche had done in his last utterances before the complete darkness of his madness enveloped him, with God.

In December 1928, a few days after Christmas, Harry Kessler attended a performance of the Diaghilev company at the Opéra in Paris.

Afterward, as I was waiting for Diaghilev in the corridor behind the stage, he approached together with a short haggard youngster in a tattered coat. 'Don't you know who he is?' he asked. 'No,' I said, 'I really can't think.' 'But it's Nijinsky!' *Nijinsky!* I was thunderstruck. His face, so often radiant as a god's, for thousands an unforgettable experience, was now gray, flabby, empty, only fleetingly lit by a blank smile, a brief gleam as of a flickering flame. Not a word crossed his lips. Diaghilev had hold of him under one arm and, to go down the three flights of stairs, asked me to support him under the other, because he who formerly seemed able to leap over rooftops now feels his way uncertainly, anxiously, from step to step. I took hold of him, squeezed his thin fingers, and tried to cheer him with friendly words. Uncomprehending, he looked at me with big eyes that were infinitely touching and reminded me of a sick animal.[4]

And what had happened to spring? In 1913, just before the first performance of *Le Sacre*, Isadora

Duncan's children had died; the car in which they were left unattended had rolled into the Seine. Now in 1927, in Nice, the 'divine Isadora' stepped into a Bugatti for a drive along the promenade des Anglais. A long fashionable scarf trailed behind her. It caught. In a wheel. She died instantly of a broken neck.

T.S. Eliot had an answer for the problem of spring. He was from St Louis, as was Josephine Baker. And Lindbergh flew in the Spirit of St Louis. They had all come to Europe.

> April is the cruellest month, breeding
> Lilacs out of the dead land, mixing
> Memory and desire, stirring
> Dull roots with spring rain.[5]

IX

Memory

We who have known war must never forget war. And that is
why I have a picture of a soldier's corpse nailed to the door of
my library.

HARRY CROSBY

Soyons, à notre tour, le printemps qui reverdit les grises terres
de mort, et de notre sang versé pour la justice, faisons après les
veilles d'horreur surgir des lendemains de beauté.*

JOSÉ GERMAIN
1923

At school, and in books written for boys, one was so constantly
reminded that we had won the war that my school friends and I
found our curiosity excited by those who had lost it. Losing
seemed much more original and stimulating than winning.

RICHARD COBB
1983

Qui aurait pensé, il y a dix-sept ans, qu'on pourrait louer
l'harmonie du Sacre? C'est un fait. On ne songe plus à ses
audaces, on admire ses perfections.**

ANDRÈ ROUSSEAU
February 1930

WAR BOOM

Erich Maria Remarque's *Im Westen nichts
Neues*, or *All Quiet on the Western Front*, as

---

*Let us in turn be the spring, which brings green new life to the
gray terrain of death, and with the blood we gave for justice let us, after
sleepless nights full of horror, give rise to new days of beauty.

**Who, seventeen years ago, would have ever thought that you could
praise the harmony of *Le Sacre*? But that's the case. One no longer thinks of
its presumption; one admires its perfection.

Cubist war. A gas sentry sounds the alarm, near Fleurbaix, June 1916.

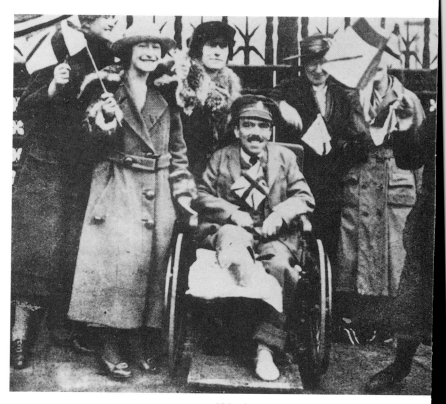

Victory!

Berlin dances, at the Eldorado on the
Motzstrasse. There is only one woman
in this picture.

Tanz in Baden-Baden
by Max Beckmann, 1923

Sur les toits de Berlin. The Charleston as
rite of spring? Compare the position
of the feet here with that of the corps
de ballet in the previous illustration.

Lindbergh: man and machine

Fame: Lindbergh arrives at the Croydon airfield, May 29, 1927.

Erich Maria Remarque

Air aces: Lindbergh and Goering. Lindbergh inspects Goering's ceremonial sword.

Man of the people: Hitler at the Feldherrnhalle, August 1, 1914

German dance champions, 1934

Spring without end: the last photo of Hitler, in the garden of the Reich Chancellery, decorating Hitler Youth with the Iron Cross

the English translation would be entitled, was published first in Berlin by the house of Ullstein at the end of January 1929. Twenty months later, in October 1930, the *Nouvelles littéraires* in Paris would refer to Remarque as the 'author today with the largest audience in the world.'[1]

When the book was published, accompanied by an advertising campaign larger than any ever before launched by a German publisher, about ten thousand advance orders had been placed. For weeks Berlin's advertisement pillars had been plastered with posters, each week a different one. First week: 'It's coming.' Second week: 'The great war novel.' Third week: 'All Quiet on the Western Front.' Fourth week: 'By Erich Maria Remarque.' The novel had by then appeared in serialized form in Ullstein's most distinguished newspaper, the *Vossische Zeitung*, from 10 November, the day before the tenth anniversary of the Armistice, to 9 December. While the paper's circulation did not skyrocket dramatically, as some have claimed, sales did rise slightly and daily editions usually sold out.

But now, after publication, the rush began. Within three weeks 200,000 copies were sold. The sale of 20,000 copies in one day was not unusual. By early May, 640,000 copies had been sold in Germany. English and French translations were hastily prepared. The English edition appeared in March, the American at the end of May, and the French in June. The American Book-of-the-Month Club selected the novel as its choice for June and ordered 60,000 copies for its 100,000 subscribers. The Book Society, a comparable book club in Great Britain, 'recommended' the novel to its members. By the end of the year sales neared a million in Germany, and another million in Britain, France, and the United States together. In Germany the Ullsteins were using six printing and ten bookbinding firms to try to keep abreast of demand. In Britain the Barrow public library announced to its members in November that *All Quiet* had been reserved in advance for two years! Within the year the book had been translated into about twenty languages, including Chinese and Esperanto, and the Ullsteins, in their remarkable promotional effort, even had a German Braille edition prepared and sent without charge to every blind veteran who requested it.[2]

Almost overnight Remarque's novel had become, as one comment put it, 'the postwar phenomenon of book-selling.' That was an understatement. Remarque's success was unprecedented in the entire history of publishing. In England and Germany the book trade, which had suffered throughout the decade but now was in even worse straits because of the general downturn in the economy in 1928–1929, gave thanks. 'Remarque is our daily bread,' quipped booksellers in Berlin.[3]

Remarque's spectacular success brought on a flood of war books and other material dealing with the war and ushered in what came to be known as the 'war boom' of 1929–1930. War novels and war memoirs suddenly dominated the lists of publishers. Robert Graves, Edmund Blunden, Siegfried Sassoon, Ludwig Renn, Arnold Zweig, and Ernest Hemingway, among others, became familiar names. They were so in demand, as public speakers and radio performers, that they could not cope with the glut of invitations. The sudden public interest in the war meant that moldy manuscripts, previously rejected by wary publishers who thought that the war would not sell, were now rushed into print. New books, too, were quickly commissioned and quickly written.

Translators were in great demand. The stage readily made room for war drama, and R.C. Sherriff's *Journey's End*, in which Laurence Olivier played the lead in the latter part of the London run, became an international hit. By November 1929 it was being staged in twelve foreign countries. The cinema, which had not been quite as reluctant as the publishing industry to deal with war material – Hollywood had started a small wave in 1926 with films like *What Price Glory?*, *The Big Parade*, and *Wings* – the cinema now joined in with a rash of war films. Galleries exhibited paintings and photographs from the war. Newspapers and periodicals gave much space to discussions about war, past and future. What some felt to have been a deliberate silence about the war was now shattered with a vengeance.

What provoked the sudden revival of interest in the war at the end of the twenties? And what did the war boom reveal? A look at the motivations of Remarque in writing his novel may yield some clues.

LIFE OR DEATH

Until the publication of *All Quiet*, Erich Maria Remarque had led a moderately successful, though unsettled, life as a dilettante intellectual and aspiring author. He was born on 22 June 1898, in Osnabrück, the son of a Catholic bookbinder, Peter Franz Remark, and his wife, Anne Maria. Christened Erich Paul, he adopted a pen name after the war by dropping the Paul – the main character in *All Quiet* is named Paul and dies toward the end of the war – adding his mother's name, and Gallicizing his surname. Remarque did not have a happy childhood. His lower-middle-class milieu apparently depressed him. He was, he said later, deeply moved as a youth by the sorrows of Goethe's sensitive and splenetic Werther; he professed to be a romantic; and he often toyed with the idea of suicide. This mood of existential doubt was never to leave him. It pervades his entire *oeuvre*. In public, though clearly craving recognition, he always assumed the manner of a recluse. Even though he would marry Paulette Goddard, the film star and former wife of Charlie Chaplin, live extravagantly in New York, and surround himself with the trappings of success, he would remain – so it appeared – desperately unhappy, a chain smoker, a heavy drinker, fixated by fast cars, speedboats, and escape.

371

Remarque's class background bears emphasis. He was the product of a social group strongly affected by technological and social change. John Middleton Murry, who also suffered in his youth from an intense anxiety born, he suspected, of his social background, called the urban lower middle class 'the most completely disinherited section of modern society.'[1] It was a stratum that the war and especially the economic instability of the twenties would assault with ferocity.

Considerable mystery surrounds Remarque's war experience. Aged sixteen when war broke out, in August 1914, he was conscripted two years later, in November 1916, while training as a teacher, and he first saw front-line action in Flanders in June 1917. At the front he was wounded, according to his own testimony, either four or five times, but according to other evidence, only once seriously. The German army minister, General Groener, was to inform his cabinet colleagues in December 1930 that Remarque had been wounded in the left knee and under one arm on 31 July 1917, and that he had remained in a hospital in Duisburg from 3 August 1917, to 31 October 1918. The minister dismissed as false the reports that Remarque had been either decorated or promoted.[2]

Little else is known about Remarque's days as a soldier. After he was catapulted to international fame, he proved reluctant to give interviews, let alone precise information about his war career. He showed little interest in countering any of the scurrilous rumors that circulated about his earlier life, and many of his critics found his aversion to publicity suspicious. There was a sustained attempt in 1929 and 1930 to uncover the 'real' Remarque, especially to disprove the claim of his publisher, Ullstein, that he was a seasoned soldier. A man named Peter Kropp maintained that he had spent a year in a hospital with the author during the war and that one of the characters in *All Quiet*, Albert Kropp, was modeled on him. The leg wound that hospitalized Remarque,

Kropp alleged, was self-inflicted, and he insisted that once the wound healed, Remarque had become a clerk in the hospital. In the end, argued Kropp, Remarque had no special qualifications for representing the feelings and behavior of the front soldier.[3] While many of the allegations of Remarque's critics and opponents were malicious and prompted by envy, opportunism, and political intent, there do appear to be grounds for suspecting that Remarque's war experience was not as extensive as his successful novel, and particularly the promotional effort surrounding it, implied.

After the war Remarque returned briefly to the Osnabrück Catholic seminary for teachers, and early in 1919 he became a village schoolmaster. He soon abandoned this occupation and took up freelance journalism and odd jobs to meet financial necessity. He published articles on cars, boats, cocktail recipes; he worked for a while for a tire-manufacturing company in Hanover, writing advertising jingles; and eventually he became a picture editor in Berlin for a publication owned by the right-wing firm Scherl. The glossy, high-society magazine *Sport im Bild* was a German version, despite its misleading title, of *The Tatler*. All the while, he tried to write seriously, working on novels, poetry, and a play. Two of his novels were published, *Die Traumbude** in 1920 and *Station am Horizon*** in 1928, but he seems to have derived little satisfaction from them. Trite sentimentality relegated the first work to the rank of pulp fiction. Of *Die Traumbude* Remarque was to say later:

A truly terrible book. Two years after I had published it, I should have liked to buy it up. Unfortunately I didn't have enough money for that. The Ullsteins did that for me later. If I had not written anything better later on, the book would have been a reason for suicide.[4]

*Dream Lodgings.
**Horizon Station.

In 1921 he sent a number of poems to Stefan Zweig for comment and attached a letter of near despair: 'Remember that this is a matter of life or death for me!' An attempt to write a play left him in deep depression.[5]

The death motif here is striking: thoughts about suicide in his youth and threats of it as an adult. Together with the derivative romanticism and the itinerant existence the motif points to a deeply disconsolate man, searching for an explanation for his dissatisfaction. And in his search Remarque eventually hit upon the *Kriegserleben*, the war experience.

The idea that the war was the source of all ills struck him suddenly, he admitted. 'All of us were,' he said of himself and his friends in an interview in 1929, 'and still are, restless, aimless, sometimes excited, sometimes indifferent, and essentially unhappy.' But in a moment of inspiration he had at least found the key to the malaise. The war![6]

That he was not truly interested, after his 'discovery,' in exploring the variety of war experience, but that his main purpose was simply to describe the terrible effects of the war on the generation that grew up during it, is revealed in a review he wrote of war books by Ernst Jünger, Franz Schauwecker, and Georg von der Vring, among others, for *Sport im Bild* in June 1928. It is even possible that these books were the source of his inspiration. Jünger's exuberant, intoxicating vitalism and brutal grandeur, Schauwecker's breathless, mystical nationalism, and von der Vring's lyrical simplicity were lumped together in a rather bland discussion that displayed little appreciation for these distinctive interpretations of the war experience.[7] Remarque was, one must conclude, more interested in explaining away the emotional imbalance of a generation than in a comprehensive or even accurate account of the experience and feelings of men in the trenches. Many of the metaphors and images that Remarque used in his book are strikingly similar to those used by the authors he had discussed, Jünger in particular, and it is not unreasonable to suggest that he took many of his ideas from these sources.

In July 1928 Remarque published another article in *Sport im Bild* that throws more light on his frame of mind at the time. This was a short, rather ingenuous piece about modern photography, in which he regretted the injustice that most professional photographers did to reality. By isolating their subjects from a wider context, by turning the world into a neat and rosy '9 × 12 or 10 × 15 format,' photographers created an illusionary world.[8] The point was a simple and honest one, but coming from a picture editor of a snobbish and expensive magazine, it had a pathetic poignancy; it indicated how unhappy the author was in his work and environment.

Having fixed upon the 'war experience,' Remarque sat down in mid 1928 to write. Working in the evenings and on weekends, he completed his book, so he claimed, in six weeks. The suddenness of the inspiration, the speed of composition, and the simplicity of the theme all indicate that Remarque's book was not the product of years of reflection and digestion but of impulse born of personal exasperation.

Remarque stated the purpose of *All Quiet* in a brief and forceful prefatory comment:

> This book is to be neither an accusation nor a confession, and least of all an adventure ... It will try simply to tell of a generation of men who, even though they may have escaped its shells, were destroyed by the war.[9]

The story then recounts the experiences of Paul Bäumer and his schoolmates, who move from the classroom to the trenches, bursting with energy and conviction, enthusiastic knights of a personal and national cause. One by one they are ripped apart at the front, not only by enemy fire but also by a growing sense of futility. The war is transformed from a cause into an inexorable, insatiable Moloch. The soldiers have no escape from the routinized slaughter; they are condemned men. They die screaming but unheard, they die resigned but in vain. The world beyond the guns does not know them; it cannot know them. 'I believe we are lost,' says Paul.

Only the fraternity of death remains, the comradeship of the fated. At the end Paul dies, forlorn yet strangely at peace with his destiny. Peace has become possible only in death. The final scene of the American film version of the novel was to be a masterly evocation of the mood of Remarque's work: a sniper's bullet finds its mark as Paul is reaching from the trench to touch what the war had rendered untouchable, a butterfly. All the shibboleths lose their meaning as the men die violent deaths – patriotism, national duty, honor, glory, heroism, valor. The external world consists only of brutality, hypocrisy, illusion. Even the intimate bonds to family have been sundered. Man remains alone, without a foothold in the real world.

The simplicity and power of the theme – war as a demeaning and wholly destructive, indeed nihilistic, force – are made starkly effective by a style that is basic, even brutal. Brief scenes and short crisp sentences, in the first person and in the present tense, create an inescapable and gripping immediacy. There is no delicacy. The language is frequently rough, the images often gruesome. The novel has a consistency of style and purpose that Remarque's earlier work had lacked and that little of his subsequent work would achieve.

Despite Remarque's introductory comment and his reiteration of the point in later statements, very few contemporary reviewers noted, and later critics have generally ignored, that All Quiet was not a book about the events of the war – it was not a memoir, much less a diary[10] – but an angry declaration about the effects of the war on the young generation that lived through it. Scenes, incidents, and images were chosen to illustrate how the war had destroyed the ties, psychological, moral, and real, between the generation at the front and society at home. 'If we go back,' says Paul, 'we will be weary, broken, burnt out, rootless, and without hope. We will not be able to find our way any more.' The war, Remarque was asserting in 1928, had shattered the possibility of pursuing what society would consider a normal existence.

Hence, *All Quiet* is more a comment on the postwar mind, on the postwar view of the war, than an attempt to reconstruct the reality of the trench experience. In fact that reality is distorted, as many critics insisted – though with little effect on the initial acclaim for the novel. Remarque's critics said that at the very least he misrepresented the physical reality of the war: a man with his legs or his head blown off could not continue to run, they protested vehemently, referring to two of the images Remarque had used. But far more serious than such shoddiness, they claimed, was his lack of understanding of the moral aspects of soldiers' behavior. Soldiers were not robots, devoid of a sense of purpose. They were sustained by a broad spectrum of firmly established values.[11]

Although his publisher did not like such admissions, because they undermined the credibility of the novel, Remarque was prepared to say that his book was primarily about the postwar generation. In an exchange in 1929 with General Sir Ian Hamilton, the British commander at Gallipoli in 1915 and now head of the British Legion, Remarque expressed his 'amazement' and 'admiration' that Hamilton for one had understood his intentions in writing *All Quiet*:

I merely wanted to awaken understanding for a generation that more than all others has found it difficult to make its way back from four years of death, struggle, and terror, to the peaceful fields of work and progress.[12]

It was in part the misinterpretation of his purpose that led Remarque to write a sequel to *All Quiet*. *Der Weg zurück* (*The Road Back*), a novel published in 1931, explicitly argued the case of the 'lost generation.'

All Quiet can be seen not as an explanation but as a symptom of the confusion and disorientation of the postwar world, particularly of the generation that reached maturity during the war. The novel was an emotional condemnation, an assertion of instinct, a *cri d'angoisse* from a malcontent, a man who could not find his niche in society. That the war contributed enormously to the shiftlessness of much of the postwar generation is undeniable; that the war was the root cause of this social derangement is at least debatable; but Remarque never took part in the debate directly. For Remarque the war had become a vehicle of escape. Remarque and his book were, to borrow from Karl Kraus, symptoms of the disease they claimed to diagnose.

Notwithstanding Remarque's opening declaration of impartiality – that his book was 'neither an accusation nor a confession' – it was in fact both. And it was more. It was a confession of personal despair, but it was also an indignant denunciation of an insensate social and political order, inevitably of that order which had produced the horror and destruction of the war but particularly of the one that could not settle the war and deal with the aspirations of veterans. Through characters identifiable with the state – the schoolmaster with his unalterable fantasies about patriotism and valor, the former postman who functions like an unfeeling robot in his new role as drill sergeant, the hospital orderlies and doctors who deal not with human suffering, only bodies – Remarque accused. He accused a mechanistic civilization of destroying humane values, of negating charity, love, humor, beauty, and individuality. Yet Remarque offered no alternatives. The characters of his *generazione bruciata* – the Italian notion of a 'burned generation' is apt – do not act; they are merely victims. Of all the war books of the late twenties – the novels of Arnold Zweig, Renn, R.H. Mottram, H.M. Tomlinson, Richard Aldington, Hemingway, and the memoirs of Graves, Blunden, Sassoon, to name but a few of the more important works – Remarque's made its point, that his was a truly lost generation, most directly and emotionally, even stridently, and this directness and passion lay at the heart of its popular appeal.

But there was more. The 'romantic agony' was a wild cry of revolt and despair – and a cry of exhilaration. In perversion there could be pleasure. In darkness, light. The relation of Remarque and his generation to death and destruction is not as straightforward as it appears. In his personal life and in his reflections on the war Remarque seemed fascinated by death. All of his subsequent work exudes this fascination. As one critic put it later, Remarque 'probably made more out of death than the most fashionable undertakers.'[13] Like the Dadaists, he was spellbound by war and its horror, by the act of destruction, to the point where death becomes not the antithesis of life but the ultimate expression of life, where death becomes a creative force, a source of art and vitality. A young Michel Tournier, on meeting Remarque, noted the paradoxical nature of this modern author-hero: world famous for his antimilitarism, Remarque, 'with his stiff posture, his severe and rectangular face, and his inseparable monocle,' looked like a larger-than-life Prussian officer.[14]

Many of Remarque's generation shared his apocalyptic post-Christian vision of life, peace, and happiness in death. George Antheil would, when appearing in concert to play his own music, carry a pistol in his evening jacket. As he sat down to play, he would take out the pistol and place it on the piano. The .25 caliber Belgian revolver that Harry Crosby used in December 1929 to kill himself and his mistress had a sun symbol engraved on its side. A year earlier, while saluting Dido,

Cleopatra, Socrates, Modigliani, and Van Gogh among others, he had promised soon 'to enjoy an orgasm with the sombre Slave-Girl of Death, in order to be reborn.' He yearned to 'explode . . . into the frenzied fury of the Sun, into the madness of the Sun, into the hot gold arms and hot gold eyes of the Goddess of the Sun!'[15]

Success would not mellow Remarque or still his chronic anxiety. The very vital Countess Waldeck, née Rosie Gräfenberg, who in 1929–30 was the wife of Franz Ullstein, later had this to say of the young author at the height of his success:

> Remarque was in his thirties. He had a pretty boy's face with a defiant soft mouth. The Ullsteins thought him a little difficult. But that was merely the result of Remarque's having almost rejected the motor-car with which the grateful firm presented him, because it lacked the travelling luggage which, in his opinion, belonged on the luggage rack. I myself thought this and other traits charmingly childlike in Remarque; he wanted his toy to be exactly as he had imagined it. He was a hard worker. Often he would shut himself up for seventeen hours at a stretch in a room where not even a chaise-longue was permitted, because it might possibly be a temptation to laziness. He was immensely sorry for himself because he worked so hard – was Remarque.[16]

FAME

According to Remarque, his completed manuscript lay in a drawer for six months. In fact it was probably only a couple of months. His employer, the Scherl firm, an important part of Alfred Hugenberg's right-wing nationalist press empire, could not even be considered a potential publisher of the work. Finally Remarque approached the S. Fischer Verlag, the most reputable literary publisher in Germany, but Samuel Fischer was still convinced that the war would not sell. He turned the manuscript down.

Through an acquaintance word reached Remarque that Franz Ullstein, by contrast, did feel that it was time to publish books on the war. Remarque tried the Ullstein Verlag. There the manuscript was passed around to various editors. Max Krell was 'gripped by the unusual tone'; Cyril Soschka, head of the production department and a war veteran, was convinced that it would be a great success because it told 'the truth about the war' – a phrase on which the controversy about the book would turn; Monty Jacobs, *feuilleton* editor of Ullstein's *Vossische Zeitung*, accepted the novel for serialization. The Ullsteins developed great confidence in the book, and, led by Franz Ullstein, one of the five brothers who ran the large newspaper- and book-publishing operation, they proceeded to launch their flamboyant and expensive advertising campaign.[1]

The initial critical response to Remarque's novel was very enthusiastic, not only in Germany, where the playwright Carl Zuckmayer wrote the first review for the Ullsteins' large-circulation *Berliner Illustrirte Zeitung* and called *All Quiet* a 'war diary,' but also when it appeared in English and French translations. Remarque's supposedly frank portrayal of human responses to war and the depiction of a pitiful dignity under suffering were praised with gusto. 'The greatest of war novels' was a phrase that appeared over and over again in the reviews. Its 'holy sobriety' would bring about 'the rehabilitation of our generation,' predicted Axel Eggebrecht, a well-known and respected German critic. Herbert Read, veteran, poet, and art historian, heralded Remarque's account as 'the Bible of the common soldier' and struck, thereby, a religious note that would recur frequently in the commentary. 'It has swept like a gospel over Germany,' wrote Read, 'and must sweep over the whole world, because it is the first

381

completely satisfying expression in literature of the greatest event of our time.' He added that he had by then read the book 'six or seven times.' An American rhapsodized about 'its blasting simplicity' and called it the 'Book of the Decade': 'I should like to see it sell a million copies,' concluded Christopher Morley. Daniel-Rops, philosopher, theologian, and historian, shared such sentiments in Switzerland: it was 'the book we waited for' for ten years, he said. Bruno Frank, Bernhard Kellermann, G. Lowes Dickinson, and Henry Seidel Canby were other eminent literary figures among the early enthusiasts. Several people suggested that Remarque be awarded the Nobel Prize for literature.[2]

In the initial reviews, then, there was rarely a note of vigorous criticism, and there was near unanimity in the belief that the book presented 'the truth about the war,' or, as the London *Sunday Chronicle* put it, 'the true story of the world's greatest nightmare.'[3] The exuberance, especially the extravagant use of superlatives and absolutes, and the shrill insistence that this book told 'the truth,' indicated how sensitive a nerve Remarque had touched and how completely many people shared his frustration – his postwar frustration. The tone of the novel and the tone of the early reviews were very similar.

But what was this 'truth' to which almost all referred? That the war had been a nihilistic slaughter without rationale? That its front-line protagonists and chief victims had no sense of purpose? That, in short, the war had been in vain? Few said so outright, but the liberal left and moderate socialists throughout Europe, and even here and there in America and the dominions, were now inclined to view the war as, in the end, a tragic and futile civil conflict in Europe, one that need not have occurred.

However, as sales mounted through the spring and summer of 1929, an opposition began to organize and to voice its opinions as shrilly as the early supporters. The communist left derided the novel as an example of the sterility of bourgeois intelligence: the bourgeois mind, incapable of locating the real source of social disorder, resorted, in its treatment of the war, to tearful sentimentality and regret. The book was seen as a fine illustration of the 'decline of the west' mentality.[4] To those at the other end of the political spectrum, the conservative right, Remarque's work was pernicious because it threatened the entire meaning of postwar conservatism, the idea of regeneration based on traditional values. In the eyes of conservatives in all belligerent countries the war had been a necessity, tragic of course, but nonetheless unavoidable. If the war was now found to have been an absurdity, then conservatism as a set of beliefs was an absurdity. Consequently, *All Quiet* had to be rejected – as deliberately 'commercialized horror and filth' and as the outgrowth of a degenerate mind that could not rise above the inevitable horror of war to see 'the eternal issues involved,' the grandeur of an idea, the beauty of sacrifice, and the nobility of collective purpose.[5]

The fascist opposition to the novel blended often with that of the conservatives and presented many of the same arguments, but there was an essential difference in the reasoning. The fascists sanctified not so much the purpose of the war as the 'experience' of the war, the very essence of the war, its immediacy, its tragedy, its exhilaration, its ultimate ineffability in anything but mystical and spiritual terms. The war, as we shall see, gave meaning to fascism. Thus, any suggestion that the war had been purposeless was a slur against the very existence of this form of extremism. It is here, on the extreme right, that the most active opposition to Remarque, and to the whole wave of so-called negative war books, films, and other artifacts, assembled.

Both traditionalists and right-wing extremists were incensed by what they saw as a completely one-sided portrait of the war experience. They objected to the language in the novel, to the horrifying images, to the frequent references to bodily functions, and, especially, to a scene involving a jovial group perched on field latrines. Little, Brown and Company of Boston, the American publisher, actually deleted the latrine scene at the insistence of the Book-of-the-Month Club, cut an episode concerning a sexual encounter in a hospital, and softened certain words and phrases in A.W. Wheen's British translation.[6] The latrine passage, retained in the British edition, was harped on by a large number of British critics, who began to refer to Remarque as the high priest of the 'lavatory school' of war novelists. In November 1929, *The London Mercury* felt the need to editorialize on this school.

> 'Criticism,' wrote Anatole France, 'is the adventure of the soul among masterpieces.' The adventure of the soul among lavatories is not inviting: but this, roughly, is what criticism of recent translated German novels must be . . . The modern Germans . . . suppose that lavatories are intensely interesting. They are obsessed by this dreary subject, and they are obsessed by brutality.[7]

An Australian, writing in *The Army Quarterly*, asked how British firms could publish 'unclean war books'; in his view the translation and publication of 'filthy foreign books' was an act of treason.[8]

The denunciation of the book as a piece of propaganda – pacifist, Allied, or German, depending on the critic – was the other main form of attack on the right. Franz von Lilienthal noted in the conservative financial daily, *Berliner Börsen-Zeitung*, that if Remarque did in fact receive the Nobel Prize, Lord Northcliffe, the press baron, would have to be applauded as well, because Remarque had nothing to say that Northcliffe, master propagandist that he was, had not said earlier. To the German military the novel was 'a singularly monstrous slander of the German army' and thus a piece of 'refined pacifist propaganda.' The military everywhere for that matter was inclined to support such a view. In November 1929, the Czechoslovak War Department banned *All Quiet* from military libraries. Outside Germany many conservative critics looked on the novel as part of a clever German campaign of cultural dissimulation. In a speech at Armistice celebrations at Folkestone in 1929, a Baptist minister deplored the tenor of the popular novels and plays on the subject of the war. He certainly had *All Quiet* in mind, as well as Robert Graves's recently published *Goodbye to All That* and R.C. Sherriff's *Journey's End*, when he said, 'I did not think I should ever live to read books written by my own countrymen which are like the dirty work done by enemy propagandists.'[9]

Earlier in the year G. Lowes Dickinson, Cambridge humanist and ardent promoter of the League of Nations, had sensed that Remarque's book might be subjected to this type of attack. Urging all those to read the book 'who have the courage and honesty to desire to know what modern war is really like,' he added, 'They need not fear German propaganda. The book is far above all that. It is the truth, told by a man with the power of a great artist, who is hardly aware what an artist he is.'[10]

But J.C. Squire and *The London Mercury* would have none of this. 'This is not the truth,' they retorted, referring to the work of Remarque and other German war novelists and warned against the apparent tendency among the British public 'to sentimentalize over the Germans' and to neglect the French. Then, with a stunning burst of ferocity, reminiscent of the war itself, they continued:

We repeat . . . (being cosmopolitans and pacifists, but facers of facts) that the Germans (many of whom were not even Christianized until the sixteenth century) have contributed very little indeed to European culture . . . In war we exaggerated the defects of the enemy; do not let us, in peace, exaggerate his merits; above all, do not let us, in a wanton reaction, take more interest in the enemy than in the friend. The cold truth is that the Russians, who are still largely barbaric, contributed far more, in music and literature, to culture in the nineteenth century than the Germans, let alone the square-head Prussians, have contributed in hundreds of years . . . Peace with the Germans, by all means; understanding with the Germans, if possible; but let us not, out of mere sentimentality, concentrate our gaze upon the Germans at the expense of more cultivated, productive and civilized peoples. Let us welcome, by all means, whatever good may come from Germany; but the present tendency is to think that anything that comes out of Germany must be good. 'Omne Teutonicum pro magnifico' seems the motto of the publishers and the press: it is a grotesque motto.[11]

Paradoxically, when in February 1930 Wilhelm Frick, the newly appointed Nazi minister of the interior in the state government of Thuringia, banned All Quiet from schools in that state, a Nazi paper, announcing the decree, commented, 'It is time to stop the infection of the schools with pacifist Marxist propaganda.'[12]

Both the critical praise and the scurrility that All Quiet provoked had, in the end, little to do with the substance of the novel. As All Quiet was a reflection more of the postwar than of the wartime mind, so the commentary, too, was a reflection of postwar political and emotional investments. Yet everyone pretended to be arguing objectively about the essence of the war experience. The critical dialogue was worthy of characters in a Chekhov play. They talked past each other. The wider public response was similar.

Remarque's success came at what we now see was a crossroads in the interwar era: the intersection of two moods, one of vague, imploring hope and the other of

386

coagulating fear; 'the Locarno spirit' and a fling with apparent prosperity intersecting with incipient economic crisis and mounting national introspection.

Accompanying the efforts at international détente after 1925 was a wave of humanism that swept the west. A wishful rather than assertive humanism this was, however. In 1927 Thornton Wilder ended his Pulitzer Prize-winning novel, *The Bridge of San Luis Rey*, with the sentence: 'There is a land of the living and a land of the dead and the bridge is love, the only survival, the only meaning.' Melancholy, sentimentality, and wish constitute the dominant mood here. Two years later, in 1929, the disastrous economic slump brought the underlying doubt starkly to the surface. The popular cultural activities of the twenties as a whole were, more or less, a bewildered salute to a bygone age when the individual had had a recognized social purpose.

The war boom of the late twenties and early thirties was a product of this mixture of aspiration, anxiety, and doubt. All the successful war books were written from the point of view of the individual, not the unit or the nation. Remarque's book, written in the first person, personalized for everyone the fate of the unknown soldier. Paul Bäumer became Everyman. On this level only could the war have any meaning, on the level of individual suffering. The war was a matter of individual experience rather than collective interpretation. It had become a matter of art, not history.

Art had become more important than history. History belonged to an age of rationalism, to the eighteenth and particularly the nineteenth century. The latter century had shown great respect for its historians. The Guizots, Michelets, Rankes, Macaulays, and Actons were read and appreciated, especially by a bourgeoisie bent on expansion and integration. Our century has, by contrast, been an antihistorical age, in part because historians have failed to adapt to the sentiments of their century but even more so because this century has been one of dis-integration rather than integration. The psychologist has, as a result, been more in demand than the historian. And the artist has received more respect than either.

It is noteworthy that among the mountains of writing built up on the subject of the Great War, a good many of the more satisfying attempts to deal with its meaning have come from the pens of poets, novelists, and even literary critics, and that professional historians have produced, by and large, specialized and limited accounts, most of which pale in evocative and explanatory power before those of the *littérateurs*. Historians have failed to find explanations to the war that correspond to the horrendous realities, to the actual experience of the war. The spate of official and unofficial histories that issued forth in the twenties was largely ignored by the public. By contrast, Remarque's *All Quiet* became, virtually overnight, the best seller of all previous time. Imaginative, not historical, literature it was that sparked the intense reconsideration of the meaning of the war at the end of the twenties. The historical imagination, like so much of the intellectual effort of the nineteenth century, had been sorely challenged by the events of the war; and it was consistent with the subsequent self-doubt of the discipline that H.A.L. Fisher's 1934 lament, in the preface to his *History of Europe*, should have become one of the most frequently quoted theoretical statements by a historian of our century:

> Men wiser and more learned than I have discerned in history a plot, a rhythm, a predetermined pattern. These harmonies are concealed from me. I can see only one emergency following upon another as wave follows upon wave.[13]

Whether the poems, novels, and other imaginative efforts provoked by the war stand as 'great' art is a debatable matter. William Butler Yeats, in his idiosyncratic 1936 edition of *The Oxford Book of Modern Verse*, omitted Wilfred Owen, Siegfried Sassoon, Ivor Gurney, Isaac Rosenberg, Robert Graves, Herbert Read, and others, on the grounds that passive suffering could not be the stuff of great poetry, which had to have a moral vision. But he was imposing his critical vision on a public that felt otherwise. Ten years after the war, amidst the glut of war novels that appeared during the war boom, the *Morning Post* bemoaned in an editorial that 'the great novel of the Great War, which will show all things in a true perspective, has yet to be written.'[14] The great war novel, explaining all, was a constant vision among intellectuals in the twenties and even the thirties. Mottram's *Spanish Farm* trilogy, Tomlinson's *All Our Yesterdays*, Aldington's *Death of a Hero*, and, in a different vein but with similar intent, Renn's *Krieg* and Remarque's *All Quiet*, to cite but a few, were motivated by this challenge and quest. 'The witness of a hundred thousand nobodies,' wrote André Thérive in *Le Temps* in December 1929, 'isn't worth the semifiction conceived by a great man.'[15] This attitude, that art might be truer to life than history, was hardly a new notion, but never before had it been so widespread, in fact so dominant.

Ironically, during the war French and British soldiers had become the 'frontier' personalities identified with the avant-garde and with German *Kultur* as a whole before the war; they were the men who had experienced the very limits of existence, who had seen no man's land, who had witnessed horror and agony, and who, because of the very experience that made them heroes, lived on the edge of respectability and morality. Given the failure of the postwar era to produce the apocalyptic resolution promised by wartime propaganda, the whole social purpose of the war – the content of duty and *devoir* – began to ring hollow. Since the tangible results of the war could never justify its cost, especially its emotional toll, disillusionment was inevitable, and soldiers in the postwar world withdrew from social activity and commitment. Only a minority bothered even to join veterans' organizations. Relatively few were able to articulate their alienation, but the statistics speak loudly: of those unemployed between the ages of thirty and thirty-four in Britain at the end of the twenties, 80 per cent were ex-servicemen. The incidence of mental illness among veterans was also staggering. 'The worst thing about the war generation of introspects,' said T.E. Lawrence, 'is that they can't keep off their blooming selves.' Aldington talked about the 'self-prisons' in which former soldiers had become trapped, and Graves wrote about his 'cage-mates.'[16]

Yet, while former soldiers suffered from a high incidence of neurasthenia and sexual impotence, they realized that the war, in the words of José Germain, was 'the quivering axis of all human history.'[17] If the war as a whole had no objective meaning, then invariably all human history was telescoped into each man's experience; every person was the sum total of history. Rather than being a social experience, a matter of documentable reality, history was individual nightmare, or even, as the Dadaists insisted, madness. One is again reminded of Nietzche's statement, on the very edge of his complete mental collapse, that he was 'every name in history.'

The burden of having been in the eye of the storm and yet, in the end, of having resolved nothing, was excruciating. The result often was the rejection of social and political reality and at the same time the rejection even of the perceptual self – only dream and neurosis remained, a world of illusions characterized by a pervasive negativism. Fantasy became the mainspring of action, and melancholy the general mood. *Nous vivons une triste époque . . . Tout est foutu – Quoi? Tout un monde . . . Il fait beau, allons au cimetière.** Carroll

---

*We live a melancholy era . . . Everything is screwed up. What? A whole world . . . It's nice out. Let's go to the cemetery.

Carstairs ended his book *A Generation Missing* in 1930 with the words 'It's a weary world and the raspberry jam sent me from Paris is all finished now.'[18]

What was true of the soldiers was true with somewhat less immediacy and poignancy of civilians. The crowded nightclubs, the frenzied dancing, the striking upsurge of gambling, alcoholism, and suicide, the obsession with flight, with moving pictures, and with film stars evinced on a popular level these same tendencies, a drift toward irrationalism. Of course bourgeois Europe tried to 'recast' itself, but it was capable of doing so only superficially. The modern temper had been forged; the avant-garde had won. The 'adversary culture' had become the dominant culture; irony and anxiety, the mode and the mood. 'The war is breaking us but is also reshaping us,' Marc Boasson had written in July 1915. Fifteen years later Egon Friedell, the cultural historian, asserted emphatically, 'History does not exist.'[19]

All Quiet captured for the popular mind some of the same instincts that were being expressed in 'high art.' Proust and Joyce, too, telescoped history into the individual. There is no collective reality, only individual response, only dreams and myths, which have lost their nexus with social convention.

In the tormented and degraded German front soldier depicted in *All Quiet* – and he could just as easily have been a Tommy, *poilu*, or doughboy – the public saw its own shadow and sensed its own anonymity and yearning for security. A small number of critics perceived this at the time. 'The effect of the book springs in fact,' wrote a German commentator,

> from the terrible disillusionment of the German people with the state in which they find themselves, and the reader tends to feel that this book has located the source of all our difficulties.[20]

An American noted, 'In Remarque the sentiment of the epoch comes to bloom.'[21] *All Quiet* seemed to encapsulate the whole modern impulse as it manifested itself in the postwar world: the amalgamation of prayer and desperation, dream and chaos, wish and desolation.

In each country there was a specific variation on this general theme. In Germany after 1925 one noticed a distinct relaxation of political tension, evidenced by the lowest turnout at the polls in the whole of the Weimar period in the national elections of May 1928, the first since December 1924. The government that was formed in June 1928 was appropriately a 'grand coalition,' ranging from Social Democrats on the left, who led the government, to the moderate right-wing People's Party of Gustav Stresemann. The government began its life in a conciliatory mood. However, in May 1930 it fell, the victim of revived nationalist and conservative sentiment.

Nineteen twenty-nine was the critical year. That the economic situation deteriorated drastically in a year that marked the tenth anniversary of the Treaty of Versailles was an unfortunate coincidence. Reparations were on the public mind. Alfred Hugenberg, press lord and leader of the right-wing Nationalist People's Party, campaigned for his referendum against the Young Plan, the new Allied proposal for reparations, and accepted Adolf Hitler into his camp. The right, in its spirited new offensive against the republic, blamed Germany's renewed economic difficulties on the draconic peace settlement and on the blood lust of the Allies. Public demonstrations against the 'war guilt lie' grew in number and frenzy through the early part of 1929 and climaxed in a flood of meetings in June. The government declared June 28, the anniversary of the treaty, a day of national mourning. Remarque was able to capitalize on both remnants of political moderation and the heightened sensitivity to the question of the war.

Remarque blamed the war for his personal

disorientation; the German public, too, assumed that its suffering was a direct legacy of the war. *All Quiet* actually raised the consciousness of Germans on the issue of the war as the source of their difficulties.

In Britain, where the economy took a very bad turn in late 1928 and where unemployment dominated the election campaign in the spring of 1929, Remarque's portrayal of the German front-line soldier as a miserable, downtrodden pawn, striving to retain some dignity and humanity, met with sympathy. By the late twenties much of British opinion had become favorable toward Germany. French pettiness and obstreperousness earlier in the decade and then 'the Locarno spirit' had drawn the British away from the French and closer to the Germans. 'In foreign affairs the psychological drama of British politics is precisely that we like the Germans more, and the French less,' *The Fortnightly Review* mused, 'but with the first we fall out and the latter we are obliged to accept as partners.' However, even this partnership with France was under question in some quarters. J.C.C. Davidson, confidant of the conservative leader, Stanley Baldwin, spoke about the advantages of loosening the tie with France, a 'parochial and highly cynical' nation 'whose population is declining and whose methods are so little in harmony with our own.' Douglas Goldring, who described himself as a 'crusted libertarian and little Englander of ingrained Tory instincts,' suggested that some terrible errors had been made by British statesmen: 'Any intelligent undergraduate, interpreting the past in the light of recent happenings, would probably arrive at the conclusion that our entry into the war was a blunder ... My generation,' he concluded, 'was betrayed, swindled, exploited and decimated by its elders in 1914.' And Robert Graves, in his memoir, *Goodbye to All That*, which he wrote in the spring and summer of 1929, thought it fit to quote Edmund Blunden: 'No more wars for me at any price! Except against the French. If there's ever a war with them, I'll go like a shot.'[22]

The undercurrent of suspicion and scorn in the Anglo-French alliance naturally did not flow only in one direction. In the twenties Frenchmen were convinced that it was mainly they who had won the war; the British contribution had never been equal to the French. How could it have been? The French had held three quarters of the line on the Western Front. British concerns, moreover, had always been overseas and not in Europe. Even during the war the French were prone to accuse the British of fighting to the last drop of other people's blood. Joffre said of the British in 1915: 'I'd never let them hold the line on their own – they'd be broken through. I trust them only when they are held up by us.' During the mutinies of June 1917 a French soldier was heard to say, 'We have to have the Boche on our side within a month to help us kick out the British.' By 1922, even before the Ruhr crisis, when the British failed to back French and Belgian punitive measures against the Germans over reparations, General Huguet, the former French attaché to the British armies, could describe Britain as an 'adversary.'[23] As the decade wore on the relationship deteriorated further. So Frenchmen, while generally calmer in their response to Remarque's novel, were nevertheless drawn to a book that portrayed the mutual hell through which the principal combatants, French and German soldiers, had gone. Perhaps the *poilu* and the *boche* were not irreconcilable. The success of *À l'ouest rien de nouveau* brought a flood of French translations of German works on the war, and, appropriately, in the initial phases of the war boom at least, British war books were neglected by French publishers.[24]

The great discovery that foreign readers said they made through *All Quiet* was that the German soldier's experience of the war had been, in its essentials, no different from that of soldiers of other nations. The German soldier, it seemed, had not wanted to fight either, once the emotional decoration put on the war by the home front had been shattered. Remarque's novel did a great deal to undermine the view that Germans were 'peculiar' and not to be trusted. Furthermore, *All Quiet* promoted at a popular level what historical revisionism was achieving at an academic and political level: the erosion of the idea of a collective German war guilt. But on this score too 'art' was clearly more effective than 'history.' Remarque alone accomplished much more than all the revisionist historians in America and Europe put together.

Who read *All Quiet* with most interest? Veterans and young people appear to have been the most avid readers of war books as a whole. By the end of the decade the disillusionment of former servicemen with postwar society had matured into vituperative scorn for the so-called peace, not only in the defeated countries but also in the victor states. *All Quiet* and other war books of 'disenchantment,' as C.E. Montague's early venture in this genre was actually entitled, elicited many a 'bravo' from embittered and saddened veterans. Yet there were also frequent denunciations from veterans who regarded the spirit and success of *All Quiet* as a manifestation of the malaise that had engulfed the postwar world, as a symptom of the spirit that had betrayed a generation and its hopes. Where exactly the balance lay is difficult to ascertain. What is clear, however, is that the interest of veterans in the literary protest was based largely on their postwar experience. They were reacting to the disappearance, in the course of the decade, of the vision the war had promised.

Youths who had matured after the war were naturally curious about the war. Many commentators noted that fathers who had survived the front were reluctant to talk about their experience even with their families, which is why young people, wishing to penetrate the silence, constituted a sizable part of the readership. And having grown up in the shadow of the hero-father, they were also fascinated by the 'negative' portrayal of the war. The literature of disenchantment offered a less ascetic, more humane, and hence more interesting portrait of the warrior-father.[25] In a straw vote among senior *Gymnasium*, or secondary school, students in Düsseldorf in January 1930 on favorite authors, Remarque topped the poll, outstripping Goethe, Schiller, Galsworthy, Dreiser, and Edgar Wallace. It is worth noting, however, that alongside war diaries and memoirs, works on economics elicited most interest among the students polled.[26] Obviously the economic insecurity felt by students in depression-ridden Germany and the fascination with accounts of horror and death in the trenches were linked. Youth, too, was prone to blame uncertain employment prospects on the war.

The 'real war' had ceased to exist in 1918. Thereafter it was swallowed by imagination in the guise of memory. For many the war became absurd in retrospect, not because of the war experience in itself but because of the failure of the postwar experience to justify the war. For others the same logic turned the war into ultimate experience, again in retrospect. William Faulkner was hinting at this process of metamorphosis when he wrote, in 1931, 'America has been conquered not by the German soldiers that died in French and Flemish trenches, but by the German soldiers that died in German books.'[27] The journey inward that the war had initiated for masses of men was accelerated by the aftermath of the war.

All Quiet, contrary to the claims of many of its enthusiastic readers, was not 'the truth about the war'; it was, first and foremost, the truth about Erich Maria Remarque in 1928. But equally, most of his critics were no nearer 'the truth' of which they too spoke. They expressed merely the tenor of their own endeavors. Remarque used the war; his critics and the public did the same. Hitler and National Socialism were to be, in the end, the most obsessive and successful exploiters of the war. The war boom of the late twenties

reflected less a genuine interest in the war than a perplexed international self-commiseration.

CLOUD JUGGLER

Hart Crane's elegy for Harry Crosby was called 'The
Cloud Juggler.' The title would have suited Erich Maria
Remarque as well. Crosby put a pistol to his head, literally, and pulled the trigger. Remarque did so figuratively, again and again. The paradoxical figure of the
vital victim – squirming, twitching, pleading, cursing in
the face of annihilation – preoccupied both. For both, art
had become superior to life. In art resided life.

Virtually everything Remarque wrote after *All Quiet*
was concerned with disintegration and death. Yet virtually everything he wrote was an international success.

The film version of *All Quiet* was a fine effort,
directed by Lewis Milestone for Universal Studios, and
released in May 1930. It met rave reviews and played to
crowded cinemas in New York, Paris and London and
was accorded Hollywood's highest accolade, the Academy Award for best picture of 1930. In Berlin, however,
after several performances were disrupted by Nazi hoo-
ligans led by Joseph Goebbels, it was banned in December, ostensibly because it slandered the German image
but actually because it was a threat to internal security
and order owing to the controversy it provoked.[1]

On 11 May 1933, after Hitler's takeover in Germany,
Remarque's books were among those burned symbolically at the University of Berlin as 'politically and
morally un-German.' 'Down with the literary betrayal of
the soldiers of the world war!' chanted a Nazi student.
'In the name of educating our people in the spirit of
valor, I commit the writings of Erich Maria Remarque to
the flames.'[2]

On November 20 1933, 3411 copies of *All Quiet* were
seized at the Ullstein publishing house by the Berlin

police, on the basis of the presidential decree of 4 February, which was drawn up 'for the protection of the German people.' In December the Gestapo instructed that these copies be destroyed.[3] On 15 May Goebbels, who had been a mere stripling during the war, had told representatives of the German book trade that the *Volk*, the German people, were not supposed to serve books, but books were to serve the *Volk*; and he had concluded, *Denn es wird am deutschen Wesen noch einmal die Welt genesen.*'*[4]

Erich Maria Remarque had sought refuge in Switzerland in 1930. After a long journey to New York, Hollywood, and back, he would die there in his mountain retreat in 1970, still handsome and still unhappy.

*See page 121.

X

Spring Without End

Elle [la guerre] a donné son empreinte aux âmes, et toutes ces
visions d'horreur, qu'elle a fait jaillir autour de nous, ces corps
à corps sauvages, ces éclairs que l'obus nous jetait à la face,
toutes ces nuits fulgurantes de Verdun, nous les retrouverons,
un jour, dans les yeux de nos fils.*

PIERRE DE MAZENOD
1922

I have long realized that actors and artists often have such
fantastic ideas that one is compelled from time to time to shake
an admonitory finger at them and bring them back to earth.

ADOLF HITLER
1942

We protest energetically that the [foreign] press should now
accuse us of all people of being anarchists who have plunged
Europe into this fearful disaster. That is the well-known method
of blaming the murdered man rather than the murderer . . . We
live in such crazy times that human reason counts for nothing.
Reason has no say any more.

JOSEPH GOEBBELS
16 March and 1 April 1945

GERMANY, AWAKE!

Berlin, Monday, 30 January 1933.
Near 11:00 a.m. Adolf Hitler is appointed chancellor

*The war has left its imprint on our souls, and all these visions of horror it
has conjured up around us, the savage hand-to-hand fighting, the shells
bursting in front, all those lightning-lit nights of Verdun, we shall find them
again one day in the eyes of our sons.

of Germany. In his cabinet of eleven ministers are only two other Nazis, Wilhelm Frick and Hermann Goering. In the last national elections, in November, Hitler's National Socialist German Workers' Party (NSDAP) captured one third of the vote. The party maintained its position as by far the largest group in the Reichstag.

Despite their minority in the legislature, Hitler and his cohort look on their accession to power and responsibility as victory at last, after fourteen years of struggle, the *Kampfzeit*, as they would call it, most of it in the political wilderness. The 'national renewal' has begun. The mood among Nazis is ecstatic. In his diary for that day Joseph Goebbels, Hitler's propaganda artist, will note jubilantly, 'It's like a dream . . . The great decision has been taken. Germany stands at a historic turning point . . . The nation erupts! Germany is awake! . . . We have reached our goal. The German revolution begins!'[1]

On the morning of the thirtieth, however, there is no time for diaries. Goebbels is a whirling dervish. He goes into action and quickly organizes a gigantic torchlight parade for the evening. Brown Shirts and Black Shirts, SA and SS, are mobilized. They are joined by members of the Stahlhelm, the paramilitary organization affiliated with conservative nationalism in the country. The Stahlhelm is invited to participate because Alfred Hugenberg, leader of the Nationalist People's Party, and other right-wing elements have joined the government. Around twenty-five thousand men assemble and march into Berlin from surrounding areas. Through the Brandenburg Gate they move, along Unter den Linden, and then down the Wilhelmstrasse past the Chancellery. Beginning at seven in the evening, after winter darkness has set in, they parade for five hours, singing their martial songs: *Es zittern die morschen Knochen . . . Heute gehört uns Deutschland und morgen die ganze Welt.**

*The old fogies quake . . . Today Germany, tomorrow the world.

400

André François-Poncet, French ambassador to Berlin, witnesses the events. The columns march past his office. They appear to him to be endless. Row upon row of humanity. Boots, drums, songs, lights, rhythms. Crowds line the route. Boundless enthusiasm. Two radio reporters, describing the events, are caught up in the excitement: 'Cheers continue to well up,' they tell their listeners.

> Adolf Hitler stands at a window . . . his eyes shine over the awakening Germany, over this sea of people from all walks of life, from all strata of the population, who parade before him, workers of the mind and of the fist – all differences among classes have been erased . . . A wonderful picture, the likes of which we shall not see again soon! These outstretched arms, these calls of 'Heil!'. . . . I hope that our listeners receive just an idea, an inkling, of this great spectacle, of how immeasurably great this moment is![2]

Harry Graf Kessler takes a walk through the streets that evening and notes a 'carnival atmosphere.'[3]

The end came a little over twelve years later. In the mid 1930s Hitler said that within ten years Berlin would be so transformed that no-one would recognize it. During the war that followed he predicted that Berlin would soon be the capital of the world. By 1945 Berlin was unrecognizable and it had become an emblem of the European crisis and indeed of the general crisis of the western world – a vista of endless rubble and devastation. By the end of the war, for every ton of bombs the Germans had dropped from the sky on Britain, the Allies – mainly Britain and America – had dropped 315 tons on Germany.

Of the drama that ended in May 1945 Malcolm Muggeridge saw 'blitzed Berlin' as the 'centrepiece.' 'Who that set eyes on this extraordinary spectacle can ever forget it?' The first impression was one of utter desolation, a barren moonscape, where the sour smell of rotting corpses dominated the senses. But closer inspection revealed human badgers burrowing and surviving in the ruins. These were the 'liberated citizens of Berlin.' 'Was all this,' Muggeridge asked himself, 'the realization of our war aims . . . ? Did it represent the triumph of good over evil?'[4]

British, American, and Russian soldiers who liberated Nazi death camp survivors had no such doubts. Instead of mountains of rubble they found mountains of corpses, stacked high, with emaciated limbs protruding in myriad contortions, like cords of ill-pruned firewood. Ovens still smoldered. Typhus threatened. Here too the dwellers emerged slowly to greet their liberators. They appeared like misshapen creatures from another planet, gaunt, tattooed, walking like mechanical toys designed by some gruesome imagination. It was as if Hades had erupted and regurgitated its contents.

Slowly the scale of Nazi atrocity began to surface. The toll had been horrendous: millions of Jews, millions of foreign slave laborers, Gypsies, homosexuals, Jehovah's Witnesses, the infirm. Auschwitz, too, became an emblem of the western spirit. After Auschwitz, for Theodor Adorno, poetry was no longer possible. Words, the main vehicles hitherto of western sensibility and rationalism, were no longer adequate or appropriate. For many, silence seemed the only proper response.

The scenes uncovered by the Allied armies in 1945 were not the inevitable outgrowth of the events that took place in early 1933, but they were a probable outcome. National Socialism was yet another offspring of the hybrid that has been the modernist impulse; irrationalism crossed with technicism. Nazism was not just a political movement; it was a cultural eruption. It was not imposed by a few; it developed among many. National Socialism was the apotheosis of a secular idealism that, propelled by a dire sense of existential crisis, lost all trace of humility and modesty – indeed, of reality. Borders and limits became meaningless. In the end this idealism completed its circle, turned upon itself, and became anthropophagous. What began as idealism ended as nihilism. What began as celebration ended as scourge. What began as life ended as death.

Contrary to many interpretations of Nazism, which tend to view it as a reactionary movement, as, in the words of Thomas Mann, an 'explosion of antiquarianism,' intent on turning Germany into a pastoral folk community of thatched cottages and happy peasants, the general thrust of the movement, despite archaisms, was futuristic. Nazism was a headlong plunge into the future, toward a 'brave new world.' Of course it used to full advantage residual conservative and utopian longings, paid its respect to these romantic visions, and picked its ideological trappings from the German past, but its goals were, by its own lights, distinctly progressive. It was not a double-faced Janus whose aspects were equally attentive to the past and the future, nor was it a modern Proteus, the god of metamorphosis, who duplicates pre-existing forms. The intention of the movement was to create a new type of human being from whom would spring a new morality, a new social system, and eventually a new international order. That was, in fact, the intention of all the fascist movements. After a visit to Italy and a meeting with Mussolini, Oswald Mosley wrote that fascism 'has produced not only a new system of government, but also a new type of man, who differs from politicians of the old world as men from another planet.'[5] Hitler talked in these terms endlessly. National Socialism was more than a political movement he said; it was more than a faith; it was a desire to create mankind anew.[6]

Nazism involved, perhaps first and foremost, a love of self, not the reality of the self but the self that is reflected in the mirror. This narcissism was projected into a political movement and eventually came to encompass an entire nation. The reflection in the mirror, the image the Nazis had of themselves – blond, blue-eyed, strong as Krupp steel, eternally youthful, with a Nietzschean will to power – that was the myth. Behind the myth, though, was a total inability to define self in any conventional terms. Yet in the narcissistic complex, existence becomes a matter of aesthetics, a matter of turning life into a *thing* of beauty, not of right, or of good, but of beauty. Walter Benjamin pointed in this direction when he said that fascism was the 'aestheticizing of politics.'[7] But fascism was more than just an aestheticizing of politics: it was an aestheticizing of existence as a whole. 'The German everyday shall be beautiful,' insisted one Nazi motto.[8]

Nazism was an attempt to lie beautifully to the German nation and to the world. The beautiful lie is, however, also the essence of kitsch.[9] Kitsch is a form of make-believe, a form of deception. It is an alternative to a daily reality that would otherwise be spiritual vacuum. It represents 'fun' and 'excitement,' energy and spectacle, and above all 'beauty.' Kitsch replaces ethics with aesthetics. Kitsch is the mask of Death.

Nazism was the ultimate expression of kitsch, of its mind-numbing, death-dealing portent. Nazism, like kitsch, masqueraded as life; the reality of both was death. The Third Reich was the creation of 'kitsch men,' people who confused the relationship between life and art, reality and myth, and who regarded the goal of existence as mere affirmation, devoid of criticism, difficulty, insight. Their sensibility was rooted in superficiality, falsity, plagiarism, and forgery. Their art was rooted in ugliness. They took the ideals, though not the form, of the nineteenth- and early-twentieth-century avant-garde, and of the German nation in the Great War, and by means of technology – the mirror – they suited these ideals to their own purpose. Germany, the home of *Dichter und Denker*,* of many of the greatest

*Poets and thinkers.

cultural achievements of modern man, became in the
Third Reich the home of *Richter und Henker*,* the
incarnation of kitsch and nihilism.

VICTIM HERO

Adolf Hitler's early life seems to have been one of
anguish, failure, and burgeoning phobias. His repeated
attempts, in 1907 and 1908, to gain entry, as a student
from the provinces, to the Vienna Academy of Arts met
with rejection, and for six years he led a disconsolate,
vagrant existence in the Austrian capital, absorbing the
tremulous atmosphere of a city whose grandeur evoked
past glory rather than future promise and of an urban
politics in which a growing middle-class paranoia was
accompanied by an escape into a strange mixture of
aestheticism and hatred. He immersed himself in art
and music, dreamed of being a free spirit, but remained
painfully aware of the setbacks he had suffered at the
hands of the establishment. Had he met with any commercial success in his private artistic endeavors, he
might have lived out his days as the archetypical bohemian, who through personal talent, initiative, and will
bucks the establishment and achieves a livelihood in
countercultural creativity. In search of opportunities,
he moved in 1913 to Munich, and there, still without
employment, he frequented the taverns and coffee
houses of Schwabing, Munich's bohemian quarter, and
the beer halls of the city center.

From an early age, then, Hitler certainly had the temperament, exacerbated by his social circumstances, to
become an artist of the 'adversary culture.' What he
lacked was any exceptional talent as a painter or drafts-
man. Even though some, like the architect Albert Speer,
the painter and sculptor Arno Breker, and the set

*Judges and hangmen.

designer Gordon Craig, were to claim later that his work showed considerable talent, no-one has ever suggested that this was a potential artistic genius who was frustrated by the establishment. The best grade Hitler was ever accorded in art at school was 'good.'[1] Yet in spirit an artist was what he was and, as he would insist to the end, what he always remained. He would later simply turn his artistic inclinations to wider pursuits. He would, so he claimed, turn politics and life into art. It was the war, the Great War, that broadened his canvas so immeasurably.

Like many in the artistic, intellectual, and radical community, he saw the outbreak of the war in August 1914 as a sudden liberation from stultifying bourgeois constraints, as an opportunity for a new beginning, as a means of bringing about a revolution of one sort or another. The remarkable picture we have of Hitler as a part of the crowd in the Odeonsplatz in Munich cheering the announcement of war speaks volumes. He is standing in one of the front rows, this misfit, without friends, without women in his life, without a job, without a future. And yet his face is ecstatic, radiant. The eyes seem to sparkle. He looks as if – suddenly and as a complete surprise – he has just been informed that all those rejections from the Vienna Academy of Arts have been a terrible mistake, and that he, Adolf Hitler, has in fact submitted, with his applications, the finest samples of work the academy has ever received. 'To me those hours,' he declared later,

> seemed like a release from the painful feelings of my youth. Even today I am not ashamed to say that, overpowered by a mighty enthusiasm, I sank to my knees and thanked heaven from an overflowing heart that it had granted me the good fortune to be alive at such a time.[2]

On 3 August he petitioned to enlist, despite his Austrian citizenship, in a Bavarian regiment. The answer came the next day. He had been assigned to the 16th Bavarian

Reserve Infantry Regiment. 'It was,' he said, 'with feelings of pure idealism that I set out for the front in 1914.'[3]

The war was to be, in his own words, 'the greatest and most unforgettable time of my earthly experience.'[4] All available evidence suggests that he remained a loner in his regiment and even in front-line duty, preferring to be by himself, receiving little mail while his comrades were often inundated with letters from home, and refusing, even at Christmas, when he received no parcels, to accept gifts from his fellows.[5] He served through most of the war as a dispatch runner, taking messages between staff positions in the rear and the front lines. Runners had a high casualty rate, especially in Flanders, Artois, Champagne, and the Somme, the areas where Hitler's regiment spent most of the war, because they frequently had to move in the open in order to get around flooded and impassable communications trenches. He arrived at the front at Ypres in October 1914, was wounded in the left leg in October 1916, and was gassed in a British attack a month before the Armistice; and so, with the exception of nine months, made up of training, recuperation, and leave, he spent the entire war on active service, and all of that in the hell of the Western Front. He was decorated three times for bravery, receiving the Iron Cross Second Class as early as December 1914, a regimental certificate in May 1918, and the Iron Cross First Class in August of that last year of the war. This was no Erich Maria Remarque, who extrapolated several months' experience into a general account of the war. There was never any suggestion of Adolf Hitler's being a shirker or a coward. He lived the front-line experience from almost the beginning to the end.

He invested in that experience emotion, courage, and unquestioning commitment, and in turn he drew from it a sense of purpose, belonging, acceptance, and the highest recognition for fortitude and excellence to which a German soldier could aspire. No wonder that he came to regard his war experience as his education, his training for life, worth more than any number of years of university study, and no wonder that his subsequent descriptions of that experience bubbled with exclamatory exuberance – 'mighty impression,' 'overwhelming,' 'so happy.'[6]

Hitler drew from this formative war experience the basic inspiration and organizational guidelines for his vision of a society of the future: 'Only by understanding the *Fronterlebnis* [the front experience] can one understand National Socialism,' said one of his followers.[7] The total mobilization of society in the interests of a greater metaphysical good, the fatherland, was to serve as his general blueprint for a future German order. The specifics of that good, like German aims during the war, were secondary considerations, if not immaterial. That good did not involve bits of territory or borders or individuals. What was important was the Idea. What was important was the act of assertion, of conquest, of victory, of struggle, and of dynamic life in war. What was important was the destruction of all that stood in the way of that dynamism – the materialists, the pedants, the infirm, the irresolute. Traditional morality, which was equivalent to bourgeois or slave morality, ceased to have a function in this forge of the future. His pedagogy is hard, he would say. He wanted to train young people to be violent and cruel and to terrorize the world. They would be free – free as beasts of prey – these youths. They would bear no trace of the centuries of domestication, of slavery.

Of course the constraints of practical politics and, later, of government responsibility would lead to tactical retreats, a tempering on occasion of the flamboyant rhetoric, a masking of energy, but the vision would never change. The war experience, more than anything else, became Hitler's model and his reservoir of inspiration. His views on social organization – the niche in the system required of everybody; on the economy – the need for national self-sufficiency; on politics – the need for eliminating subversive criticism and all decadent manifestations of unresolve, weakness, pacifism; on leisure – as a form of leave from front-line duty; on technology – as a means of liberation from the sterility of the bourgeois imagination; on race – 'I learnt that life is a cruel struggle and has no other object but the preservation of the species';[8] all these views were shaped by what he experienced between 1914 and 1918.

Even the use of gas against the enemies of the Reich was rooted in his personal experience. His own gassing had had a traumatic effect physically and emotionally. He, a visual creature, an artist dependent on his eyes, was temporarily blinded. The passage in *Mein Kampf* often quoted by historians though rarely underlined by contemporaries, takes on special significance in this context:

> If, at the beginning and during the war, someone had only subjected about twelve or fifteen thousand of these Hebrew destroyers of the people to poison gas – as was suffered on the battlefield by hundreds of thousands of our best workers from all social classes and all walks of life – then the sacrifice of millions at the front would not have been in vain.[9]

Hitler constantly referred to the Jews as 'vermin,' And he remembered that the most effective instrument during the war against vermin – rats and other pests – had been gas. The extermination of the Jews by means of gas Hitler would describe as a form of 'delousing.'

For Hitler the war did not end in 1918. He simply was incapable of accepting that the most invigorating experience of his life should end in defeat. While for over a decade most Germans could see no practical alternative to acceptance of defeat, in their hearts all Germans were inclined to sympathize with the radical elements that at least had the courage vigorously and publicly to deny that the war effort had been in vain. All political parties in Weimar, without exception, denounced the Treaty of Versailles, but only the radical right claimed that the peace treaty was the product of the same treacherous domestic elements, in league with the enemy, that had undermined the German war effort and stabbed the victorious army in the back. If one could unseat the traitors, the 'November criminals' who had engineered the defeat and ushered in the republic of shame, then one could begin to eradicate the blight that had attacked the 'ideas of 1914,' the 'spirit of the front,' and the 'community of the trenches.' Friedrich Wilhelm Heinz, veteran of the war and subsequently the SA leader in western Germany, asserted:

> Those people told us the war was over. That was a laugh. We ourselves are the war: its flame burns strongly in us. It envelops our whole being and fascinates us with the enticing urge to destroy.[10]

One had to return somehow to that supreme exultation which was the war before the defeat. To do that one had to employ methods taught by the war: one had to destroy.

If in the years immediately after the war people were still shaken by the horrors, the time would come, wrote Ernst Jünger in 1921, when the war would take on the character of the 'crucifixion paintings of the old masters: as a grand idea whose brilliance overwhelms night and blood.'[11] For the Nazis, however, and for other right-wing groups, the war was already an inspiration. 'National Socialism is in its truest meaning, the domain of the front,' insisted Gottfried Feder, one of the original members of the party. The socialism of National Socialism, said Robert Ley, was meant to duplicate the community of the trenches. Gregor Strasser, Hitler's adjutant in Berlin, constantly exalted the front soldier, to whom he promised leadership in the new Reich. All this was comparable to Mussolini's notion of a *trincerocrazia*, a 'trenchocracy,' which would be the elite of Fascism. And Hitler personally saw himself as the embodiment of the unknown soldier, the personification of that anonymous strength which had been unleashed and then shaped by the war.[12]

To reawaken that spirit and sense of commitment was the aim of all nationally minded elements in Weimar Germany, even of political moderates in the center, but it was the radicals on the right who pursued the goal with the least equivocation. What the war boom of the late twenties, with its wave of literary disillusionment, did was, paradoxically, prepare the way for a nationalist blacklash. By 1930, as the economic depression deepened, a literature of 'national reawakening' blossomed. Ernst Jünger began to be read eagerly. Franz Schauwecker gained a large audience. And a host of lesser nationalist authors prospered as well. It was in this context of growing economic despair and a newly articulated interest in the war that the Nazis registered their phenomenal gains in the state and local elections of 1929 and 1930 and especially in the national elections of September 1930.

Then, amidst the new respectability that accompanied success, while some of the party's programmatic statements – on the Jewish question, for instance – were toned down, the urgent need to stamp out the republic of shame, corruption, and national abnegation, and to replace it with a genuine *Volksgemeinschaft*, which would resurrect the mood and unity of 1914, and of the trenches, was invoked shrilly to ever-larger audiences. The word *Kultur* was used constantly by the Nazis to summon up the spirit of the war. They claimed to be the true heirs of that *Kultur*, of a spirit of selfless devotion to the idea of the nation and of German destiny. When Hitler decided to stand as a candidate for the presidency of the republic in the spring of 1932, the only way his opponents could find to counter his appeal was to persuade the old war leader Hindenburg to stand

411

again, despite his eighty-four years. The field marshal alone had the stature to defeat the 'Bohemian corporal.' Hindenburg did defeat Hitler in that election, but support for the Nazis continued to grow. In the national elections in July the party became, with 37.4 per cent of the votes and 230 seats, the largest single party ever to sit in a German Reichstag. Six months later Hitler was appointed chancellor by the very same Hindenburg who had been enlisted to keep him out of office. Thus, finally, on 30 January, 1933, that first major plateau in the rejuvenation of Germany, in the national awakening, was reached.

Within weeks of Hitler's appointment Philipp Witkop brought out a new edition, a *Volksausgabe* or popular edition, of the letters of German students who fell in the war. His new preface stated:

These letters are a legacy to us, so that we may realize that ideal fatherland which the writers envisioned longingly and for which they gave their lives. These young dead men are the martyrs not of a lost but of a new Germany, whose creators and citizens we are to become.

He pointed out that the letters contained an 'indubitable personal and historical truth' that was far more profound than that to be learned from any novels or histories of the war. And he added:

In these days of national self-awareness we bow to these students and swear in memory of them that they did not die in vain, that we shall discharge their testament, and that we through incessant effort shall be worthy of them.[13]

Christopher Isherwood was walking down the Bülowstrasse in Berlin shortly after the Nazi takeover and observed a Nazi raid on a liberal publishing house.

412

Books were being loaded on to a truck and the titles were being read out. 'Nie wieder Krieg' one brownshirt shouted, holding the book by a corner with stiff, elongated fingers. 'No more war!' echoed a fat, well-dressed woman, with a scornful, savage laugh. 'What an idea!'[14]

Four years later Thomas Mann reflected on the whole Nazi enterprise: 'If the idea of war, as an aim in itself, disappeared, the National Socialist system would be . . . utterly senseless.'[15]

ART AS LIFE

Nazism was a popular variant of many of the impulses of the avant-garde. It expressed on a more popular level many of the same tendencies and posited many of the same solutions that the avant-garde did on the level of 'high art.' Above all, it, like the moderns it claimed to despise, tried to marry subjectivism and technicism.

Nazism took as its point of departure the subjective self, feeling, experience, Erlebnis, and not reason and the objective world. That objective world was simply discarded. It could provide no hope, no warmth, no consolation. When Hitler returned from the war he had no job, no homeland, no profession, not even an address. In conventional terms he was a nothing, a nullity. All that he possessed of a positive nature was his conviction of his merit as an artist and his war experience. He was able to define himself not in any standard social terms, only in terms of personal emotions and a style – an aesthetic sense about how things must be done and the way in which meaning ought to be given to life.

It was Hitler's style, his oratorical talents and his remarkable ability to transmit emotions and feelings in his speeches, that took him to the leadership of the ragtag party of misfits and adventurers that he joined in Munich in 1919 and that called itself the German Workers' Party. The ideas he and the party spouted were all

413

tattered; they were nothing but jargon inherited from the paranoid Austro-German border politics of the pre-1914 era, which saw 'Germanness' threatened with inundation by 'subject nationalities.' Even the combination 'national socialist,' which Hitler added to the party's name when he became leader in 1920, was borrowed from the same era and same sources. It was not the substance – there was no substance to the frantic neurotic tirades – that allowed the party to survive and later to grow. It was the style and the mood. It was above all the theater, the vulgar 'art,' the grand guignol productions of the beer halls and the street. It was the provocation, the excitement, the frisson that Nazism was able to provide, in the brawling, the sweating, the singing, the saluting. Nazism, whether one wore brass knuckles and carried a rubber hose or simply played along vicariously, beating up communists and Jews in one's mind, was action. Nazism was involvement. Nazism was not a party; Nazism was an event.

Early on, to arouse a sense of belonging, of 'community,' the party began to emphasize the importance, above everything else, of ritual and propaganda – the flags, the insignia, the uniforms, the pageantry, the standard greetings, the declarations of loyalty, and the endless repetition of slogans. Nazism was a cult. The appeal was strictly to emotion. The assault was on the senses, primarily visual and aural. The spoken word took precedence over the written. Drama, music, dance and later radio and film were accorded more importance than literature. Nazism was grand spectacle, from beginning to end. In a country devoted for centuries to its 'poets and philosophers,' all this was new. When the legislature, elected on 5 March 1933, had to find a new meeting place because the Reichstag building had burned during the campaign, the choice fell on the Kroll Opera House. That was no accident and certainly not a question merely of convenience, space, and seating. Politics was now to become 'genuine' theater, as opposed to the pompous posturing of the democratic era. During the 1939–45 war, as Allied bombing raids on German cities and the corresponding destruction mounted, Hitler insisted on the immediate reconstruction of theaters and opera houses as a first priority. To the suggestion that the mood and morale of the populace demanded other priorities, Hitler would reply, 'Theatrical performances are needed precisely because the morale of the people must be maintained.'[1] From first to last, the Third Reich was spectacular, gripping theater. That is what it was intended to be.

Myth took the place of objectively conceived history. Myth, Michel Tournier has said, is 'history everyone already knows.'[2] As such, history becomes nothing but a tool of the present, with no integrity whatsoever of its own. Although Hitler was not as ignorant of historical detail as is often claimed, he subjected that detail, and the past as a whole, to the test of his personal experience. All historical concepts were drawn to that experience – the nation, the state, politics, culture, society, and economics. His personal experience became the lodestar of life, both national and international. When the end was near, he lost interest in history, even in the career of Frederick the Great, whose miraculous victories, snatched from the jaws of defeat, had provided much solace for him, particularly Thomas Carlyle's version of them. 'Even my historical examples do not make much impression on him,' wrote Goebbels in his diary on 21 March 1945.[3] History, then, became merely an extension of Hitler's own personality and his own fate.

In this context the deed took the place of deliberation, action replaced ethics. The program of the party, the so-called Twenty-five Points, issued in 1920 and subsequently declared immutable, was a declamatory act rather than a statement of principles and goals. It was a propagandistic and tactical gesture, and all subsequent declarations of immutability were similar acts. It was the act, the declaration, the theatrical pronouncement

415

that was important, not the content. The same was true of all of Hitler's speeches. They too were acts rather than speeches in the traditional sense. No wonder that Hitler insisted that the NSDAP was a 'movement' rather than a party. Parties were tied to rules, platforms, and agendas. The very essence of National Socialism, by contrast, was perpetual motion, vitalism, revolt. Hitler himself personified the imprecision. He seemed congenitally incapable of an orderly routine of work. He was notorious for missing appointments, for treating paperwork in a slap-dash manner, and for keeping odd hours – staying up until the early morning and sleeping late – which exhausted his inner circle. Again, this style, like the unruly forelock on his brow, was always attributed to the artist in him.

The Nietzschean invocation to 'live dangerously' became the sole commandment of Nazism. To live dangerously means, of course, consciously to court objection and resistance, to transgress against accepted social norms, to reject inherited morality. To live dangerously means never to accept the status quo; it means to act the adversary constantly, it means to exaggerate, to provoke. It means permanent conflict. 'Nazism is,' said Hitler, 'a doctrine of conflict.'

In this *Weltanschauung*, pity, compassion, the Sermon on the Mount, all become relics. Pity was nothing but bourgeois sentimentality, said Goebbels, an expression of the inequality that the Nazi community was eliminating. The bourgeois literature of disenchantment with the war wallowed in pity. If this kind of memory of the war and if bourgeois decadence in general were to be overcome, there could be no room for pity. Ezra Pound, in his fascist phase, also railed against pity. And Yeats, when he was editing *The Oxford Book of Modern Verse*, had no tolerance for so ignoble a sentiment as pity. He excluded Wilfred Owen, who had said of his verse: 'The poetry is in the pity.' To Yeats, true art could not be rooted in so ignoble a sentiment as pity.

The titanic conceit at work here is not a 'heroism of the will,' as claimed, but a 'heroism of the absurd,' a monumental egocentrism that excluded compromise, debate, conciliation – any recognition, in short, of a dialectical 'I and Thou' existence, of an objective world in response to which character and personality constantly develop. This was a realm of illusion which invented the outside world in its own image. If the tendency of modernism, from its roots in romanticism, was to 'objectify the subjective,' to translate into symbol subjective experience, Nazism took this tendency and turned it into a general philosophy of life and society. For the French collaborator Robert Brasillach, fascism was poetry – 'the poetry of the twentieth century.'4 For Hitler, life was art, his movement a symbol. At the 'day of Potsdam,' the superbly stage-managed official opening of the new Reichstag session, on 21 March 1933, when Hitler, the petit bourgeois Austrian corporal, shook hands with Hindenburg, the aristocratic Prussian field marshal and Reich president, over the tomb of Frederick the Great, the new chancellor attributed to art the responsibility for generating the redemptive phenomenon that was National Socialism. Out of art grew 'the longing for a new rising, for a new Reich, and therefore for new life.'5 The German effort in both wars and his own party's struggle for acceptance Hitler would equate with 'beauty.'6 He looked on himself as the incarnation of the artist-tyrant Nietzsche had called for, as the executor of the 'dictatorship of genius' Wagner had craved. In dealing with foreign policy, he boasted that he was 'the greatest actor in all Europe.' Banal his evil may in the end be judged, but he, no less than Tosca, could say that he lived for 'art.'

Fascism, in its German form and in others, was of course a political reality, but it was a political reality that emanated a frame of mind. Social and economic considerations naturally helped shape that frame of mind, but in the final analysis it was the existential void, not specific material concerns, that determined the response. Nazism was not simply a coercive system imposed on people by powermongers, less still by industrialists and financiers or by reactionary elites. Terror and violence were indeed political tools of the system, but despite their efficacy in containing serious opposition – at least until July 1944, when Hitler barely escaped an attempt on his life – they were peripheral to the acceptance of Nazism by the mass of Germans. In 1933 Goebbels had said that there were two ways of going about the 'revolution':

> You can go on shooting up the opposition with machine-guns until they acknowledge the superiority of the gunners. That is the simpler way. But you can also transform the nation by a mental revolution and thus win over the opposition instead of annihilating them. We National Socialists have adopted the second way and intend to pursue it.[1]

Germans were not forced to become Nazis. But they were attracted by the force of the movement.

The SS, Gestapo, and other security and police agencies in Germany, while extremely effective in rooting out and destroying potential opposition, were more symbolic for most Germans of the vitality of the regime than indispensable practical instruments for its security. Similarly, the war, when it finally came, was not the result of a master scheme followed resolutely by a master schemer but the unexpected – at that particular moment – outcome of an irrepressible dynamism bringing with it unavoidable confrontation. Germans were convinced that the war in 1939 was a question of survival, an inescapable continuation of the 1914–18 struggle. Either Germany would assert herself, territorially and politically, in Europe or she would be destroyed. Those were the alternatives presented to Germans not only by Hitler but by, so it was thought, the British, the French, and the Russians, among others; in short, by historical and geopolitical realities. As a result, this phase of the struggle, which began in September 1939, was greeted with stoical resignation, in contrast to the exuberance of August 1914; but the loyalty of the Germans was never in doubt. They fought the war with resolve and out of conviction that their existence was at stake. World power or extinction seemed the only possibilities.

Still, if violence and terror were not indispensable instruments of social control in the Third Reich, they were essential attributes of the Nazi cult. Violence was glorified. Terror, like everything else, was turned into an art form. The most ardent Nazis reveled in the aesthetics of murder. In the wake of the attempt on his life in July 1944, Hitler had the executions of the conspirators filmed for his own viewing pleasure – bodies racked by the most excruciating contortions dangling from meat hooks. Goebbels then insisted that these films be shown publicly. Obviously they were meant to cow opponents of the regime, but at the same time they were meant to transmit a sense of the resolve and ruthlessness of Nazism.

Hitler's confrère, Mussolini, and Italian fascism as a whole, also aestheticized brutality. When Italy attacked Ethiopia in 1935 and waged war, with bombers and modern weapons, on natives armed often only with spears, fascist writers vied with each other to evoke the 'beauties' of this conflict. 'Do you want to fight? To kill? See rivers of blood? Great heaps of gold? Herds of female prisoners? Slaves?' asked d'Annunzio.[2] 'War is

419

beautiful,' bellowed Marinetti in turn, 'because it combines the gunfire, the cannonades, the pauses, the scents, and the stench of putrefaction into a symphony.'[3]

The theme of death exercised a powerful grip on the fascist imagination. Much of Nazi ritual was enacted at night: torches and pyres figured prominently in the apparatus of the liturgy. The grandest of Nazi ceremonies seemed to focus on the laying of wreaths, on the celebration of heroes or martyrs, whether they were Frederick the Great, the fallen of the war, the party dead of the 1923 Munich putsch, or Horst Wessel. 'Propaganda of the corpse' was how Harry Kessler described this aspect of Nazism.[4] A crucial criterion for Nazi architecture, insisted Hitler, was its ability to survive as a ruin, like the Pyramids of Luxor, and thus to inspire awe. Nazi buildings were to be mausoleums, intended as such directly or not.

And what about the so-called ideology of Nazism? Because Nazism was above all, despite its fascination with death, a question of 'experience,' a pursuit of authenticity, the specifics of the 'program' always took a back seat to the notion of the movement as energy, of conflict as liberation. What was important was constant confrontation, an unflinching adversarial posture, not the details of that posture. Thus the party before 1933 and then the administration of the Third Reich could sustain a remarkable divergence, characterized by hundreds of petty jealousies, rivalries, disagreements, and a chaotic jostling for power and influence. Goebbels despised Goering; Goering hated Hess; they all loathed Rosenberg; and on it went, endless whirlpools of internecine spite and animus. Contrary to surface impressions of monolithic unity centered on the Führer and of administrative efficiency, if not wizardry, the party and the Reich represented an 'authoritarian anarchy.'[5]

The movement displayed striking contradictions between programmatic statements and actual policy.

The peasantry was heralded as the 'lifeblood of the nation,' but depopulation of rural areas continued and Germany actually became more urbanized during the Third Reich. Promises to provide every German with 'a little house in the country' to the contrary, Nazi building plans were focused almost exclusively on monumental urban architecture. Women were to remain in the home and devote themselves to their role as mothers, but even before the outbreak of the war in 1939 there were more women in the work force than ever. The small businessman was supposed to prosper in the Third Reich, but in reality business and industry became more concentrated. The contradictions, like the animosities, were countless.

To outsiders, perhaps the most ironic of Nazi asseverations was the race thesis. That the supremacy of the Aryan race should be propounded by the likes of Hitler, Goebbels, Goering, and the rest was simply ludicrous. Take Hitler, with his dark hair, small eyes, low brow, broad cheekbones, with his effeminate hand gestures, the jaw always on the verge of dissolving into an irrepressible tremble; or Goebbels, the conspicuously ugly 'superdwarf' with the club foot; or Himmler, the monocled chicken farmer, failed veterinarian, who looked like a caricature of Hollywood caricatures of the Nazis; or Goering, the avuncular buffoon; or Ley, the varicose-veined drunkard whose nickname was 'Reich boozer'; or Rosenberg, whom even his colleagues mocked unremittingly, saying he looked Jewish; or Streicher, the sadistic Bavarian oaf and expert pornographer. The 'racial hygienist' Max von Gruber declared in 1924 that Hitler's appearance was decidedly un-Nordic, suggestive more of Alpine-Slavic stock.[6] The rest of the Nazi hierarchy was equally unconvincing as an advertisement for racial purity. Yet none of these contradictions or ironies seemed to make any difference. The energy and fanatical faith invoked by Hitler overrode them all.

Nazi faith had no real direction or definition other than its vulgar affirmation of self. That faith was pointed at the 'nation,' but its locus was the individual. Even though eugenics was added to the curricula of schools and universities, the subject could never escape its circular arguments. Aryanism defied definition and was little other than an article of faith. Nazi master-race theory, with its emphasis on fabulously beautiful prototypes, flawless youths and maidens, was nothing but a banal aestheticism. A mindless, simple notion of beauty was all there was at the heart of Aryanism. Racism is related to narcissism, and there was a striking similarity to the paths followed by Maurice Barrès in France, Gabriele d'Annunzio in Italy, and Hitler. They were all myopic, frustrated egocentrics who appeared to move, to borrow terminology from Barrès, from a *culte du moi* to a preoccupation with *l'énérgie nationale*. In fact the apparent shift from aestheticism to nationalism was simply a reordering of terminology rather than a change of focus, an egomaniacal transference of one's own illusions of self to the nation.

And the Jew? Nietzsche had remarked that anti-Semitism was the ideology of those who felt cheated. The Jew was the most convenient, most visible, scapegoat available to western Christian culture to explain away the ills and failings of society and individuals. The Jew had after all killed Jesus Christ; therefore the Jew must be the Antichrist. But such a general resentment, prevalent in western society for centuries, does not explain the dimensions of Nazi viciousness toward the Jew and cannot begin to explain the Holocaust. Here, again, the notion of transference is useful. If a racial nationalism consisted of a projection of personal fantasy and illusion on to a national level, anti-Semitism was similarly a projection of profound individual self-hatred and self-doubt on to the Jew. Hitler's paragon Karl Lueger, the mayor of Vienna, once said, 'I decide who is a Jew.' The Jew, in other words, became a negative function of the self.

422

To Hitler, the Jew came to be associated with all the dark instincts of his own personality and sexuality. The sexual motif in his anti-Semitism, in his ranting about the Jews, is unmistakable. They are the carriers of syphilis, the organizers of prostitution, the swarthy, hairy, race defilers lurking in shadows, in wait of blond, blue-eyed, virginal prey. Whether Hitler had one or two testicles, whether he indeed was an 'undinist' or coprophiliac who achieved sexual gratification by having women urinate and defecate on him, as some have claimed on rather slight evidence, is in itself incidental. What is clear beyond doubt is that Hitler projected his own failings and guilt, sexual and otherwise, on to the Jew. The 'universal enemy' represented what he most hated in himself.[7]

In personal as well as social terms Hitler was a failure. There was nothing natural or straightforward about him. He was humorless, always awkward, always performing. Even his eroticism, said Putzi Hanfstaengl, was 'purely operatic, never operative.'[8] Everything was artificial and surreptitious. He was incapable of friendship or love or even a genuine smile. Authenticity, which he advertised to the nation, was completely foreign and frightening to him. If he was provoked to laugh, he always put his hand in front of his face. He took pills for gas, terrified as he was of farting. He changed his underwear as often as three times a day. All was symbol, substitution, abstraction. At the center there was nothing, an utter vacuum. Only an audience could give Hitler meaning; he had none himself.

If darkness was to be turned into light, the Jew, the symbol of darkness, had to be eliminated. When Walther Rathenau, the Jewish foreign minister, was murdered in June 1922, the youths responsible timed the act to coincide with summer solstice. The Jew, the agent of darkness, was sacrificed to the Germanic sun god. Hitler thought in similar terms. Just what form 'elimination' or 'removal' – Hitler used the world *Entfernung* –

would take was, during the twenties and thirties and even at the beginning of the war, not clear. Resettlement, to Madagascar or a part of Poland or to Siberia, and ghettolike isolation were talked about. However, when the possibility surfaced, in the second half of 1941, after Britain had refused to capitulate and after the German attack on Russia had stalled, that Nazism might not achieve its goals in the east, the process of transference took its logical course. What until the end of 1941 had been sporadic killing of eastern European and Russian Jews was turned into systematized slaughter. In Auschwitz the mass murders began in February 1942. As military failures accumulated, the pace of genocide accelerated. As the Russian armies advanced toward Germany in 1944 and early 1945, the 'Jewish problem' took precedence over everything else; to Hitler and his henchmen it became more important than the preservation of Germany.

On 14 March 1945, Goebbels remarked in his diary on the 'grotesque impression' created by the news that Palestinian Jews had called a one-day strike in sympathy with the Jews of Europe.

The Jews are playing a wicked and thoughtless game. No-one can say with certainty which nations will be on the losing side and which on the winning at the end of the war; but there can be no doubt that the Jews will be the losers.[9]

Given the mass slaughter of European Jews that was going on at the very moment Goebbels wrote, the entry is totally incomprehensible unless one substitutes 'Nazis' for 'Jews.' The Jew was the representative of everything the Nazi refused to accept about himself. It was the Nazis who were playing the 'wicked and thoughtless game,' and by March 1945 there could be 'no doubt' that it would be the Nazis who would be 'the losers.' In the end the process of reversal, which characterized

Nazism, meant the light would be turned into darkness. In the Nazi flag, the swastika, a sun symbol, was in black.

The manner in which Hitler carried out the 'final solution' was monomaniacal but efficient. There was a gigantic impersonal bureaucracy of death – the ultimate bureaucracy – that may have encompassed as many as eighty thousand 'employees.' Each had a set task to perform, and few were openly informed of the purpose of the task except in vague, euphemistic terms. Train conductors, railway maintenance men, camp guards, and 'scientists' went about their work as they would have any other. Goebbels often noted in his diary that secrecy was essential for the sake of efficiency. The technology of destruction was improved with alacrity. The mass shootings were soon replaced by gassings in mobile vans and then gas chambers and crematoria in camps designed for killing. The obsession with efficiency in the extermination of the Jews climaxed the regime's general preoccupation with technique. This was the other side of the coin of life as myth. As the journey inward proceeded, as the fantasy deepened, there was a corresponding accentuation of technique.

Without the emphasis on technique, Hitler's rise to power is inconceivable. The devotion to enhancing the appeal of ritual, the obsession with propaganda, and the interest in technology and in the applications, as opposed to the substance, of science, all fitted under this rubric of technicism. The 'friendship' of sorts that Hitler developed with Albert Speer was based on their mutual fascination with the instruments of power. Speer created the staggeringly successful palaces of light for the Nuremberg rallies, designed a number of the monumental buildings of the Reich, made plans for a future Berlin, and later, during the war, became minister of munitions. Similarly, the productive relationship Hitler had with Leni Reifenstahl, the filmmaker who, especially in *The Triumph of the Will*, evoked the 'beauty' of

Nazism, sprang from a joint fascination with the 'art' of social control.

Propaganda was to Hitler not just a necessary evil, a question of justifiable lies, of warranted exaggeration. Propaganda was to him an art. Again it was the war experience that brought this home. The propaganda apparatus of the party and later of the regime was as a result truly impressive, even awesome. The party and its propaganda blended into one: they became indistinguishable. This kind of fusion of technique and substance was also the basis of the *Führerprinzip*, the leadership principle: the leader and the led became one. Not surprisingly, in the party initially, and then in the Third Reich, the technicians and the managers moved to the forefront. They were much attracted to the idea of National Socialism, and Nazism in turn was very much a movement of technicians, of one sort or another.

Nazi fascination with technique affected all aspects of social organization and institutional life in the Third Reich, none more so than the military. The manner in which the Great War had been fought, with mass formations and direct frontal assaults, Hitler regarded as 'degenerate.' That form of warfare would not return, he promised. The next war would be quite different, and of course it was. It was a war of movement, of mechanized divisions, a *Blitzkrieg*, prepared carefully in advance. Tanks and airplanes were the key to this war, which Hitler directed in large part himself because of firmly implanted suspicions about the unreliability of the high command.

Given the importance of 'communication' in his movement, Hitler was intrigued by the technology of transportation and information, and he took pains to associate himself with these advances. He was frequently photographed in his Mercedes-Benz and relished the sensation of driving, often at considerable speed, through crowds. He could go on at length in monologues to his associates about the art of driving an automobile.

The road network he had built in Germany he regarded as one of his greatest achievements and legacies, saying that 'the beginnings of every civilization express themselves in terms of road construction.' The building of roads, as opposed to railways, which belonged to the last century, would be a first priority in a conquered Russia. He made, in this connection, one particularly striking remark about the *Autobahnen*: 'Even in the more thickly populated areas they reproduce the atmosphere of the open spaces.'[10] Technology, it is clear, was a means of escaping from the confines of reality, a way of liberating the imagination.

For this reason flying also intrigued him, even though his stomach was less tolerant of the sensation than his mind. One of the most successful of all Nazi slogans was from the presidential election campaign of 1932: 'Hitler over Germany.' It was of course based on his frequent use of the airplane in his whirlwind campaign that spring. He flew about thirty thousand miles and spoke at about two hundred meetings. He was the first politician to use the airplane so extensively.

The air, as an arena of combat, also naturally interested Hitler, as it did all foot soldiers of the Great War, and the Luftwaffe became, after its creation in 1935, in open contravention of the Versailles Treaty, a favored branch of the armed services. Hitler wanted the largest air force in the world and the best pilots. War in the air he viewed as a Germanic form of battle.[11]

Charles Lindbergh, when he showed an interest in visiting Germany, was greeted with open arms, in 1936 and again in 1937 and 1938, not simply because of the propaganda benefits the regime would derive from such visits but because of genuine respect for the air ace. In October 1938, on the flyer's third visit, Goering pinned the Service Cross of the German Eagle on Lindbergh, 'by order of the Führer.' The admiration was reciprocated. In 1938 Lindbergh would seriously consider taking up residence in Berlin, and there can be no question that at least part of the reason for his advocacy of American neutrality after the outbreak of war stemmed from a sympathy with Fascism. He viewed the western democracies as degenerate and incapable of competing with Germany. His wife, Anne, was to publish in 1940 an eloquent anti-interventionist tract, *The Wave of the Future*, whose style was hers but whose ideas reflected the views of her husband. The book argued that Fascism was just that, the wave of the future, and that even with the rough edges it had shown in the process of establishing itself, its ideas were sound. Fascism was the only alternative to communism, the other manifestation of the political future. To resist Nazism was to resist change, and 'to resist change is to sin against life itself.'[12] As blackness closed in on Germany in 1945, Goebbels even then saw in Lindbergh a glimmer of hope. 'Isolationism,' he noted in his diary on 22 March in reference to the United States, 'is raising its head again. Moreover Colonel Lindbergh is becoming active in politics again.'[13]

Mussolini, Mosley, and other fascist leaders were also enamored of technology. Mussolini loved to fly. Mosley, after a stint in the trenches, had served in the Royal Flying Corps. By comparison, the leaders of the 'decadent' democracies were technological antediluvians. Neville Chamberlain and Sir Horace Wilson, when they went to Munich in 1938 to negotiate the Sudeten question, both flew for the first time.[14]

Radio and film played an indispensable role in the consolidation of the Third Reich. The purchase of radio sets, or 'people's receivers' *(Volksempfänger)*, as they were called, was subsidized by the Reich. Film production was centralized and encouraged. Hitler was an avid film viewer, much preferring films to literature as entertainment.

As the years went by, more and more attention was paid to the staging of party functions, particularly the annual September rallies at Nuremberg. These became the *pièces de résistance* of the Nazi festal cycle. 'Seven days yearly,' as François-Poncet put it after finally attending one of these staged festivals, 'Nuremberg was a city devoted to revelry and madness, almost a city of convulsionaries.'[15] The enthusiasm was kindled by meticulous attention to detail: high-precision parades, forests of banners, carefully rehearsed catechetical speeches. At the end came Hitler. His concluding oration was timed to end as night fell. The rally would close under the magical spell of Speer's 'cathedral of ice': hundreds of searchlights pointing to the sky. Of the grandeur of the rally he witnessed, Nevile Henderson said, 'I had spent six years in St Petersburg before the war in the best days of the old Russian ballet, but for grandiose beauty I have never seen a ballet to compare with it.'[16] That he should have been provoked to such a comparison is not accidental. Albert Speer, who designed the visual effects for the rallies, was very interested in the dance theories of Mary Wigman.[17] Her ideas about 'choirs of movement' that would 'conquer space' were in turn influenced by Émile Jaques-Dalcroze, whom we met earlier, and Rudolf von Laban, who became ballet master of the Prussian state theaters. All these people had either worked with or been stimulated by the Russians.

Now, where does Hitler, the individual, stand in relation to the Nazi phenomenon as a whole? It must be said that the diabolical brilliance of his perversity is unique, and that it is indeed impossible to imagine the movement's being quite the same without his charismatic imprint. Certainly no-one else in the Nazi hierarchy exercised anywhere near the influence or demonstrated any comparable appeal. But that said, Hitler remains undeniably the creation of his time, a creature of German imagination rather than, strictly speaking, of social and economic forces. He was never regarded in the first instance as the prospective agent of social and economic recovery – that was a *post facto* interpretation –

but rather as a symbol of revolt and counteraffirmation by the dispossessed, the frustrated, the humiliated, the unemployed, the resentful, the angry. Hitler stood for protest. He was a mental construct in the midst of defeat and failure, of inflation and depression, of domestic political chaos and international humiliation. Before his speaker's podium, as Joachim Fest has noted, the masses actually celebrated themselves.[18] Hitler produced millions of little clones in the orgiastic religiosity of his movement. He played to this imagery of the common man. He, Hitler, he often said in his speeches, was a 'lonely wanderer out of nothingness.' He was the 'unknown soldier,' the 'anonymous warrior,' the 'worker,' the 'man of the people.' His dress was always austere. His speeches had no room for jokes or flippancy. And he saw the political advantage of remaining unmarried. A single-minded devotion was what he meant to suggest and what he evoked in his audiences. They responded ecstatically, witnesses of a sacred vision. But in all this the need and the imagination of the audience were parents to the reality of Hitler. And to this day, in his evocative powers, as symbol of 'evil' genius, he remains a creation of our imaginations. He is indeed, as Syberberg's engrossing film of the late 1970s affirmed, 'our Hitler.'[19] He is antithesis. The ultimate kitsch artist, he filled the abyss with symbols of beauty. The victim he turned into the hero, hell into heaven, death into transfiguration.

The emphasis of Nazism was not on the past but in 'breaking out' to the future – *Aufbruch* was one of the movement's prized words, capturing the notion of eruption, the exuberant eruption of life that comes with the awakening of spring. One spoke of the 'eruption of the nation,' the 'eruption of spirit.' Just as the overriding theme of *Die Meistersinger* – according to Hanfstaengl, Hitler's favorite opera – is the awakening of life and art that comes with spring, so too was that of Nazism.

Much of the intellectual and artistic community became caught up in the drama of Nazism and the Third Reich. In its early days in Munich the party drew a significant number of members from the artistic community in Schwabing.[1] By 1931 the Nazis enjoyed about twice as much support in universities as in the country as a whole. And on 3 March 1933, three hundred university teachers openly declared themselves for Hitler in an election statement.[2] If considerable numbers of talented and renowned people left Germany after January 1933, it was for the most part either because they were Jewish or because they feared, for one reason or another, for their livelihood. Those who left for moral reasons, as a statement of opposition, constituted a tiny fraction. In relation to those who remained, the exiles were a small minority.[3]

For every non-Jew of international stature who left, many, like Gottfried Benn, Richard Strauss, Gerhart Hauptmann, Emil Nolde, and Martin Heidegger, remained. A number of these, inherently shy of overt political involvement because of the negative connotations of politics, in fact became publicly involved, initially at any rate, in the excitement of 1933. 'All is permissible that leads to experience,' Benn had written earlier.[4] That kind of amorality and adventurism, so Nietzschean in inspiration, came home to roost in 1933 and characterized the intellectual response to Nazism. For Rudolf Binding the advent of the Third Reich represented the actualization of a 'great longing.' 'This longing is not external but internal, and whoever draws it to the exterior desecrates it.'[5] As was the case for Robert Brasillach, Fascism for Binding was a poetical construct. In the Third Reich poet and soldier became one. Very few of the prominent intellectuals actually became party members, and it is undeniable that the organization of cultural life was left to second-rate

431

talents. But creative minds have always shied away from entanglements with the mundane and routine, and party membership should not be the measuring rod of support or acceptance.

Outside Germany, too, there was much interest and sympathy in intellectual and artistic quarters for the experiment taking place in central Europe, as there had been earlier for the advent of Bolshevism in Russia and then Fascism in Italy. All these experiments seemed to capture the mystique of the avant-garde movements of an earlier day: to embrace life, to rebel against bourgeois sterility, to hate respectable society, and above all to revolt – to bring about a radical revaluation of all values. Misfortune became grace; need became salvation; despondency, intoxication; weakness, strength. In April 1917 Paul Morand had heard Misia Sert, Diaghilev's admirer and patron, 'speak enthusiastically of the Russian Revolution, which appears to her like an enormous ballet.'[6] Her friend Serge Lifar, one of Diaghilev's early protégés, who was to be made director of the Paris Opéra Ballet under the German occupation, would repeatedly refer in conversation to a meeting he had with Hitler: 'Only two men in my life have caressed me like this,' he would say as he slid his hand down the arm of his interlocutor, 'Diaghilev and Hitler!'[7] The vitalism, the heroism, the eroticism of first Bolshevism and then Fascism produced a very strong brew indeed for artists and intellectuals. Nietzsche had asserted that the only way to justify the world was as an aesthetic phenomenon, and Benn thought in 1933 that Germany was about to realize the meaning of that statement.[8] Maurice Mandelbaum was with W.H. Auden at Swarthmore between 1942 and 1945. In conversation one day Auden asked whom one would trust if Fascism came to America. Both men decided they would much rather trust nonacademics than academics.[9]

Of course there was a steady attrition of intellectual support for the Nazi regime. Jünger, Benn, Strauss,

Heidegger, all retreated from their early enthusiasm. The massacre of the Night of the Long Knives, 30 June 1934, when the leaders of the SA were killed off to appease the major-domos of the army, who saw the Brown Shirts and their ambitions as a threat, and when several other old scores were settled with the murders of Gregor Strasser, General Kurt von Schleicher and his wife, Gustav von Kahr, Edgar Jung, Erich Klausener, and, through mistaken identity, the music critic Willi Schmidt; those murders appalled many. The steady progression of anti-Semitic measures, culminating before the war in Crystal Night, in November 1938, when synagogues and Jewish stores were smashed and burned, this frightened others. Outside Germany the same process of distancing occurred. In 1934 James Joyce noted sarcastically, 'I am afraid poor Mr Hitler will soon have few friends in Europe apart from my nephews, Masters W. Lewis and E. Pound.'[10]

The gradual falling-out was occasioned, however, less by what National Socialism represented as a general phenomenon than by its treatment of the intelligentsia: the insolence of party cadres toward intellectuals, their distrust of them, and their feelings of inferiority toward them. The former second-rate expressionist turned ardent Nazi, Hanns Johst, termed intellectualism a combination of 'the art of persuasion and Jewish pettifoggery.'[11] Speer related how uncomfortable Hitler felt with distinguished guests. He preferred, as a result, not to invite them for private audiences or even to party functions. Those people he did invite were more often artists or film stars than writers or thinkers. Many of the latter were alienated by what they saw as the vulgar style of the regime, the aggressive and opportunistic tactics of the 'spiritual SA,' the young arrivistes who took control of the academies and cultural institutions of the Reich.

The ambitions of many German intellectuals to be hailed as national heroes were thus dashed. Mussolini honored Marinetti and d'Annunzio, and futurism received a quasi-official recognition as spiritual forebear of Italian Fascism. Many German expressionists, among them Benn, hoped something similar would happen in Germany. It did not. Instead the quip 'When I hear the word *culture* I reach for my gun' became so popular that its origin was attributed to virtually every leading Nazi. It captured the petit bourgeois resentment of the regime toward intellectuals and also expressed the movement's refusal to allow itself to be associated with any traditional social group. *Kultur* was to be stripped of its elitist implications and given a genuinely populist meaning. Culture was a matter of people, the *Volk*, not of intellectuals.

In such an atmosphere intellectuals invariably started to turn away from the party, though not necessarily the uprising of the nation it stood for. What ensued was ambivalence and ambiguity. The party and its leadership began to be scorned as cheap. Their goals, however, remained legitimate. The result was not opposition but what the Germans came to call 'internal exile' – a withdrawal from public life. Yet when the war came in 1939 many of these exiles returned to enlist and fight for the national cause, which Hitler of course still led. The divorce had not been complete.

One is tempted initially to accept the designation of Nazism as 'reactionary modernism,'[12] but the implication of such a description is that Nazism used the tools and technology of modernity in an attempt to impose on Germany a vision of the past. As we have argued, that would be to misinterpret, in fact to reverse, the central thrust of the movement in the context of its age. Postwar Germany inherited from the imperial era, especially its last decades, an aggressive urge to expand, to establish its predominance, at least on the continent of Europe, which was still regarded as the center of the world. She had been in the pre-1914 age the national incarnation of rebellion against the bourgeois Anglo-French epoch of materialism, industrialism, and imperialism. At the same time, she was also its offspring: the personification of youth, rejuvenation, and technical efficiency. Her defeat in the war paralleled the death of a young generation, and her frustrations were emblematic of the frustrations of the confused, neurotic, rebellious survivors who in droves everywhere in the twenties took up the torch of the prewar avant-garde and turned rebellion against the hated bourgeois into a matter no longer of individuals, or even of one nation, but of an entire generation. Germany remained the foremost national representative of that revolt. The Great War was the psychological turning point, for Germany and for modernism as a whole. The urge to create and the urge to destroy changed places. The urge to destroy was intensified; the urge to create became increasingly abstract. In the end the abstractions turned to insanity and all that remained was destruction, Götterdämmerung.

'Under the debris of our shattered cities,' wrote Joseph Goebbels in 1945 with a breathless intoxication reminiscent of expressionist plays of the twenties, and indeed of his own diaries of that decade,

the last so-called achievements of the middle-class nineteenth century have been buried ... Together with the monuments of culture there crumble also the last obstacles to the fulfilment of our revolutionary task. Now that everything is in ruins, we are forced to rebuild Europe. In the past, private possessions tied us to bourgeois restraint. Now the bombs, instead of killing all Europeans, have only smashed the prison walls which held them captive . . . In trying to destroy Europe's future, the enemy has succeeded in smashing its past; and with that, everything old and outworn has gone.[13]

These statements were meant for public consumption on radio and in the press. In his diary the tone was more somber but the gist was the same. In mid March, on learning of a raid on Würzburg that demolished the center of the city, he commented:

> So the last beautiful German city still intact has now gone. Thus we say a melancholy farewell to a past which will never return. A world is going down but we all retain a firm faith that a new world will arise from its ashes.[14]

In mid April 1945, when the end was imminent, Goebbels – who too had enjoyed the Russian ballet a score of years earlier[15] – was still thinking in terms of 'art,' a grand color film that would eventually be made about the Twilight of the Gods in Berlin.

> I can assure you that it will be a fine and elevating picture, and for the sake of this prospect it is worth standing fast. Hold out now, so that a hundred years hence the audience does not hoot and whistle when you appear on the screen![16]

Was he thinking of the performance of the film *All Quiet on the Western Front*, in the Mozartsaal of the Theater am Nollendorfplatz in Berlin, which he had helped interrupt so rudely in December 1930? He was certainly thinking of his own reflection on that modern mirror of civilization, the picture screen. The thought that the Third Reich would survive in this modern art form provided solace for him. Along with Hans Sachs, he might have said:

> *Zerging' in Dunst*
> *Das heil'ge römische Reich*
> *Uns bliebe gleich*
> *Die heil'ge deutsche Kunst!**

*Though should dissolve
The Holy Roman Empire,
Still would remain
Our sacred German Art!

On 1 May, Goebbels, the Reich Funeral Master, as he was often called, whose forte had always been the funeral oration, poisoned his six children. Then after his wife, Magda, had taken a fatal dose, too, he shot himself. A few days earlier, on 28 April, confined to the Führer bunker by fighting in the streets above, Magda had composed a letter of farewell to Harald Quandt, a son by her first marriage.

> Our splendid concept is perishing and with it goes everything beautiful, admirable, noble and good that I have known in my life. The world which will succeed the Führer and National Socialism is not worth living in and for this reason I have brought the children here too. They are too good for the life that will come after us . . . Harald, my dear – I give you the best that life has taught me: be true – true to yourself, true to mankind, true to your country – in every respect whatsoever.[17]

The kitsch, the transvaluation, the death in life, continued to the very end.

On the same day that Magda Goebbels wrote to her son, Hitler began a last series of gestures to the world that had created him. Late on the twenty-eighth he married his mistress, Eva Braun. The marriage was not an act of abdication; it did not mark the end of the posturing. The reversal of norms continued. Marriage is meant to mark a beginning. Here it signaled the end. In the early hours of the twenty-ninth, after the ceremony, Hitler drew up his testament. It contained the old tirades against the Jews and the need for territory in the east, but there was one interesting passage that hinted at his thoughts on the relationship between life and death. 'Death,' he said of himself and his new wife, 'will compensate us for what my work in the service of my people robbed from us both.'[18] Death was to be looked on, it seems, as a reward, as 'compensation' for sacrifice.

Death was the antithesis of work. Death was the supreme manifestation of life.

In the bunker day and night blended. In the early hours of the thirtieth, Hitler summoned the staff of his underground shelter for final farewells. There were secretaries, orderlies, officers – some twenty men and women. A round of hand shaking took place. Hitler was silent. He then withdrew. Everyone was aware that the Führer was planning to commit suicide.

Whereupon a strange 'happening' occurred. In the canteen of the chancellery, within earshot of the Führer bunker, a dance began. Soldiers, secretaries, orderlies, menial staff, and other bunker dwellers began to frolic. A general slapped a tailor on the back. They talked. Distinctions of rank broke down. The noise reached the Führer's quarters, and a message came to tone down the commotion. But the dance continued.[19]

Twelve hours later, the Red Army knot had tightened. The Russians had taken the Tiergarten. They now occupied the railway tunnels in the Friedrichstrasse. They had reached the Weidendammer bridge over the Spree. From the Führer's subterranean suite a single shot was heard. Years earlier Karl Kraus had written, 'When I think of Hitler, nothing comes to mind.'

A popular German song in 1945 was entitled 'Es ist ein Frühling ohne Ende!'*

*'It Is Spring Without End!'

438

Acknowledgements
Notes
Selected Sources
Index

Acknowledgements

A book that has been in the making as long as this one belongs to many people besides the author, whether they want credit for it or not. It is a pleasure to acknowledge assistance.

The Social Sciences and Humanities Research Council of Canada provided funds, in the form of a leave fellowship and research grants, for work in Europe at several stages. Without this generous support I could not, quite simply, have written the book. My academic home, the Scarborough Campus of the University of Toronto, gave encouragement in many ways.

To the archivists, librarians, and staff of the institutions listed in the note on sources I owe thanks. Mention must, however, be made of some individuals who went out of their way to help: Clive Hughes, Philip Reed, and Peter Thwaites at the Imperial War Museum, that extraordinary repository of documents of the Great War; Général Delmas at the Service historique de l'armée de terre at Vincennes; M. Duchêne-Marullaz, a private scholar who gave me valuable leads; Hans-Heinrich Fleischer of the West German military archives at Freiburg; Gerhard Heyl of the military section of the Bavarian state archives in Munich; and Parmenia Migel Ekstrom of the Stravinksy-Diaghilev Foundation in New York.

James Joll, George Mosse, and Fritz Stern assisted as much by example as by encouragement. Robert Spencer,

John Cairns, and Martin Broszat smiled benignly on, perhaps also at, my efforts.

To Martin Landy and Ruth Caleb, Nigel Thorpe and Susan Bamforth, Michael and Colette Llewellyn Smith, Russell and Lulu Hone, Suzanne Weinberg and François Bursaux, Susan Meisner and Thomas Brown, Volker Klein, and Ernst-Günther Koch, to all these friends I bow for important favors. Before John and Valerie Bynner, however, I prostrate myself. Their kindness has been exceptional.

Of my colleagues, I single out William Dick, who read the manuscript with his critical eye, Thomas Saunders, who tracked down some material, and Paul Gooch, Wayne Dowler, and Paul Thompson, who extended administrative backing to my endeavors. David Harford provided help with the illustrations and Lois Pickup with sundry vital tasks.

Crown copyright material in both the Imperial War Museum and the Public Record Office is reproduced by permission of the Controller of Her Majesty's Stationery Office. For permisssion to cite from various private papers, I thank L.W. Galer, B.C. Gregson, Paul P.H. Jones, R. McGregor, N.J. Mountfort, Sybil O'Donoghue, W.E. Quinton, F.H.T. Tatham, and A. Walker. The editors of *The Journal of Contemporary History* and *The Canadian Journal of History* have been kind enough to permit me to use here segments of articles that first appeared in the pages of their publications.

For his confidence in the prospects of this book I thank Malcolm Lester. But that this lucky manuscript found its way eventually to Peter Davison, poet and confrère, for his care and tact, and then to Frances Apt, manuscript editor *sans pareil*, is due to the good sense of Beverley Slopen, my agent.

In the course of our mutual labors, my wife, Jayne, often cited to me the sentiments of Rudyard Kipling's 'If.' To her I now cite James Joyce's words in 1921, to

Harriet Shaw Weaver: 'I am very grateful for your unremitting loyalty to my troublesome self and interminable composition.'

M.E.
Toronto and Maussane-les-Alpilles

Notes

pages 23–8

1. This and the other quotations from the novella are taken from the translation of *Death in Venice* by H.T. Lowe-Porter (New York, 1954).
2. Misia Sert, *Misia* (Paris, 1952), 229–30.
3. Heinrich Mann, 'Der Tod in Venedig,' *März*, 7/13 (1913), 478.
4. Thomas Mann, 'Lebensabriss' (1930), *Gesammelte Werke*, 14 vols. (Frankfurt am Main, 1960–1974), XI:123–24; Karl Ipser, *Venedig und die Deutschen* (Munich, 1976), 90–91; and Peter de Mendelssohn, *Der Zauberer* (Frankfurt am Main, 1975), 869–73.
5. In Carl Schorske, *Fin-de-siècle Vienna* (New York, 1980), 164; and J.E. Chamberlin, 'From High Decadence to High Modernism,' *Queen's Quarterly*, 87 (1980), 592.
6. John Hellmann, *Fables of Fact: The New Journalism as New Fiction* (Urbana, Ill., 1981).
7. John Ruskin, *The Stones of Venice*, in *The Complete Works*, 13 vols. (New York, n.d.), VII:15.
8. In Ipser, *Venedig*, 93.

pages 31–2

1. Vera Stravinsky and Robert Craft, *Stravinsky* (New York, 1978), 75.

pages 32–40

1. *Le Figaro*, May 17, 1913.
2. Gabriel Astruc, *Le Pavillon des fantômes* (Paris, 1929), 286–87.

444

3. Jean Cocteau, *Oeuvres complètes*, 11 vols. (Geneva, 1946–1951), IX:43–49.
4. Carl Van Vechten (ed.), *Selected Writings of Gertrude Stein* (New York, 1946), 113.
5. *Le Figaro*, May 31, 1913.
6. For Cocteau see n.3 above; for Stravinsky, his *Conversations* (London, 1959), 46.
7. My italics. Cited in Richard Buckle, *Nijinksy* (Harmondsworth, 1980), 357.
8. Carl Van Vechten, *Music and Bad Manners* (New York, 1916), 34.
9. Bronislava Nijinska, *Early Memoirs* (New York, 1981), 470.
10. My italics. Carl Van Vechten, *Music After the Great War* (New York, 1915), 88.
11. In Nigel Gosling, *Paris 1900–1914* (London, 1978), 217. Also John Malcolm Brinnin, *The Third Rose: Gertrude Stein and Her World* (London, 1960), 190–91.

pages 40–6

1. J.M. Richards for one, in his edition of *Who's Who in Architecture* (New York, 1977), 252.
2. In Nikolaus Pevsner, *Pioneers of Modern Design* (Harmondsworth, 1970), 181.
3. In Peter Collins, *Concrete, the Vision of a New Architecture* (London, 1959), 153.
4. In Daniel Bell, *The Cultural Contradictions of Capitalism* (New York, 1976), 110–11.
5. In Pierre Lavedan, *French Architecture* (Harmondsworth, 1956), 227; Collins, *Concrete*, 191.
6. Astruc, *Le Pavillon*, 240–59.
7. Her name was pronounced Greffeuille, as Jacques-Émile Blanche informs us in *La Pêche aux souvenirs* (Paris, 1949), 202. Albert Flament, *Le Bal du Pré Catalan* (Paris, 1946), 258; Gorge D. Painter, *Proust: The Early Years* (Boston, 1959), 115.
8. Astruc, *Pavillon*, 282.
9. Ibid., 283–84; Blanche, 'Un Bilan,' *Revue de Paris*, t.6 (November 15, 1913), 283–84.

1. In Arnold Haskell, *Diaghileff* (London, 1935), 87.
2. Romola Nijinsky, *Nijinksy* (New York, 1934), 49. Richard Buckle's *Diaghilev* (New York, 1979) contains a wealth of biographical detail.
3. John E. Bowlt, *The Silver Age: Russian Art of the Early Twentieth Century and the 'World of Art' Group* (Newtonville, Mass., 1979), 166-67.
4. Misia Sert, *Misia*, 151.
5. In Janet Kennedy, *The 'Mir iskusstva' Group and Russian Art, 1898-1912* (New York, 1977), 343.
6. In Robert Craft, 'Stravinsky's Russian Letters,' *New York Review of Books*, February 21, 1974, 17.
7. Buckle, *Nijinksy*, 92.
8. Tamara Karsavina, *Theatre Street* (London, 1981), 236.
9. Marcel Proust, *À la recherche du temps perdu*, 3 vols. (Paris, 1954), III:236-37.
10. Letter, March 4, 1911, Marcel Proust, *Correspondance*, ed. Philippe Kolb, 15 vols. (Paris, 1970-1987), X:258.
11. Harold Acton, *Memoirs of an Aesthete* (London, 1948), 113.
12. In Edward Marsh, *Rupert Brooke* (Toronto, 1918), 75.
13. *Le Figaro*, May 31, 1912.
14. In his diary entry for March 17, 1914: Charles Ricketts, *Self-Portrait*, ed. Cecil Lewis (London, 1939), 189.
15. In Cyril W. Beaumont, *Michel Fokine and His Ballets* (London, 1935), 23-24.
16. In Buckle, *Nijinsky*, 346.
17. E.G.V. Knox, 'Jeux d'Esprit at Drury Lane,' *Punch*, 145 (July 16, 1913), 70.
18. In Vera Krasovskaya, *Nijinsky*, trans. John E. Bowlt (New York, 1979), 91.
19. In *Revue de Paris*, t.6, 525.
20. 'Serge de Diaghilew,' *Revue musicale*, XI/110 (December 1930), 21.
21. In Bowlt, *Silver Age*, 169-70.

1. Ludwig Feuerbach, *The Essence of Christianity*, trans. George Eliot (New York, 1957), 185.

2. Wedekind's line is in his *Marquis of Keith*, and Eastman is cited in John P. Diggins, *Up From Communism* (New York, 1975), 5.
3. In Leon Edel, *Bloomsbury* (Philadelphia, 1979), 149.
4. See the exchange of letters between Gide and Paul Claudel, March 2 and 7, 1914, in their *Correspondance 1899–1926*, ed. Robert Mallet (Paris, 1949), 217–22.
5. Igor Stravinsky, *Memories and Commentaries* (New York, 1960), 40.
6. *The Diary of Vaslav Nijinsky*, ed. Romola Nijinsky (London, 1937), 154.
7. Cocteau, *Oeuvres complètes*, IX:42.
8. Prince Peter Lieven, *The Birth of the Ballets-Russes*, trans. L. Zarine (London, 1936), 126–27.
9. In Charles Spencer et al., *The World of Serge Diaghilev* (Chicago, 1974), 51.
10. Stravinsky, *Memories*, 38.
11. In Michael Holroyd, *Lytton Strachey*, 2 vols. (New York, 1968), II:95.
12. Pierre Lalo in *Le Temps*, June 5, 1913.
13. 'The Old Ballet and the New: M. Nijinski's Revolution,' *Times* (London), July 5, 1913, 11d. This article and Jean Marnold's review in *Mercure de France*, CV (October 1, 1913), 623–30, remain among the best analyses of Nijinsky's accomplishments that we possess.
14. Stanley J. Fay, 'All the Latest Dances,' *Punch*, 141 (November 1, 1911), 311.

pages 69–75

1. Stravinsky, *Memories*, 29; Vera Stravinsky, *Stravinsky*, 76–105.
2. In Craft, *New York Review*, February 21, 1974, 19.
3. Ibid.
4. Hugo von Hofmannsthal and Richard Strauss, *The Correspondence*, ed. and trans. Hanns Hammelmann and Ewald Osers (London, 1961), 150.
5. In Robert Craft, 'Le Sacre and Pierre Monteux,' *New York Review of Books*, April 3, 1975, 33.
6. In Craft, *New York Review*, February 21, 1974, 17.
7. Ibid. The reference to *la sale musique* is in a letter from Monteux to M. Fichefet, October 28, 1911, to be found in

the Astruc Papers, file 61, p.7, Dance Collection, New York Public Library.

8. In Craft, *New York Review*, February 21, 1974, 18.
9. *New York Times*, January 23, 1916.
10. Buckle, *Diaghilev*, 88; Haskell, *Diaghileff*, 150.
11. In Bowlt, *Silver Age*, 202.
12. D.H. Lawrence, *The Rainbow* (Harmondsworth, 1977), 184.

pages 76–83

1. William L. Shirer, *20th Century Journey* (New York, 1976), 216.
2. Harold Rosenberg, *The Tradition of the New* (New York, 1959), 209.
3. In Agathon, *Les Jeunes Gens d'aujourd'hui* (12th ed., Paris, n.d. [1919]), 4–5.
4. Oliver Wendell Holmes, *One Hundred Days in Europe* (1891), in *The Writings of Oliver Wendell Holmes*, 14 vols. (Boston, 1899–1900), X:177.
5. Jack Kerouac, *Satori in Paris* (New York, 1966), 8.
6. Georges Clemenceau, *Dans les champs du pouvoir* (Paris, 1913), 82.
7. *Le Crapouillet*, October 1931, 14.
8. Artur Rubinstein, *My Young Years* (Toronto, 1973), 132.
9. In George P. Gooch, *Franco-German Relations, 1871–1914* (London, 1928), 26.
10. Alexandre Benois, 'Lettres artistiques: les représentations russes à Paris,' typewritten manuscript in the Astruc Papers, 30, 11–14, with inscription 'Journal de St Pétersbourg,' along with the date July 2, 1909.
11. Samuel Rocheblave, *Le Goût en France* (Paris, 1914), 323–28.
12. Jean Cocteau, *Professional Secrets*, ed. Robert Phelps, trans. R. Howard (New York, 1970), 70–71.
13. Blanche, *Revue de Paris*, t.6, 279.
14. Ibid., 276–77.

pages 83–9

1. Jacques Rivière's discussion, 'Le Sacre du printemps,' *Nouvelle Revue Française*, X (November 1913), 706–30,

remains perhaps the most penetrating appreciation we have of the work. It is available in English in Jacques Rivière, *The Ideal Reader*, trans. Blanche A. Price (New York, 1960), 125–47.

2. In Arthur Gold and Robert Fizdale, *Misia: The Life of Misia Sert* (New York, 1980), 151.

3. Truman C. Bullard reprints most of the French reviews in his superbly researched thesis, 'The First Performance of Igor Stravinsky's "Sacre du Printemps,"' 3 vols., Eastman School of Music, University of Rochester, 1971.

4. *Le Figaro*, May 31, 1913.

5. In Buckle, *Nijinksy*, 361.

6. Louis Laloy ibid.

7. Marie Rambert, *Quicksilver* (London, 1972), 61.

8. Maurice Dupont, 'Les Ballets russes: l'orgie du rythme et de la couleur,' *Revue Bleue*, 52a., II (July 11, 1914), 53–56.

9. Charles Nordmann, 'La Mort de l'univers,' *Revue des deux mondes*, t.16 (July 1, 1913), 205–16.

pages 90–101

1. *The Diaries of Franz Kafka, 1910–1923*, ed. Max Brod, trans. M. Greenberg (Harmondsworth, 1964), 301.

2. In Georg Kotowski et al. (eds.), *Das wilhelminische Deutschland* (Munich, 1965), 145.

3. *Vossische Zeitung*, 374, July 26, 1914.

4. Entry for July 27, 1914, Kurt Riezler, *Tagebücher, Aufsätze, Dokumente*, ed. K.D. Erdmann (Göttingen, 1972).

5. *The Letters of Charles Sorley* (Cambridge, 1919), 211–12.

6. In Fritz Klein et al., *Deutschland im ersten Weltkrieg*, 3 vols. ([East] Berlin, 1968–1970), I:262–63.

7. *Frankfurter Zeitung*, 211, August 1, 1914.

8. In Martin Hürlimann, *Berlin* (Zürich, 1981), 193.

9. *Frankfurter Zeitung*, 212, August 2, 1914.

10. In *Frankfurter Zeitung*, 213, August 3, 1914.

11. In Dieter Groh, *Negative Integration und revolutionärer Attentismus* (Frankfurt am Main, 1973), 675.

12. Diary entry, August 15, 1914, *Tagebücher*. Also, Konrad H. Jarausch, *The Enigmatic Chancellor* (New Haven, Conn.: 1973), 177.

13. Thomas Mann in his foreword in 1924 to *Der Zauberberg*. Cf. *The Magic Mountain*, trans. H.T. Lowe-Porter (New York, 1969), ix. Friedrich Meinecke, *Strassburg-Freiburg-Berlin, 1901–1919* (Stuttgart, 1949), 137–38.

pages 101–8

1. In Norbert Elias, *The Civilizing Process*, trans. E. Jephcott (New York, 1978), 11–12.
2. Friedrich Schiller and J.W. von Goethe, 'Das Deutsche Reich,' *Xenien*, in Schiller, *Gesamtausgabe*, 20 vols. (Munich, 1965–1966), II:30.

pages 108–13

1. In Gordon A. Craig, *The Germans* (New York, 1982), 27.
2. David Landes, *The Unbound Prometheus* (Cambridge, 1969), 342.
3. In Paul M. Kennedy, *The Rise of the Anglo-German Antagonism, 1860–1914* (London, 1980), 110.
4. In Klaus Dockhorn, *Der deutsche Historismus in England* (Göttingen, 1950), 217.
5. Landes, *Prometheus*, 354.
6. In Kennedy, *Rise*, 71.
7. In Fritz Fischer, *Krieg der Illusionen* (Düsseldorf, 1969), 154–55.

pages 113–16

1. In Rolf H. Foerster, *Die Rolle Berlins im europäischen Geistesleben* (Berlin, 1968), 115.
2. Moritz J. Bonn, *Wandering Scholar* (London, 1949), 44–45.
3. Friedrich Sieburg, *Gott in Frankreich?* (Frankfurt am Main, 1931), 120.

pages 116–21

1. In Richard Ellmann, *James Joyce* (New York, 1959), 116.
2. In Geoffrey G. Field, *Evangelist of Race* (New York, 1981), 43.

3. In ibid., 216.
4. Friedrich Nietzsche, *Twilight of the Idols*, trans. R.J. Hollindale (Harmondsworth, 1968), 23.

pages 122–34

1. Katherine Anthony, *Feminism in Germany and Scandinavia* (New York, 1915), 169–204.
2. In William Rubin (ed.), *Pablo Picasso: A Retrospective* (New York, 1980), 18.
3. In Samuel Hynes, *The Edwardian Turn of Mind* (Princeton, 1968), 334.
4. In Marshall Berman, *All That Is Solid Melts into Air* (New York, 1982), 239.
5. Pevsner, *Pioneers*, 32. Also, Joan Campbell, *The German Werkbund* (Princeton, 1978).
6. In Buckle, *Nijinksy*, 316.
7. Emil Nolde, *Das eigene Leben* (Flensburg, 1949), 238.
8. In John Russell, *The Meanings of Modern Art* (New York, 1981), 83.
9. In James D. Steakley, *The Homosexual Emancipation Movement in Germany* (New York, 1975), 49.
10. Ibid., 24–27.
11. Marc to Macke, January 14, 1911, August Macke and Franz Marc, *Briefwechsel* (Cologne, 1964), 40.
12. Emil Nolde, *Briefe aus den Jahren 1894–1926*, ed. Max Sauerlandt (Hamburg, 1967), 99.
13. George Santayana, 'English Liberty in America,' *Character and Opinion*, in *The Works of George Santayana*, 14 vols. (New York, 1936–1937), VIII:120.
14. George Santayana, 'Egotism in German Philosophy,' in ibid., VI:152.
15. In *New York Times*, August 5, 1914, cited in Barbara Tuchman, *The Guns of August* (New York, 1962), 312.
16. Letter to Maximilian Steinberg, in Craft, *New York Review*, February 21, 1974, 18.
17. Walther Rathenau, 'Der Kaiser,' in *Gesammelte Schriften*, 6 vols. (Berlin, 1925–1929), VI:301.
18. Bertrand Russell, *Freedom Versus Organization, 1814–1914* (New York, 1962), 430.
19. Prince Bernhard von Bülow, *Memoirs, 1849–1897*, trans. G. Dunlop and F. A. Voigt (London, 1932), 637.

20. 'Spectator,' *Prince Bülow and the Kaiser*, trans. O. Williams (London, n.d.), 71; and Isabel V. Hull, *The Entourage of Kaiser Wilhelm II, 1888–1918* (Cambridge, 1982), 69–70.
21. Viktoria Luise, Princess of Prussia, *The Kaiser's Daughter*, trans. R. Vacha (London, 1977), 76.
22. Julius Meier-Graefe, *Wohin treiben wir?* (Berlin, 1913); Theodor Fontane, in a letter, April 5, 1897, *Briefe an Georg Friedlaender*, ed. Kurt Schreinert (Heidelberg, 1954), 309.
23. Diary, May 29, 1888, in Helmuth von Moltke, *Erinnerungen, Briefe, Dokumente 1877–1916*, ed. Eliza von Moltke (Stuttgart, 1922), 139.

pages 134–40

1. Friedrich von Bernhardi, *Germany and the Next War*, trans. Allen H. Powles (New York, 1914), 18.
2. In Wolfgang Rothe, *Schriftsteller und totalitäre Welt* (Bern, 1966), 19.
3. Theodor Heuss, 'Der Weltkrieg,' *März*, 8/3 (August 5, 1914), 221–25.
4. Conrad Haussmann, 'Europas Krieg,' *März*, 8/3 (August 22, 1914), 250.
5. Friedrich Meinecke, *Die deutsche Erhebung von 1914* (Stuttgart, 1914), 29.
6. In Groh, *Integration*, 704.
7. In Konrad Haenisch, *Die deutsche Sozialdemokratie in und nach dem Weltkriege* (Berlin, 1919), 20–26.
8. Eduard David, diary entry, August 4, 1914, *Das Kriegstagebuch des Reichstagsabgeordneten Eduard David 1914 bis 1918*, ed. Susanne Miller (Düsseldorf, 1966), 12.
9. Ludwig Thoma, 'Stimmungen,' *März*, 8/3 (September 5, 1914), 296–99.
10. Magnus Hirschfeld, *Warum hassen uns die Völker?* (Bonn, 1915), 11, 18, 33.
11. 'Burschen heraus!' *Vossische Zeitung*, 391, August 4, 1914.
12. Carl Zuckmayer, *Als wär's ein Stück von mir* (Frankfurt am Main, 1969), 168; Schauwecker and Hirschfeld in Eric J. Leed, *No Man's Land* (Cambridge, 1979), 21, 46–47.

13. Emil Ludwig, 'Der moralische Gewinn,' *Berliner Tageblatt*, 392, August 5, 1914; and Emil Ludwig, *Juli 1914* (Hamburg, 1961), 7–8, and chap. 13.
14. Ernst Glaeser, *Jahrgang 1902* (Berlin, 1929), 191–95.
15. In a letter, November 18, 1914, in Philipp Witkop (ed.), *Kriegsbriefe deutscher Studenten* (Gotha, 1916), 25.
16. In Erich Kahler, *The Germans* (Princeton, 1974), 272.
17. In a letter, December 26, 1914, in Ralph Freedman, *Hermann Hesse: Pilgrim of Crisis* (New York, 1978), 168.
18. Diary entry, September 17, 1914, in Guy Chapman, *Vain Glory* (London, 1937), 107.

pages 141–45

1. 'An Armistice,' *Western Times* (Exeter), January 1, 1915, 3a.
2. 'Leicestershire and the War,' *Leicester Mail*, January 6, 1915, 5c.
3. Captain Sir Edward H.W. Hulse, 'Letters Written from the English Front in France Between September 1914 and March 1915,' published privately in 1916 by the family, 56–70. Excerpts from the letters are more readily available in F. Loraine Petre et al., *The Scots Guards in the Great War, 1914–1918* (London, 1925), 67; and Guy Chapman, *Vain Glory*, 100–103. Hulse was killed at Neuve Chapelle, March 12, 1915, trying to assist a wounded fellow officer.
4. Diary entry, December 25, 1914, Gustav Riebensahm Papers, Bundesarchiv-Militärarchiv, Freiburg (hereafter BAM).
5. In Fridolin Solleder (ed.), *Vier Jahre Westfront: Geschichte des Regiments List R.I.R. 16* (Munich, 1932), 92.
6. 'Our Day of Peace at the Front,' *Daily Mail*, January 1, 1915, 4d.
7. In a letter, December 27, 1914, O. Tilley, Imperial War Museum, London (hereafter IWM).
8. Contrary to the impression left by, among many others, Barbara Tuchman in *The Guns of August* and Samuel Hynes in *The Edwardian Frame of Mind*.
9. W.A. Quinton in his unpublished memoirs (1929), 28, IWM.
10. Memoirs of R.G. Garrod, IWM.

1. Most of the casualty figures are taken from official regimental, brigade, and divisional war diaries, in this instance in the Public Record Office, London (hereafter PRO).

2. Diary entry, September 13, 1914, in C.E. Callwell, *Field-Marshal Sir Henry Wilson: His Life and Diaries*, 2 vols. (London, 1927), I:177.

3. Edward Grey, *Twenty-Five Years*, 2 vols. (New York, 1925), II:68.

4. 'Programme d'une causerie à faire aux officiers et hommes au repos,' 24N346, Service historique de l'armée de terre, Vincennes (hereafter SHAT).

5. Note from the Quartier Général (QG), 1st Corps d'Armée (CA), January 1, 1915, 22N10, SHAT.

6. Diary, January 22, 1915, *The Private Papers of Douglas Haig*, 1914–1919, ed. Robert Blake (London, 1952), 84.

7. Diary, 20th Infantry Brigade, December 26, 1914, WO95/1650, PRO.

8. Diary entry, December 25, 1914, P. Mortimer, IWM. Diary, 7th Division, December 30, 1914, WO95/1627, PRO.

9. Diary, 2nd Notts and Derby, January 8, 1915, WO95/1616, PRO.

10. Diary, 1st Army, WO95/154.

11. Lt. Gen. W.P. Pulteney, to Smith-Dorrien, GOC 2nd Army, January 12, 1915, WO95/669.

12. Letter, December 19, 1914, in Christopher Isherwood, *Kathleen and Frank* (London, 1971), 308.

13. Diary entry, December 23, 1914, P.H. Jones, IWM.

14. Carl Groos (ed.), *Infanterie-Regiment Herwarth von Bittenfeld (1. Westfälisches) Nr. 13 im Weltkriege 1914–1918* (Oldenburg, 1927), 70. Also Solleder (ed.), *R.I.R 16*, 93; and diary, 1st Royal Irish Fusiliers, WO95/1482, PRO.

15. Gustav Riebensahm, *Infanterie-Regiment Prinz Friedrich der Niederlande (2. Westfälisches) Nr. 15 im Weltkriege 1914–18* (Minden i. W., 1931), 94.

16. Diary, 6th Division, January 17, 1915, WO95/1581. Also, letter from Private H. Hodgetts, 2nd Worcestershires, printed in the *Morning Post*, December

24, 1914, 4a. Diary, 2nd Army, January 22, 1915, WO95/268. The French material is full of similar evidence: Note de service, 4th CA, December 29, 1914, 22N556; 68th Infantry Regiment report, December 24, 1914, 22N557; and dispatch of le Chef d'État-Major Louis, December 30, 1914, 22N1134, SHAT.

17. Order of Corps Commander, II Corps, to Divisional Commanders, December 4, 1914, WO95/268, PRO.
18. Sorley, *Letters*, 283.
19. *The Scotsman* (Edinburgh), where the letter was published on January 2, 1915, 9e, gave it the headline GERMAN SOLDIERS WANT PEACE. Here is a basic example of how the home front could misconstrue evidence and jump to completely unwarranted conclusions about reality in the fighting lines.
20. Solleder (ed.), *16 R.I.R.*, 88.
21. Diary, 12th Brigade, December 10, 1914, WO95/1501, PRO.
22. Diary, 4th Division, December 1, 1914, WO95/1440, PRO.
23. Ibid.
24. Order, dated November 28, 1914, is to be found in the files of the 6th Bavarian Reserve Division, Bd. 5, Bayerisches Kriegsarchiv (hereafter BKA).
25. Just how this was envisaged is shown in a picture in *The Illustrated London News*, January 6, 1915, 37.
26. Diary, 11th Brigade, WO95/1486, PRO.
27. Diary, 15th Brigade, December 23, 1914, WO95/1566, PRO.
28. S.R. de Belfort, January 10, 1915, 18N302, SHAT.
29. Diary entry, December 24–26, 1914, Albert Sommer Tagebuchauf-zeichnungen, MSg 1/900, BAM.

pages 159–66

1. Diary entry, December 27, 1914, P.H. Jones, IWM.
2. Curt Wunderlich, *Fünfzig Monate Wehr im Westen: Geschichte des Reserve-Infanterie-Regiments Nr. 66* (Eisleben, 1939), 280–81.
3. Wilhelm, Crown Prince of Germany, *My War Experiences* (London, n.d.), 122–23.
4. Letter of December 26, 1914, BAM.

5. Diary, 1st Somerset Light Infantry, WO95/1499; the letters of James M'Cormack in *The Scotsman*, January 9, 1915, 12d, and of J. Dalling in *The Western Times*, January 11, 1915, 3g.
6. 'Letters from the Trenches,' *Daily Mail*, January 4, 1915, 9cd.
7. Diary, 2nd Scots Guards, December 25, 1914, WO95/1657; letter in the *Daily Mail*, January 1, 1915, 4d; D. Mackenzie, *The Sixth Gordons in France and Flanders* (Aberdeen, 1921), 23–24; Riebensahm, *Infanterie-Regiment 15*, 96.
8. *Daily Mail*, January 4, 1915, 9cd; *The Scotsman*, January 4, 1915, 8g.
9. Diary, 10th Brigade, WO95/1477. Also Diary, 20th Brigade, WO95/1650, PRO.
10. Diary, December 28, 1914, Samuel Judd, IWM.
11. *Glasgow Herald*, January 14, 1915, 9fgh.
12. Report of Capt. Beckett, 1st Hants, WO95/1488, PRO.
13. Diaries, regimental and individual, December 25, 1914, in WO95/1413, PRO.
14. Diary, 20th Bavarian Infantry Regiment, December 25, 1914, Bd.8, BKA.
15. Diary, 56th Brigade, December 25, 1914, 26N511, SHAT.
16. WO95/1496, PRO.

pages 166–83

1. WO95/1657, PRO.
2. Mackenzie, *6th Gordons*, 26.
3. In George Watson, *The English Ideology: Studies in the Language of Victorian Politics* (London, 1973), 61–62.
4. Ford Madox Ford, *Thus to Revisit* (London, 1921), 136–37; Virginia Woolf, 'Mr Bennett and Mrs Brown' (1924), in *The Captain's Death Bed and Other Essays* (London, 1950), 91.
5. Walter Sickert, 'Post Impressionists,' *Fortnightly Review*, 89 (January 1911), 79.
6. Stanley Weintraub, *The London Yankees* (New York, 1979).
7. Acton was citing Froude: Lord Acton, *A Lecture on the*

Study of History, delivered at Cambridge, June 11, 1895 (London, 1895), 72.

8. In Watson, *Ideology,* 60.
9. Thomas Mann, 'Gedanken im Kriege,' *Gesammelte Werke,* XIII:530–32. The essay first appeared in *Die Neue Rundschau* in November 1914.
10. A.E. Housman, '1887,' *The Collected Poems* (London, 1962), 10.
11. A.D. Gillespie, in John Laffin (ed.), *Letters from the Front, 1914–1918* (London, 1973), 12.
12. Pattenden's diary is now a part of the regimental record, 1st Hants, WO95/1495, PRO.
13. In James Walvin, *Leisure and Society, 1830–1950* (London, 1978), 85.
14. In Tony Mason, *Association Football and English Society, 1863–1915* (Brighton, 1980), 224.
15. In Peter Bailey, *Leisure and Class in Victorian England* (London, 1978), 128.
16. In Mason, *Football,* 228.
17. In Donald Read, *Edwardian England, 1901–15* (London, 1972), 53–54.
18. Letter to Sir Claude Phillips, July 31, 1914, in *The Letters of Henry James,* ed. Percy Lubbock, 2 vols. (London, 1920), II:389–92.
19. In his poem 'Peace,' from Rupert Brooke, *The Collected Poems,* ed. G.E. Woodberry (New York, 1943), 111.
20. *The Letters of Rupert Brooke,* ed. Geoffrey Keynes (New York, 1968), 625.
21. 'One Day of Peace at the Front,' *Daily Mail,* January 1, 1915, 4d.
22. 'The Christmas Truce in the Trenches,' *Chester Chronicle,* January 9, 1915, 5c.
23. Jerome K. Jerome, 'The Greatest Game of All: The True Spirit of the War,' *Daily News and Leader,* January 5, 1915, 4ef.
24. In Paul Fussell, *The Great War and Modern Memory* (New York, 1975), 27.
25. Letter, July 1916, p.163, R.D. Mountfort, IWM.
26. *Western Times,* January 19, 1915, 6f, based on a report in the *Berliner Tageblatt.*
27. Diary entry, August 27, 1916, Louis Mairet, *Carnet d'un combattant (11 février 1915–16 avril 1917)* (Paris, 1919), 212–13.

28. P.B. Ghéusi, *Cinquante ans de Paris: mémoires d'un témoin, 1892–1942*, 4 vols. (Paris, 1939–1942), IV:185–97.

29. Walvin, *Leisure*, 129.

30. War diary of the 17th Middlesex, WO95/1361, PRO. Also the papers of W.G. Bailey, a forward formerly with Reading, and those also of R. Stafford, who commanded the Footballers Battalion from August 1917 to February 1918; both in IWM.

31. In Mason, *Football*, 225.

32. W.R.M. Percy in H.E. Boisseau (ed.), *The Prudential Staff and the Great War* (London, 1938), 18. Percy was killed near Ypres, April 28, 1915.

33. Diary, December 27, 1914, P.H. Jones, IWM.

34. *Western Times*, January 11, 1915, 3g.

35. Diary, 2nd Scots Guards, December 25, 1914, WO95/1657, PRO.

36. 'The Christmas Truce in the Trenches,' *Chester Chronicle*, January 9, 1915, 5e.

37. *La Vie de tranchée* (Paris, 1915), 35.

38. *History of the 1st and 2nd Battalions the North Staffordshire Regiment ('The Prince of Wales') 1914–1923* (Longton, 1932), 14–15.

39. 'Letters from the Trenches,' *Daily Mail*, December 31, 1914, 8a.

pages 183–7

1. See Gertrude Himmelfarb, 'The Victorian Ethos: Before and After Victoria,' in her *Victorian Minds* (New York, 1968), 276–78.

2. In H.E. Meller, *Leisure and the Changing City, 1870–1914* (London, 1976), 248–49.

3. Robert Roberts, *The Classic Slum: Salford Life in the First Quarter of the Century* (Manchester, 1971), 15–16.

4. J.B. Priestley, *Margin Released* (London, 1962), 46–47.

5. Gerald Gould, 'Art and Morals,' *New Statesman*, August 23, 1913, 625–26.

pages 187–92

1. In Christopher Hassall, *Rupert Brooke* (London, 1964), 456.

2. In John Grigg, *Lloyd George: From Peace to War, 1912–1916* (Berkeley, 1985), 166.
3. *La Vie de tranchée*, 71–72.
4. In a letter to E.M. House, December 7, 1915, in Burton J. Hendrick, *The Life and Letters of Walter H. Page*, 3 vols. (New York, 1922–1925), II:108.
5. Guy Pedroncini, *Les Mutineries de 1917* (Paris, 1967), 177.
6. Charles Smith, *War History of the 6th Battalion: The Cheshire Regiment* (Chester, 1932), 5.

pages 195–9

1. In John Keegan, *The Face of Battle* (New York, 1976), 264.
2. Charles Delvert uses the word *troglodyte* in his diary, February 11, 1916, *Carnets d'un fantassin* (Paris, 1935), 145; and Peter McGregor uses it in a letter, August 6, 1916, P. McGregor, IWM. Hence the term is hardly an invention, as some have claimed, of the postwar era.
3. In a letter to his wife, July 24, 1916, P. McGregor, IWM.
4. H. Winter, in Denis Winter, *Death's Men: Soldiers of the Great War* (Harmondsworth, 1979), 177.

pages 199–216

1. Charles Sorley, in a letter to his mother, July 10, 1915, *Letters*, 284.
2. In Alistair Horne, *Death of a Generation* (London, 1970), 104.
3. Ivan Goll, 'Requiem for the Dead of Europe' (1917), in Jon Silkin (ed.), *The Penguin Book of First World War Poetry* (Harmondsworth, 1979), 232.
4. Ernst Jünger, *In Stahlgewittern* (Berlin, 1931), 100.
5. In Ordre général, N°32, December 17, 1914, 16N1676, SHAT.
6. Keegan, *Face of Battle*, 227–37.
7. In John Ellis, *Eye-Deep in Hell* (London, 1977), 94.
8. Roger Campana, *Les Enfants de la 'Grande Revanche': Carnet de route d'un Saint-Cyrien, 1914–1918* (Paris, 1920), 204.
9. Herbert Read, 'In Retreat: A Journal of the Retreat of the Fifth Army from St Quentin, March 1918,' in *The*

    Contrary Experience (London, 1963), 248.
10. Paul Rimbault, in Jean Norton Cru, *Témoins* (Paris, 1929), 465.
11. In a letter to his wife, November 16, 1917, in Paul Nash, *Outline: An Autobiography and Other Writings* (London, 1949), 210–11.
12. In Alistair Horne, *The Price of Glory: Verdun 1916* (London, 1962), 173.
13. Herbert Read, diary, January 10, 1918, in *Contrary Experience*, 116.
14. Diary, September 27, 1915, Mairet, *Carnet*, 96.
15. Guy Buckeridge, 'Memoirs of My Army Service in the Great War,' 65, IWM.
16. In Horne, *Price of Glory*, 62.
17. Letter, February 14, 1915, J.W. Harvey, IWM.
18. Letters, June 7 and 11, 1916, P. McGregor, IWM.
19. In Silkin (ed.), *Poetry*, 91.
20. Jünger, *In Stahlgewittern*, 163–64.
21. Campana, January 19, 1915, *Enfants*, 69.
22. Letter, November 27, 1915, Marc Boasson, *Au Soir d'un monde: lettres de guerre* (Paris, 1926), iii–iv.
23. Wilfred Owen, *The Collected Poems*, ed. C. Day Lewis (London, 1964), 48–49.
24. Siegfried Sassoon, *Memoirs of a Fox-Hunting Man* (London, 1960), 300.
25. Diary, March 29, 1916, Delvert, *Carnets*, 184.
26. Letter, August 19, 1916, R.D. Mountfort, IWM.
27. Campana, diary entries, November 1915, *Enfants*, 115.
28. Letter, June 16, 1916, R.D. Mountfort, IWM.
29. Diary, December 16, 1915, and letter, January 3, 1916, P.H. Jones, IWM.
30. Diary, January 12, 1916, Delvert, *Carnets*, 129–30.
31. In Winter, *Death's Men*, 101.
32. Diary, December 8, 1915, Delvert, *Carnets*, 101.
33. Wilfred Owen, 'Dulce et Decorum Est,' *Collected Poems*, 55.
34. W.C.S. Gregson, Papers, IWM.
35. Letter, August 2, 1916, F.H.T. Tatham, IWM.
36. Letter, July 31, 1916, in C.E.W. Bean, *The Official History of Australia in the War of 1914–1918*, 6 vols. (Sydney, 1929–1942), III:659.
37. In Ellis, *Eye-Deep in Hell*, 59.

38. Jünger, *In Stahlgewittern*, 123, 207.
39. In Horne, *Price of Glory*, 187.
40. Diary, January 27, 1916, Delvert, *Carnets*, 138–39.
41. Diary, June 16, 1916, César Méléra, *Verdun* (Paris, 1925), 34–35.
42. Horne, *Price of Glory*, 99.
43. Diary, October 16, 1916, Paul Morand, *Journal d'un attaché d'ambassade* (Paris, 1963), 39.
44. See the informative analysis, 'Kurzschüsse der Artillerie,' September 16, 1918, in the files of the 16th Bavarian Reserve Infantry Regiment, Bd. 13, BKA.
45. Siegfried Sassoon, 'Counter-Attack,' *Collected Poems 1908–1956* (London, 1961), 68.
46. Diary, March 10, 1917, Mairet, *Carnet*, 294.
47. Fritz Kreisler, *Four Weeks in the Trenches: The War Story of a Violinist* (Boston, 1915), 65–66.
48. Letter, December 20, 1914, J.W. Harvey, IWM.
49. Kreisler, *Four Weeks*, 66.
50. Letter to Frank N. Doubleday, Christmas 1915, in Hendrick, *Life and Letters of Walter H. Page*, II:111.

pages 216–33

1. See Geoffrey Best, 'How Right Is Might? Some Aspects of the International Debate About How to Fight Wars and How to Win Them, 1870–1918,' in *War, Economy and the Military Mind*, ed. G. Best and A. Wheatcroft (London, 1976), 120–35.
2. Henry James in a letter to Edith Wharton, September 21, 1914, *The Letters of Henry James*, II:420–21.
3. Meinecke, *Erhebung*, 71–72. Also, Max R. Funke, 'In Rheims,' *März*, 8/4 (December 19, 1914), 242–45.
4. *Kölnische Zeitung*, January 29, 1915.
5. Klaus Schwabe, *Wissenschaft und Kriegsmoral: Die deutschen Hochschullehrer und die politischen Grundfragen des Ersten Weltkrieges* (Göttingen, 1969), 23.
6. Reprinted in Ernst Johann (ed.), *Innenansicht eines Krieges: Deutsche Dokumente, 1914–1918* (Munich, 1973), 47–48.
7. Jünger, *In Stahlgewittern*, 114–15.
8. Jean-Jacques Becker, *1914: Comment les Français sont*

entrés dans la guerre (Paris, 1977), 46–47; and Pierre Miquel, *La Grande Guerre* (Paris, 1983), 145.

9. In Jean Lestoquoy, *Histoire du patriotisme en France des origines à nos jours* (Paris, 1968), 207.

10. Henri Bergson, *La Signification de la Guerre* (Paris, 1915), 19.

11. In a letter to the Hon. Evan Charteris, January 22, 1915, in Henry James, *Letters*, II:453.

12. Miquel, *La Grande Guerre*, 327.

13. Basil H. Liddell Hart has made this argument, in his *History of the First World War* (London, 1972), 145; as has Peter Graf Kielmansegg, *Deutschland und der Erste Weltkrieg* (Frankfurt am Main, 1968), 91.

14. Letter, May 5, 1915, V.M. Fergusson, IWM.

15. Ulrich Trumpener, 'The Road to Ypres: The Beginnings of Gas Warfare in World War I,' *Journal of Modern History*, 47 (September 1975), 468.

16. From an autobiographical sketch by G.W.G. Hughes, n.d., n.p., IWM.

17. Wilfred Owen, 'Dulce et Decorum Est,' *Collected Poems*, 55.

18. Robert Graves, *Goodbye to All That* (Harmondsworth, 1960), 123.

19. In Horne, *Price of Glory*, 286.

20. Ronald Dorgelès, *Souvenirs sur les Croix de bois* (Paris, 1929), 18.

21. Frank Fox, *The British Army at War* (London, 1917), 35–36.

22. From a commemorative pamphlet prepared by Leonard Levy and printed for private circulation, 'Some Memories of the Activities of the R.E. Anti-Gas Establishment During the Great War,' n.d. [November 1938], in the Foulkes Papers (J41), Basil Liddell Hart Archives.

23. 'Report of the Committee on Chemical Warfare Organization,' Foulkes Papers (J18), Basil Liddell Hart Archives.

24. Diary, December 26, 1916, Mairet, *Carnet*, 269–70.

25. In E.L. Woodward, *Great Britain and the War 1914–1918* (London, 1967), 40.

26. In André Ducasse et al., *Vie et mort des français 1914–1918* (Paris, 1968), 72.

27. In Woodward, *Great Britain and the War*, 40.

28. In ibid., 167.
29. Letter to L.P. Jacks, June 1915, in *The Letters of Josiah Royce*, ed. John Clendenning (Chicago, 1970), 628–29.
30. Diary, W.C.S. Gregson, IWM.

pages 234–42

1. In Ellis, *Eye-Deep in Hell*, 100.
2. Ibid.
3. Ibid., 101.
4. Letter of April 4, 1915, from France, in Philipp Witkop (ed.), *Kriegsbriefe deutscher Studenten* (Gotha, 1916), 45–46.
5. Letter, March 26, 1917, Boasson, *Au Soir*, 218–19.
6. Kreisler, *Four Weeks*, 2–3.
7. In Horne, *Price of Glory*, 227.
8. J.L. Jack, *General Jack's Diary*, ed. John Terraine (London, 1964), 188–89.
9. Diary, July 23, 1916. G. Powell, IWM.
10. Dorgelès, *Souvenirs*, 20.
11. André Bridoux, *Souvenirs du temps des morts* (Paris, 1930), 16.
12. 'Dictée,' *Nouvelle Revue Française*, 33 (July 1, 1929), 21–22.
13. Letter, August 25, 1916, the Rev. J.M.S. Walker, IWM.
14. Jacques Rivière, 'French Letters and the War,' *The Ideal Reader*, 271.
15. In Ducasse, *Vie et mort*, 94.
16. Diary, June 12, 1916, Delvert, *Carnets*, 286.
17. Letter, July 23, 1917, to Ronald Rees, R.D. Rees, IWM.
18. This emphasis on duty has been badly understated in the subsequent literature on the war, which has been dominated by the 'disenchantment' school of thought. Charles Delvert was one who did point to the importance of duty: 'L'histoire de la guerre par les témoins,' *Revue des deux mondes*, 99a. (December 1929), 640.

pages 242–62

1. In Asa Briggs, *Victorian People* (Harmondsworth, 1965), 124.
2. Ian Hay, *The First Hundred Thousand* (London, 1916), xi.

463

3. Anthony Powell, *The Kindly Ones* (London, 1971), 161.
4. Woodward, *Great Britain and the War*, xv–xvi.
5. In Bill Gammage, *The Broken Years: Australian Soldiers in the Great War* (Canberra, 1974), 47.
6. David Jones, in D.S. Carne-Ross, 'The Last of the Modernists,' *New York Review of Books*, October 9, 1980, 41.
7. Mairet, *Carnet*, 32.
8. Jean-Marc Bernard, '*De Profundis*,' in Ducasse, *Vie et mort*, 102.
9. Letter, October 28, 1915, P.H. Jones, IWM.
10. In a letter to his father, September 2, 1915, Sorley, *Letters*, 307.
11. Vera Brittain, *Testament of Youth* (London, 1933), 259.
12. Diary, August 4, 1916, G. Powell, IWM.
13. Diary, May 11, 1916, Abel Ferry, *Carnets secrets, 1914–1918* (Paris, 1957), 140.
14. In Ducasse, *Vie et mort*, 159–60.
15. Letter, April 28, 1918, Herbert Read, *Contrary Experience*, 127.
16. Letters, January 15 and 20, 1915, in Christopher Isherwood, *Kathleen and Frank* (London, 1971), 312.
17. Letters, August 28 and December 20, 1917, R.R. Stokes, IWM.
18. Diary, June 26, 1916, P.H. Jones, IWM.
19. Diary, July 1, 1916, E. Russell-Jones, IWM.
20. QG IIIe Armée, 'Contrôle de la Correspondance,' report dated May 31, 1917, 16N1521, SHAT.
21. In Stephen R. Ward, 'Great Britain: Land Fit for Heroes Lost,' in S.R. Ward (ed.), *The War Generation* (Port Washington, N.Y., 1975), 28.
22. Humbert, letter, June 1, 1917, 16N1521, SHAT.
23. Wilfred Owen, 'Apologia Pro Poemate Meo,' *Collected Poems*, 39.
24. Letter, December 29, 1916, Mairet, *Carnet*, 273.
25. Letters, September 15, 1916, P. McGregor, IWM.
26. In Brittain, *Testament of Youth*, 316.
27. In Keegan, *Face of Battle*, 275.
28. Diary, June 14, 1916, Méléra, *Verdun*, 30–31.
29. Letter, July 27, 1917, Read, *Contrary Experience*, 107.
30. In Charles, S. Maier, *Recasting Bourgeois Europe* (Princeton, 1976), 32.
31. Benjamin Crémieux, 'Sur la guerre et les guerriers,'

Nouvelle Revue Française, 34 (1930), 147.

32. J.S. Mill, 'Coleridge,' in John Stuart Mill: A Selection of His Works, ed. John M. Robson (Toronto, 1966), 445–48.
33. Sassoon, Memoirs of a Fox-Hunting Man, 271.
34. Basil Liddell Hart called Haig 'the quintessence of pre-War Britain' in Through the Fog of War (London, 1938), 57.
35. In Ducasse, Vie et mort, 150.
36. In ibid., 104.
37. In Ellis, Eye-Deep in Hell, 81–82.
38. These remarks by Captain Laffargue of the 153e RI were composed August 25, 1915, and discovered by the Germans exactly one month later after an attack. They are to be found in a German translation 'Studie über den Angriff im gegenwärtigen Zeitabschnitt des Krieges,' in the Nachlass of Franz von Trotta gen. Treyden, N234/3, BAM.
39. In Horne, Death of a Generation, 39.
40. Robert Graves, 'The Dead Fox Hunter,' Poems (1914–26) (London 1927), 48–49.
41. Bean, Official History, III:873.
42. In Martin Middlebrook, The First Day on the Somme (London, 1975), 28.
43. Guy Hallé, in Horne, Price of Glory, 237.
44. Letter to Colin Owen, May 14, 1917, Wilfred Owen, Collected Letters, ed. Harold Owen and John Bell (London, 1967), 458.
45. In Ellis, Eye-Deep in Hell, 187.
46. 'Rapport de contrôle postal du 129e RI,' June 4, 1917, 16N1521, SHAT.
47. Diary, September 14, 1917, Michael MacDonagh, In London During the Great War (London, 1935), 24.
48. Jean Norton Cru, Du témoignage (Paris, 1930), 23.
49. J.M. Winter, 'Britain's "Lost Generation" of the First World War,' Population Studies, 31/3 (1977), 454.
50. Henri Berr, La Guerre allemande et la paix française (Paris, 1919), xvii.
51. Louis Huot and Paul Voivenel, La Psychologie du soldat (Paris, 1918).
52. Letter, May 7, 1917, Mairet, Carnet, xiv.
53. The Private Papers of Douglas Haig, 1914–1919, 10.
54. The Bodley Head Scott Fitzgerald, 6 vols. (London, 1963–1967), II:67–68.

1. Ernst Schultze, *Die Mobilmachung der Seelen* (Bonn, 1915), 58.
2. In Field, *Evangelist*, 378–79.
3. Letter, August 7, 1914, of Walter Limmer, in Philipp Witkop (ed.), *Kriegsbriefe gefallener Studenten* (Munich, 1928), 8.
4. E. Küster, *Vom Krieg und vom deutschen Bildungsideal* (Bonn, 1915), 24.
5. Schultze, *Mobilmachung*, 26.
6. 'Fünf Gesänge,' in Thomas Anz and Joseph Vogl (eds.), *Die Dichter und der Krieg: Deutsche Lyrik, 1914–1918* (Munich, 1982), 31–32.
7. Arthur Schopenhauer, *Ein Lesebuch*, ed. Arthur and Angelika Hübscher (Wiesbaden, 1980), 168.
8. Burckhardt's letter to Preen, December 31, 1870, in *The Letters of Jacob Burckhardt*, ed. and trans. Alexander Dru (London, 1955), 145; and Burckhardt, *Force and Freedom*, ed. J.H. Nichols (New York, 1943), 153.
9. Theodor Mommsen, *Reden und Aufsätze* (Hildesheim, 1976), 91.
10. Letter, January 6, 1889, in *The Portable Nietzsche*, ed. and trans. Walter Kaufmann (New York, 1954), 686.
11. Letter, April 16, 1915, Witkop (ed.), *Kriegsbriefe* (1916), 49–51.
12. In his poem 'Anrufung,' in Anz (ed.), *Dichter und Krieg*, 51.
13. Leopold Ziegler, *Der deutsche Mensch* (Berlin, 1915), excerpt in Johann (ed.), *Innenansicht*, 65. A popular slogan was '*Jeder Deutsche ist Deutschland, Deutschland ist in jedem Deutschen.*'
14. Schultze, *Mobilmachung*, 67.
15. In Schwabe, *Wissenchaft und Kriegsmoral*, 25.
16. Letter, October 14, 1914, in Witkop (ed.), *Kriegsbriefe* (1916), 71.
17. Ibid., 70.
18. Letters, September 23 and 24, 1914, in Witkop (ed.), *Kriegsbriefe* (1928), 20–21.
19. Letter, August 28, 1914, in Witkop (ed.), *Kriegsbriefe* (1916), 61.
20. Letter, October 2, 1914, in ibid., 13–15.

21. Letter, March 11, 1915, in ibid., 44–45.
22. Fritz Stern, 'Capitalism and the Cultural Historian,' in *From Parnassus: Essays in Honor of Jacques Barzun*, ed. Dora B. Weiner and William R. Keylor (New York, 1976), 219. For an elaboration on this theme see Stern's *Gold and Iron* (New York, 1977).
23. J.S. Mill, 'Civilization,' in Robson (ed.), *Mill*, 444–45.
24. Letter, October 7, 1915, in Witkop (ed.), *Kriegsbriefe* (1916), 113–14.
25. Magnus Hirschfeld, *Kriegspsychologisches* (Bonn, 1916), 7.
26. Agnes von Zahn-Harnack, *Adolf von Harnack* (Berlin, 1936), 444.
27. The poem is entitled 'Edward Grey' and is to be found in the Nachlass Gerhard von Nostitz-Wallwitz, N262/1, BAM.
28. Diary, December 31, 1914, in the Kriegstagebuch of the 15th Bavarian Infantry Regiment, Bd. 1, BKA.
29. Ernst Wurche, quoted by Walter Flex in a letter, March 14, 1916, in *Briefe von Walter Flex* (Munich, 1927), 184–85.
30. Letter, April 16, 1915, in Witkop (ed.), *Kriegsbriefe* (1916), 49–51.
31. Daniel R. Borg, *The Old-Prussian Church and the Weimar Republic* (Hanover and London, 1984), 39.

pages 276–82

1. Files of the 4th Bavarian Infantry Division, Bd. 102, BKA.
2. Order from K.H.Qu., August 18, 1917, 1st Bavarian Infantry Division, Bd. 90, BKA.
3. Order of Armee-Oberkommando, July 31, 1917, 1st Bavarian Infantry Division, Bd. 90, BKA.
4. Diary, July 19, 1918, Rudolf Binding, *A Fatalist at War*, trans. I.F.D. Morrow (London, 1929), 237.
5. In a letter, October 13, 1918, D.L. Ghilchik, IWM.
6. Evelyn, Princess Blücher, *An English Wife in Berlin* (New York, 1920), 35.
7. F.L. Carsten, *War Against War: British and German Radical Movements in the First World War* (London, 1982), 76–77.

8. Ibid., passim.
9. In Schwabe, *Wissenschaft und Kriegsmoral*, 104–105.
10. Delbrück, letter, February 4, 1918, in ibid., 166.

pages 283–92

1. In George D. Painter, *Proust: The Later Years* (Boston, 1965), 223.
2. In Weintraub, *The London Yankees*, 350–51.
3. Dorgelès, *Souvenirs*, 8.
4. In Klein et al., *Deutschland im ersten Weltkrieg*, I:xvii.
5. In Gold and Fizdale, *Misia*, 166.
6. In Johann (ed.), *Innenansicht*, 163.
7. In ibid., 164.
8. John Galsworthy, *A Sheaf* (London, 1916), 208.
9. David Jones, *In Parenthesis* (London, 1982), ix; and D.S. Carne-Ross, 'The Last of the Modernists,' *New York Review of Books*, October 9, 1980, 41.
10. James Joyce, *Ulysses* (Harmondsworth, 1968), 40.
11. Letter, June 21, 1916, P. McGregor, IWM.
12. Letter, November 18, 1914, in Witkop (ed.), *Kriegsbriefe* (1916), 25.
13. Letter, July 10, 1916, Boasson, *Au Soir*, 127.
14. Letter, December 22, 1917, ibid., 299–300.
15. In Leed, *No Man's Land*, 183–84.
16. In Roland N. Stromberg, *Redemption by War: The Intellectuals and 1914* (Lawrence, Kan., 1982), 152.
17. Diary, March 4, 1917, Mairet, *Carnet*, 291.
18. Graves, *Goodbye to All That*, 98.
19. Wyn Griffith, *Up to Mametz* (London, 1931), 187, 212.
20. Jacques-Émile Blanche, *Portraits of a Lifetime*, ed. and trans. Walter Clement (London, 1937), 259–60.
21. Diary, October 28, 1915, and letter, December 12, 1915, P.H. Jones, IWM.
22. Letter, December 23, 1915, J.W. Gamble, IWM.
23. Diary, August 28, 1916, G. Powell, IWM.
24. David Jones, *In Parenthesis*, x.
25. In Heather Robertson, *A Terrible Beauty: The Art of Canada at War* (Toronto, 1977), 92.
26. In Malcolm Cowley, *Exile's Return* (New York, 1934), 256; and Geoffrey Wolff, *Black Sun: The Brief Transit and Violent Eclipse of Harry Crosby* (New York, 1976), 59.

1. Letter, December 29, 1916, Mairet, *Carnet*, 270–71.
2. In a letter to his wife, November 16, 1917, in Nash, *Outline*, 210.
3. In his introduction to an exhibition catalogue of Gino Severini's futurist works, Marlborough Gallery, April 1913, cited in John Rothenstein, *Modern English Painters*, 2 vols. (New York, 1976), II:129.
4. Memorandum, October 16, 1917, C.R.W Nevinson file, Department of Art, IWM.
5. This foreword, along with the objections to Nevinson's work cited above, are to be found in ibid., IWM.
6. *Daily Express*, May 30, 1919.
7. In Michael L. Sanders and Philip M. Taylor, *British Propaganda During the First World War, 1914–18* (London, 1982), 157.
8. Dorgelès, *Souvenirs*, 10.
9. From a letter to his wife, October 21, 1916, in Constance B. Smith, *John Masefield: A Life* (New York, 1978), 164.
10. T.S. Eliot, 'Burnt Norton,' *Collected Poems: 1909–1962* (London, 1963), 194.
11. Letters, April 17, 1917, November 26, 1917, October 2, 1918, R.R. Stokes, IWM.
12. Letter to his parents, December 23, 1915, J.W. Gamble, IWM.
13. Jünger, *In Stahlgewittern*, 198; Graves, *Goodbye*, 97; Horne, *Price of Glory*, 147, 259; Marie-Émile Fayolle, *Les Carnets secrets de la Grande Guerre*, ed. Henry Contamine (Paris, 1964), 259.
14. Diary, November 29, 1914, P. Mortimer, IWM.
15. Basil H. Liddell Hart, *The Memoirs of Captain Liddell Hart*, 2 vols. (London, 1965), I:21–23.
16. Diary, March 10, 1916, W.C.S. Gregson, IWM.
17. *Wipers Times*, February 12, 1916.
18. *Somme Times*, July 31, 1916.
19. Diary, n.d., Mairet, *Carnet*, 129.
20. Letter, August 1918, D.L. Ghilchik, IWM.
21. Letter, Easter 1915, Binding, *Fatalist*, 60.
22. Marcel-Edmond Naegelen, *Avant que meure le dernier* (Paris, 1958), 222.
23. Letter, March 19, 1918, Boasson, *Au Soir*, 311.

24. In Gaston Esnault, *Le Poilu tel qu'il parle* (Paris, 1919), 160–61.
25. In Ellis, *Eye-Deep in Hell*, 102.

pages 303–7

1. Letter, September 14, 1915, P. McGregor, IWM.
2. Letter, November 21, 1915, ibid.
3. In Michael Moynihan (ed.), *People at War 1914–1918* (Newton Abbot, 1973), 107.
4. Winter, *Death's Men*, 150.
5. Huot, *Psychologie*, 156–57.
6. Frederic Manning, *The Middle Parts of Fortune* (London, 1977), 50.
7. Diary, Ocotber 24–25, 1914, P.H. Jones, IWM.
8. Diary, February 18, 1916, Delvert, *Carnets*, 149.
9. *Their Crimes* (London, 1917), 14.
10. Humphrey Cobb, *Paths of Glory* (New York, 1935), 4–5.
11. Philippe Girardet, *Ceux que j'ai connus, souvenirs* (Paris, 1952), 104–105.
12. E.E. Cummings, *The Enormous Room* (New York, 1922, repr.1978), 17.

pages 307–21

1. Letter to mother, July 23, 1916, R.D. Mountfort, IWM.
2. Graves, *Goodbye*, 188, 194.
3. Diary, March 5–12, 1916, Mairet, *Carnet*, 131–32.
4. *Literary Digest*, 60/10 (March 8, 1919), 105.
5. Jünger, *In Stahlgewittern*, ix.
6. Letter, July 1, 1915, Boasson, *Au Soir*, 10.
7. In Pedroncini, *Les Mutineries*, 271.
8. Diary, March 26, 1916, Delvert, *Carnets*, 182–83.
9. Diary, March 29, 1916, ibid., 185.
10. Diary, July 13, 1916, ibid., 311.
11. Diary, July 2 and 23, 1916, G. Powell, IWM.
12. Siegfried Sassoon, ' "Blighters," ' *Collected Poems*, 21.
13. Jean Galtier-Boissière, *Le Crapouillet*, IV/5 (August 1918), 7–8.
14. Pierre Drieu la Rochelle, *Interrogation* (Paris, 1917), 55.
15. Bridoux, *Souvenirs*, 39, 45.

16. Especially his letter of May 29, 1917, Boasson, *Au Soir*, 235–36.
17. Graves, *Goodbye*, 78.
18. Diary, June 15, 1917, Read, *Contrary*, 97.
19. In Ducasse, *Vie et mort*, 96; and G.L. Dickinson, *War* (London, 1923), 6–7.
20. Henri de Montherlant, *Chant funèbre pour les morts de Verdun* (Paris, 1924), 115.
21. Diary, May 9, 1918, Read, *Contrary*, 128.
22. Dickinson, *War*, 5–6.
23. Diary, October 7, 1917, Read, *Contrary*, 110.
24. Diary, February 27, 1918, Fayolle, *Carnets*, 257.
25. 'Rapport du Capitaine Canonge,' June 1, 1917, 3e Armée, 16N1521, SHAT.
26. Letter to his father, August 1, 1918, R.R. Stokes, IWM.
27. *L'Intransigeant*, August 17, 1914.
28. Letter, December 29, 1915, J.W. Harvey, IWM.
29. Letter, June 2, 1916, J.M.S. Walker, IWM.
30. Letters, September 1 and 3, 1914, in *The Letters of Henry James*, II:414–19.
31. In Roland H. Bainton, *Christian Attitudes to War and Peace* (New York, 1960), 207.
32. In Ray H. Abrams, *Preachers Present Arms* (New York, 1933), 28.
33. Isadora Duncan, *My Life* (New York, 1927), 349.
34. Letter, April 22, 1915, to his parents, Mairet, *Carnet*, 42.
35. Ian Hamilton, *The Soul and Body of an Army* (London, 1921), 92.
36. Robert Graves, 'Recalling War,' in *Collected Poems, 1959* (New York, 1959), 121.
37. John Brophy and Eric Partridge, *The Long Trail* (London, 1965), 27.
38. Diary, November 11, 1918, Carnet de route du lieutenant René Hemery, Dons et Témoignages 170, SHAT.
39. Edward Thomas, 'Roads,' in *Collected Poems* (London, 1969), 163–64.

pages 326–33

1. In Wolff, *Black Sun*, 260.
2. *Daily Mail*, May 23, 1927, 14d.
3. Harold Wheeler, a reporter for the *Herald* of Paris and a

'plain New Yorker,' as the *Morning Post* (May 23, 1927) described him, was among the first to reach the plane. He is credited by some accounts with saving Lindbergh from the hordes by impersonating him and distracting attention from the real hero. For his humanitarian and perhaps patriotic gesture he was almost torn to shreds. See Jack Glenn, 'Reeling Round the World,' *Lost Generation Journal*, IV/2, (1976) 2–4.

4. *Morning Post*, May 30, 1927.
5. *Berliner Tageblatt*, 252, May 30, 1927.

pages 333–9

1. In his preface to Charles A. Lindbergh, *Mon avion et moi*, trans. L. Lemonnier (Paris, 1927), viii.
2. In Edmund Wilson, *The Twenties*, ed. Leon Edel (New York, 1976), 317.
3. Cited in *Journal des débats politiques et littéraires*, May 23, 1927.
4. *Times of London*, June 1, 1927, 21a.
5. *L'Humanité*, issues of May 22–27, 1927.
6. Waverley Root, *The Paris Edition*, ed. Samuel Abt (San Francisco, 1987), 36; Leonard Mosley, *Lindbergh* (New York, 1976), 406; William Wiser, *The Crazy Years: Paris in the Twenties* (London, 1983), 189.
7. *The Observer*, June 12, 1927, 17d.
8. Root, *Paris Edition*, 29.
9. *Daily Express*, May 31 and June 2, 1927, 4d.
10. *Manchester Guardian*, June 2, 1927, 10ef.
11. *Léger et l'esprit moderne (1918–1931)*, exhibition catalogue, Musée d'art moderne de la ville de Paris (Paris, 1982), 149.
12. In Janet Flanner, *Paris Was Yesterday, 1925–1939*, ed. I. Drutman (New York, 1972), 23.

pages 339–350

1. Ilya Ehrenburg, *Men, Years – Life*, 6 vols., trans. T. Shebunina (London, 1962–1966), III:11–12.
2. Stephen Spender, *World Within World* (London, 1951), 2–3.

3. Paul Valéry, *Variety*, trans. Malcolm Cowley (New York, 1927), 27–28.
4. Michael Arlen, *The Green Hat* (New York, 1924), 53.
5. Aldous Huxley, *Point Counter Point* (Harmondsworth, 1971), 138.
6. In Beverley Nichols, *The Sweet and Twenties* (London, 1958), 18.
7. Christopher Isherwood, *Lions and Shadows* (London, 1953), 73–74.
8. Ehrenburg, *Men, Years*, III:129.
9. Isherwood, *Lions and Shadows*, 217.

pages 350–8

1. One of the more detailed and nuanced accounts of the arrival is to be found in the *Berliner Tageblatt*, 241, May 23, 1927, 4.
2. Groupe sénatorial de l'aviation, *Réception par le sénat de l'aviateur américain Charles Lindbergh* (Paris, n.d. [1927]), n.p.
3. The comment was quoted approvingly by *Vowärts*, 241, May 23, 1927, 5.
4. *Manchester Guardian*, May 23, 1927, 8b.
5. In J.P. Dournel, 'L'Image de l'aviateur français en 1914–1918,' *Revue historique des armées*, 4 (1975), 62.
6. *Daily Express*, May 23, 1927, 10b.
7. Paul Claudel, *Journal, vol.I: 1904–1932*, ed. F. Varillon and J. Petit (Paris, 1968), 772.
8. In René Weiss, *Les premières traversées aériennes de l'Atlantique* (Paris, 1927), 21.
9. In ibid., 22, 28.
10. Alexandre Guinle, *Ode à Charles A. Lindbergh* (Paris, 1927).
11. *Journal des débats politiques et littéraires*, May 23, 1927.

pages 359–64

1. 'New York,' *Cahiers d'Art*, 1931, cited in *Léger et l'esprit moderne*, 197.
2. Lucien Romier, *Qui sera le maître: Europe ou Amérique* (Paris, 1927), 155–58.

3. In Allan Nevins (ed.), *America Through British Eyes* (New York, 1948), 396.
4. Mary Borden, 'The American Man,' *The Spectator*, 140 (June 30, 1928), 958.
5. Ivan Goll, *Transition*, 13 (1928), 256.
6. In Haskell, *Diaghileff*, 296.
7. Letter to Boris Kochno, August 7, 1926, in Buckle, *Diaghilev*, 473.
8. Margaret Halsey, *With Malice Towards Some* (New York, 1938), 194.
9. B. Henriques, cited in *The Observer*, June 19, 1927, 21b.
10. Octave Homberg, *L'Impérialisme américain* (Paris, 1929), 22.
11. Ernest Hemingway, *A Moveable Feast* (New York, 1965), 71; and Wayne E. Kvam, *Hemingway in Germany* (Athens, Ohio, 1973).
12. In Freedman Hesse, 227.
13. Letter ('Brief an einen Opernleiter'), November 15, 1927, Mann, *Gesammelte Werke*, X:894.

pages 364–7

1. *Le Figaro*, May 30, 1927.
2. Adolf Weissmann, *Vossische Zeitung*, 121, May 25, 1927.
3. Romola Nijinsky, *Nijinsky*, 361.
4. Diary, December 27, 1928, Harry Graf Kessler, *Tagebücher 1918–1937*, ed. Wolfgang Pfeiffer-Belli (Frankfurt am Main, 1961), 612–13.
5. T.S. Eliot, 'The Waste Land,' *Collected Poems*, 63.

pages 368–71

1. *Nouvelles littéraires*, October 25, 1930.
2. *Börsenblatt für den deutschen Buchhandel*, June 10, 1930, 540; *Die Literatur*, 31 (1928–29), 652; *Publisher's Weekly*, September 21, 1929, 1332; *Daily Herald*, November 23, 1929.
3. Friedrich Fuchs in *Das Hochland*, 2 (1929), 217.

pages 371–80

1. John Middleton Murry, *Between Two Worlds* (London, 1935), 65.
2. Cabinet minutes, December 19, 1930, Reichskanzlei files, R431/1447, 383, Bundesarchiv Koblenz (hereafter BAK).
3. Peter Kropp, *Endlich Klarheit über Remarque und sein Buch 'Im Westen nichts Neues'* (Hamm i. W., 1930), 9–14.
4. *Der Spiegel*, January 9, 1952, 25.
5. In D.A. Prater, *European of Yesterday: A Biography of Stefan Zweig* (Oxford, 1972), 140.
6. Interview with Axel Eggebrecht, *Die Literarische Welt*, June 14, 1929.
7. *Sport im Bild*, June 8, 1928.
8. Ibid., July 20, 1928.
9. I have used the A.W. Wheen translation (London, 1929) for quotations. Wheen was himself a veteran of the war; see R. Church, *The Spectator*, 142 (April 20, 1929), 624.
10. Hanna Hafkesbrink, for instance, called *All Quiet* a 'genuine memoir of the war'; see *Unknown Germany: An Inner Chronicle of the First World War Based on Letters and Diaries* (New Haven, Conn., 1948), ix.
11. For examples of the criticism see Jean Norton Cru, *Témoins*, 80; and Cyril Falls, *War Books* (London, 1930), x–xi, 294.
12. E.M. Remarque and Gen. Sir Ian Hamilton, 'The End of War?' *Life and Letters*, 3 (1929), 405–406.
13. *Time*, March 24, 1961, in its review of *Heaven Has No Favorites*.
14. Michel Tournier, *Le vent Paraclet* (Paris, 1977), 166.
15. Harry Crosby, 'Hail: Death!' *Transition*, 14 (1928), 169–70.
16. R[osie] G[räfenberg], *Prelude to the Past* (New York, 1934), 320–21.

pages 380–97

1. The legends about Remarque and *All Quiet* are many. One is that he offered his manuscript to forty-eight publishers. See the obituary in *Der Spiegel*, September 28, 1970. For accounts of the publication see Peter de

Mendelssohn, *S. Fischer und sein Verlag* (Frankfurt am Main, 1970), 1114–18; Max Krell, *Das gab es alles einmal* (Frankfurt am Main, 1961), 159–60; Heinz Ullstein's version in a *dpa* release, June 15, 1962, as well as his letter to the *Frankfurter Allgemeine Zeitung*, July 9, 1962; and the remarks of Carl Jödicke, an Ullstein employee, in his unpublished 'Dokumente und Aufzeichnungen' (F501), 40, Institut für Zeitgeschichte, Munich.

2. Carl Zuckmayer, *Als wär's ein Stück von mir*, 359–60; Axel Eggebrecht, *Die Weltbühne*, February 5, 1929, 212; Herbert Read, 'A Lost Generation,' *The Nation & Athenaeum*, April 27, 1929, 116; Christopher Morley, *The Saturday Review*, April 20, 1929, 909; Daniel-Rops, *Bibliothèque universelle et Revue de Genève*, 1929, II, 510–11.

3. The *Sunday Chronicle* is cited in *The Saturday Review*, June 1, 1929, 1075.

4. See Antkowiak's survey of the communist reviews in Pawel Toper and Alfred Antkowiak, *Ludwig Renn, Erich Maria Remarque: Leben und Werk* ([East] Berlin, 1965).

5. Freiherr von der Goltz, *Deutsche Wehr*, October 10, 1929, 270; Valentine Williams, *Morning Post*, February 11, 1930; *The London Mercury*, 21 (January 1930), 238; and *Deutschlands Erneuerung*, 13 (1929), 230.

6. See the reports in the *New York Times*, May 31, June 1, July 14, July 29, 1929.

7. *The London Mercury*, 21 (November 1929), 1.

8. *The Army Quarterly*, 20 (July 1930), 373–75.

9. *Berliner Börsen-Zeitung*, June 9, 1929; *New York Times*, November 17, 1929; *Daily Herald*, November 12, 1929.

10. *The Cambridge Review*, May 3, 1929, 412.

11. *The London Mercury*, 21 (January 1930), 194–95.

12. Reported in the *New York Times*, February 9, 1930.

13. H.A.L. Fisher, *A History of Europe*, 3 vols. (London, 1935), I:vii.

14. 'War Novels,' *Morning Post*, April 8, 1930.

15. André Thérive, 'Les Livres,' *Le Temps*, December 27, 1929.

16. Robert Wohl, *The Generation of 1914* (Cambridge, Mass., 1979), 120; A.C. Ward, *The Nineteen-Twenties* (London, 1930), xii; Robert Graves, 'The Marmosite's Miscellany,' *Poems (1914–26)* (London, 1927), 191.

17. José Germain, in his preface to Maurice d'Hartoy, *La Génération du feu* (Paris, 1923), xi.
18. Carroll Carstairs, *A Generation Missing* (London, 1930), 208.
19. Letter, July 2, 1915, Boasson, *Au Soir*, 12; Egon Friedell, *A Cultural History of the Modern Age*, trans. C.F. Atkinson (New York, 1954), III:467.
20. W. Müller Scheid, *Im Westen nichts Neues – eine Täuschung* (Idstein, 1929), 6.
21. *Commonweal*, May 27, 1931, 90.
22. *The Fortnightly Review*, October 1, 1930, 527; Davidson, in John C. Cairns, 'A Nation of Shopkeepers in Search of a Suitable France: 1919–40,' *The American Historical Review*, 79 (1974), 728; Douglas Goldring, *Pacifists in Peace and War* (London, 1932), 12, 18; Graves, *Goodbye*, 240.
23. Joffre, in Marc Ferro, *La Grande Guerre 1914–1918* (Paris, 1969), 239; Pedroncini, *Les Mutineries*, 177; General Huguet, *L'Intervention militaire britannique en 1914* (Paris, 1928), 231.
24. See the introductory remarks by René Lalou to R.H. Mottram's *La Ferme espagnole*, trans. M. Dou-Desportes (Paris, 1930), i–iv.
25. Isherwood, *Lions and Shadows*, 73–76, and also his *Kathleen and Frank*, 356–63; and Jean Dutourd, *Les Taxis de la Marne* (Paris, 1956), 189–93.
26. *New York Times*, January 18, 1930.
27. William Faulkner, *The New Republic*, May 20, 1931, 23–24.

pages 397–8

1. See my 'War, Memory, and Politics: The Fate of the Film *All Quiet on the Western Front*,' *Central European History*, 13/1 (March 1980), 60–82.
2. In Henry C. Meyer (ed.), *The Long Generation* (New York, 1973), 221.
3. See the correspondence between the Polizeipräsident in Berlin and the Geheime Staatspolizeiamt, December 4 and 16, 1933, Reichssicherheitshauptamt files, R58/933, 198–99, BAK.

4. Wolff'sche Telegraphen Büro report, May 15, 1933, in the Neue Reichskanzlei files, R43II/479, 4–5, BAK.

pages 399–405

1. Diary, January 30, 1933, Joseph Goebbels, *Vom Kaiserhof zur Reichskanzlei* (Munich, 1934), 251–54.
2. In Hannah Vogt, *The Burden of Guilt*, trans. H. Strauss (New York, 1964), 118.
3. Diary, January 30, 1933, Kessler, *Tagebücher*, 747.
4. Malcolm Muggeridge, *The Infernal Grove: Chronicles of Wasted Time, Part 2* (London, 1975), 283–84).
5. In Colin Cross, *The Fascists in Britain* (London, 1961), 57.
6. ZHermann Rauschning, *Hitler Speaks* (London, 1939), 242. If Rauschning has been discredited of late as an accurate transmitter of Hitler's words, he is still a fairly reliable delineator of Hitler's ideas.
7. Walter Benjamin, *Das Kunstwerk im Zeitalter seiner technischen Reproduzierbarkeit* (Frankfurt am Main, 1963), 48.
8. Anson G. Rabinbach, 'The Aesthetics of Production,' *Journal of Contemporary History*, 11/4 (1976), 43–74.
9. Matei Calinescu, *Faces of Modernity: Avant-Garde, Decadence, Kitsch* (Bloomington, 1977), 229.

pages 405–13

1. Jacques de Launay, *Hitler en Flandres* (Brussels, 1975), 103–108.
2. Adolf Hitler, *Mein Kampf* (Munich, 1943), 177.
3. *Hitler's Table Talk, 1941–1944*, intro. H.R. Trevor-Roper, trans. N. Cameron and R.H. Stevens (London, 1953), 44.
4. Hitler, *Mein Kampf*, 179.
5. Hans Mend, *Adolf Hitler im Felde 1914–1918* (Diessen, 1931), 47–58.
6. In Joachim C. Fest, *Hitler*, trans. Richard and Clara Winston (New York, 1975), 70.
7. In Peter Merkl, *Political Violence Under the Swastika* (Princeton, 1975), 167.
8. *Hitler's Table Talk*, 44.
9. Hitler, *Mein Kampf*, 772.

10. In Robert Waite, *Vanguard of Nazism* (New York, 1969), 42.
11. In his preface to the second edition, Jünger, *In Stahlgewittern*, xii.
12. Feder is cited in *Le Crapouillet*, July 1933, 40; Ley in Richard Grunberger, *The 12-Year Reich* (New York, 1971), 51; Strasser in Barbara Miller Lane, 'Nazi Ideology: Some Unfinished Business,' *Central European History*, 7/1 (1974), 23.
13. Philipp Witkop (ed.), *Kriegsbriefe gefallener Studenten* (Munich, n.d. [1933]), 5–6.
14. Christopher Isherwood, *Goodbye to Berlin* (Harmondsworth, 1965), 202.
15. In a letter to the Dean, Bonn University, January 1, 1937, Thomas Mann, *Briefe 1937–1947*, ed. Erika Mann (Frankfurt am Main, 1963), 13.

pages 413–17

1. In Albert Speer, *Inside the Third Reich*, trans. Richard and Clara Winston (New York, 1970), 299.
2. Michel Tournier, *Le vent Paraclet*, 189.
3. Joseph Goebbels, *Final Entries 1945: The Diaries*, ed. Hugh Trevor-Roper, trans. Richard Barry (New York, 1978), 194.
4. In René Rémond, *La Droite en France*, 2 vols., (Paris, 1968), II:384.
5. In Fest, *Hitler*, 381.
6. Ibid., 142.

pages 418–30

1. In Michael Balfour, *Propaganda in War 1939–1945* (London, 1979), 48.
2. Gabriele d'Annunzio, in Alexander Rüstow, *Freedom and Domination*, trans. S. Attanasio (Princeton, 1980), 586.
3. In Benjamin, *Das Kunstwerk*, 49.
4. Diary, February 2, 1933, Kessler, *Tagebücher*, 748; see also Saul Friedländer, *Reflections of Nazism: An Essay on Kitsch and Death*, trans. T. Weyr (New York, 1984), 41–53.

5. W. Petwidic, *Die autoritäre Anarchie* (Hamburg, 1946).
6. In Konrad Heiden, *Der Fuehrer: Hitler's Rise to Power*, trans. Ralph Manheim (Boston, 1944), 190, 378; and Hans Peter Bleuel, *Sex and Society in Nazi Germany*, trans. J.M. Brownjohn (Philadelphia, 1973), 38.
7. Robert G.L. Waite, *The Psychopathic God: Adolf Hitler* (New York, 1977); Rudolph Binion, *Hitler Among the Germans* (New York, 1976); and Norbert Bromberg and Verna V. Small, *Hitler's Psychopathology* (New York, 1983).
8. Ernst Hanfstaengl, *Hitler: The Missing Years* (London, 1957), 124.
9. Goebbels, *Final Entries*, 133.
10. *Hitler's Table Talk*, 309–12, 537, 577–78, 707.
11. Rauschning, *Hitler Speaks*, 18–19.
12. Anne Morrow Lindbergh, *The Wave of the Future: A Confession of Faith* (New York, 1940).
13. Goebbels, *Final Entries*, 205.
14. Nevile Henderson, *Failure of a Mission* (New York, 1940), 151–52.
15. André François-Poncet, *The Fateful Years*, trans. J. LeClercq (London, 1949), 209.
16. In Alan Bullock, *Hitler: A Study in Tyranny* (Harmondsworth, 1962), 379.
17. George Mosse, *The Nationalization of the Masses* (New York, 1975), 155–58.
18. Joachim C. Fest, 'On Remembering Adolf Hitler,' *Encounter*, 41/4 (October 1973), 20.
19. See also Alvin H. Rosenfeld, *Imagining Hitler* (Bloomington, 1985).

pages 431–8

1. Donald M. Douglas, 'The Parent Cell: Some Computer Notes on the Composition of the First Nazi Party Group in Munich, 1919–1921,' *Central European History*, 10 (1977), 55–72; and Michael H. Kater, *The Nazi Party* (Cambridge, Mass., 1983), 29.
2. Joachim C. Fest, *The Face of the Third Reich*, trans. M. Bullock (London, 1970), 252.
3. Of 400,000 German emigrants between 1933 and 1941 only about 10 per cent could be termed political

refugees. The majority were racial refugees. Hans-Albert Walter in Walter Zadek (ed.), *Sie flohen vor dem Hakenkreuz* (Reinbek bei Hamburg, 1981), 10–11.

4. Gottfried Benn, 'Über die Rolle des Schriftstellers in dieser Zeit' (1929), *Gesammelte Werke*, 4 vols. (Wiesbaden, 1958–1961), IV:211.

5. Rudolf G. Binding et al., *Sechs Bekenntnisse zum neuen Deutschland* (Hamburg, 1933), excerpted in Josef Wulf (ed.), *Literatur und Dichtung im Dritten Reich* (Reinbek bei Hamburg, 1966), 107.

6. Diary, April 10, 1917, Paul Morand, *Journal*, 209.

7. In Gold and Fizdale, *Misia*, 296.

8. Benn, 'Lebensweg eines Intellektualisten' (1934), *Gesammelte Werke*, IV:64–65.

9. Maurice Mandelbaum, in Stephen Spender (ed.), *W.H. Auden: A Tribute* (London, 1975), 121.

10. In Irving Howe, *The Decline of the New* (New York, 1970), 42.

11. In Wulf (ed.), *Literatur*, 150.

12. Jeffrey Herf, *Reactionary Modernism: Technology, Culture, and Politics in Weimar and the Third Reich* (Cambridge, 1984).

13. In Hugh Trevor-Roper, *The Last Days of Hitler* (London, 1950), 57–58. See also Stern, *Hitler*, 34.

14. Goebbels, *Final Entries*, 174.

15. Diary, September 14, 1925, Joseph Goebbels, *The Early Goebbels Diaries, 1925–1926*, ed. Helmut Heiber, trans. O. Watson (London, 1962), 35.

16. In H.R. Trevor-Roper's introduction to the last volume of Goebbels's diaries, *Final Entries*, xxxii.

17. Goebbels, *Final Entries*, 330–31.

18. In Fest, *Hitler*, 746, and Trevor-Roper, *Last Days*, 199.

19. Trevor-Roper, *Last Days*, 217–18.

Selected Sources

The sources for this work are extremely varied. They consist of published and unpublished items, consulted and collected over many years of reading and rummaging in libraries and archives in Europe and North America. To list all the material I consulted in the research would be an impossible task. To list even the major published works on this period would require a volume of its own. Therefore, only those collections of primary sources which I have used to considerable advantage are recorded here. Some of the more significant secondary sources are mentioned in the notes.

New York, New York Public Library, Performing Arts Research Center, Dance Collection.
    Gabriel Astruc, Papers.
    Jacques-Émile Blanche, Miscellaneous manuscripts.
    Sergei Pavlovich Dyagilev, Papers 1910–1929 and Correspondence.

London, Imperial War Musuem.
    Papers: W.G. Bailey, A.G. Bartlett, H.R. Bate, H.D. Bryan, Guy Buckeridge, F.L. Cassel, Iain Colquhoun, E.B. Cook, Elmer W. Cotton, R. von Dechend, T. Dixon, David H. Doe, B.W. Downes, H.V. Drinkwater, J.S. Fenton, V.M. Fergusson, J.W. Gamble, R.G. Garrod, Kenneth M. Gaunt, David L. Ghilchik, Arthur Gibbs, William C.S. Gregson, John W. Harvey, R.G. Heinekey, Edward R. Hepper, Edmund Herd, C.E. Hickingbotham, Harold Horne, Walter Hoskyn, Alfred Howe, G.W.G. Hughes, Percy H. Jones, Samuel Judd, Leslie H. Kent, E.D. Kingsley, Peter McGregor, P. Mortimer, Roland D. Mountfort, Richard Noschke,

M.W. Peters, P.H. Pilditch, Garfield Powell, W.A.
Quinton, I.L. Read, John R. Rees, Ronald D. Rees,
Arthur G. Rigby, Frank M. Robertson, G.R.P. Roupell,
Alexander Runcie, E. Russell-Jones, Siegfried Sassoon,
Eric Scullin, A. Self, R. Stafford, Richard R. Stokes,
Hiram Sturdy, F.H.T. Tatham, Harold A. Thomas,
Oswald Tilley, John M.S. Walker, M. Leslie
Walkinton, H.G.R. Williams. Miscellaneous Item
469.

Oral History Recordings: Philip Neame, James D.
Pratt, J.P.O. Reid.

Department of Art. Papers: John Nash, Paul Nash,
C.R.W. Nevinson, William Roberts. Christmas Card
Collection.

London, Public Record Office.
    War Diaries (WO95). Military Headquarters Papers
    (WO158).
    Directorate of Military Operations and Intelligence
    (WO106).
    Kitchener Papers (WO159). Maps and Plans (WO153).
    Intelligence Summaries (WO157). War Office Council
    (WO163).

London, Liddell Hart Centre for Military Archives, King's
College, University of London.
    Papers: C.H. Foulkes, Basil Liddell Hart, Ian Hamilton,
    Edward L. Spears.

Paris, Service historique de l'armée de terre, Château de
Vincennes.
    Journaux des Marches et Opérations (22N, 24N, 25N,
    26N). Grand Quartier Général (16N). Dossier
    Montlebert (1K143). Papiers Mealin (1K112). Dons et
    Témoignages: Chansons de tranchée (87), Carnet de
    route d'un combattant allemand en 1914 (103), Carnet
    de route du lieutenant René Hemery (170).

Koblenz, Bundersarchiv.
 Reichskanzlei (R43I), Neue Reichskanzlei (R43II),
 Reichssicherheitshauptamt (R58), UFA files (R109I),
 Filmoberprüfstelle protocol, December 11, 1930
 (Kl.Erw.457).

Freiburg i. B., Bundersarchiv-Militärarchiv.
 Papers: Émile-Marcel Décobert, Karl von Einem,
 Hermann Ritter von Giehrl, Frithjof Freiherr von
 Hammerstein-Gesmold, Henry Holthoff, Rudolf
 Müller, Gerhard von Nostitz-Wallwitz, Gustav
 Riebensahm, Paul Schulz, Bernhard Schwertfeger,
 Gerhard Tappen, Ferdinand von Trossel, Franz von
 Trotta gen. Treyden, Erwin von Witzleben.
 Manuscript collections (MSg2): Georg Eberle,
 Annemarie Heine, Felix Kaiser, the brothers
 Bernhard, Clemens, and Aloys Lammers, Lücke, Ernst
 Prasuhn, Gerhard Schinke, Heinrich Schlubeck, Ernst
 Wisselnick, Karl Zieke, Erinnerungsfeier 'Goldene
 Monstranz.'

Bonn, Politisches Archiv, Auswärtiges Amt.
 Schuldreferat. Botschaft London Geheimakten.
 Botschaft Paris. Kunst und Wissenschaft. Bücher und
 Zeitschriften. Wissenschaft – Reisen. Presse-
 Abteilung.

Munich, Bayerisches Kriegsarchiv.
 Kriegstagebücher.
 Papers: Oberst von der Aschenauer (HS2047), Gustav
 Baumann (HS2646), Otto Weber (HS1984), Georg Will
 (HS2703).

Munich, Institut für Zeitgeschichte.
 Carl Jödicke, Dokumente und Aufzeichnungen betr.
 Ullstein-Verlag (F501).

Index

Acton, Harold, 53
Acton, Lord, 170
Adams, Reverend J. Esslemont, 162
Adorno, Theodor, 402
'Aerial Locomotion' (Grand Palais, Paris), 338
aestheticism: of life, 118; and politics, 73
agents provocateurs, 314, 318
AGFA firm, 106
airplane: fascist enthusiasm for, 428; fatality rate among flyers, 353–4; military potential of, 353, 355 (see also air raids); Nazi use of, 427; symbolism of, 338–9, 355; symbolism of Lindbergh's flight, 337–9, 350–58
air raids: of Great War, 219–21, 258, 290
Aisne front, 147
Aitken, Alexander, 236
Akenbrand, Alfons, 272
À la recherche du temps perdu (Proust), 284
Albert, king of Belgium, 331
Albert cathedral: destruction of, 220
Alcock, John, 333
Aldington, Richard, 379, 389, 390
Alfonso XIII, king of Spain, 54
alienation: and soldiers' sense of camaraderie, 310–14; and trench warfare, 287–8
Allgemeine Elektrizitäts-Gesellschaft, 44
All Our Yesterdays (Tomlinson), 389
All Quiet on the Western Front (Remarque): accusations in, 378–9; as best seller, 388; criticisms of, 376–7, 384–5, 395; defecation imagery in, 307, 384; film of, 376, 397, 436; as great war novel, 389; language of, 383–4; lost generation theme of, 377–8, 379; military objections to, 384–5; and modernism, 392; Nazi banning of, 386, 397–8; and postwar mentality, 377, 378, 386, 389–90, 395, 396; as propaganda, 384–5; publishing history of, 381–3; reception and reviews of, 382–6; and revisionist history, 395; sales of, 369–70, 382, 388; serialization of, 369; themes of, 375, 376, 378; translations of, 370, 381, 384; truth of, 382–6, 396–7; veterans' response to, 390, 395, writing of, 375–80
Almond, H.H., 174
Alsace, 82
America. See United States
American Civil War, 134

Americanization: of Europe, 359–64
anarchism, 79
Anschütz, Gerhard, 268
Antheil, George, 379
Anti-Machiavel (Frederick II), 109
anti-Semitism, 45, 402–3, 409, 411, 422–5, 433; Nazi final solution, 425; as self-hatred, 422–3, 424–5
antiwar demonstrations: in Germany, 99–100
Apollinaire, Guillaume, 34, 204
Appleton, Thomas, 76
Après-midi d'un faune, L' (Debussy/Nijinsky), 54–5, 64, 71, 123
Arabic: sinking of, 231
architecture: *art nouveau*, 41; German, 43–4, 122–3; modernism, 41–4, 122–3; Nazi, 421; Parisian, 40–43, 76–7; postwar international style, 348–9
Aristotle, 266
Arlen, Michael, 348
armchair strategists: dislike of soldiers for, 309
Arminius, 127, 267
Armistice, 272, 282, 321, 339–40, 343
Army Quarterly, The, 384
Arnold, Sir Thomas, 173–4
Arp, Hans, 285
Arras: battle of, 200
art: distinctions blurred between life and, 27; experimental forms of, 293; as form, 292–302; vs. history, 387–8, 389; kitsch, 404–5; and morality, 303–7; Nazi, 404, 413–17; new aesthetic from war, 290–92; Paris as cultural center, 80–83; radicalist, Great War and, 284–7; as regeneration, 58–61; role of audience in, 75, 76–83; and socialism, 289;

total, 51, 60–62; war as, 283–92; *see also specific movements and styles*
artillery: in Great War, 195–6, 202, 213, 214; short shelling, 213
art nouveau, 41, 54
Artois front, 199
Aryanism, 421–2
Aschenhauer, Major von Der, 163
Association of German Jews, Berlin, 98
Astor, John L., 45
Astor, Lady, 333
Astruc, Gabriel, 32, 33, 37, 38, 44–5, 50, 51, 89, 123
Atkins, Thomas, 155, 168, 179
atrocity stories: and propaganda, 315, 318
Auden, W.H., 432
Auric, Georges, 359
Auschwitz death camp, 402, 424
Australian troops: in Great War, 258
Austria: architecture in, 44; Prussian war against, 103; ultimatum to Serbia, 91–2
Austrian army, 144, 272
Austrian Secessionists, 70, 285
authority: failure of, in Great War, 289
Autobahnen, 427
automobiles, 78–9; graveyard at Verdun, 15–16; Hitler's enthusiasm for, 426
avant-garde: and lower classes, 74; use of term, 18

Badische Anilin firm, 106
Baker, Josephine, 280, 346, 359, 365, 367
Bakst, Léon, 50, 52, 53, 54
Balanchine, George, 365
Baldwin, Stanley, 393
Balkan War (1913), 87
Ball, Hugo, 285

ballet: historical evolution of, 65–9; see also specific compositions

Ballets russes, 51–8, 80, 88, 123, 339, 429; aestheticism and politics, 73; gas warfare shares novelty with, 226–7; homosexuality amongst, 63–4; postwar loss of attention, 364–6; and Rite of Spring, 32–40, 72–3 (see also Rite of Spring)

Barbusse, Henri, 239, 241

Barrès, Maurice, 77, 422

Bauer, Colonel Max, 217

Bauhaus school, 350

Bavarians: vs. Prussians, 190

Bayard, Émile, 43

Bayreuth festival, 83, 118, 119

Beardsley, Aubrey, 186

Beaverbrook, Lord, 294

BEF. See British army

B.E.F. Times, 300

Behrens, Peter, 44

Belgian army, 146

Belgium: and 1914 Christmas truce, 164–5; German occupation policy, 218–19, 221, 318; in Great War, 133, 146–7, 274

belle époque, 79, 82

Benjamin, Walter, 404

Benn, Gottfried, 431, 432, 434

Benois, Alexandre, 50, 51, 52, 58, 71, 74, 81

Bentham, Jeremy, 185

Benvenuto Cellini (Berlioz), 46

Berger, Marcel, 358

Bergson, Henri, 60, 223

Berlin: Allied bombing of (WWII), 401; anti-Serbian demonstrations in, 91–4; antiwar demonstrations in, 99–100; aura of newness in, 114–15; Ballets russes in, 53; as capital city, 113–16, 122; compared with New York, 113;

as cosmopolitan immigration center, 113, 115; dynamics of, 113–16; homosexuality in, 125; Moabit criminal courts, 96; popular feelings for war in, 90–101; population of, 101, 102, 114; prewar marriages in, 98; see also Germany

Berliner Börsen-Zeitung, 384

Berliner Illustrirte Zeitung, 381

Berliner Lokal-Anzeiger, 95, 138

Berliner Tageblatt, 99, 127, 138, 332, 358

Berlioz, Hector, 46

Bernanos, Georges, 289

Bernard, Jean-Marc, 246

Berners, Gerald, 364

Bernhardi, Friedrich von, 135

Bernstein, Eduard, 281

Berr, Henri, 260

Bethmann Hollweg, Theobald von, 91, 92, 93, 95, 96, 229, 232, 271

Bethune front, 151

Better Times, 300

Big Parade, The, 371

Bildung: German concern with, 117

Binding, Rudolf, 279, 301, 431

Bismarck, Otto von, 82, 96, 103, 131, 135, 264, 267; and unification of Germany, 103–5, 109

Blachon, Georges, 233

black humor: expressing new sensibility, 298–301

Blanche, Jacques-Émile, 46, 58, 82, 83, 285, 290

Blasis, Carlo, 67

Blass, Ernst, 263

Blast, 126

Bleak House (Dickens), 105

Blériot, Louis, 330, 338

Blitzkrieg, 426

Blumenfeld, Franz, 269

Blunden, Edmund, 341, 370, 379, 393

Boasson, Marc, 206, 237, 288, 301–2, 308, 311, 312, 391
Boccioni, Umberto, 60
body culture, 67–8, 126, 127, 128
Boer War, 134, 176, 222
Bois, Ilse, 325
Bois sacre, Le (Flers/Cavaillet), 65
Bolsheviks, 242, 281, 341; accepted by artistic and intellectual community, 432
Bonn, Moritz Julius, 115
Book-of-the-Month Club, 369, 384
Book Society (Great Britain), 369
book trade: and war books, 370
Borden, Mary, 361
Boris Godunov (Mussorgsky), 50
Boston: dance halls in, 69
Bourdelle, Antoine, 42, 46
bourgeois values: education and, 254–5; in Great War, 242–6, 252–7, 260–61
Box, Charles, 174
Boxer Rebellion, 127
Boyd, Thomas, 306
Boy Scouts, 67
Braque, Georges, 226
Brasillach, Robert, 417, 431
Braun, Eva, 437
Braun, Otto, 139
Breker, Arno, 405
Bremer Bürger-Zeitung, 100
Brest-Litovsk, Treaty of (1918), 242
Bridge of San Luis Rey, The (Wilder), 387
Bridoux, André, 239, 311
Briefe an das Leben (Eichacker), 279
Britain. See Great Britain
British army: attacks and counter-attacks, 156–8; attitudes toward Germans, 181–3; casualties of, 148, 200, 201; and Christmas 1914 truce, 141–5, 159–83; conscription introduced, 249, 250; enlistment in, 148, 180, 259; exposure casualties, 151; introduction of new technology by, 228–9; leadership of, 256; loyalty in, 240; at Mons, 146, 148; morale and motivation in, 234–62; mutiny in, 240; official artists in, 293–5; reasons for fraternization of Christmas 1914, 167–83; sporting organizations in volunteer recruitment, 180; and trench warfare, 148–59 (see also trench warfare); use of gas by, 224–5, Victorian social code and sense of duty, 183–7; see also Great Britain; Great War
British Expeditionary Force (BEF). See British army
British navy: blockade of Germany, 229, 271, 340; convoy system, 232; and German submarine warfare, 230–32
British Red Cross Society, 234
Brittain, Vera, 246, 252
Brooke, Rupert, 53, 176, 187–9
Brown, Arthur Whitten, 333
Brussel, Robert, 55
Buchanan-Dunlop, Major A.H., 162
Bucher, Lothar, 123
Buckle, Richard, 52
Bülow, Prince Bernhard von, 131
Burckhardt, Jacob, 121, 266, 267
Byron, George Gordon, Lord, 23, 137

Caillaux, Henriette, 55
Caillaux, Joseph, 55
Calmette, Gaston, 55
cameras: forbidden on front lines, 315

Camondo, Count Isaac de, 44
Campana, Roger, 207, 212
Canadian troops: in Great War, 316
Canby, Henry Seidel, 382
Canetti, Elias, 90
Capote, Truman, 27
Capus, Alfred, 87
Carlyle, Thomas, 415
Carr (flyer), 354
Carstairs, Carroll, 390
Caruso, Enrico, 44
Casement, Roger, 233
Cassel, Sir Ernest, 45
Castle, Irene, 348
Catherine II, the Great, tzarina of Russia, 49
Catholic Center Party (Germany), 112
Cavaillet, Gaston de, 65
Cavalieri, Lina, 44
Caves du Vatican, Les (Gide), 60
Céline, Louis-Ferdinand, 31
censorship: in Great War, 238, 316–19
Chaliapin, Feodor, 50, 80, 366
Chamberlain, Houston Stewart, 118–20, 124, 133, 266, 357
Chamberlain, Joseph, 175
Chamberlain, Neville, 428
Champagne front, 199
Chanel, Coco, 348
Chaney, Bert, 304–5
Charleston (dance), 337, 347, 362
Charpentier, Gustave, 80
Chartier, Émile, 313
Chatte, La (Sauguet/Balanchine), 365
chemical warfare. See gas
Chemin des Dames: battle of, 203, 240, 249
Chemnitzer Volksstimme, 136
Cherfils, General, 228
Chesterton, G.K., 175
Chevallier, Gabriel, 240
Chiappe, Jean, 357

Chicago Tribune, 335
chlorine gas, 225; see also gas
Christmas 1914 truce, 141–5, 159–83, 189–92; Anglo-German, 159–65, 189–91; bartering during, 163–4; British values and, 172–81, 188, 189–90; burial parties during, 162; events leading to, 141–59; football match during, 164; Franco-German, 165–6; main meal of, 162; music playing during, 160–61; press on, 166, 190–91; reasons for, 166–83, 187–91
cinema: American in Germany, 363; film version of All Quiet, 376, 397, 436; and Great War, 302; in twenties, 347, 350, 363; use by Nazis, 425–6, 428, 436; on war experience, 370–71
civilization, 117, 121, 124, 137, 168–9, 172, 185–8, 244–6, 252–4; and bourgeois values in Great War, 242–6, 252–6, 260–61; and sense of history, 265; values undermined by Great War, 260–61
Clarendon Commission of 1864, 174
Claudel, Paul, 330, 356
Clausewitz, Karl von, 263
Clemenceau, Georges, 77, 340, 342
Cléopatre (ballet), 54, 63
coal-tar industry: in Germany and Britain, 111
Cobb, Humphrey, 306
Cobb, Richard, 368
Cocteau, Jean, 32, 33, 34, 35, 39, 60, 64, 82, 204
Code of Terpsichore, The (Blasis), 67
Coli, François, 353
colonialism, 79; German, 129
Communist Party (Germany), 342

communists: opposition to *All Quiet*, 383

compulsory service: in Great War, 250, 255

Conrad von Hötzendorf, Count Franz, 147

conscripts: in Great War, 250, 255

Coolidge, Calvin, 333, 334

Courbet, Gustave, 81

Cousin, Victor, 110

Covent Garden, London, 54

Craig, Gordon, 406

Crane, Hart, 397

Crémieux, Benjamin, 254

cricket, 174–5

Crimean War, 134

Crosby, Caresse, 327

Crosby, Harry, 292, 327, 339, 368, 379, 397

Cru, Jean Norton, 259

Crystal Night (Nov.9, 1938), 433

Crystal Palace, 123

cubism, 126, 293

cultural history, 16–17

Cummings, E.E., 295, 306

Cunard, Nancy, 359

Czechoslovak War Department, 385

Dadaists, 280, 285, 298, 301, 345, 379, 390

Daily Express, 295, 337, 355

Daily Herald, 352

Daily Mail, 182–3, 190, 225, 317, 328

Dalling, Private, 181

dance: Charleston, 337, 347, 362; historical evolution of, 65–9; popular, 69; *see also* Ballets russes

Daniel-Rops, 382

d'Annunzio, Gabriele, 419, 422, 434

Dardanelles front, 199, 320

David, André, 358

David, Eduard, 136

Davidson, J.C.C., 393

Dawes loan, 363

Death in Venice (Mann), 24–6

Death of a Hero (Aldington), 389

Debussy, Claude, 51, 54, 57, 80, 83, 84

Declaration of London of 1909, 230

Décobert, Émile Marcel, 160

defecation imagery: among soldiers, 305–7

Degas, Edgar, 170

Delage, Maurice, 39

Delaunay, Robert, 338

Delbrück, Hans, 281–2

Delvert, Charles, 207, 209–10, 212, 240, 306, 309–10

Demian (Hesse), 349

Denis, Maurice, 42

Denmark: German war against, 103

de Pinedo (flyer), 354

Derby Eve Ball, 333, 337

Derrick, T., 294

Descartes, René, 120

d'Espérey, Marshal Franchet, 364

Devine, Frank, 154

Dherbécourt, Senator, 357

Diaghilev, Sergei Pavlovitch: as aesthetician and propagandist, 59–62; and ballet as total art form, 50–51, 118; and Ballets russes, 51–7, 204, 339, 364–5; death in Venice, 23, 25; and *Death in Venice*, 24–6; family background of, 23; and Faustian moment, 139; in Germany, 123; homosexuality of, 24–5, 63–5, 432; life in Venice, 23–5; postwar loss of attention, 365–6; relations with Nijinsky, 24, 63–5, 89; and *Rite of Spring*, 39, 67, 69, 71, 73, 85; youth and early successes of, 46–52

Dickens, Charles, 105
Dickinson, G. Lowes, 313, 382, 385
'Die Hards, The' (battalion), 180
Dilthey, Wilhelm, 120, 266
Disraeli, Benjamin, 141
Dobujinski, Mstislav, 50
Dodge, Mabel, 36
Döhring, Licentiate, 98
Dolin, Anton, 25
Dompierre front, 165
Donnay, Maurice, 191
Dorgelès, Roland, 238, 284, 296
Dostoevsky, Fyodor, 82
Doumergue, Gaston, 55, 330
Dreiser, Theodore, 396
Dresden, 115, 122
Drieu la Rochelle, Pierre, 310, 311
Droysen, Johann G., 120, 266
Duchamp, Marcel, 27
du Maurier, Major Guy, 186
Duncan, Isadora, 66–7, 75, 123, 320, 326, 348, 366–7
Dupont, Maurice, 88–9
Dürer, Albrecht, 267
duty, sense of: German, 242–4, 265, 267–8, 269; in Great War, 241, 242–62
dyestuff industry, 106

Eastern Front: collapse of Russian army, 241–2, 272; tactics on, 156, 200
Eastman, Max, 63
Eaton, Reverend Charles Aubrey, 319
École des Beaux-Arts, Paris, 42
education: and bourgeois values, 254; compulsory elementary, 110, 254; in Germany, 110–11, 122; secondary and higher, 110
Edward, Prince of Wales, 333
Edwardian morality: and Great War, 183–7

Eggebrecht, Axel, 381
Ehrenburg, Ilya, 341, 350
Eichacker, Reinhold, 279
Einstein, Albert, 60, 111, 350
Einzige und sein Eigentum, Das (Stirner), 74–5
élan vital, 60
electrical manufacturing, 106, 114
Elektra (Strauss), 72, 128–9
Eliot, T.S., 170, 296, 325, 340, 367
Elizabeth, princess of England, 335
emancipation movements, 18; homosexual, 18, 63, 122, 125, 136; women, 18, 122, 125; youth, 18, 63, 81, 122, 125, 127
empiricism: and Anglo-French civilization, 117
employment: division of, 255
energy: and industrial development, 106
Enfant et les sortilèges, L' (Ravel), 359
England. See Great Britain
Englishman's Home, An (du Maurier), 186
Enormous Room, The (Cummings), 306
Epstein, Jacob, 170
Ethiopia, 419
Eulenburg, Prince Philipp zu, 131
euphemisms: used to describe war, 296–8, 315
eurhythmics, 67, 85
Exil, L' (Montherlant), 82
Exiles (Joyce), 82
expressionism, 345, 433–4; violence in, 126

Falaba: torpedoing of, 230
Falkenhayn, Erich von, 147, 155, 201, 232
Fargue, Léon-Paul, 39
Farmer, Rifleman G.A., 142–3
farming: postwar, 347

Fascism: accepted by artistic and intellectual community, 431–3; and aestheticizing of politics and violence, 404, 419–20; enthusiasm for flying, 428; eroticism of, 432; futuristic outlook of, 403–4; Lindbergh's relations with, 427–8; opposition to *All Quiet*, 383; *see also* Nazis

fashion: trim silhouette look, 67–8, 347–8; in twenties, 347–8

Fatherland Party (Germany), 271

Faulkner, William, 396

Fauré, Gabriel, 80

Faust (Goethe), 134

Faustian moment, 139

Fauves, 81

Fayolle, Marie Émile, 314

Feder, Gottfried, 410

Ferry, Abel, 247

Fest, Joachim, 430

Festubert: battle of, 200

Feu, Le (Barbusse), 239, 241

Feuerbach, Ludwig, 62

Figaro, Le, 87, 191, 357, 365

film. *See* cinema

Filosofov, Dmitri, 23–4

Firebird (Stravinksy), 69–70, 365

First World War. *See* Great War

Fischer, Rudolf, 139, 288

Fischer, Samuel, 381

Fischer Verlag, S., 380–81

Fisher, H.A.L., 388

Fitzgerald, F. Scott, 261, 359

flame throwers: in Great War, 218, 227–8

Flanders front: trench warfare in, 148–59, 168, 199

Flanner, Janet, 339

Fleischer, Hans, 269–70

Flers, Robert de, 65

Flex, Walter, 279

flyers. *See* airplane; Lindbergh, Charles Augustus

Foch, Marshal Ferdinand, 330

Fokine, Michel, 52, 56, 67, 71, 365

Folies Bergères, Paris, 359

folk traditions: art and, 60–61

Fontane, Theodor, 111, 133

food rationing: for Great War, 200

football, 173–5, 180

Footballers Battalion, 180

Forain, J.L., 43

Ford, Ford Madox, 170

Fortnightly Review, The, 393

France: anti-German feeling in, 83; bourgeois values in Great War, 253–4; civilization vs. German *Kultur*, 117–18, 121, 124, 137; as cultural arbiter, 80–83; declining birth rate of, 80; at *fin de siècle*, 76–83; Germany declares war on, 99; industrial output of, 106; modernist exiles in, 81–2; and Peninsular War, 173; population of, 107; postwar anti-British feelings, 394; postwar conditions in, 394; postwar politics in, 342; Second Empire, 79; sense of duty from middle class values, 242–6; Third Republic, 79; *see also* French army; Great War; Paris

François-Poncet, André, 401, 429

Franco-Prussian War (1870–71), 79, 82, 103, 110, 116, 121, 218

Franco-Russian treaty (1893), 82

Frank, Bruno, 382

Frankfurter Zeitung, 97

Franz Ferdinand, archduke of Austria, 88, 91

Fredenburgh, T., 306

Frederick II, the Great, king of Prussia, 99, 102, 109, 267, 415, 417, 420; Testament of 1752, 109

Frederick Barbarossa, Holy Roman emperor, 132, 267
Freikörperkultur, 126
Freischütz, Der (Weber), 46
French army: atrocities by, 222; casualties of, 148, 200, 201; and Christmas 1914 truce, 144–5, 191; collapse of, 200; fraternization with Germans during truce, 165, 182; fronts of, 158; introduction of new technology by, 228; leadership of, 256; morale and motivation in, 234–62; mutinies in, 203, 205, 240–41, 249–50, 259, 307, 310, 314, 394; psychology of soldier, 260; see also Great War; trench warfare
French Revolution of 1789, 77
Freud, Sigmund, 60, 62, 344, 350
Frick, Wilhelm, 386, 400
Friedell, Egon, 391
Fromelles front, 156
Frühlingserwachen (Spring Awakening) (Wedekind), 70
Fry, C.B., 175
Fry, Roger, 122
Fudakowski, Janek, 26
Fürstenberg, Max Egon Fürst zu, 132
futurism, 49, 60, 61, 126, 293, 295, 434; in Nazi outlook, 403–4, 430
'Futurism and Futurists' (Grassi Palace, Venice, 1986), 28

Gabo, Naum, 365
Gallieni, Joseph Simon, 256
Gallipoli campaign, 189, 200
Galsworthy, John, 286, 396
Gamble, J.W., 291, 297
Garnier, Tony, 41
Garrod, R.G., 144
gas: Hitler's experience of, 407, 409; in Nazi death camps, 425; used in Great War, 197, 209, 218, 223–7, 231, 232, 270, 297, 315, 320
Geibel, Emanuel, 121
general staffs: attitudes toward war, 314
Generation Missing, A (Carstairs), 390–91
George, Stefan, 121, 125
George V, king of England, 54, 244, 333
Germain, José, 368, 390
German air force: air raids by, 219–20, 285, 290; in Second World War, 427
German army, 145–6; attacks on civilians, 218–20; British attitudes toward, 180–82; casualties of, 148, 201; and Christmas 1914 truce, 144–5, 159–66, 189–92, 278; collapse of Western Front, 271, 279; enlistment by social class, 259; flame throwers used by, 227–8; gas used by, 223–7, 232 (see also gas); letters of student casualties published, 412; loyalty in, 240, 277–8, 281; military records of, 277–8; mobilization orders issued for, 97, 145; morale and motivation in, 234–62, 276–82; and new technology of warfare, 216–33; objections to All Quiet, 384–5; and opposition to war, 280–81; plundering for clothes by, 152–3; Schlieffen plan, 133, 146, 147, 217; sniping by, 228; Stellungskrieg, 232; tactics and attitudes to war, 216–33; and total war, 217–18; trench mortars used by, 228; and trench warfare, 148–59 (see also trench warfare); and war of attrition, 216–18; see also Great War
German idealism, 121, 265, 272

493

German language, 101–2

German music, 57

German navy: mutiny in, 282; policy of, 129; and submarine warfare, 230–32

German Workers' Party, 413–14

Germany: anti-British feeling in, 130, 137, 273–4; architecture in, 43–4, 122; association between war and art in, 138–9, 170–72, 265, 275–6; blames Britain for war, 273–4; boundaries of, 102; British naval blockade of, 229, 271; British war attitudes to, 168–73; concern with *Bildung*, 117; concern with *Macht*, 117, 121; concern with *Technik*, 108–13, 402–3, 413, 425–7; customs union, 114; declaration of war on Russia and France, 97, 99; demographic changes in, 107; depersonalization in, 108; economic protectionism in, 112; education in, 109–11, 122; elections of 1912 in, 112; fabulation in, 116–17; in face of defeat, 271–2; food riots in 1916, 281; Franco-Prussian War, 79, 82, 103, 110, 116, 121; fusing of society and culture in Great War, 263–76; historians justifying attacks on civilians, 220–21; Hitler becomes chancellor of, 399, 412; individualism and personal honor, 267–8; industrial output of, 106; *Kultur* as ideal, 105, 116–21, 129, 135–6, 279; as leading economic and military power, 116; modern dance in, 123; modernism of, 17–19, 402–5, 417, 435; modernist architecture in, 43; nationalism in, 112, 120, 264–7; nationalist societies in, 112; official histories of war,

343; opposition to war in, 280–82; political system of, 112–13, 122; popular acceptance of Nazism, 418; popular feelings for war in, 90–101, 134–40, 263–76; population of, 107; postindustrial advances of, 105–7; postwar Americanization of, 363–4; postwar economy of, 363, 392, 396, 411; postwar nationalist literature, 411; postwar political realignments in, 342–3; postwar radicalism in, 19; postwar reparations, 392–3, 394; prewar foreign relations and policy of (*Weltpolitik*), 129–30; propaganda in Great War, 220–23; regionalism of, 102; responses to cultural effervescence in, 128–9; role of Bismarck in unification of, 103–5; secular idealism in, 117; sense of duty (*Pflicht*) in, 242–6, 265, 267–9, 276; sense of mission in, 124; society vs. community in, 107–8; spirit of revolt in, 122–34; spiritual approach to war, 134–40, 170–73, 216–21, 263–76, 318–19; as threat to British values, 187–9; totalitarianism in war effort, 270–72; tribal origins of, 127; unification into state, 101–8, 266–7; urbanism in, 107; veneration of management in, 108–9; Versailles terms on defeat of, 340; views on history, 266–7, 269; *Volk* culture, 61; and war god, 263–76; Weimar Republic, 19, 392, 411; will and honor in, 268; working women in, 122; xenophobia and racism in, 119–20; youth movement in, 63, 122, 125, 127; *see also* Berlin;

German army; Great War; Nazis

Gesamtkunstwerk, 51, 99, 118, 119

Gestapo, 398, 418

Ghéusi, P. B., 365

Ghilchik, David, 279, 301

Gide, André, 59, 60, 65, 239, 325, 338

Gilman (flyer), 354

Giraudoux, Jean, 213

Giselle, 64

Glaeser, Ernst, 139

Glazunov, Aleksandr, 50

Goddard, Paulette, 371

Godin, Pierre, 356–7

Goebbels, Joseph, 397, 398, 399, 400, 415, 416, 418, 419, 420, 421, 424, 425, 428, 435–6, 437; organizes election celebrations, 400–401

Goebbels, Magda, 437

Goering, Hermann, 400, 420, 421, 427

Goethe, Johann Wolfgang von, 15, 102, 134, 137, 267, 269, 270, 371, 396

Goldring, Douglas, 393

Goll, Ivan, 201, 358, 361

Goncharova, Natalia, 61, 365

Goodbye to All That (Graves), 385, 393

Gosse, Edmund, 284

Gosset, Alphonse, 43

Gould, Gerald, 187

Grahame, Kenneth, 188

Grand Palais, Paris, 42; 'Aerial Locomotion' exhibition at, 338

Granville, Lord, 229

Graves, Robert, 241, 257, 290, 308, 310, 312, 321, 341, 370, 379, 385, 389, 393

Great Britain: architecture in, 122–3; art and culture in, 169–70; blamed for war by Germany, 273–4; bourgeois values in Great War, 242–5, 252–4; civilization vs. German *Kultur*, 117–18, 121, 124, 136–7, 168; conformity in, 185; as conservative power, 18, 169–70; German fear and hatred of, 130, 137, 273–4; and German submarine warfare, 229–31; German threat to values of, 187–9; industrial output of, 106; insularity of, 184; millenarian attitudes to war, 137; mission in Great War, 168–83; Pax Britannica, 18, 124, 168; and Peninsular War, 173; population of, 107; postwar anti-French feelings, 393–4; postwar conditions in, 393; postwar politics in, 342–3; quality of life in, 184–5; sense of duty from middle class values, 171, 242–5, 252; social code at time of Great War, 183–7; sportsmanship and war, 173–81; Victorian/Edwardian morality and Great War, 170, 183–7; Zeppelin raids on, 220; see *also* British army; Great War

Great War: air raids, 219–20, 285, 290; Armistice, 272, 282, 321, 339–40, 343; artillery in, 195–6, 202; bourgeois values in, 242–5, 252–6, 260–62; British and German attitudes to cause of, 167–73; British social code at time of, 183–7; British sportsmanship and, 173–81; casualties of, 148, 200–201, 210–13, 215, 242, 258, 259,341–2; censorship in, 238, 315–16; Christmas 1914 truce, 141–5, 159–83, 189–92; civilian attacks in, 218–20, 231; commemorations of unknown soldier, 343, 351; compulsory service introduced, 249, 250, 255; courtsmartial in, 235, 250; desertion in, 235, 259; develops own momentum, 251; diaries and letters, 235, 238, 246–7; exposure casualties, 151–2; flame throwers in, 218, 227–8; fore-planned brevity of, 134–5; fraternization during, see Christmas 1914 truce; gas used in, 197, 209, 218, 223–6, 232, 270; German attitudes to rules of war, 216–33; German spiritual approach to, 134–40, 170–72, 216–22, 263–76, 319; Germany's Schlieffen plan, 133, 146, 147, 217; home front, 247–8, 296–7; home leave, 308–10; immediate after-effects of, 339–50; insubordination in, 235, 240, 242, 249–50; in literature, 369–98; looting, 152; military leadership in, 255–6, 289; millenarian attitudes to, 137, 170–72, 264–5; mobilization of troops, 45; morale and motivation in, 234–62; morality as decorum, 252; new technology introduced by Germans, 216–33; in 1914, 147–92; official histories of, 343–4; peace terms of, 340; and personal character, 252; popular feelings for, 90–101; population on eve of, 107; position warfare, 201; postwar political realignments, 342–3; propaganda in, 145, 220–23, 248–9, 284, 315–19; reasons for Christmas 1914 truce, 166–83; repression of memory of 344; sense of duty in, 241, 242–62; significance of, 16; stalling with winter rains of 1914, 150–59; strate-gies of, 199–216; submarine warfare in, 218, 229–32; summer of 1914, 90–92; tanks introduced, 229; as total war, 217–18, 230–31; trench warfare, 147–59, 195–216 (see also trench warfare); truces of 1915, 192; ultimatum to Serbia, 91–2; as war of attrition, 200, 217–18, 241; winter rains of 1914, 150–59; see also British army; French army; German army; Western Front

Greece: war with Turkey, 341

Greek art, 51

Greek dance, 65, 67

Green Hat, The (Arlen), 348

Greffuhle, Comtesse, 45, 50

Gregson, William, 231

Grey, Sir Edward, 149, 274

Grey, Lady de, 45

Griffith, Wyn, 290

Groener, General Wilhelm, 372

Gropius, Walter, 44

Gross, Valentine, 32, 35–6, 37, 39

Group of Soldiers, A (Nevinson), 294

Gruber, Max von, 421

Grundlagen des neunzehnten Jahrhunderts (Chamberlain), 119

guerrilla warfare, 218

Guinle, Alexandre, 357

Gundolf, Friedrich, 124

Gurkha troops: in Great War, 318

Gurney, Ivor, 389

gymnastic societies: in Germany, 127

Gypsies: in Nazi death camps, 402

Haber, Fritz, 223

Hague Convention of 1907, 223, 227

Hague Declaration of 1899, 223

Hahn, Reynaldo, 53

Haig, Field Marshal Sir Douglas, 150, 229, 250, 256, 261, 314
hair styles: postwar, 348
Hallam, Henry, 110
Halsey, Margaret, 362
Hamilton, General Sir Ian, 320, 377
Hanfstaengl, Ernst, 423, 430
Harden, Maximilian, 125
Hardy, Thomas, 188
Harich, Walter, 268
Harnack, Adolf von, 221, 274, 281
Hartlepool: bombing of, 220
Harvey, John W., 205, 214, 316
Hauptmann Gerhart, 221, 270, 431
Haussmann, Conrad, 135
Haussmann, Baron Georges, 76, 78, 80
Hay, Ian, 244
hedonism: postwar, 344
Hegel, G. W. F., 121
Heidegger, Martin, 431, 433
Heine, Heinrich, 76
Heinz, Friedrich Wilhelm, 410
Hemery, René, 321
Hemingway, Ernest, 334, 359, 363, 370, 379
Henderson, Nevile, 429
Herder, Johann von, 61
Hermann monument, Teutoburg Forest, 127
Herrick, Myron T., 334, 335, 352
Herzl, Theodor, 26, 118
Hess, Rudolf, 420
Hesse, Hermann, 139, 349, 363–4
Heuss, Theodor, 135
Himmler, Heinrich, 421
Hindenburg, Paul von, 147, 271, 342; elected president of Germany, 411–12, 417
Hines, Lance Corporal, 177, 182
Hirschfeld, Magnus, 125, 136, 138
historians: vs. artists, 387–8;

on military leadership of Great War, 255–6; official versions of Great War, 343
history: and Anglo-French sense of identity, 245; vs. art, 387–8, 389; as art not science, 266; cultural, 16–17; denial of, in civilian attacks of Great War, 221; vs. fiction, 19; German views on, 265–6, 269; military, 16–17, 343; vs. myth, 415; official versions of Great War, 343–4; and revisionism of All Quiet, 395
History of Europe (Fisher), 388
Hitler, Adolf, 119, 392, 396, 397, 399–400; anti-Semitism of, 409, 422–5; appearance of, and racial theories, 421; appointed chancellor, 399–400, 412; assassination attempt against, 418, 419; death of, 438; early life of, 405–6; enthusiasm for film, 425–6, 428; fascination with autos and flying, 426–7; gassing of, 407, 409; leadership skills of, 413–14; on life as art, 417; personality of, 423–4; personalizing of history, 415–16; sexuality of, 423; speeches of, 416, 429; symbolism to Germans, 429–30; as unknown soldier, 411; views on politics, 408–9; views on social organization, 408–9; views on technology, 408–9; war experience of, 406–9
Hobbes, Thomas, 320
Höchst firm, 106
Hoffmann, E. T. A., 61
Hofmannsthal, Hugo von, 72
Hohenzollern dynasty, 103, 267
Holland report on chemical warfare, 227

'Hollow Men, The' (Eliot), 340
Holmes, Oliver Wendell, 77
Holocaust, 402–3, 422
Holy Roman Empire, 101, 102, 109
home front of Great War, 247–8, 296–7; armchair strategists, 309; dislike of soldiers for civilians, 310; letters from, 309; reading matter from, 309–10; see also press; propaganda
home leave: from trench warfare, 307–8
homosexuals, 24–5, 63–5, 81, 432; emancipation of, 18, 63, 122, 125, 136; in Germany, 122, 125, 131, 136; in Nazi death camps, 402; support for Great War, 98
Hope, T. S., 259
Houghton, Alanson B., 332
Housman, A. E., 188
Huelsenbeck, Richard, 285
Hugenberg, Alfred, 392
Hughes, Colonel G. W. G., 224–5
Huguet, General, 394
Huizinga, Johan, 141
Hulse, Edward, 143, 181
Hülsen-Häseler, Dietrich Count von, 132
humanism: death of, 301–2
Humanité, L', 335
Humbert, General, 250
Humperdinck, Engelbert, 221
Huot, Louis, 260
Huxley, Aldous, 349

Ibsen, Henrik, 122
Illustrated London News, 54
Imperialism: British, 128
Imperial War Museum, London, 294
impressionism, 49, 81; in music, 57
Im Westen nichts Neues. See All Quiet on the Western Front

Independent Social Democratic Party (USPD), 281
industrialism: in Germany, 105 –8
industrial mobilization: for Great War, 200
influenza: epidemic of 1918–19, 341
intellectuals: and the Great War, 284; support for Nazis in Germany, 431–4
international style: postwar, 348–9
inward turning: among soldiers, 289–302, 315
Ionesco, Eugène, 297
Ireland, 186; German support for nationalists, 233
iron industry, 106
irony: expressing new sensibility, 297–301; sense of, in Great War, 241
Isherwood, Christopher, 349, 350, 412
Isherwood, Frank, 152, 248
Italy: invasion of Ethiopia, 419; see also Fascism

Jacobs, Monty, 381
Jacobsen, Friedrich, 274
Jahn, Turnvater, 127
Jahrgang 1902 (Glaeser), 139
James, Henry, 176, 220, 223, 284, 286, 317
Jaques-Dalcroze, Emile, 67, 85, 429
Jarry, Alfred, 307
jazz, 359
Jehovah's Witnesses: in Nazi death camps, 402
Jerome, Jerome K., 177–8, 180
Jeux (Debussy/Nijinsky), 33, 34, 56, 63, 64
Jews: anti-Semitism, 45, 402, 409, 411, 422–4, 433; Crystal Night, 433; German support for Great War, 98; Holocaust,

401–3, 422; Palestinian, 424

Joffre, General Joseph, 202, 256, 330, 394

Johannet, René, 254

Johannsen, Christian, 66

Johst, Hanns, 433

Jones, David, 245, 287, 291

Jones, Percy, 152, 159–60, 163, 181, 208, 246, 248, 291

Journey's End (Sherriff), 370, 385

Joyce, James, 82, 118, 287, 307, 391, 433

Judd, Samuel, 163

July 1914 (Ludwig), 138

Jung, Edgar, 433

Jünger, Ernst, 201, 206, 212, 221, 278, 308, 310, 311, 374–5, 410

Jutland: battle of, 230, 232

Kafka, Franz, 90, 338

Kahn, Otto H., 45

Kahr, Gustav von, 433

Kaiser Wilhelm Memorial Church, Berlin, 133

Kangaroo (Lawrence), 75

Kardorff, Wilhelm von, 112

Karsavina, Tamara, 52, 53, 64

Kellermann, Bernhard, 382

Kemmel Times, 300

Kerouac, Jack, 77

Kessler, Harry Count, 366, 401, 420

King, Mackenzie, 352

Kipling, Rudyard, 169, 179, 286

Kirchhoff (singer), 160

Kirchner, Ernst Ludwig, 124

Kitchener, Horatio Herbert, 149, 228, 244, 303, 318

kitsch: Nazism as, 404–5, 430

Klatt, Fritz, 269

Klausener, Erich, 433

Klee, Paul, 283, 349

Klemm, Wilhelm, 267

Klimt, Gustav, 63

Kluck, Alexander von, 146

Kochno, Boris, 25

Kraus, Karl, 438

Kreisler, Fritz, 214–15, 237

Krell, Max, 381

Krieg (Renn), 389

Kroll Opera House, Berlin, 414

Kropp, Peter, 372–3

Kultur: vs. Anglo-French civilization, 117–18, 121, 124, 137, 168, 172, 186–8, 389, 434–5; as German ideal, 105, 116–21, 129, 135–6, 279; and *Gesamtkunstwerk*, 118; Nazis and, 411, 434

Kuznetsova (singer), 80

Laban, Rudolf von, 429

La Bassée front, 150

labor: division of, 255

Labour Party (Great Britain), 342

Lafayette Escadrille, 352

Laloy, Louis, 85

Landowska, Wanda, 44

Langbehn, Julius, 118, 124, 266, 357

Langemarck, Flanders: gas first used at, 223

language: inadequacy of traditional, to describe trench warfare, 296–7

Larionov, Mikhail, 50, 61, 365

latrine imagery: among soldiers, 306–7

Lawrence, D. H., 75, 284

Lawrence, T. E., 341, 390

Lawson, Dillon, 240

League of Nations, 340

Leane, B. B., 245

Lebensreformbewegung, 122

Le Bon, Gustave, 260

Le Cateau: battle of, 148

Le Corbusier (Charles-Édouard Jeanneret), 41

leftist parties: postwar, 342, 343–4

Léger, Fernand, 360

Leibeskultur, 67, 125

Lenin, Nikolai, 233, 285

Lessing, G. E., 137
Le Touquet front, 156
Levaillant, Maurice, 357–8
Lewis, Wyndham, 126, 433
Ley, Robert, 410, 421
Liberal Party (Great Britain), 342
liberation: as motif, 17
Liddell Hart, Basil, 146, 299
Liebknecht, Karl, 281
Liège: forts at, 196, 202
Lieven, Peter, 64
Lifar, Serge, 25, 432
Lindbergh, Anne Morrow, 428
Lindbergh, Charles Augustus: awarded honors, 330–31, 427; and commemorations of war, 351–3; kidnapping of his child, 333; and modern sensibility, 338–9; personality of, 336–7; poets on, 356–8; press on, 326, 328, 332, 333, 334–7; reception in Belgium, 331, 351; reception in London, 331–3, 351; reception in New York, 333; reception in Paris, 326–30, 350–51, 364–5; relations with Nazis and Fascism, 427–8; as star, 333–9; symbolism of his flight, 337–9, 350–58, 367; as symbol of America, 359–60
literature of disenchantment, 241
Little, Brown and Company, 384
Lloyd George, David, 137, 189, 340, 342
Locarno spirit, 393
Loder, Captain, 167, 181
London: Ballets russes in, 53–4, 57; music halls in, 68; Zeppelin raids on, 220
London Mercury, The, 384, 385–6
London Observer, 335
London Times, 54, 174, 300, 335
Lonsdale, Earl of, 333

Loos, Adolf, 41
Loos: battle of, 200, 224, 257
Lorraine, 82
lost generation, 310, 378–9
Louis Napoleon. See Napoleon III
Louis Philippe, king of France, 169
Louvain: bombing of, 219
Ludendorff, Erich, 147, 217–18, 271, 278, 342
Ludwig, Emil, 138
Lueger, Karl, 422
Luftwaffe, 427
Lulu, 126
Lusitania: sinking of, 231, 319
Luther, Martin, 267
Lutheranism, 104
Luxemburg, Rosa, 281

MacDonagh, Michael, 234, 259
Mackay, Clarence, 45
Macke, August, 126, 127, 128
Maeterlinck, Count Maurice, 134
Mahler, Gustav, 26
Mailer, Norman, 27
Mairet, Louis, 179, 205, 213, 246, 251, 260, 290, 293, 301, 308, 320
male bonding: in trench warfare, 310–14
Mallarmé, Stéphane, 51, 54, 83
Manchester Guardian, 354
Mandelbaum, Maurice, 432
Mann, Heinrich, 26
Mann, Thomas, 364, 413; and the Great War, 101, 171; sexuality in work of, 26, 126; and Venice, 24–6
Marc, Franz, 126, 127, 128, 139
Marinetti, Filippo Tommaso, 126, 420, 434
Markevitch, Igor, 25
Marne: battle of, 147, 149, 172, 352
Marsh, Edward, 187

Marx, Karl, 169
Masefield, John, 296
Masterman, Charles, 294
Maud'huy, Colonel, 256
Mazenod, Pierre de, 226, 399
McGill, Patrick, 236
McGregor, Peter, 197, 206, 251, 288, 303
Meier-Graefe, Julius, 132–3
Meinecke, Friedrich, 90, 101, 135, 220, 281
Mein Kampf (Hitler), 409
Meistersinger, Die (Wagner), 430
Méléra, César, 212, 252
Metropolitan Opera, New York, 44
Metternich, Prince Klemens von, 102, 169
middle class. See bourgeois values; civilization
Mies van der Rohe, Ludwig, 44
Milestone, Lewis, 397
military history, 16–17; of Great War, 343–4
military leadership: in Great War, 255–6, 289, 343–4
Mill, John Stuart, 169, 171, 185, 254, 273
Minenwerfer (Minnies), 228
Miquel, Pierre, 223
Mir iskusstva. See World of Art
modernism: American, 359–64; in architecture, 41–4; and exiles, 81–2; German, 43–4; and Lindbergh's flight, 338–9; and Nazis, 402–5, 417, 434–5; and All Quiet, 392; soldiers' experience and, 289; in statecraft, 320; of twenties, 344–50; use of term, 18–19
Modigliani, Amedeo, 82, 293
Moes, Wladyslaw, 26
Moltke, Helmuth von, 95, 97, 134, 147, 217; and Schlieffen plan, 133, 146

Moltke, Helmuth von (elder), 96
Mommsen, Theodor, 266
Mondrian, Piet, 347
Mons: battle of, 146, 316
Montague, C. E., 395
Monteux, Pierre, 35, 72–3
Montherlant, Henry de, 82, 313, 349
morality: and art, 303–7; and character, 252; destruction of perspective in Great War, 290; see also sexual morality
Morand, Paul, 213, 432
Morgan, Pierpont, 45
Morley, Christopher, 382
Morning Post, 389
Mortimer, Brigadier P., 298–9
Moscow: as modernist center, 360
Mosley, Sir Oswald, 428
Mottram, R. H., 379, 389
Mountfort, Roland D., 178, 208, 307
Mozart, Wolfgang Amadeus, 57
Muggeridge, Malcolm, 401
Munch, Edvard, 122
Munich, 114, 122; Nazi putsch in, 420
Munro, Colin, 163
Münster, Count Georg, 80
Münster Anabaptists, 272
Murry, John Middleton, 372
music: nineteenth-century evolutions in, 57; see also specific compositions
Musil, Robert, 349
Mussolini, Benito, 410, 419, 428, 433–4
Mussorgsky, Modest, 50, 80
mustard gas, 225; see also gas
mystical nationalism: in Germany, 120
myth: vs. history, 415; as reality, to Nazis, 418–30

Napoleon I, 83, 102, 110, 127, 218, 267

501

Napoleon III, 79, 169
narcissism: of Nazis, 403–5, 422; postwar, 344; and racism, 422
Nash, Paul, 204, 293
National Association of Boys Clubs, 362–3
National Gallery, London, 170
nationalism: in Germany, 112–13, 120, 264–7
Nationalist People's Party (Germany), 392
National Socialist German Workers' Party (NSDAP). See Nazis
National War Museum, London, 294
Naumann, Friedrich, 113, 264
Navy League, 217
Nazis, 19; anti-Semitism of, 422–5; architecture of, 421; and the avant-garde, 413–14; banning of *All Quiet*, 386, 397–8; book bannings and burnings, 386, 397–8, 413; celebration of death by, 420; celebrations of 1933 victories, 400–401; as cult, 414; death camps of, 402, 424; as doctrine of conflict, 416; and elections of 1929 and 1930, 411; evolution of party, 414; futuristic outlook of, 403–4, 430; gains in 1933 election, 400, 412; and Great War experience, 410; ideology of, 420; internecine conflicts among, 420; kitsch and, 404–5, 430; and *Kultur*, 411, 434; Lindbergh and, 427–8; and modernism, 402–5, 417, 434–5; as movement, 416–21; myth as reality to, 418–30; and nationalist literature, 411; Night of the Long Knives, 433; Nuremberg rallies, 428–9; popular acceptance of, 418; principles of, 413–17; program-policy

contradictions of, 420–21; propaganda by, 426; race thesis of, 421–4 (*see also* anti-Semitism); relations with artistic and intellectual community, 431–4; socialism of, 410–11; as spectacle, 414–15, 428–9; symbolism of Hitler to Germans, 429–30; technicism of, 402–3, 413, 425–7; Twenty-five Points program of, 415–16; use of cinema, 425–6, 428, 436; *see also* Hitler, Adolf
Neuve Chapelle: battle of, 200; front, 156
Nevill, Captain W. P., 178
Nevinson, C. R. W., 293–4, 360
Nevinson, Henry W., 360
Newbolt, Sir Henry, 175
'New Church' *Times*, 300
new conservatism, 342
New Statesman, 186
New York: as modernist center, 360, 362
New York Times, 73
Nietzsche, Friedrich, 28, 59, 61, 66, 74, 88, 121, 137, 253, 266, 267, 268, 307, 338, 339, 366, 416, 417, 431, 432
Night of the Long Knives, 433
Nijinska, Bronislava, 32, 37
Nijinsky, Romola, 32, 35, 47, 89
Nijinsky, Vaslav: as Ballets russes dancer and choreographer, 52, 54–7, 61, 67, 75, 89; eroticism of, 54–6, 64; and *Faune*, 54–6; madness of, 64, 366; relations with Diaghilev, 24, 63–5, 89; and *Rite of Spring*, 33, 35, 38, 39, 67, 71–2, 85, 87–8
Noailles, Anna Comtesse de, 339
Nolde, Emil, 123–4, 127, 431
no man's land, 197–9, 203, 287–8
Nordmann, Charles, 89
Northcliffe, Lord, 384

Noske, Gustav, 100
Notre Dame Cathedral, Paris, 220
Nouvelles littéraires, 369
NSDAP. See Nazis
nudism: in Germany, 126; in twenties, 346
Nungesser, Charles, 353
Nuremberg rallies, 428–9

'Ode to Charles A. Lindbergh' (Guinle), 357
Oiseau de feu. See Firebird
Olivier, Laurence, 370
Olympics, 68
Opéra, Paris, 42, 45, 50
Opéra Comique, Paris, 45
Orlando, Vittorio, 342
Otto the Great, king of Germany, 267
Owen, Wilfred, 206, 210, 241, 250, 259, 389, 416
Oxford Book of Modern Verse (Yeats ed.), 388–9, 416

Packer, Corporal, 141–2
'Pack Up Your Troubles' (song), 299
Page, Walter H., 192
painting: in fin-de-siècle France, 81; see also specific movements
Pan-German movement, 217, 271
Parade (Stravinsky/Satie), 204
Paris: architecture of, 40–43, 76–8; Ballets russes in, 51–6, 364–6; bombing of, 220, 285, 290; compared with Berlin, 115; as cultural center, 76–83; first performance of Rite of Spring in, 16, 32–40; foreign theatrical seasons in, 80; German attack plan on, 133; international exhibition (1900) in, 42; modernist exiles in, 81–3; Russian arts and artists in,

49–56; urban blight of, 77; see also France
Paris Commune of 1871, 78
Parsifal (Wagner), 118
Passchendaele: battle of, 201, 203
passports: introduction of, 320
Pastors, Gerhart, 267, 273
patents: development in Germany and Britain, 111
Paths of Glory, The (Nevinson), 294
patricide, 348–9
patriotism: and sense of duty, 245
Pattenden, Private, 172
Pavillon d'Armide, Le (ballet), 52
Pavlova, Anna, 52, 64, 365
Pax Britannica, 18, 124, 168
Péladan, Joséphin, 283
Pelléas et Melisande (Maeterlinck), 134
Peninsular War, 173, 218
People's Party (Germany), 392
Percin, General, 213
Percy, W. R. M., 181
Pergaud, Louis, 222
Péronne: bombing of, 218
Perret, Auguste, 41, 43, 44
Pétain, General Philippe, 237, 247, 314
Peter the Great, tzar of Russia, 48
Petipa, Marius, 66
Petit Palais, Paris, 42, 49
Petrushka (Stravinsky), 63, 69
Pflicht (duty): German sense of, 242–4, 265, 267–9, 276
phosgene gas, 225; see also gas
photography: as medium, 291, 371, 375
Picardy front, 199
Picasso, Pablo, 82, 122, 204, 226
Piltz, Maria, 36
Pirandello, Luigi, 297
Planck, Max, 60, 111

Poelzig, Hans, 44
poetry: vs. history, 266; modernist, 290; on symbolism of Lindbergh's flight, 357–8
Point Counter Point (Huxley), 349
poison gas, See gas
Populaire, 353
Portland, Duchess of, 45
postimpressionism, 42, 122
Potemkin, Grigori, 49
Poulenc, Francis, 359
Pound, Ezra, 170, 416, 433
Pourtalès, Comtesse de, 35
Pourtalès, Count Friedrich von, 97
Powell, Anthony, 244
Powell, Garfield, 238, 247, 291, 310
press: and bourgeois values, 255; British anti-German, 180; censorship and propaganda in Great War, 315–18; on Christmas 1914 truce, 166, 190–92; dislike of soldiers for, 309; and Lindbergh's flight, 326, 328, 332, 333, 334–5; on postwar Ballets russes, 364–6; on Rite of Spring, 38; on war themes, 371
Priestley, J. B., 186
primitivism: German interest in, 127–8, 133
Prince Igor (Borodin), 39, 52
Prohibition, 363
propaganda: All Quiet on the Western Front denounced as, 384–5; and bourgeois values, 255; and British artists, 293–5; French wartime, 182; in Great War, 145, 221–3, 248, 284, 315–19; Nazi, 426, 427; see also press
prostitution: in Germany, 126; on Western Front, 304–5
Proust, Marcel, 45, 53, 59, 65, 70, 83, 284, 391

Prussia, 102; education in, 110; industrialism of, 114; management in, 109, 114; vs. Saxony, 181–2, 190; and unification of Germany, 102, 103–4, 105, 109, 114; see also Germany
psychoneurosis: among soldiers and veterans, 288, 289, 389–90; see also shell shock
public good: sense of, 243
Punch, 54, 56–7, 68, 164, 175
Pushkin, Aleksander, 39

Quandt, Harald, 437
Quinton, W. A., 144
Quittard, Henri, 33, 34, 85

Rachmaninov, Sergei, 50
racism, 421–4; in Germany, 119–20; see also anti-Semitism
Radbruch, Gustav, 281
radicals: and the Great War, 284–6; postwar, 342, 344, 349
radio: in twenties, 347; use by Nazis, 428
Rag-Time (Auric), 359
Rag-Time (Stravinsky), 359
Rainbow, The (Lawrence), 75
Rambert, Marie, 32, 85, 87
Raper, Colonel Henry S., 227
Rathenau, Walther, 130, 271, 340, 423
rationalism, 59–60; and Anglo-French civilization, 117, 272
Ravel, Maurice, 39, 80, 359
Raws, J. A., 211
Ray, Man, 27
Read, Herbert, 189, 203, 205, 241, 247, 253, 310, 312, 314, 381, 389
Reformation, 101
Regnier, Pierre de, 357
Reichstag, Berlin, 414, 417
Relève du matin, La (Montherlant), 349
religion: in Germany, 101, 104

Remark, Peter Franz, 371
Remarque, Erich Maria, 307, 368–98; background of, 371–2; borrowings of, 374–5; fame comes to, 380–97; fascination with death, 374, 379; postwar career of, 373–4; suggested for Nobel Prize, 382, 384; war experience of, 372–3; writes *The Road Back*, 378; and writing of *All Quiet on the Western Front*, 375–80
Rembrandt als Erzieher (Langbehn), 118
Renan, Ernest, 110
Renn, Ludwig, 370, 379, 389
revolutionary renewal: Great War and, 284–6; *see also* radicals
Revolution of 1848, 78
Revue des deux mondes, 233
Revue Nègre, La, 365
Rhapsodie nègre (Poulenc), 359
Rheims cathedral: bombing of, 219, 220
Rhodes, Cecil, 176
Richepin, Jean, 69
Richter, Hans, 285
Rickert, Heinrich, 120
Ricketts, Charles, 55
Riebensahm, Gustav, 143, 153, 161, 179
Riefenstahl, Leni, 425
Riezler, Kurt, 93, 100
Rilke, Rainer Maria, 265, 286
Rimsky-Korsakov, Nicholai, 50, 53
Rimsky-Korsakov, Vladimir, 51
Ring cycle (Wagner), 83, 117–18, 270
Rite of Spring, The (Stravinsky/Nijinsky), 56, 67, 77, 276, 290, 365–6; creation of, 69–73; critical reception of, 32–40, 85–9, 364–5; first performance of, 16, 32–40, 83–4; libretto for, 31–2; theme of, 83–9

Rivière, Jacques, 59, 84, 86, 240
Road Back, The (Remarque), 378
Roberts, Robert, 185
Robertson, General Sir William, 229
Rocheblave, Samuel, 81
Rodin, Auguste, 55
Roerich, Nicholas, 50, 52, 71, 85–6
Rolland, Romain, 270
romanticism, 59, 61
Romier, Lucien, 360
Röntgen, Wilhelm Conrad, 111
Root, Waverley, 335, 336
Rosenberg, Alfred, 421
Rosenberg, Harold, 76, 77
Rosenberg, Isaac, 389
Rostand, Edmond, 339
Rostand, Maurice, 325, 339, 352
Rousseau, André, 368
Rousseau, Jean-Jacques, 61, 268
Royce, Josiah, 231
Rubinstein, Arthur, 44, 64, 79
Ruffo, Titta, 44
Rupprecht, Crown Prince of Bavaria, 146, 224
Ruskin, John, 27, 170
Russell, Bertrand, 131
Russell-Jones, E., 249
Russia: industrial output of, 106; mobilization for Great War, 94, 97, 99 (*see also* Great War)
Russian army, 144, 146, 147, 200; in Berlin (WWII), 438; casualties of, 242; collapse of, 241–2, 272; myth of Western Front destination, 316–17
Russian arts: in Paris, 49–62
Russian ballet, 32–40, 51–8, 65; *see also* Ballets russes
Russian-Japanese war (1905), 49
Russian revolution of 1905, 49, 74
Russian Revolution of 1917, 77, 233, 242, 341, 432
Rutland, Duchess of, 45

Sachs, Hans, 436
Sacre du printemps, Le. See Rite of Spring, The
St. Petersburg, Russia, 49, 50, 66
Saint-Saëns, Camille, 40
Saint-Simon, Henri de, 31, 62
Salomé, 126
Salon d'Automne exhibition, Petit Palais, Paris, 49
Samson, Captain A. L., 257
Santayana, George, 128
Sassoon, Siegfried, 207, 213, 241, 255, 310, 370, 379, 389
Satie, Erik, 204
Sauguet, Henri, 365
Saxony: education in, 110; industrialism in, 114; vs. Prussia, 182, 190
Sazonov, Sergei, 97
Scarborough: bombing of, 220
scatology imagery: among soldiers, 305-7
Schauwecker, Franz, 138, 374, 411
Schéhérazade (Rimsky-Korsakov), 53, 63
Scherl publishers, 373, 380
Schiller, Johann von, 102, 396
Schleicher, General Kurt von, 433
Schlieffen, Count Alfred von, 217
Schlieffen plan, 133, 146, 147, 217; abandoned, 147
Schmidt, Willi, 433
Schmitt, Florent, 39, 80
Schopenhauer, Arthur, 121, 265-6, 268, 287
science: education in, 111
Scotsman, 352
Scott, Canon F. G., 291
Seaman, Owen, 164
Secessionist art, 70, 285
Second World War: Allied bombing of Berlin, 401; as continuation of Great War, 419; Nazi death camps, 402, 424

secular idealism: Nazis and, 402-3
Sedan: battle of, 218
Seeley, John, 110
Self-Help (Smiles), 183
Senegalese troops: in Great War, 318
Serbia: Austrian ultimatum to, 90-92
Serov, Valentin, 50
Sert, Misia, 25, 32, 47, 50, 64, 285, 432
sexual impotence: among soldiers and veterans, 289, 390
sexual morality, 62-5; in art and literature, 126-7; in Germany, 124-6; repudiated among soldiers, 304-7; *see also* homosexuals
Shakespeare, William, 189
Shaw, George Bernard, 118, 186
Shelley, Percy Bysshe, 27, 137
shell shock, 237-8, 288-9; *see also* psychoneurosis
Sherriff, R. C., 370, 385
Shirer, William, 76
Sickert, Walter, 170
Sieburg, Friedrich, 115
Siegesallee, Berlin, 133
Sikh troops: in Great War, 318
Silesia, 109, 114
Sitwell, Sacheverell, 365
Smiles, Samuel, 183, 242-3
soccer, 173-5, 179-80
social classes: aestheticism and, 74
Social Democratic Party (S P D) (Germany), 99-100, 112-13, 122, 135-6, 392; and Great War, 270, 281
socialism: among soldiers, 288-9; in Germany, 113, 122 (*see also* Nazis)
Société Musicale, 44
Soissons: bombing of, 218
Somme: battle of, 149, 195, 201, 202-3, 214, 229, 278, 298;

front, 165, 180, 205, 207, 236, 248, 261, 287, 296, 310
Sommer, Albert, 158
Somme Times, 300–301
Somov, Konstantin, 74
Sorley, Charles, 94, 154, 189, 246
Soschka, Cyril, 381
sozialer Volkstaat, 264
So ziehen wir aus zur Hermannsschlacht (Strobl), 127
Spain: Peninsular War in, 173, 218
Spanish Farm (Mottram), 389
Spectre de la rose, Le (ballet), 39, 61, 64
Speer, Albert, 405, 425, 429, 433
Spender, Stephen, 344
Spessivtseva, Olga, 365
Sport im Bild, 373, 374, 375
sporting organizations: and volunteer recruitment for war, 180
sportsmanship: and war, British sense of, 173–81, 189
Squire, J. C., 385
Staël, Madame de, 110
statecraft: Great War's effects on, 320
Station am Horizont (Remarque), 373
Stechlin, Der (Fontane), 111
steel industry, 106
Stein, Gertrude, 34, 37–8, 39
Steinthal, Hugo, 237
Stillman, James, 45
Stirner, Max, 74–5
Stokes, Richard, 248, 297
Strachey, Lytton, 65
Strasbourg: bombing of, 218
Strasser, Gregor, 410, 433
Strauss, Richard, 63, 72, 80, 126, 128–9, 431, 432
Stravinsky, Igor, 82, 204, 359, 365; and ballet as art form, 51; on German culture, 128–9;

and *Rite of Spring*, 16, 17, 31–2, 35, 38, 39, 40, 69–73, 290, 364–5
Streicher, Julius, 421
Stresemann, Gustav, 392
Strindberg, August, 122
Strobl, Karl Hans, 127
students: enthusiasm for war among German, 94, 138
submarine warfare: in Great War, 218, 230–32, 270
Sudermann, Hermann, 221
sulfuric acid: production of, 106
Sunday Chronicle (London), 382
surrealism, 345; and Western Front, 204
Swabia, 101
Sybel, Heinrich von, 266
Syberberg, Hans-Jurgen, 430
Sylphides, Les (ballet), 39
Symons, Arthur, 118
Szögyény-Marich, Count Laszlo, 92

Tägliche Rundschau, 92
Taine, Hippolyte, 83
'Take It to the Lord in Prayer' (hymn), 299
tango, 69
tanks: in Great War, 229
Tatham, F. H. T., 210–11
Tauride Palace, St. Petersburg, 49
taxation: for Great War, 320
Tchaikovsky, Peter, 63
technical education: in Germany, 111
Technik. See technology
technology: as artistic inspiration, 61; education in, 111; German fascination with, 109–15; and Nazi outlook, 402–3, 413, 425–7; postindustrial advances of German, 105–8
Temps, Le, 389

Tender Is the Night (Fitzgerald), 261

Tennyson, Alfred, Lord, 105

Teutonic Knights, 267

Théâtre des Champs-Élysées, Paris, 32, 40–46, 83, 123, 364–5

'There's a Girl for Every Soldier' (song), 305

Thérive, André, 389

Third Reich. See Nazis

thirties: Nazi rise in, see Nazis; war boom of, 387

Thoma, Ludwig, 136

Thomas, Alan, 235

Thomas, Edward, 206

Three Men in a Boat (Jerome), 177–8

Tilley, Oswald, 143

Tirpitz, Alfred von, 97, 134

Tissot, Victor, 114–15

Titian, 124

Toklas, Alice B., 38

Toller, Ernst, 264

Tolstoy, Count Lev Nikolaevich, 82

Tomlinson, H. M., 379, 389

Toscanini, Arturo, 44

total art, 51, 60–62; see also Gesamtkunstwerk

total war, 217–18, 270–71; and submarine warfare, 231

Tournier, Michel, 379, 415

Traumbude, Die (Remarque), 373

Treitschke, Heinrich von, 266

trench mortars, 228

trench warfare, 147, 195–216; advances into no man's land, 198–9; as aesthetic experience, 290–92; and artillery barrage, 195–9, 202, 213; artists on, 285–6; banter between lines, 154–5; barter during truce, 163–4; blamed on Germans, 228; boredom in, 215; breakdown of social barriers in, 311–12; and British sporting sense, 173–81; burial parties during truce, 162; casualties of, 148, 201, 211–13, 215, 258; Christmas 1914 truce, 141–5, 159–83; cold in, 206–7; comradeship in, 247–8; conditions with winter rains of 1914, 150–59; defense as offense in, 202–4; depicted in art, 293–5; desensitization in, 235–40; desertions, 259; dirt and filth of, 205–6, 207–9; dislike of soldiers for civilians, 310; early battles establishing, 147–9 (see also specific battles); eating in, 207; exchanges of rations, 155; exposure casualties, 151–2; flame throwers in, 218, 227–8; football match during truce, 164; gas attacks, 197, 209, 218, 223–7, 232, 270, 297, 315, 320; going over the top, 234, 235–6, 258; historical criticism of, 255–7; home leave from, 307–9; horror vs. boredom in, 214–15; immunization to brutality, 214; inadequacy of traditional language to describe, 295–7; killing of officers, 259; length of tour of duty, 205; letters from home, 309–10; machine gunners in, 203; male bonding in, 310–14; material concerns foremost in, 238, 246; morale and motivation in, 234–62; mud and, 205–7; mutilation in, 211–12; nighttime work, 209–10; pack-loads, 197, 257; as position warfare, 201–3; reading matter from home for, 309; rebuilding of trenches, 154; reflex responses in, 235–41; relations between soldiers and officers, 155–6, 158, 257–

508

8; rules of behavior, 236; and sense of alienation, 287–8; sense of camaraderie in, 310–14; sense of duty in, 240, 242–62; shell shock from, 237–8, 288–9; short shelling, 213; sleep deprivation in, 209–10; sniping and night raids, 153–4, 228; stench of death in, 198, 210–13; and tactics of Western Front, 156–9, 200–204; and total war concept, 217–18; trench mortars used, 228; vermin in, 207–9; weather and morale, 153–4, 205–7; see also British army; French army; German army

Tribune (Paris), 335

Tristan und Isolde (Wagner), 23, 25, 83

Triumph of Neptune, The (Berners/Balanchine), 364

Triumph of the Will (Riefenstahl), 425

Troeltsch, Ernst, 281

Trotsky, Leon, 49

Turckheim, Baron de, 270

Turkey: in Great War, 199, 272; war with Greece, 341

turkey trot (dance), 69

twenties: as denial of Great War, 344–5; fads and cynicism of, 346; fascination with death, 379; fashions of, 347–8; flight from reality in, 346–7; international style of, 348–9; reality vs. myth of, 344–5; sense of transitoriness in, 347–8; war books of, 379 (see also *All Quiet on the Western Front*); war boom of, 387; youth worship of, 344–5, 348–9

Tzara, Tristan, 285–6

U-boats, 230–32

Ubu Roi (Jarry), 307

Ullstein, Franz, 380, 381

Ullstein Verlag, 369, 372, 380, 381, 397

Ulysses (Joyce), 307

unemployment: postwar, 341, 345, 390, 393

United States: aid in Great War from, 272, 352; Americanization of Europe, 359–64; enters Great War, 232, 271; as postwar symbol, 359–64; retreat to isolationism after war, 340

unknown soldier: commemoration of, 343, 351

urbanism: in Germany, 107; in Great Britain, 184; postwar, 346–7

utilitarianism: and Anglo-French civilization, 117, 186

Valéry, Paul, 345

Vanderbilt, William K., 45

Van de Velde, Henry, 43, 44

Van Vechten, Carl, 32, 36, 38

Varus, 127

Vatican, 145

venereal disease: among soldiers, 305

Venice, 23–8, 76

Verdun: battle of, 195–6, 200–201, 202–3, 204–5, 207, 212, 214, 247, 252, 256, 278, 292; memorial cemetery at, 15–16; use of gas at, 226

Verlaine, Paul, 63

Ver Sacrum, 70

Versailles, Treaty of, 340, 392, 427

veterans: behavior in twenties, 341–50; postwar mentality of, 389–91; response to *All Quiet*, 391, 395

veterans' organizations, 341, 351, 390

Victim, The. See Rite of Spring, The

Victorian morality, 62–3, 170; and Great War, 183–7

Vidrac, Charles, 238
Vienna, 115, 116
Vienna, Congress of, 102
Vie Parisienne, 309
Vieux Volontaires de la Grande Guerre, 351
violence: of Nazi cult, 419; and sexuality, 126
Viollet-le-Duc, Eugène, 76
'Vitaï Lampada' (Newbolt), 175
Vladimir, Grand Duke, 50
Voivenel, Paul, 260
Volk culture, 61
Voltaire, 109
Vossische Zeitung (Berlin), 93; serializes *All Quiet*, 369, 381
Vring, Georg von der, 374
Vrubel, Mikhail, 50

Wagner, Richard, 23, 26, 61, 83, 139, 270, 417, 430; and *Gesamtkunstwerk*, 51, 99; influence of, 117–20, 133; and *Kultur*, 117–18
Waldeck, Rosie Gräfenberg, Countess, 380
Walker, Reverend John, 239, 316
Walküre, Die (Wagner), 270
Wallace, Edgar, 396
Wall Street, New York, 360
war: as art, 283–92; and art, German associations of, 138–9, 170–71; British sportsmanship and, 173–81
Waste Land, The (Eliot), 325, 367
Watts, Isaac, 234
Wave of the Future, The (A. M. Lindbergh), 428
weather: and morale in trench warfare, 153–4, 205–7; and politics, 90–91
Weber, Karl Maria von, 46
Weber, Max, 281
Wedekind, Frank, 63, 70, 126, 128

Weg zurück, Der (Remarque), 378
Weimar Republic, 19, 392, 411
Wells, H. G., 128, 186, 349
Weltpolitik, 129–30
Wenzl, Josef, 143
Werkbund, 44
Wesley, John, 185
Wessel, Horst, 420
Western Front: battles of, *see specific battles*; gas warfare on, 223–6, 232; German failure on, 271; morale and motivation in, 234–62; periods of, 202; surrealism and, 204; tactics on, 156, 200; *see also* British army; French army; German army; Great War; trench warfare
Wharton, Edith, 317
What Price Glory? (film), 371
Wheen, A. W., 384
Whistler, James A. M., 170
Whitby: bombing of, 220
Wigman, Mary, 429
Wilde, Oscar, 26, 59, 63, 137, 186
Wilder, Thornton, 387
Wilhelm I, kaiser of Germany, 96
Wilhelm II, kaiser of Germany, 54; abdication of, 340; dismisses Bismarck, 104, 131; homosexuality in entourage of, 125, 131; interest in arts and dance, 131–2; personality of, 131–3; and popular feeling for war, 92, 94, 95, 97, 99; as puppet during war, 271; xenophobia of, 119
Wilson, Archdeacon, 185
Wilson, Major General Henry, 149
Wilson, Sir Horace, 428
Wilson, Woodrow, 319, 340, 342
Windelband, Wilhelm, 120

510